This book is dedicated in loving memory of my friend, Phil May.

The Rustling of Angels

Discovering the Power of Unconditional Love

By

Helen Heinmiller

ISBN: 0-7596-9715-9 (softcover)
ISBN: 0-7596-9714-0 (ebook)

Library of Congress Control Number: 2002100568

This book is printed on acid free paper.

Printed in the United States of America
Bloomington, IN

1stBooks - rev. 3/26/02

Acknowledgments

My deepest love and gratitude is sent to the following people who have helped me in my three-year long journey that has become this story, *The Rustling of Angels*. First, I would like to thank my husband, Paul, who is not only a great husband and father, but, also, my best friend. Thank you for believing in my potential, when I could not see it myself. I am so grateful to my daughters, my own little angels, Katie and Elizabeth, for sharing Mommy's time with this book. This project would never have gotten started without the encouragement and courageous editing help from Marlene Linke. You taught me more lessons about friendship than you could ever know. I also want to thank, from the bottom-of-my heart, my dear friend, Sally McQuail, for her help in editing the last three drafts and her support in every other area of my life. Thank you for your honesty and your kindness. I would have never finished this book without you. A special thank you goes to Judy Davis, my soul sister. Thanks for your love and encouragement and your faith in my abilities—it means so much to me.

I would also like to thank Clif Niblock for all of the time that he invested in helping me understand the complex world of motorcycle racing. Your help was priceless! Thanks must also go to The Reverend Dr. James E. Morris for the inspirational book title that added so much to the story line. My sincere appreciation goes to Mike Thomas, Paramedic, Peg Zazo, Hospice Coordinator, Rosemary Conway, Dr. Edwin Abbott, M.D., and Liz Allen, RN for their expertise and direction in my various research requirements.

Finally, I thank God for my life, my family, my health and my talents. I thank my angels for their inspiration every day and everyone who has touched my life in any way.

To love for the sake of being loved is human,
but to love for the sake of loving is angelic.

—Alphonse de Lamartine, Graziella

Chapter 1

"**W**hat could possibly go wrong on a beautiful day like today?" The stout security guard mused on his way to making his third and final check in the main building of the new state-of-the-art superspeedway. The stormy skies had cleared out at daybreak and the sun cast a brilliant gleam on everything left damp from the rain. Even the humidity that had stifled the East Coast all summer was holding off until mid-afternoon.

The old guard was thinking about how anxious everybody was this morning in the Security Office and how many guards were assigned to duty today. "You would think we were guarding the President of the United States today! People are too damn paranoid these days, if you ask me." As he stepped off the elevator onto the upper mezzanine, he scratched the back of his neck and cursed with annoyance at the new, stiff uniform shirt that he wore unwashed against his wife's better judgment. It was enough of a distraction to keep him from noticing how unusually quiet that end of the hall was for opening day.

Old Joe Peterson lumbered down the hall toward the suites and the press box with the thumb of his left hand tucked into his belt and his trigger hand poised over his gun. It was the same way he always walked for twenty-five years on the force in the streets of West Philadelphia.

Many things had changed since retiring as a police officer five years ago. Instead of a nightstick and a 38-calibre revolver, he now carried a cell phone and a laser stun gun. It wasn't easy getting used to these new-fangled gadgets at his age, especially the stun gun. It looked like something out of a Star Trek episode to him and felt awkward to use; but at least he had a job that gave him something to do, after retiring to Harrisburg. His wife, Claire, wanted to go someplace quiet near the mountains to get away from twenty-five years of city life. But the Harrisburg area was too quiet for Joe. He hated being retired. Despite the protests of Claire, he got a job with Secure-It-T Guards just before they landed the contract with the new superspeedway. She thought he was getting too old for this kind of work, but that was pure nonsense to Joe.

He grimaced as he checked the lock on the maintenance supply closet at the end of the hall. All this fuss being made by the owner over security for the complex! Hell, in his days, no one worried about protecting company executives at a sporting event, but these days everyone is worried about terrorists and half-cocked employees going postal.

Everything seemed to be in order on this end of the corridor. The last three executive suites would be empty today. They were still unfinished, waiting for some special molding that was on back order. Only 75 percent of the suites were reserved anyway. This owner was a real optimistic fellow, Joe thought, if he thinks he can book the speedway solid.

The superspeedway was built to hold 200,000 people. It was the largest complex in the U.S, built solely for motorcycle racing. "How's he gonna get that many people interested in motorcycle racing?" he wondered to himself as he continued down the hall.

Joe brushed his hand over the doorknob of the first unfinished suite until he felt it click and let it go. His attention was drawn to the noise coming from the press box in the middle of the mezzanine. He quickened his pace past the second suite, barely checking the knob and suddenly halted before the last empty room. The door stood ajar and Joe heard two men speaking inside. He glanced at the blank suite ID on the wall—no one should be in there. He thought that maybe the contractor was working overtime, but no one had mentioned it at the security office. He inched toward the door to hear the conversation better. A younger man was talking to an older man inside, but he couldn't see them from where he stood.

"We made our last attempt to change his mind, but it looks like he's going to race." The younger man was saying.

"Very well, then. You better inform headquarters. Tell them to alert Anna." The older man responded in a commanding voice.

The young man hesitated. "So that's it? We just let him do it?"

The older man's voice was steadfast in his command. "Of course. It's out of our hands now. We can't control his actions. It's his choice. We did everything we could. Now we must prepare for delivery."

The young man's voice was strained. "But.."

"No buts. We follow orders. If you want to do well in this job, you better get used to this. Now, you have your instructions."

"Are you coming?"

"In a minute. There's something else I need to complete first."

Joe was confused. Were these guys from the racing organization? Before he could gather his thoughts on his next action, he heard a high-pitched whirring sound and instinctively threw open the door to see what was going on.

A tall, well-built middle-aged man dressed in a navy blue delivery uniform stood with his back to Joe looking out the window down onto the racetrack below. He seemed totally undisturbed by the intrusion and continued looking out the window. Joe was crouched down with both hands holding his gun straight out in front of him. His eyes darted left and right, looking for the younger fellow. The room was completely devoid of furniture and no one else was there.

The whirring sound had ceased the moment Joe opened the door and a faint, crackling noise fizzled away in the air, too quickly for him to notice. Joe's heart was racing, as he demanded, "What are you doing in here?"

The deliveryman turned toward the guard. He was wearing a baseball cap and mirrored sunglasses that shielded his eyes. He was holding a clipboard. His face remained expressionless, as he viewed the shaky guard pointing his gun at him, and he politely answered him. "Overseeing a delivery, sir."

Joe straightened up but kept his gun directed at the strange man. "Deliveries go around the back, buddy; you need to leave now." And then he added, "What happened to the young fellow who was with you?"

The deliveryman turned and looked back down at the track. "It's not that kind of delivery, Sir. And there is no one else here."

Now Joe was upset. "I don't care what kind of delivery you have, buddy. This is a restricted area and you have to leave now! What company are you from?"

The deliveryman turned back toward the guard and straightened his cap. "That's not important."

The flustered guard moved closer to read the man's nametag sewn onto his shirt. It simply said Sage. "What in the hell kinda name is Sage? Your first or last?"

Now the deliveryman seemed a little annoyed. "It's just Sage."

Joe could feel the intense stare coming from behind the silver glasses. The situation felt very uneasy. "Stay right there and don't move, fella. I'm calling my office. You're gonna have a lot of explaining to do." The old guard fiddled with his holster, trying to pull his cell phone out of its leather holder. The damn thing was too tight. He looked down as he freed it and flipped it open to dial, trying to remember the autodial code. Just as he was hitting #3, he heard the deliveryman reply. "That won't be necessary, Mr. Peterson. It's time for you to go home now."

A tremendous gust of swirling wind blew up around Joe, sending the cell phone flying across the room. He looked up and the deliveryman was gone. A crackling noise filled the air and a sensation of electricity passed right through his body and out the door. The wind disappeared and Joe looked around the empty room with bulging eyes, trying to make sense of what had just happened. The only evidence from the whole incident was his broken cell phone on the floor by the window. "For Christ's sake! How did he know my name? What did he mean it was time for me to go home now? No one is going to believe what just happened." He realized he was talking to himself. He felt a glimmer of hope when he spotted the security camera in the corner, but remembered it wasn't turned on yet in the main office.

3

Slowly, he put his stun gun away and picked up his cell phone and proceeded to back out of the room.

Creeping backwards like a cat out of an alley full of dogs, Joe became aware of the tingling sensation still present in every cell of his body. He licked his dry, cracked lips and swallowed to remoisten his parched throat. His hands still shook as he grabbed the doorknob to draw the door closed while he stepped out into the hall.

A sudden slap on the shoulder sent Joe's arms flailing, and startled an obscene curse out of him. He pulled out his gun and swung around to ward off the attack, only to find that it was one of the cable sportscasters from the press box. The well-known Burt Highland was standing with his arms raised high in the air, appearing as offended as a formally dressed debutante invited to a burger joint could be. Joe realized he almost wet his pants.

"Good God, old man!" snapped the sportscaster while he adjusted his silk tie and flattened the lapels of his gray Armani suit, as if somehow they could have been damaged. Burt was WYYM Cable Sports Channel's prima donna announcer and displayed his usual melodramatic reaction. "Put that thing of yours away! You could have killed me! You look like you've seen a ghost, for God's sake."

Joe tried to recover. "I'm, I'm sorry, Mr. Highland, I didn't hear you coming. I was just, just making my rounds." Annoyed that he was caught off guard, Joe became a little defensive. "You shouldn't sneak up on a person like that!"

Burt Highland didn't have time to argue with the old goat. "Just what I get for trying to keep in touch with the public." He thought as he adjusted his silk tie again. "You might want to try walking out the door the right way, like everyone else next time." A young woman leaning out of the press box saved him from further bother.

"Burt, we need you in here. You're on in two minutes."

"Coming!" was all that he said as he left the pale-faced guard leaning against the wall in the hallway.

Joe reached back for the doorknob without looking and pulled it until he heard the click. He headed straight for his locker to gather his composure. Sweat poured down the sides of his face. When he pulled out his handkerchief to mop his brow, he noticed how hard his right hand was shaking. In all of the dangerous confrontations he experienced on the force—and there were many—he never lost his wits like he did this time. He asked himself. "What the hell am I doing here? I almost stunned that fellow! Maybe I am getting too old for this kind of work." Joe reached for a flask of whiskey that he had stashed in his locker and sat down on the bench in front of him to contemplate retirement one more time.

4

At that precise moment, in another part of the stadium, Sage checked off the completed box, next to the first of two names on his assignment sheet.

♥ ♥ ♥ ♥ ♥ ♥ ♥ ♥

The press box was buzzing with activity. Burt walked around the technician's table to a seat in front of the booth window, where every point of the racetrack was in full view. Already seated next to him was Bobby Baker, a recently retired Superbike National Champion, acting as a color commentator for today's big racing events. The producer was briefing him.

Burt smiled briefly and shook Bobby's hand lightly after placing his headset on his head and then looked over the stats one more time. His producer interrupted him. "Nice of you to join us Burt. Could you cut it any closer?"

He raised his hands in the air in self-defense. "Not my fault, Jackie. I was coming back from the little boy's room when I spotted an old guard coming out of one of the rooms down the hall. I just touched his shoulder and said hi as I went by and the old fool nearly blew my head off! I thought he was going to have a heart attack right in front of me. You keep telling me, Sugar, that I need to do more PR work and look where it gets me!" Burt took time to notice his attractive producer's long legs dangling from the table where she was perched.

"I'm sure you were as charming as always with him!" She looked over at the clock. "Phil, how much time?"

"We've got thirty seconds to go."

Jackie looked at Burt. "Okay, get ready guys! Let's have a good show. Bobby, just relax and enjoy yourself. Burt, you okay with the stats?" Jackie knew Burt detested doing today's show, having no interest in motorcycle racing; but the station felt the opening exhibition races for the new racing complex was important enough to warrant his presence and it was required as part of his lucrative contract.

"As always beautiful! But do me a favor, call Security and tell them to send us a younger guard. Maybe they can use the old guy out in parking." Burt chuckled at his own comment and settled in as he heard Phil run the countdown in his ear. "Ready in Five, four, three, two..."

Without missing a beat, Burt smiled into the camera and opened the broadcast with the fast, smooth-talking style that had made him famous.

"Welcome fellow racing fans! This is Burt Highland and WYYM Sennnnsational Sports coming to you LIVE from the most increeedible state-of-the-art racing complex built in the U.S. of A. We're right outside Harrisburg, Pennsylvania, in the new and I must say spectaaacular Capitol

View Superspeedway, just off the Pennsylvania Turnpike. And folks, I gotta tell you, this is a superspeedway to see!"

"Sitting with me today, to fill us in on this inaugural event, is recently retired three-time AMRA Superbike Champion, the incredible Bobby Baker. Thanks for being with us, Bobby."

"Thank you Burt, it's a pleasure to be here."

"That's great Bobby. From the look of the new track, I bet you wish you were still racing today."

"Well, Burt, I gotta tell you, I do and I don't. This racing course is considered to be one of the, if not *the,* most difficult tracks built in the world today. The track is made from an entirely different surface using recycled rubber tires and how the bikes will handle on it remains to be seen. It's a whole new concept in racing for both the riders and the bikes. So maybe I'm lucky my career has been spared the new phase in track racing."

"That's surprising to hear! Can you explain to me and everyone watching why this new surface is so challenging?"

"Sure. You see, this track was designed by Rodney Davis, who is a very wealthy racing enthusiast. He was also a design engineer for Metcor Tires, before venturing out on his own as an entrepreneur. His dream was to design a track that would be the ultimate challenge for a racer's talent, the bike's performance and the tires. Rodney feels there should be more endurance races like the Daytona 200. And I think he's built a hell-of-a-track to race on. This new surface track will be the ultimate conquest that the racers, the sponsor teams, and the bike and tire manufacturers will work towards. Personally, I don't think any other track, including the Daytona Speedway, could come close to this one."

"It's that tough!" Burt scanned his stats quickly to try to add something, wishing he studied up more on motorcycle racing. At a loss, he threw out another question to Bobby. "So, what are the big challenges on this track?"

"Well for the racers, stamina is going to be important. The track is 3 miles long and the race is 70 laps. Physically, this is a lot of riding, considering as a racer you are maneuvering a 350 pound bike going at speeds of up to 185 miles an hour on the straightaways. And this track has 14 turns. Six of them are critical turns with steep banking at 35°. There's a right, left, right combination at the beginning of the course that is a challenge. And an even tougher left, right, left combination at the end that they've already knick-named *The Serpent.* These six turns are sharp and each one carries a different degree of difficulty, with the severest being the last left turn of The Serpent. For the bike, the team mechanics have to make sure that every single part is in perfect working order to withstand such a long race. The racers are going to be pushing their bikes to the limit. It's a long track and parts get hot fast. The racers must maintain total concentration on just about every spot on the track. One minor problem, even trouble with a footpeg, could be detrimental to the racer's chances of winning. You only have two pit stops available, and the crews are gonna want to concentrate on changing tires and getting the bike back on the track as quickly as possible. Any major problems and the racer pretty much loses a chance at placing."

Burt began to like the way the conversation was going. Bobby was a natural and it made his own job easy. They had fifteen long minutes to kill before the first event, so he let Bobby go on.

"Interesting, Bobby. Explain what's involved with the tires."

"Sure!" Bobby couldn't wait. "Your tires are just as important as everything else. In fact, they are pivotal. What most people don't realize is that racing tires are rounded, instead of flat like a car tire. There are a variety of tires to choose from. Slicks are used in dry weather; intermediate rain tires are used on a track that is wet but has no standing water; and full rains are used for really wet tracks. This new road surface has kept the tire manufacturers frustrated this past month, trying to figure out which tire compound will work best on this new surface.

"Another critical factor that affects how well the tires wear is the racer's riding style. For instance, some racers go into the corners hard and that's harder on the front tire, while racers who use a lot of throttle while at maximum lean wear out the back tire faster. If the tires wear out, the heat of the track can turn it to mush, and if the tire falls apart, you don't have to be a rocket scientist to guess his chances of winning."

Burt laughed a little more than necessary. That was his style. "Bobby, thanks for helping us understand the complex details of this sport." (*And doing my job for me!*)

"Oh, there's so much more to racing than that, of course. It's an incredibly competitive motorsport that takes a great deal of drive and talent."

Burt took a cue from his producer to move on. "Speaking of competition, it looks like a veritable who's who in racing down there."

"Yeah, everyone is here. A lot of personalities from the European Grand Prix circuit and the World Superbike series have popped over to view this event. I heard Claude Van Husen with the Dutch racing team, who's currently leading the GP circuit, is here. And Eddie Ried from England is in the pits, too!"

"Are they racing today, Bobby?"

"Noooo...No Way! This is a money event only today. None of the top guys in the GP or the World Superbike competition will touch this track. First, most of their contracts wouldn't allow it and the ones that have special clauses to race special events like the Daytona 200 may be leery of the track right now. Because of it's complexity, and the fact that the track hasn't been broken in, they can't take a chance of injury or damaging their bikes in any way. There's only a small point spread between the top three teams in the Grand Prix. And the same thing goes for the National and World Superbike competition. Ricky Evans from California leads Mike Monahan from Texas by eighteen points. With only a few races left in both championships, they have no room for errors. They're using this event strictly for PR today."

"So, if the big names aren't out there today, then who are we going to see?"

"Oh, the competition is gonna be tough." Bobby gulped a sip of coffee fast and didn't give Burt a chance to talk. You could hear the excitement in his voice. "This race is really important! Anyone not in the top ten seats in any of the professional road racing levels has a lot at stake. With an event this big, anyone on the factory second level teams or the privateer racers will get noticed today, *if* they race well. There are scouts here from all of the American racing teams, and the Japanese and European factory teams to check out the upcoming talent. This will be a great opportunity for the class rookies, too. There is so much talent coming up the ranks now that the professional teams literally have too much talent to choose from. One of the goals of Rodney Davis is to increase public awareness to draw in more investors and create more professional teams, now that motorcycle racing is drawing the same level of interest as car racing."

Burt was glad to finally have an opening. The producer had been whining in his ear all through Bobby's explanation. "And with that, we can move on to give you what's coming up in the first race that will begin in about four or five minutes. This race will be in the 750CC Superbike category and there are forty riders."

Bobby jumped back in without a cue. "This is a really interesting race today, because four of the racers will be racing 750CCs for the very first time professionally. What a way to start your professional career!"

"You think they'll have trouble on this track?"

"It's hard to say. It depends on how aggressive they get. Remember, this is their golden chance to get noticed, but the 750CC is a faster bike than they're used to racing. All four racers are crossing over from dirt bike competition, which is a totally different kind of racing using a much lighter bike. And I hear two of them are real risk takers, although I haven't seen them in action myself."

"Do you know which ones they are?"

Bobby looked down at his list of entries. "Yeah, here they are. The first guy is Brian Cox from Milpitas, California. He's wearing number 7. And the other is number 15, Matt Bradley, from Forrest Hills, Pennsylvania. Bradley's currently leading the U.S. Dirt Bike Championship. I'm really surprised that he would risk injury today. What's interesting about Bradley is that he's only been racing for three years and has moved up quickly in the ranks."

Inside, Burt was starting to get annoyed at his co-host's enthusiasm, but he knew it made for a great show. "Well, we'll see who's the real talent shortly, because the racers are lining up at the start."

Burt checked the starting stats as he spoke. "At the front of the pack we have Ossie Humphrey, River Collins, Jeff White—one of the rookies, and Sammy "Sparks" Anderson. Jeff White, by the way, is the son of Bob White, who raced for a short time with Ducari back in nineteen seventy-six before losing a part of his leg in an unfortunate street accident that took him out of the game. Bradley and Cox are actually at the back of the pack. Why's that Bobby?"

"Both Bradley and Cox had difficulties in the warm-up and timed laps. Bradley was all over the turns. He seemed to have trouble controlling the bike. And Cox was having rear tire problems. He blew out his back tire during his timed lap, fortunately right before the finish line, but it cost him valuable time. At least he finished the race. His mechanics were scrambling to figure out if it was a tire defect and it appeared that it was, so they had to change the type of tire he would be riding to a stiffer all dry surface tire. Now Cox has to hope that they made the correct choice. It's the timed warm-ups that determine what position you are in at the start of the race. It'll be hard for either Bradley or Cox to catch up to the guys in front, if they haven't worked out their problems."

Burt interrupted, lowering his voice to build tension for his home audience. "I'm being told the race is about to start. The flagman has raised the starting flag now. Let's watch." Burt and Bobby traded off calling the race as the laps went on. By the end of the sixty-fifth lap, three bikes were out of the race: Two because of mechanical problems and one went down coming out of the last left turn in The Serpent. Four riders were neck-and-neck for first place, well ahead of the other racers.

Burt and Bobby's voices grew excitedly louder as tension mounted going into the final lap. Neither could stay in their seats. Burt was totally mesmerized by the action and he passed on his newfound zeal to his audience. "This has been an increeedible race, folks, with only three and a half miles of track to go. It's anyone's guess who'll break free at the finish. I've never seen four riders stay so tight in the turns like this."

Bobby jumped in, unable to control his excitement. "It's truly incredible Burt! Normally, a rider gets uneasy when one guy is constantly leaning on him in the turns, especially towards the end of a race, but *four bikes* riding that close is asking for trouble." Burt expertly fed off of Bobby's words.

"Especially when two of those riders are first timers. Ossie Humphrey and River Collins must be holding their breath, praying these new guys keep their composure."

"Well, so far, Burt, White and Bradley are holding their own. White is a fairly consistent rider and has been able to hold on to his position in the leading pack. Bradley has shown tremendous talent coming from behind. He's been aggressive in the turns, usually sliding the back wheel, which is something dirt bikers do all the time, but it's risky on highspeed road surfaces. I've also noticed that he likes to make his move going into the last three turns of the track. That's how he jumped ahead of every rider he's passed so far. If Humphrey, Collins or White don't make a move before then, I think Bradley might be able to win this race."

As the race neared its end, Burt made sure his audience would hear his voice calling the last unforgettable lap of this race. "Okay, we're in the straight-away before the last three critical turns folks and its neck-and-neck all the way! Look at this! White has moved up a little on the bank coming out of the first left-hand turn and that's caused him to slip back behind Bradley! It's Collins on the outside! Bradley and Humphrey pressing him on the inside coming out of the turn! Collins is making a move now and he's moved up a half of a bike length on the straight track! They're coming up to the next turn now; and, oh no! Humphrey is slowing down! Humphrey's bike is smoking and he appears to be out of the race, folks!"

"That smoke is from his tire, Burt. Looks like he gambled and lost."

"Not only that, Bobby, but Collins went into that turn a little high and has dropped down to the inside! He tried to knock Bradley back with that move but Bradley wouldn't budge from his spot and Collins just lost the lead! That Bradley has guts!" Burt and Bobby talked as fast as they could, using the short straightaways between the turns to catch the viewers up on the action taking place.

"Yeah, it was a big risk for both riders to come so close. I bet you Bradley's leathers will show a burn mark from Collins' exhaust pipe pressing on his leg like that. And that maneuver allowed White to tighten up the gap in the straight coming out of that turn and we're now coming into the last turn before the finish. Here's where Bradley usually makes his move, but I'm not sure Collins knows it. Bradley is braking early coming into the turn and has given Collins room. White has dropped directly behind Bradley and he won't be able to gain anything there. Collins leads and look! Collins is banking high, *a big mistake,* Burt, and Bradley's taken the lead! Amazing! White has moved right beside Collins! *But wait!* Bradley's pulled

10

right! Oh no, he's flipped off the bike head first coming out of the last turn and is flipping over and over. His bike is cartwheeling after him and, good Lord, has come crashing down on top of his chest!"

Burt grabbed Bobby's arm to stop him from talking, afraid of losing the race ending. He screeched into the microphone, "White and Collins are fighting for first place with less than a quarter of a mile to go! Both riders are gunning it for the finish line and it looks like White has won! Incredible, a first time superbike ride for White and he has won the race!"

"What an ammaazing chain of events, folks and you saw it here on WYYM, your number one cable sports channel! I can't believe it! Whoa! Bradley is still lying on the gravel and he's not getting up. The bike literally bounced off his body and kept going until it hit the haybail in front of the grandstand. The medics have just reached him and we'll find out what's going on down there. What an unfortunate chain of events for the young Bradley. What could have gone wrong? White's bike was awfully close. Maybe their tires touched. Let's replay that last turn and maybe you can shed some light for us, Bobby."

"Okay, right here when he goes into the turn, he looks good. He has the lead and he starts sliding the rear wheel. No, it wasn't White's tire that did it. It looks like he just turned his front wheel to move over for some unexplainable reason, just as he was getting on the throttle. Sometimes when you do that while you're maintaining high speeds right there at mid-corner, your tires can regrip the surface of the road and the bike flicks the rider off on the high side. There appears to be a wet spot on that part of the track and it looks like he overcompensated when he turned his front wheel, something he would be able to get away with on a dirt bike track, but not on a smooth surface riding a superbike. That's what caused him to fall forward over the bike, instead of coming down on his left side and sliding. But there was no reason for him to move over in the first place. It was like he was giving the race away to White! He showed so much talent handling that bike up until that moment. It was clearly just an amateur mistake that cost him the race."

Burt took over. "What a shame! White won the race, but what a hollow victory. Such a tragic way to begin this opening day here at Capitol View Superspeedway. In case you just joined us, we're watching the paramedics work on Matt Bradley, who crashed in the last turn of the final lap of the 750CC Superbike race at the new Capitol View Superspeedway. Excuse me folks." Burt put his hand over his microphone and listened through his headset as his producer updated him on the situation down on the track.

"Well fans, I just received truly disturbing news on Matt Bradley. It appears his injuries are severe and he has not responded to the paramedics' treatments. It won't be confirmed until he arrives at the hospital, but his injuries are severe and possibly fatal." Dramatically lowering his voice, Burt played into the camera. "It is a sad opening day at the beautiful, new superspeedway that will be forever haunted by the tragic memory of its very first superbike race. Stay tuned for the 600CC Supersport race coming next. But first, we take you down on the field with our roving reporter, Jimmy Powell, who is with Clyde Cantwell, the track official representing Rodney Davis, designer and owner of this new track." Burt took off his headset and rubbed his eyes. Bobby had already left to go down onto the track and check out what was happening there. He looked over to his producer, Jackie, and smiled. "That should bring the ratings up on the six o'clock news today!"

Jackie blanched at Burt's callous remarks. "He's such a jerk! Nothing was going right today." She thought. She wasn't the only one who felt that way.

♥ ♥ ♥ ♥ ♥ ♥ ♥

Nothing had gone right for Matt Bradley that morning, either. In fact, his whole week had been a string of errors and mishaps that unsettled his normally calm facade. Matt arrived at the racetrack at nine o'clock that morning, instead of eight o'clock as he had originally planned. First, he left his racing gloves and had to go back to his house for them. Then he was caught in a backup on the turnpike because of an overturned tractor trailer carrying maple syrup that spilled all over the highway. He waited nearly thirty minutes for the gooey mess to be cleaned up enough to let cars go by. Matt was exceedingly agitated by the time he pulled into the racer's entrance of the new speedway. He could hear other racers already warming up on the track and cursed his luck. This was too important of a day to have all this happen to him. His bad start began to melt away as he drove past stall after stall of professional teams already hard at work, preparing their top racers' bikes. Some of his favorite professionals were just inches away from him and it gave him butterflies in his stomach to think he was finally living his dream. Sparks Anderson was walking out of his stall and waved to him as he drove by. He wished his family knew how exciting today was to him. He pulled over at the second to last stall and began to unload his bike. His best friend, Jeff White, came out of the stall and offered to give him a hand. Matt was so preoccupied that he hardly acknowledged Jeff's presence.

Jeff grabbed the back tire of the bike and helped ease it down off the truck. The two guys had been close friends for four years and Jeff knew Matt better than anyone right now. Although they had quite opposite personalities, they shared a passion for motorcycle racing that bonded them like brothers. Matt was popular, fiercely competitive and good-looking. Jeff was quiet, reclusive and average. If it weren't for racing, most people would think they had little in common. But the truth was they both had another aspect of life that was very similar—their relationship with their fathers. Matt's relationship with his father was outwardly strained from years of conflict. Jeff's relationship with his father looked normal to everyone around them, but Jeff felt the cloud of disappointment his father held over him because he was not the premium racer that his dad hoped he would be.

Jeff was the one who introduced Matt to motorcycle racing when they met in college. He had already been an amateur racer for several years. His father, Bob, and his Uncle Wayne both had prominent careers as professional, factory team superbike racers and racing went back two generations in his family. Bob was in his prime racing for the number one Ducari team back in the mid-seventies when he was involved in an accident with a pickup truck that left him with a crushed right foot and shin bone. His leg was so badly mangled that it was amputated just below the knee, tragically ending his promising career. Ducari hired Bob as a mechanic for a while, but Bob had a difficult time getting along with the team manager. He ended up opening a cycle repair shop and transferred all his hopes and dreams onto the shoulders of his only son. Jeff loved racing but never felt the competitive drive that his father and his uncle had. When Jeff was twelve, he dreamt of becoming an architect and designing skyscrapers and mentioned it often. For his thirteenth birthday, however, instead of receiving scales and graph paper, Jeff received a cycle owner's manual and a racing helmet. Jeff realized on that day that his dream would never happen. His future in racing was the only thing that held back the bitterness his father had about his own life. Jeff did not feel strong enough to assert himself and felt obligated to try and succeed.

Jeff's family had always favored the road racing circuit. He was more comfortable with dirt bikes and did well in that class. He tried his best to master road racing, but he didn't like the heavier bikes and danger of the game. Banking the sharp turns at high speed seemed almost violent to him. The g-force that he experienced on the turns compressed the bike's suspension and every bump was magnified causing his head to bounce around. He hadn't mastered the technique of blipping the twist-grip on the downshift while squeezing the front brake lever, so his bike jerked in the corners. Sitting tucked so low behind the windshield with his chin almost banging the gas tank felt like a twenty-pound weight had been placed on top of his helmet. Through all of this he had to try and look up as far as possible to see where he was going. The transition on and off the banking was really eerie when the bike wobbled and shook. Jeff didn't like how sensitive the bigger bikes were and how hard it was to master the front and rear braking. It was way too easy to lose control in the turns. He could not overcome the clutch of fear he felt in his belly, every time he went into one of those turns and felt the presence of those thirty-foot walls. They reminded him of menacing giants waiting for the opportunity to crush him. His cautious approach cost him valuable time and his chance to win. Jeff was more of a mechanic than a racer. He could take apart a bike and put it back together probably better than his dad, but winning a major championship title wasn't in his heart; that was his father's dream. Jeff couldn't figure out what his father could possibly get out of this kind of racing.

Meeting Matt seemed to be the best thing that could happen to him for a while. Matt had an almost supernatural talent for racing. Jeff outwardly felt a great relief. He could see the excitement in his father's eyes when he began to teach Matt the finer points of racing.

In less than a year, Matt had exceeded Jeff's skills. In their first professional dirt bike race together, Matt's first place finish overshadowed Jeff's best performance of third place. He had never placed in the top five before. It was an awkward moment for the two friends but proved that Matt's constant drive for perfection actually goaded Jeff to excel. Something began to happen to Jeff inside. All of a sudden, beating Matt was almost as important as proving to his father that he could race. Their odd loyalty to each other was cemented by their common goal to prove something to their fathers.

A whirlwind of activity picked up outside of the long line of garage stalls as celebrities began to make their appearance. Normally, Matt and Jeff would be preparing for the race in the general pit area at the end of the private garages reserved for the stars of racing. But because some of the top racers had bowed out of the risky competition, the four superbike newcomers were assigned the last two private stalls to share. Most stalls were buzzing with a team of men preparing bikes and tires for today's race. Most of the racers were either hanging outside of their stall or performing whatever pre-race ritual they were accustomed to do. Some racers exercised or jogged to loosen up or walked the track to memorize every turn. But a few had bizarre rituals like Rocky Jones, who used to scour the track in front of the Grand Stands to find a white pebble to place in the arch of his left boot. He believed that a pebble was the reason why he won his first superbike race, because the pebble caused a pain every time he leaned over too far in the turns. He never won a major race without a pebble in his boot. And then there was old Boots Watkins, who drank a dozen raw eggs before every race on the advice of a fortune teller he met in Las Vegas. The motorcycle racing circuit had an interesting mix of people.

Matt and Jeff tried to stay focused on their bikes and block out the commotion. They were responsible for the entire race preparation, with the exception of help from Jeff's dad, who wasn't even here yet, and a couple of his mechanics who helped change their tires during pit stops. They couldn't afford a mistake today.

It became even harder to concentrate when a large group of press and promoters stopped outside of their stall with the Metcor Tire Pin-Up Girls, Ronnie and Heather. Clad in silver halter tops and barely covering shorts with white cowboy boots, the two voluptuous blondes could stop any man in his tracks. The lovely vixens immediately caught sight of Matt working on his bike and strolled in to meet him.

Ronnie strolled over behind the bike, pressing up against Matt and making sure that her voluptuous breasts that strained against the shimmering fabric were in full view for him. She ran her fingers through his thick brown hair and purred into his ear. "Now, who do we have here! I've never seen you around before, racer boy! My name is Ronnie, what's yours?" Matt was none too shy with a response.

"My name's Matt." He ran his eyes over her body with a look of approval and smiled. "I'm not going anywhere else now."

"Ohhh, I like your style, sugar." The two exchanged lusty glances, as if agreeing on a future rendezvous.

Heather, feeling left out, jumped at the chance for a photo op with the strapping young man by mounting his bike in a most provocative way and pulling Matt's head down to plant a long, wet kiss on his cheek. Jeff immediately observed the competition going on between the two girls. Ronnie whispered something into Matt's ear and slipped a business card into his shirt pocket. Matt smiled and pulled both girls closer to him while the photographers snapped away. After the press scurried to find out who the two unknown racers were, a reporter shoved a mic in his face. "How's it feel to be with these two hot ladies before your first professional race?"

Matt responded unwaveringly. "Looks like I found my lucky charms! Don't see how I can lose now." The press loved his answer.

After the girls fawned over Matt for a few more minutes, their promoter moved them on. Heather climbed off his bike and waited for Ronnie to leave. She grasped Matt's shirt at the shoulders and pulled him over his bike and gave him a long, wet, full tongue kiss, the likes of which Matt had never had before; saying with the sweetest southern drawl, "Win the race today and I'll ride you tonight, Matt." She left the stall, passing Jeff and gave him a brief good luck pat on his arm.

Jeff shook his head while he watched Heather leave. "Man, you are like a chick-magnet!" He felt annoyance mixed with envy growing inside him, but he was used to this. Everywhere they went together, Matt got all the attention from the chicks. Matt liked that kind of woman, in particular—free and easy with no commitments. Jeff was growing tired of that scene. He wanted to find someone to have a real relationship with.

Matt laughed as he reached for a can of helmet defogger that was in his tool box. "Yeah, the perks of racing just keep on getting better and better. Have you ever seen such tits?"

Jeff tried to look amused. "I wouldn't know. When are you gonna start looking for someone a little tamer? You know, to settle down with."

"You don't know, because you have a sign written all over your scruffy face that says *marry me*. And who said I was ever going to settle down?"

"I don't know, I thought that was a given. Everybody settles down eventually."

"Not me. I've seen what marriage is all about and it isn't for me." Matt looked off in the distance as he placed the can of defogger back into his toolbox without even using it.

Until now, Jeff had brushed off Matt's preoccupation when he arrived this morning. But now he was becoming concerned as he watched Matt fool around with the throttle setting on his bike. Riders *never* messed with the settings done by the mechanics. Especially when the mechanic was Bob White.

"Whoa, Matt! You want to die an early death today? Dad will rip you a new one if he catches you messing around with your bike."

"Shit!" he told Jeff. "He always makes the throttle too tight. Besides, I can't wait much longer to get out there."

"You never cease to amaze me! I would think that even you would be a little cautious on this track today. I wouldn't take a chance on those turns, till I saw how these bikes handle it. Word is it's jamming with mystery at every turn. Hell, some racers are scared to race on it!"

"Never mind what I do, where the hell is your old man? Didn't he come with you? I was expecting him to be pacing in front of the stall when I arrived."

"Me, too. He was working on that revised cylinder design on my back up bike. Mom said he never came to bed last night."

"Is he planning on showing it to Ducari today?"

"I know he'd like to, but he's got to get it to really work first or they're gonna laugh him out of this place." Jeff frowned as he thought about his father's intent to prove something to Ducari, as if they walked on water. They were the very same people that, in his opinion, had let his father down.

Jeff noticed the worried look on Matt's face. "Something bothering you?" he asked and then added in a light-hearted banter, "Don't tell me you are nervous about the race today!" Matt was never nervous before a race.

"No, I'm not worried about the race. Hell, I can't wait to burn some rubber." He mounted the bike and started the engine. He loved hearing the roar of the engine and feeling the vibration of the big bike straining to be set

16

free. It was a used bike, but the most reliable design ever built by Ducari. Until he could get his hands on his trust fund, this was all he could afford. Lucky for him, Bob White was an excellent mechanic and performed miracles with the old bike. Between the three of them, they didn't have much money, but they managed to scrape together a couple of bikes reliable enough to win. If he could get this far with this used thing, he could imagine how far he would go on one of the new bikes Ducari has out now. Realizing he had zoned out again, he continued his conversation with Jeff.

"This has just been a really shitty week. I had a fight with my mom this morning and it was weird. I never saw her get so upset." Matt rubbed his right hand over his chin. "She's been bugging me all week to go to this dinner my dad arranged at the Brandywine Grille tonight. She says he has some big announcement to make. He's probably got another big shot politician coming to visit us. Remember last year when the Ambassador from France stayed at our house and we were invaded by French security for a week? Some f'ing fun that turned out to be!"

"Tonight?" Jeff asked, "What is she, crazy? Does she know about the race today? How do you plan to make it back in time with a two hour drive ahead of you?"

"I don't. But I just couldn't tell her that, so I said I'd try not to be late."

"You said you would? Why'd you do a damn thing like that?" Jeff knew Matt and his mother had a special relationship few people ever experience.

Matt looked exasperated. "I had to. She was so freaking upset. I can't get over how insistent she was. I asked her to tell me what was so important but she said she didn't know the details."

"So, do they know you're racing in your first professional road race?"

"Yeah, I told her. And you can imagine how thrilled she was. She knows it's an optional race that doesn't count towards my dirt bike title this year. She thinks I'll have plenty of opportunities next year."

Jeff stood up and faced him. "I can't believe she would ask you to give up this chance. What if you place today? Christ, what if a scout shows interest in you? Doesn't she have any idea how big this is?"

"She doesn't understand. Neither of them will even *try* to understand. All they want is for me to go back to school and complete my degree so I can get some cushy, responsible, ass-kissing job at my dad's company. What really gets me is this is the only thing they both agree on these days. They're so worried about me getting killed."

"Well, in a way you can't blame them. I mean, it wouldn't be, you know, the first time." Jeff hesitated bringing the subject up.

Matt sighed as he checked over his racing gear. "I know, man, it's about Sarah. I understand why she fears the worst, but Sarah had an illness. This is my life and I've got to live it my own way. Christ, I'm twenty-two years old. I'd be in my own apartment right now if I could swing it along with the racing expenses."

"I agree buddy, but lying to your mom! You two are so close. I'd hate to see the problems with your dad get between you and your mom. Your old lady ain't bad."

"Well, she can be cool, but she's a rug when it comes to my dad. She let's him walk all over her. You're lucky your mom is so understanding when it comes to racing."

Jeff smirked to himself, "My mom married it. She knew what she was getting into, although she doesn't always like it. Maybe if you ask your mom to come and see how good you are, she would feel better about it."

"You know, it's funny you said that because she tried to bribe me this morning by saying she would help me get my trust money if I came to dinner tonight."

Jeff wiped his hands clean on a towel and inspected his tire treads. Both of them were using Metcor's all weather design that rode a little too slow when they were cold, but could handle a long track pretty well. They couldn't afford the luxury of bringing along a trailer of tires. As it was, Bob made half of their stock appear out of nowhere and they didn't want to know how he got them. They used the all weather tires a lot and knew how to milk them for all they were worth. "Then this dinner must really be important to her, huh."

Matt paused at the revelation, "I guess so," he guiltily admitted.

"It's a shame. I doubt she'll feel the same way after you stand her up tonight." He saw he hit a nerve with his friend.

Matt started to put on his kneepads. He wore plain black leather gear against Bob's emphatic protests. Bob got two Ducari stock outfits, hoping to impress on them how much the boys wanted to ride for them. They were simple white suits with Ducari's red and green colors and a small Ducari patch on the chest. There were no other logos and Matt felt this advertised "beginner". The black outfit looked more menacing and helped him stand out on the track. Matt said he wouldn't wear their colors until they sponsored him. He wanted to make sure he left his options open for other teams. Wearing their colors may distract the competitions' interest in him.

Jeff had a thought. "What time is dinner?"

"Six-thirty."

"Look, race time is at noon. My dad and I can load your bike on our trailer and you could split after the trophy presentation and press meeting. If you left by five, you could at least make an appearance."

Matt mulled the idea over in his head. "But what if one of the scouts comes around to talk to me?"

"You'll have time to talk to them. If it gets late, I'll interrupt and tell you that you have a home emergency. Hell! They can't be offended if you leave then. Just ask for a meeting with them on Sunday. They won't be talking contract details while the parties are going on tonight anyway. Hey, it's your choice, but if you want my advice, you can have your cake and eat it too. You get to do your first pro race and finally get your hands on that trust fund."

Matt smiled as he tapped his friend's shoulder. "Sounds like a plan, thanks."

"Don't thank me yet. Shit, they're probably gonna want to talk to me after I kick your sorry ass out there!" Jeff threw a grease rag at Matt's head.

Matt laughed and pitched it back. They were interrupted by the sound of Jeff's dad backing up his trailer.

"What took you so long, old man?" Matt harassed Bob, as he glanced at Jeff with a look of appreciation that few guys cared to show each other.

Bob White was usually a pretty scruffy character. He was a stocky man with a protruding beer belly. His gray hair was wiry and appeared unkempt because he constantly rubbed his head in a nervous manner. His dark skin was wrinkled from time and wind and his steely blue eyes gave him a toughened appearance, even though on occasion he could be as gentle as a teddy bear. His voice was loud and coarse and he cursed a lot. Today, he was incredibly light-hearted. "Old man, shit! You boys don't appreciate where you're standing right now. We're with the pros, boys, and it feels good to be back. Besides, I was up all night fine tuning the cylinder head on the backup bike." He rubbed both his hands together as he walked to the back of the trailer bed. His usual limp was hardly noticeable. "And boys, I believe I've done it."

Jeff walked over to the trailer to lend a hand. The look on his face was sheer joy. "Jesus, Dad, you think it's ready?" Jeff and Matt had the same model Ducari bike. Bob wouldn't let them ride any other manufacturer. Bob was obsessed with his new bike design, which included a revised cylinder head. He spent months shaving metal off of every part of the bike he could safely manage, just to lighten the body weight. Every reduced ounce saved time in a race. He had retrofitted Jeff's bike with his new cylinder design last month but it didn't pull out of the start smoothly. The new cylinder design definitely made the bike faster, but Jeff had trouble downshifting going in and out of sharp turns. Jeff felt his father believed it was his inability and not the bike that was at fault, but Bob said he would work on the design further. If Jeff could master this new retrofit today, he would redeem himself.

"Ready son? Holy shit, this bike could drive itself over the finish line! And wait until the Ducari boys see this beauty. Damn, I finally can show

19

that bastard, Joe Hinkle, he doesn't know shit when it comes to engines." Joe was Ducari's team manager who got Bob fired after a major disagreement over research objectives. Bob had been working on a new cylinder head design that Joe thought was impossible. Bob's passionate drive to achieve some kind of recognition in the racing industry after his failed career caused him to become too confrontational with his peers. Bob lowered Jeff's backup bike off the trailer platform.

Jeff smiled over at Matt, who was finishing dressing. "Looks like today is everybody's lucky day."

His father's smile went from ear to ear. This was the day for which he had been waiting for a long time. He knew his idea was right, even though it didn't do well on the flow bench test. The air that is forced through the cylinder head on the test bench is not an exact simulation of road racing, no matter what its designers say. Bob believed he finally found a trick to increase the air turbulence in the intake track of the fuel line for more efficient burning. This made for a smoother ride while shifting in and out of the turns. Today was his day of reckoning. He couldn't wait to see the look on Hinkle's face.

Jeff went back to his bike to move it over and make room for the backup. His father was still rambling on excitedly about his discovery. Jeff thought about the competitive edge that this more powerful model would give him in today's race. For the first time ever, he had a glimpse at victory. If he could remain calm in the turns, he'd be able to overtake the seasoned riders. He felt a surge of adrenaline race through his body. Today, all three men could experience their dreams. Placing in any of the top five positions would get Matt and Jeff noticed by the scouts. Bob would see his son join the professional ranks and also redeem himself as a top mechanic in the field.

Jeff had another selfish thought about today. Beating Matt would be his ultimate victory. He loved Matt like a brother, but as with any sibling rivalry, he felt a surge of resentment sometimes at Matt's natural talent. He grudgingly justified that Matt wouldn't even be here today, if he hadn't introduced him to racing. At last Jeff felt wisps of the competitive drive he had been missing for so long and his mind sharpened to the task ahead.

Bob White released the kickbar of the cycle and turned it toward the two guys. Jeff watched him push the bike forward and march the ultimate winning machine toward his outstretched hands that waited to grasp his prized possession. Matt was busy rechecking his tires. His father smiled down at his masterpiece, as if he was a proud king presenting his newborn prince to his subjects, and then glided the bike past Jeff's outstretched hands straight toward Matt.

Jeff's expression froze as a surge of disbelief flooded his senses. Matt looked up, first at Bob and then Jeff, and stood in stunned silence. Bob was beaming as he started to give a confused Matt the rundown on the changes. Matt's eyes darted between Jeff's devastated stare and Bob's excited ramblings.

"Now remember Matt, the Ducari boys will be here any moment and all eyes are on you. I told them you are the best here today and that you and this bike would steal the race. You better get on the track early to get a feel for it. This bike will feel a lot different than yours." Bob turned toward his son, not even aware of Jeff's shattered expression.

"Jeff'll help you make the adjustments, won't you son? You can tell him what you have trouble with on your bike." Completely oblivious, he turned back to Matt and drove the knife a little deeper into his son's back. "Don't worry, kid. I'm sure you won't have the same problems Jeff's had working out the kinks."

Matt's bewildered emotions began to fade as he started to address Bob.

"Bob, don't you think Jeff..." but his words were interrupted as Bob called out a greeting to Tony Delucci, one of the owners of Ducari.

"Tony, Tony over here!" Bob flagged down the dark-haired man in his early fifties, who was walking by the stall, and shook his hand vigorously. "Tony, I want you to meet your next star racer." He led the man straight to Matt who continued to stand looking like an idiot with his mouth agape.

The man extended his hand to Matt and gave him a hardy shake. "Nice to meet you, young man. Bob has done nothing but praise you from the moment he started working with you." The man hung his thumbs on the waist of his pants. "So, you think you can be number one someday?"

Matt's eyes jumped to Jeff's acrimonious stare. He stood dumbstruck until Bob broke the silence.

"Someday? Tony, he's gonna be number one today!" The two men laughed and then Tony looked at the two bikes parked side by side. "Which bike is the new design you were telling me about?" Bob pointed to the one he was standing next to. "Well, Bob, I guess it's time to put your money where that big mouth of yours is!"

Bob laughed and began to caress the seat of the Ducari. "This is it, Tony! Mark my word, you're in for a surprise today. Oh, by the way, this will be Matt's first ride on the new design, so expect even better performance than you see today. By next year's Championship, Matt will be a blur on the track." In an after thought, Bob turned to Jeff and added, "You remember my son, Jeff."

"Sure I do, nice seeing you again, Jeff. Now you boys take care out there. It's a hell of a course! Got my boys on their toes." Tony and Bob turned and began to walk toward the grandstands together. Bob never left the boys alone during warm ups. Usually he would be breathing down their necks every step of the way. Jeff saw the writing on the wall. All eyes would be on Matt. His father had been promoting Matt to Ducari all along. Jeff felt a pain of betrayal so deep, he thought his heart would crack.

Matt tried vainly to explain how bad he felt. In his own mind, he could not justify why he had not spoken up before the conversation got out of hand. He never expected Bob to treat Jeff as he did, yet he could not summon the courage to stop it from happening. Was he that selfish that he would sacrifice a friendship for the sake of a win today?

"Jeff, man, I'm sorry. I should have said something but I was in shock. I can't ride this bike today. Here, you take it. Bob should have never done this to you. I had no idea this was coming."

Jeff knew it wasn't Matt's fault directly for what his dad just did. Nevertheless, this incident unlocked a deep wound inside Jeff that sent a mixed bag of emotions rocketing up to his conscious level. All of the resentment, envy and jealousy that was suppressed by a sense of loyalty and love for father and friend were cut loose by the blade of a knife that now penetrated him deeply. It wasn't Matt's fault that he had better racing instincts than Jeff did. Still, it didn't make Jeff feel any better.

Jeff glared at his friend, "No man, you race it. That's what my old man wants. Far be it from me to take his damn victory away from him." Jeff started his bike up and grabbed his helmet. "I gotta get out there, apparently I need the practice."

Matt watched Jeff ride towards the track and take off popping his front wheel.

He looked over at Bob walking toward the grandstands with Tony Delucci, laughing and totally unaware of what he had just done. How can I race against Jeff like this, he thought. Why would Bob put me in such a position? Matt saw in Bob what he saw in his own father. Both had a drive to succeed so great that they would sacrifice their relationships with their only sons. But now what could he do? He had worked hard for a shot at the race. This may be his only opportunity with Ducari. Without a sponsor, he could never afford to compete seriously, even with his trust fund. And if he won, he could show his own father that he wasn't a failure. He began to rationalize about Jeff to himself, just like he had done with his mother earlier. He thought to himself, Jeff knows I didn't do this. He'll get over it. He still has his own shot at placing in the top five. Jeff's skills have improved a lot since I started racing with him. He said so himself. With that reasoning, Matt was able to clear his conscience for the moment and he headed toward the track.

♥ ♥ ♥ ♥ ♥ ♥ ♥ ♥

The rest of the morning became a nightmare for Matt. He wondered if Bob was crazy. The new bike was so sensitive, it felt like it wanted to throw him off every chance it got. It was like riding an unbroken stallion. Coming into the turns, the bike would shake almost uncontrollably if he used the brakes early, like he was used to doing. He finally figured out how to use the throttle right before the mid-section of the turn. This did not give him as much control with his slide coming out of the turn, but after practice, he got the hang of it. In his timed lap, he almost went down on turn six and ended up in last place on the starting line. Bob White was furious that Matt was taking risks attempting to slide in the turns on an unfamiliar bike. After the timed lap he flagged Matt into the stall and discovered that a worn part had caused the settings to slip. He changed the part and re-adjusted the throttle, so it wasn't so sensitive when Matt shifted gears. It was the same problem Jeff had complained about in his earlier design. Only now, Bob believed it.

Jeff, on the other hand, had a great timed run and was sitting up front at the start of the race.

Matt could see Jeff's red, green and white striped helmet, the Ducari colors, from where he sat in the back of the pack. Jeff never turned around to give him a thumb up, which is something they always did at the start of the race. There was no time to be bothered by that now. Matt adjusted his helmet strap and put on his race face. It was an imperturbable veil. His concentration was so intense that it had a menacing quality to it. His eyes focused on the starting flag and his ears listened to the sound of his bike revving. He had the uncanny ability at the start of any race to become one with the bike. He noticed every noise and vibration the bike made and knew what parts were making them. He could even feel if his tires were cold, warm or hot while sitting there. He connected to the paved road and allowed his senses to be guided by a strange unspoken language between him, the bike and the track. It was "the zone" that every rider strived to discover and it came easily to him.

When the flag dropped, only calculated thoughts of victory were left in his mind. The bike took off from the start smooth as silk. The last adjustment that Bob made to the cylinder did the trick. Matt was able to gain position on every turn. His adrenaline soared as he passed bike after bike with a pass and block maneuver that worked great going into the serpent. His performance was flawless until Jeff's bike came into view in the beginning of the last lap. Matt was impressed at Jeff's tenacity throughout the race. Maybe this was what Jeff needed to spark a fire of competitiveness in him, he thought. Surprisingly, his mind drifted from the task at hand. Matt was hanging in Jeff's draft by the time they reached the serpent, when Jeff gave him his opening by banking too high, giving him just enough room to pass him on the inside, forcing Jeff to drop behind him. Collins pulled ahead of him by half a bike length in the straight, and Matt was brushing legs with Humphrey when he saw smoke coming up between them. His breathing froze as he checked his gauges. Everything looked fine and the tires felt good. Matt exhaled when Humphrey pulled onto the grass oval inside the track and he was aware fleetingly that the smoke was from Humphrey's tire. The next turn was coming up and Matt saw Collins pull right a little, forcing him high mid-turn and then into a death drop towards Matt coming out of the turn. He recognized the defensive maneuver and moved toward him slightly, hoping to throw Collins off guard. Collins was trying to ride him off the road, never expecting this rookie to counter his move. The riders touched together briefly, but the surprise was enough of a shock to cause Collins to back off and lose his lead. Jeff moved directly behind Matt into his draft, close enough to pull on Matt's bike's momentum. Matt cursed his friend for slowing him down and letting Collins smoke past him on the short straightaway coming into the last turn.

Matt took the beginning of the turn easily and saw his opportunity for victory when Collins banked high and created the opening he needed. "Perfect, you son-of-a-bitch, I gotcha! This race is MINE now!" Matt smirked. He was ready to make his final move and started switching gears when his actions stopped cold. The sound of Jeff's bike pulling in closer amplified into every cell of his body. A sudden thought flashed through his mind that this stolen victory would put him in the same category as his father and cast a shadow on his friendship with Jeff forever, possibly even ending it in this very moment. Matt had only one brief second to decide his fate. His breath caught in his chest and his temples began to pound. Sweat broke out on his forehead and his hands remained in an iron grip on the handlebars. It was not like him to lose his focus at such a critical moment. The betrayal was more than he could bear. He suddenly realized that this race would be won for all the wrong reasons. There would be no family or friends on the other side of the checkered flag to celebrate with tonight.

Without a second to spare, Matt moved over six inches to the right to let Jeff by and slipped in a wet spot made by a rider earlier, when he ran off the track into a puddle on the side of the course. Matt's speed was too fast and his front tire was too hot and greasy and it forced his handlebars to twist to the right, sending him and the rest of the bike into the air. Matt's body cartwheeled end-over-end with his bike following in the same mode. He ended up sprawled out on his back at the edge of the gravel pit that separated the track from the Grandstands. Pain had already taken over his senses from the series of broken bones, torn muscles and wrenched ligaments each flip on the track had made. Matt was unaware of the additional damage to his kidneys, lungs and heart that the 350 pounds of bike made when it crashed down onto his broken body forcing the life out of him.

♥ ♥ ♥ ♥ ♥ ♥ ♥ ♥

Matt's eyes opened to a brilliant white light he thought to be sun glare. He started to recognize sounds of people rushing towards him yelling for help. He felt an undefinable squeezing sensation, as if someone was pulling him up by his jacket shoulders through some kind of a funnel. It was reminiscent of a birthing experience, but then, upon study, it seemed more like a genie coming out of a magic lamp. It was as if his body had become a vapor substance that allowed it to stretch at the narrowest point and re-expand in the wider areas. The stretching sensation started in his head and went completely through the body to the very last toe. When his feet came through the narrow opening he heard a popping sound and he floated gently to the ground. His body felt incredibly light and rejuvenated but he remained in a disconcerted state, unable to grasp what just happened. The white light faded away unnoticed.

Matt stood looking down at the dark form that was stretched out on the ground. He did not recognize his own body because of the three dimensional view he had of everything he saw. He saw the front of the body and also the back at the same time and it gave an entirely different appearance from the one way view we see in the mirror. Matt sighed for the poor guy lying motionless at his feet, feeling dazed himself from the crash. He did not notice that he was not in pain. He felt bad for the unfortunate fellow who must have gotten tangled up in his accident, although he could not recall anyone else other than Collins and Jeff around him when he went down. He bent down over the body and was about to check for a pulse but was distracted by blaring sirens. The ambulance had just arrived and two paramedics in dark blue uniforms and baseball caps sprang from their seats and began pulling equipment off the back of the truck. As they rushed towards Matt, he politely stepped aside so they could begin working on the accident victim. He turned to scan the area for his bike.

By now the field was filling up with bystanders and a crowd had circled around the body the paramedics were trying to revive. Matt started walking away from the accident toward the inside field and began to feel uneasy about the situation. The scene reminded Matt of an earthquake disaster, as people ran around him from different directions and sometimes almost through him, totally unaware of his presence. Matt couldn't understand why no one was asking him if he was alright. He guessed the fact that he was walking around was enough proof, besides that guy on the ground looked pretty bad. Matt smiled when he finally saw Jeff racing across the field on his bike and flagged him down. Oddly, Jeff whizzed by leaving him standing with his hand raised high in the air. "Jeff, yo, wait." Matt yelled to Jeff's back but he didn't stop. Bob White was running along the side of the track toward the accident. His reddened face looked terrified. "Bob, wait up! I can't find my bike." But Bob never acknowledged him. "What the hell is going on here!" Matt yelled, turning in a circle as he tried to make sense of this madness.

Panic swept through Matt's body as his eyes fell on Jeff and Bob frantically parting the crowd to get to the victim. The air filled with a crackling hiss that sounded like static on the phone. The buzzing grew louder and louder in Matt's head, causing him to sway off balance. He ran back and followed Bob through the crowd, afraid of what he would see. Matt heard Jeff's voice cry out his name. When he came through the parted crowd and saw Jeff kneeling beside the body, trying to stay out of the paramedics' way, his heart dropped into the pit of his stomach. Bob White leaned over Jeff, clutching his son's shaking shoulders. Jeff continued talking to the body he was calling Matt. "Matt, oh my God, what did I do!" He grabbed the body's left arm and looked up at the paramedic closest to him. "Is he okay? What's wrong with him?"

The paramedic gently removed Jeff's hand and told Jeff the news. "Your buddy suffered massive injuries. I'm afraid there's nothing we could do to save him."

Bob White brought his hands up to his face and tried to choke back his emotions. Jeff rested back on his heels and Matt watched his shoulders shake from his sobs. Matt's confused thoughts raced in his mind. He knelt down next to Jeff and quickly began to comfort him. "Jeff, buddy, it's me. You didn't do anything. Christ, I'm right here next to you! I'm alive." But his words trailed away as soon as he watched the paramedics lift the body onto a stretcher and he saw his own lifeless face. Matt jumped up in disbelief and frantically tried to understand the situation. "No, no I'm not dead, I can't be." He clutched at his clothes and scanned his body. Everything was intact. His jacket, pants, kneepads, boots, everything was real. He took off his helmet, ran his hands through his hair and felt the familiar tug on his scalp. "I'm alive, I am."

Behind him came a familiar sweet voice that startled him, "No, Matt dear, I'm afraid you're not."

Matt whirled around, shocked to see his petite great-grandmother Anna, his mother's deceased grandmother, standing calmly by the edge of the track. Matt always called her Gram. She stood with her hands folded together resting on a long tan robe that was fringed at the bottom. She was dressed like an Indian shaman, with her hair braided on each side and a turquoise necklace with a bear head pendant around her neck. It was a far cry from the normal light blue housedress that she always wore when the family came to visit, but Matt knew it was her. She was such a small woman, barely five feet tall but she had the presence of a giant.

"Gram, I don't understand, what's happening here?" Matt looked back and forth between Jeff and Anna, unwilling to accept what he knew in his heart to be true.

His great-grandmother reached out her hand. Matt was almost afraid to touch her. She had been dead for about ten years, yet she stood there with the same healthy glow as when he last saw her. And Matt could smell the lilac perfume she always wore that used to linger on his clothes after a big hug. However, there was a new soft white aura around her. She was a vision of calm in the middle of the maddening chaos.

"Touch me, Matt, I'm not gonna hurt you, son." She chuckled and stepped closer. Matt brought his quivering fingers toward her outstretched hand and lightly touched her fingertips. They were as soft as he remembered and he slid his fingers into her warm palm and she gave him a reassuring squeeze. He looked over at Jeff once more.

"I'm dead, for real?" He looked back at her gentle face; the buzzing sound in his head grew distractingly loud again, blocking out the other noises around them.

"Yes, Matt, you are." Her gaze softened. "It's time for us to go."

"Go where? I can't leave Jeff, and what about my mom and the dinner tonight? She's never gonna know I intended to come. She'll be devastated when she finds out I'm dead. What will happen to her?" Matt became almost livid. "No, I can't go with you, I'm not finished here."

"Yes you are, Matt, there's nothing you can do, you're dead." Her voice became firm.

Matt looked at Jeff still crying by his body. He walked back over next to him. Jeff was talking to his body as if he were alive. "Matt, it's my fault, it's my fault."

Matt looked back at Anna. "I gotta help him, Gram. He can't go through life thinking it was his fault. I moved over myself. It was just an accident."

"Tell him that, Matt!" she instructed.

"But I'm dead, he can't hear me."

"Yes, he will. Tell him!"

Matt put his hand on Jeff's shoulder. "It's alright Jeff, I'm okay. You didn't do anything. It was an accident." Jeff's body seemed to relax under Matt's touch and his voice became steady.

"Listen, buddy, I owe you one. I'll never forget what you did for me."
Jeff fixed Matt's crumpled jacket sleeve so it lay smooth. "I know you
opened up the hole for me. I hope you know that I won. And I'll make sure
your mom and dad know what you did, too."

Matt realized he had one hope in redeeming himself with his mother.
"Tell her that I was going to make dinner tonight, Jeff. Please tell her for
me."

Bob White helped Jeff to his feet while the paramedics placed the
stretcher on the gurney. They walked arm in arm towards the ambulance
knowing their lives would never be the same.

Matt looked back at Anna. "Did he hear me? Will he tell her?" She
waved her hand to the left of them and a small cloud appeared that showed
him his answer. He saw Jeff and Bob knocking on his front door and Janet,
Matt's mother, inviting them in. His parents were getting dressed for the
dinner. Both men waited for Matt's father to join them before they broke the
news. Jeff told them and Matt watched his mother collapse into his father's
arms. Matt heard Jeff tell them how upset he was about the fight with his
mother that morning and that he had planned on coming to dinner. He told
them how Matt sacrificed his victory that morning for Jeff. Matt felt better
but still heart sick at the sight of his emotional mother. The cloud faded
away. Anna stepped up next to him and grasped his hand. Her touch sent a
warm feeling through him.

"It's time to go, Matt. They will be alright." And they started walking
away from the crowd of people. They heard the paramedics close the door
of the ambulance and a reporter summing up his story of the accident scene,
but neither of them turned around. They kept walking hand in hand across
the field.

"Where are we going?" he asked.

"Home, Matt. Where we all came from." Her answer was as casual as
the stroll they were taking.

"How do we get there, Gram?" Anna laughed softly at his question.

"Oh, I think you are in for a treat!" They reached the end of the field and
the buzzing grew louder. The scenery dissipated into thin air and the two
stood in a misty gray cloud. His great-grandmother turned to face him and
straightened his collar in a maternal way. "Well, this is as far as I can take
you. You have to make the journey back alone."

"What do you mean alone? Where are you going?" Matt began to panic
again. He felt like he was 4 years old.

"Relax, son. It's okay. Everyone has to return home through the light by
themselves. It's part of the process. Now remember, you are never alone."

"But, where will you be? Don't you go through it too?"

28

"Yes, but in a different way." Anna squeezed his hand one more time. "Don't worry Matt, I'll see you on the other side. I think you will get a kick out of the ride. It's fast—just like you like it." She let go of his hand and walked by herself deep into the mist until she disappeared. Matt stood spellbound as the gray mist began to swirl creating a tornado-like funnel of wind around him. The buzzing sound became deafening and he felt the same tug on his shoulders pull him up into the whirling cloud. The buzzing sound quickened to a high pitched whine that got sharper as he increased speed. Matt moved faster and faster. He tried to fight the velocity by waving his arms and legs to no avail. He traveled so fast that his skin and clothes felt like they could not keep up and blurred into a trail of nothingness, until finally he felt like a pair of eyes traveling along. The cloudy mist formed a tunnel that became perfectly round inside. A blue light filled the tunnel and the buzzing noise faded into a soft whispering voice that beckoned him on. It kept saying over and over, "This way, this way." The direction of the tunnel began to shift and he propelled forward instead of upward in what felt like a maze. Matt made a sharp left and then a quick right turn before straightening out again. The pattern was repeated over and over. This went on long enough for Matt to adjust and he began to enjoy the different sensations. It felt even better than the high he used to get when he was in the "zone" on his bike in a race. Finally, he became his experience, feeling one with the sound, with the blue light and with the speed that he traveled. Instead of *moving through* the different sensations, he *moved as part of them*.

When his sensations of rapture became almost more that he could endure, Matt was jettisoned into a large area of grayish blue mist and he slowed down to an ethereal saunter. Up ahead were clusters of wavy blobs of a darker gray that seemed to move together in a pulsating rhythm. As Matt approached each group the mist parted, creating a path for him to travel. As he passed within a few feet of the first group, the face of an elderly woman emerged from one of the blobs. She smiled at him and welcomed him home. As he passed each clump another face would emerge extending a warm greeting. Some were old and some were young of various ethnic persuasions. Each group seemed to have a mix and when he passed by they would sink back into their dark miasmic form. There were about ten groups in this area. Up ahead was a pinhole of bright white light past the last group. The light was drawing Matt to itself and he floated towards it, while he watched it begin to expand. When he felt the beam of light, he was immersed in a brilliant flash and now floated alone in brilliant warm, white mist. The same voice that whispered direction in the tunnel began to whisper again. "Sleep, Matt, sleep." A light tinkling music similar to wind chimes filled the air and Matt's eyes began to close. He no longer felt the need to try

Helen Heinmiller

to control his surroundings. As he listened to the music, his apprehension melted away and he drifted into a deep and comforting sleep.

Chapter 2

Matt stirred from his long rest expecting to see the fine white mist swirling in front of his eyes. Instead, he was startled to find himself in his childhood bedroom. He jumped up from the twin bed where he had been resting and quickly scanned his familiar surroundings, trying to absorb the change. He was aware of the faded football print sheet he was laying on first, remembering how much he loved this print before realizing he was no longer dressed in his racing gear. He was wearing his favorite khaki pants and a solid navy blue short sleeve polo shirt. He glanced over at his dresser on the adjacent wall and saw the first peewee football trophy that he had ever received. He remembered as a young boy how proud he was of it. When he was little, he polished it so much that the inscription began to fade. This was the time when he was so close to his father and mother, before they moved to the bigger house where they now lived. It was before his father lost interest in him. For a moment, Matt was transported back to that time in his life. The memories brought tears to his eyes and he wondered at how the magic of those days faded away as he grew older. He hadn't thought about it in years.

Matt was so absorbed in his thoughts that he didn't notice the creaking of the rocker in the other corner of the room at first. His heart began to pound fearfully when he suddenly became aware of someone in that corner. With a sigh of relief, he smiled when he saw it was his precious great-grandmother Anna again, rocking patiently without a word.

"Gram, you scared me for a moment! I was just thinking about the good times I had here." Matt returned to a more pensive state. "What am I doing here? Why are we in my old bedroom?"

Anna rose from the rocker and sat down next to him on the bed. She began to rub his shoulder like she used to do when giving him advice. Her touch seemed to draw the uneasiness right out of him. "I am so glad to see you again, Matthew. I have missed you so much. Although I didn't expect to see you this soon!" Her eyes rolled from one side to the other, as she patted his knee. "You always managed to surprise everyone, you know. Never a dull moment around you!"

Her voice carried the same sprightliness he remembered. Matt loved his great-grandmother. Gram had lived to be ninety-five and was vivacious to her last breath. She appeared once again dressed like an Indian shaman and holding an eagle feather in her hand.

"Gram, why are you dressed like an Indian?"

"This is how I like my spirit to be seen." She reached down and lifted up the bear head pendant to show Matt. "I am from one of the soul groups representing the spirit of the Native American Indian Wisdom. Throughout my lives on Earth, I have lived under this influence. I come from a long line of healers in the Indian heritage. When I incarnate, I always stay in touch with this part of my soul in some way."

Matt remembered how Anna used to bring over various mixtures of herbs to make tea when someone in the family got sick. She would sometimes smudge their forehead or throat with sage and chant some old Indian prayer. Matt never thought she was serious. In fact, he thought she did it more for amusement, seeing how most of the grown-ups would groan when they saw her coming.

He remembered the time his father had a fit when he came home from work and found her performing a smudging ceremony on the front lawn of their new home to chase evil spirits away. His mother insisted that everyone let her do whatever she wanted. Matt thought she only said that because Gram was family and she was the closest grandchild to her grandmother. Most of the family regarded her as the quirky relative you never talked about and dreaded bringing her to public affairs. You never knew what Gram would say or do next. He loved that she always said exactly what was on her mind, but never in a way that could be taken offensively. Gram especially knew how to get his father upset and he enjoyed watching them spar at the dinner table. Gram disliked the pharmaceutical distribution business he was in. She believed it had lost its healing intentions and was driven purely by profits. It was a sore subject between them.

One thing Matt was sure of was that Gram had an exuberant outlook on life and he always looked forward to his summer visits to her house in Lancaster as a young boy. When she died he missed her, but he never thought he would see her again and now she was his lifeline.

"I really screwed up this time, didn't I?"

"No, my son, there are no mistakes in life, only detours. We are all walking the same path to God. Only some of us like to wander off onto side roads."

"Well, I messed up with Mom, really bad. I said a lot of hurtful things to her when I left the house. I can't believe that's what she'll remember me by." Matt was truly saddened by his admission.

"Oh, my poor boy—no! Not at all. Do you really think that your mother would choose to block out all of the wonderful memories of you and only remember this one? You need to give her more credit than that! We all have said things out of anger, to someone we love, but anger is a temporary thing.

Only love is permanent. That is what we are trying to learn on our journeys."

Matt tried to find comfort in Anna's words, but he couldn't. "I told her that she was a rug when it came to Dad. I brought up all those memories of Sarah and now she has to relive them all over, because of what I've done. I told her she was weak and shouldn't have let Dad ruin her life. And now I've probably done just that!" He was appalled to find that he was near tears.

"Yes, Matt. You did use some harsh words. It was a difficult time for everyone when Sarah died. It left scars on every member of your family. You chose to believe it was all your father's fault, didn't you?"

"It was—not her dying, but everything else. I used to listen at the top of the stairs at night to Mom and Dad arguing about Sarah's treatments. I know Mom wasn't happy with what the medicine was doing to Sarah, but she wouldn't stand up to him."

"And that was your father's fault?"

"Yes, of course. He wouldn't listen to her." Matt was surprised that he had to defend his mother to Anna. Anna was so close to Janet. She used to show his mother all kinds of remedies and rituals of the Indian tradition. "Why are you taking my father's side?"

"I'm not taking any side, just making an observation."

"It wasn't like she had much of a choice with Dad working for a drug distributor."

Anna felt so sorry for Matt at that moment. She saw the confusion of a little boy unable to make things better in his eyes. "Remember when I just told you that I come from a long line of healers?"

"Yes."

"Well, in our group, some of us incarnate into certain family lines every other generation. Some of us come to learn, and some of us come to teach. We take the same path as everyone else, that is, we *forget* everything when we are born and set out to discover who we are. When we are in the early stages of development, we have the same problems as any other soul in overcoming the temptations of the material world. And so some healers will falter and some will grow in a lifetime."

Matt interrupted. "You are a healer! I see that now. But, then why didn't you save Sarah—you helped Mom take care of her the whole time she was sick?"

Anna placed the eagle feather down on the bed. She faced Matt and looked him squarely in the eyes. "I did have the power to heal Sarah, son, but it wasn't up to me."

"What do you mean, it wasn't up to you! Are you telling me that God wouldn't allow you to heal my sister!"

33

"No! God wanted Sarah healed, although not only for Sarah's benefit as you might think. She knew why she had come to Earth in that life."

"Then why?"

"Because I was there as a teacher, not a student. It was up to the student to heal Sarah."

"How can that be? There was no one else there that was a healer, except for…Mom, who you were showing how to use your medicine. Oh my God, Mom? You were teaching Mom to be a healer?"

"Yes, I was."

"And she let Sarah die."

"No! She did not fully realize her own abilities at that time and she hadn't come to terms with who she was. Part of the torch that she has carried in her heart is the unconscious knowing that she could have saved Sarah. But, Matt, there is no one to blame for this. Sarah gladly took on this mission knowing that there was a good chance her mother was not ready. But Sarah has no regrets. There will be other opportunities for your mother to grow and other lifetimes. It is important not to judge these things. No one is at fault. Not your mother, not your father or you."

"Oh, God, I can't believe this. This is crazy!"

"It might seem crazy, but it's true Matt. Welcome to the real world!" Anna kissed him on the forehead. Matt sat quietly for a minute. On one hand her explanation started to make sense to him, but at the same time it didn't make any sense at all! He couldn't digest all of this news at once, so he went on to other questions.

"Have you seen Sarah?"

"Yes and your great-grandfather and Aunt Dot and everyone else."

Matt was relieved, "Can I see her, why isn't she here with you?" He couldn't imagine Sarah wouldn't want to welcome him to this strange new world.

"You will see her and others in time, but probably not right away. Sarah is preparing to incarnate into a new life on Earth and cannot be disturbed. She wants you to know how sorry she is for not being here, but her preparation comes first. It's another thing you will understand in time. Sarah is very excited about her next assignment."

Matt winced at Anna's words. He could not accept the concept of reincarnation of any sort and chose to drop the topic for now. He continued with his questions. "Why are we in this bedroom? And what happened to my body in the tunnel?"

Anna smiled and hugged him. "Oh, Matt, you are right. I do need to answer your questions. It was just so good to see you! My, how you have grown into such a handsome young man! You look so much like your father." She straightened up on the bed before continuing.

"Well, where do I begin. First, you are not in your old body or your old room. These are simply illusions. When we die, depending on the spiritual level we have achieved, we require different types of familiar surroundings in returning to our real spiritual state. We are all merely light forms. When you leave your physical body, you need an adjustment period to get used to your new lighter form. The physical body is rather heavy, don't you agree?"

Matt nodded, remembering the sensation of leaving his body. Anna went on.

"It is necessary, though, to remain in spirit form when you are crossing from one dimension to another. Once you arrive here, you turn back to the form of the physical body you are most comfortable with, until you are ready to move to the next phase. Now, in cases like yours, where you have unexpectedly died at a young age, it usually takes that soul a longer time to get over the shock of leaving the Earth so suddenly. So you are set in a familiar surrounding from your Earth life that has happy memories to help comfort you and ease your transition. The next time you return, you may not need this sort of help." Anna tried to convey the feeling that this was all quite natural.

"What are you talking about the next time I come back? How can that be so?" Matt was bewildered.

"Oh, I'm sorry Matt. I keep forgetting that you were brought up believing that we have only one lifetime on Earth. That is not so, dear. It will all come back to you as you move through processing." She noticed Matt's confused state and tried to reassure him. "It's okay to be anxious, but believe me, I promise that you will understand soon. I have to be going now, but your guides will be here in a few minutes to take you to processing."

Matt's panic grew. "Why do you have to go? Can't you come with me to processing? I don't understand."

Anna stood up and gently took both of his hands in hers and pulled him to a standing position. Her eyes twinkled with love as she smiled up at him. "Do you remember how I used to tell you that you were a child of the brown bear when you were little?"

"Sure I do."

"What did I say?"

"You said that I was born at harvest time under the influence of the brown bear and the south winds. And like the brown bear, I was self-reliant and strong, because I preferred to stand on my own two feet rather than rely on others. And that the Indians regarded the brown bear as an intense dreamer, whose beliefs were so strong that it could make any dream come true."

"Yes, but I never did get a chance to tell you more about the Brown Bear People. You lost interest by the time you were old enough to understand. Brown Bear People are very constructive by nature and are good fixers with both their hands and their hearts. They bring tenderness and understanding to human relationships. The South Winds influence their growth by allowing them to experience life through their emotions and feelings. However, they tend to over-focus sometimes on what they see in the moment and don't look beyond their own interpretation of an event to realize the whole situation. Brown bear people's walk in life is to learn to balance their emotions with truth."

"Why are you telling me this now?"

"Because you seem to have mastered working on machines like your motorcycles with your hands. Now you need to concentrate on fixing relationships with your heart. Just remember this advice and you will do just fine. I love you, my son, but I have to go now. Remember, everything is okay. There is nothing to be afraid of. We are not from the same soul group here and I must go back to my own group now. I'm so glad that I was able to be the one to welcome you home. In time you will see that this is the safest, most wonderful place to be. God has a perfect plan for all of us here! Trust God and you will never be afraid." With that she gave him a warm hug, pinched his cheek and pulled away.

With a wave of her hand, her physical body became transparent and fused into a ball of light that shrank into nothingness. Matt watched her blow a final kiss and whisper I love you to him before she disappeared and he felt reassured. "I love you, too, Gram!" Matt whispered back. He sat down on the bed and covered his face with his hands. For a few seconds, his mind emptied of questions and he enjoyed a silent peacefulness. His thoughts then returned to his great-grandmother's announcement that he would be visited by guides.

♥ ♥ ♥ ♥ ♥ ♥ ♥ ♥

After a few moments, Matt felt the now familiar feeling of a presence standing right inside the door of his bedroom. He cautiously peered between the cracks of his fingers to confirm his suspicion. He was amused to see two people of a gentle nature waiting patiently for him to become aware of their presence. Matt was not startled this time as he looked up.

An older man in his fifties stood stiffly holding a clipboard, along with a young woman, who appeared to be about twenty. The man had sandy brown hair cut short. He was much shorter than Matt and appeared frail in stature. He wore a long, brown robe that oddly faded into the ground, as if it were melded with the floor. Matt noticed that his hands looked very feminine. He wore Benjamin Franklin style wire framed glasses that exaggerated his fragile features. His nose was long and slender and curled up slightly over his pursed, thin lips, giving him a prudish appearance. The elder man spoke up in a monotone voice, "Hello, we are the caseworkers assigned to you."

"Why are you assigned to me?" Matt asked, "Where exactly am I?" He felt himself relax, although he was not sure why.

The young girl spoke up for the first time, as she moved forward. "You are in Heaven, of course!" Matt became spellbound as he studied her closely. This girl was utterly breathtaking. She had dark amethyst eyes that he had never seen on any human and they danced with an expression of joy so animated that they stirred his heart. When she spoke, her voice had a musical quality that left lingering vibrations of what sounded like a harp note at the end of each sentence. If her voice were a jewel, it would be the Hope Diamond.

Her long blond hair fell gently over her shoulders in the softest shades of yellow; wrapping around her like a mink stole. Her robe matched the older man's outfit and seemed far too drab for such incredible beauty. Her facial features were perfectly symmetrical and her skin glowed as if she were standing under a soft pink light.

The softness of her features reminded Matt of his own mother's beautiful face, especially her expressive eyes. Now he could only picture the sadness his mother's eyes would portray and his heart sank for a moment.

Matt refocused on his question. "I know this is suppose to be Heaven. I meant what part of Heaven are we in?"

"Oh, sorry!" The girl blushed at her mistake. "This is the recovery area. A place to rest after making the transition."

The older man rolled his eyes and adjusted his glasses as he pulled her back next to him. He seemed rather annoyed by her enthusiasm. He spoke again. "We just need to take down some preliminary information before we begin processing you for your return."

"Return?" Matt croaked, "Return to where? What did I do wrong?"

The young girl moved quickly to Matt's right side and placed her hand on his arm while glaring over her shoulder at the older man. Matt felt a tide of love rush through him as she touched his arm. "You didn't do anything wrong, Matt. You're just going back to Earth."

Now Matt was really confused. "What do you mean I'm going back to Earth?" He stood up and began to pace along the bed.

"Matt," the elder man said "there are many questions that need to be answered and we will get to all of them, but for now I must insist that we follow our procedures, one step at a time." The elder glanced down at his

37

clipboard and began spouting off information. "Most of these questions are just for confirmation. We already know everything about you. This is just a formality. First," he began, "your name in Matthew Stephen Bradley born September 4, 1976?"

"Hold it, hold it!" Matt spewed. "This is going too fast!" his pace quickened. "I have to know some things first. This is blowing my mind." Matt sat down on the corner of the bed and ran his fingers through his hair.

The older caseworker looked over at the young girl and shrugged his shoulders. "I knew this case wasn't going to go well. It's bad enough being assigned a rookie, and now I have an immediate return case. I should have retired!" He put down his pencil and gestured for the young girl to take over. "Go ahead, fire away," He crossed his arms and impatiently drummed his fingers.

"Don't mind him," the young girl exclaimed, "He's all bark and no bite, if you know what I mean. What is it you would like to know?"

Matt wasn't sure where to begin. He didn't fully understand what his great-grandmother had told him. "How come I can see and feel my body now and I couldn't in the tunnel? Are your bodies real or just imaginary?"

"Oh, that's an easy one," the young girl blushed. "We take on a physical form for all new arrivals. It eases the tension as you adjust to your spirit state. Especially during initial processing."

Matt glanced down at the floor where their robes blended into the wood. It was the only thing that defied his physical surroundings. The girl continued.

"Obviously, you left your physical body behind on Earth. Most people down there grow up knowing that your physical body stays on Earth. For a short time after you arrive here, you still have an attachment to seeing souls in the physical form. It makes things easier for you initially, if we all can see each other in physicality."

"Okay," Matt agreed, "So, who are you exactly? Some kind of fellow spirits like Gram or some kind of angels without wings?" His tone had traces of sarcasm.

The girl ignored his attitude and answered reassuringly. "We are angels. Here in Heaven we don't usually wear our wings unless it's a special occasion. Some souls, however, need to see the full dress to accept that this is Heaven. If you want, I can show you mine. Would you like that?" The older angel protested, "That's really not necessary, I think we have established our identity!"

Matt ignored his response. "Sure, go ahead!"

The beautiful angel moved away from Matt to allow room for her wings. She clasped her hands reverently together over her heart and bowed her head in a prayerful state. Out of nowhere a soft golden light shone directly down over her head, casting shadows over her face from the loose strands of hair that fell down in front of her. Her once dull robe glimmered with golden highlights.

As she began to raise her face toward the expanding light beam, her hands stretched out in front of her. She lifted her hands above her head and graceful white feathered wings unfolded behind her shoulders. The subtle sound of a praising choir wafted through the air until the immense wings were in full spread about ten feet across, almost filling the small bedroom.

Matt was dumbfounded as he walked around her to get a full view of her resplendent beauty. Her wings arched about eight inches over her shoulders and in full spread he could see flecks of gold on the underside of the feathers. After a minute, she folded her wings in to rest gracefully on her back, stretching down to about knee length.

Matt curiously touched the feathers on her right side and saw them bristle at his touch. They were softer than silk and, as he ran his index finger over each one, he could see the gold highlights on the underside create a rippled wave effect. It was the most magnificent sight he ever experienced.

The older angel tapped on his clipboard in an annoyed fashion for attention, disrupting the splendor of the moment. The young girl smiled sheepishly at Matt and gave him a surreptitious wink as she bowed her head once more and the light above her faded away. Her wings dissolved into golden dust and disappeared like fireworks into thin air.

"Wow, that was spectacular!" Matt stammered at a loss for words and finally asked, "What are your names?"

"My name is Anjella. This is Enon, he is my trainer." She turned to Enon with a surprisingly affectionate look and continued, "We've been together for almost a year in Earth time. Am I right, Enon?"

"Seems like a millennium, if you ask me!" he quipped, still looking at his clipboard. Anjella just smiled at him.

"Enon?" Matt scoffed, "Isn't that None spelled backwards?"

Anjella's hand covered her mouth, as her enchanting eyes grew wide. "In all our time together, I never realized that!" she laughed. Both Matt and Anjella chuckled as they looked toward Enon, who tried to appear untouched by the comment. Matt could tell by the look on his face that he had heard that joke a million times before. Enon peered over his wire frames with a disapproving look and remarked "Why do I always get the wise guys?" And then added. "Now, if the two of you do not mind, I think we need to move on to central processing. You can continue questions and answers on the way." With that he turned, as the door opened on its own, and entered what appeared to be a hallway outside. Anjella held in a giggle with her hand and began to exit, too.

Matt hesitated for a minute, unsure that he was ready to leave the security of his old room. Anjella turned and took his hand. "Trust me, Matt, it will be okay." She said. "You are in God's safe hands now!" Matt smiled and allowed her to lead him into the corridor. The three turned left and began moving down a long hallway with grayish-white walls that seemed to lead nowhere.

Chapter 3

Matt and Anjella did not waste any time returning to their conversation. Enon picked up the pace, hoping to speed through this unusual assignment as soon as possible. The corridor walls were bare and gray and rather unimpressive for Heaven, Matt thought.

Anjella responded quickly to Matt's non-verbal observation. "This may not be what you had expected Heaven to look like; but, again, we like to make the transition between Earth and Heaven as easy as possible. Many souls are still adapting to the idea of leaving Earth. Case worker angels use this time in the corridor to prepare souls for Heaven's grandeur. Everything we do here has meaning."

Matt's eyebrows raised in amazement. "You can read minds, too?"

"There's really nothing to it once you get the hang of it." Anjella chimed. "When your spirit evolves to the next frequency, you will be able to do this, too. It is usually the only way we communicate around here. Remember Matt, speech, movement and hearing are all part of your physical senses that you leave behind when you die. Knowledge is free here. You simply have to think of a question and the answer will automatically come to you. You will not receive this ability, however, until you have transitioned into the next phase. Hopefully, you will move to this level when you return."

Matt grew frustrated again. He strained to understand what was happening. "Why do you keep saying when I return? How can I go back to Earth if I've already lost my body? And why is it so damn important that I go back? I think I would really prefer to stay here and check this place out."

"Everyone prefers it here, Matt, this is Heaven!" Anjella went on. "This really isn't the time to go into questions about your return. They will be addressed during your review. I can only tell you that returning so soon is very rare. The Elders will explain this process to you. Enon and I will supervise your return to Earth and then reprocess you when you come back. That's all I have been instructed to say on the subject."

"So who are the Elders?" Matt asked.

"Everyone who enters Heaven must go before the Elders. They are a group of twelve highly evolved spirits who show you your life's accomplishments and transgressions and then place you at the proper spiritual level to continue your growth according to your life merits on Earth."

Anjella went on. "Anyway, back to your thought about this plain corridor. Heaven," she paused and smiled, "is so beautiful and so vast that

41

no words can even explain the brilliance of its many worlds. Heaven encompasses all possibilities and therefore it will take you an eternity to experience all of God's magnificent domain."

Matt was more curious than ever. "So when do I get to see all this beauty?"

Enon piped up for the first time. He halted the group and turned Matt to his right. "Simply open your heart and your mind and it will be revealed to you." As Enon finished his words, the drab corridor began to transform before them. The dull gray wall in front of them crystallized and parted forming a hallway into an enormous courtyard. Enon signaled Matt and Anjella to enter first.

Matt's heart stirred as he gazed at the sight before him. The courtyard was more majestic than the grandest palace on Earth. It was as big as a football field and more than 100 feet high. The walls were white marble with flowing lines of silver and gold veins that seemed to pulse and glow as if they were alive. As a matter of fact, everything appeared to be alive in this grand courtyard. About twenty yards away from Matt marble steps led down to a sitting area in the center of the courtyard. There were four curved marble benches forming a circle with large gothic pillars between them. Each bench could seat about twenty people. A circular marble platform rose in the center of the benches. Anjella explained that it was used for lectures. The four pillars reached up 100 feet into the air. At the top of each was a large statue of an angel, sounding a trumpet, standing twenty feet high. There was no ceiling over the center court. The sky above was dark and filled with magnificent stars. Matt could see many of the constellations that he knew. The courtyard was filled with bright sunshine despite the dark sky above and there was no lighting source to be seen. Beautiful plants lined the steps leading down to the courtyard and against the outer walls. The plants' leaves were spectacular shades of blue-greens unlike anything on Earth. In the center of each wall was a tall archway framed with detailed carvings of angels leading to more corridors. The walls of these three hallways were adorned with beautiful paintings and statues, very different from the hallway Matt just came from. Cascading flowers hanging from large pots created a waterfall effect in each corner. The flowers sparkled like jewels and swayed in time to the faint music that lingered softly in the air, adding to the underlying vibration felt in everything around them. Many of the flowers were brilliant blends of colors Matt had never seen before. The floor to the right of the central seating area displayed a large mosaic scene of the entire angel family surrounding a grand golden throne that emanated a powerful light. The great masters of Earth stood encircling the angels on the outer rim of the mosaic. Some of the masters were dressed in robes from ancient times, while others wore modern garb. Matt recognized Dr. Martin Luther King, Mahatma Ghandi and Mother Theresa among them. There were men and women dressed in very futuristic clothes. Matt wondered if these great masters were yet to come in the history of Earth. Was it possible that the entire history of the Earth was already foretold in this picture? From various angles the picture appeared three dimensional, especially the great light emanating from the center of the throne. The floor to the left of the seating area displayed another mosaic scene that looked like the Garden of Eden. A man and a woman stood on each side of a majestic tree bearing golden fruit. Animals of every kind, some unfamiliar to Matt, wandered through a rich green forest that surrounded them. Matt noticed that the serpent was not present. Again, the meaning of this picture puzzled him. Was the serpent left out for a reason, or did it even exist, he wondered.

The walkway where they were standing went all the way around the center courtyard. Matt realized for the first time that it was buzzing with activity. Angels in either brown or white robes were escorting people of all ages and races. Occasionally, groups of angels would pass by together, chatting about certain souls or procedures. The scene looked much like the first day of school on a college campus. Everyone was smiling and excited.

"Where are we?" Matt was barely able to ask.

"This is our central processing area. Each hallway leads to a different station, depending on where you need to go. The hallway over to our left leads to angel headquarters." Two angels in white robes entered that hallway as Anjella spoke. "That hall is used mostly by angels returning from a search and rescue mission or angels that fill prayer requests. The hallway directly across from us on the other side of the courtyard is the one we will use. It is called the Human Affairs station. All souls making their transition from Earth that have acclimated to their new spiritual state go on to their review. The hallway to our right is for souls that have not yet been able to adapt to their new state as spirits. Some souls do not want to part with their physical bodies and require an adjustment time. We have special healing stations that allow them to adapt. They are given as much time as they need. When they are ready, they move to Human Affairs."

"Everything appears to be so bureaucratic here!" Matt sounded almost disappointed. He thought about working at his father's company and how stifled he felt by all the formality.

Enon seemed annoyed and snipped, "What did you expect in Heaven, chaos?"

"Well I didn't expect to get an angel with an attitude!" Matt barked back.

Anjella jumped between them. "Okay you guys. Enough! Now Matt, angels have feelings, too! Enon's been processing souls for ages, so I'm sure his enthusiasm is a little worn. And Enon, just because Matt is your 455,255th case is no reason to be rude. So both of you be nice." Anjella bristled past them and started walking toward their station.

Enon turned to Matt and chided, "I guess she told you!"

"I guess she told *you*!" Matt whispered back.

Anjella just smiled at the control she showed and patted herself on the back. She had only been working with Enon for a short time, but had never seen him let his feathers get ruffled by a case before. This was Anjella's first return case ever. Maybe there is more to these cases than I realize, she thought to herself.

Anjella slowed her pace as she entered the long Human Affairs hallway to allow the others to catch up. Both were walking silently side by side. Matt walked by the first room on the right and peered in. The sign above the entranceway said Inspiration Room. Several angels and their assignments were wandering around what looked like a museum.

"What is this room for?" Matt asked.

Enon took delight in explaining. "This is just a sampling of the various inspirations that have been sent down to Earth for creation there. Everything on Earth is first created here in Heaven. There are mansions devoted to each Earth century that pay tribute to each creation. You will notice that each example here has two plaques above it. The first plaque has the name of the spirit or spirits that first created the inspiration or invention. The one below that has the name of the humans on Earth who manifested the work for them."

Matt moved closer to the first painting on the wall and recognized "Water Lilies" by Monet. Above Monet's name was the name Zacharios. Next to the painting was a display case with the model of a car belonging to the inventor Henry Ford and a plaque with the name Adonna above his name. As Matt roamed the room he saw the cotton gin, a spacecraft, various flowers and vegetables and even a paper clip. Some inventions listed the names of groups of sponsoring spirits.

"This is all too crazy." Matt exclaimed. "How are these individuals chosen to receive these inspirations on Earth?"

Anjella fielded this question. "Some individuals come to Earth for the specific purpose of inspiring or inventing some thing that will further human evolution. Other ideas are sent into the Universal conscience for any enlightened soul to grab."

The three continued through the room and returned back into the hall. Matt looked around at the various groups of people casually strolling along. "No one appears to be in much of a hurry!" he noted to Anjella.

"There is no such thing as time here. You have all of eternity to explore this world. Each soul can advance through Heaven at their own pace, once they have completed their Earth lessons. If something appeals to a soul, the soul can stay there as long as it likes. Eventually, when a soul has fully matured at that level, it will move on to the next level. At various levels, the guides instruct in small groups. These souls work together to accomplish a specific task to further their enlightenment. Usually the assignments involve missions on Earth. At the more advanced levels, souls work individually with higher level guides called masters." Anjella noticed Matt's surprised reaction. It reminded her that it was hard for those who died earlier than their planned time to recall the process, because they lacked the proper closure on Earth. This block normally is corrected by the time they finished their review. Anjella wondered if this would happen in Matt's case.

Enon suggested that they make their way towards central processing. Matt's case was very different from the other souls exploring the halls. He must return to Earth. There was a lot of coordination involved in this effort. At the end of the hallway was a large room about a quarter of the size of the courtyard. The room was decorated like the inside of a bank. The walls were painted a soft two tone blue color which gave the room a serene feeling. There were five booths off to the right of the entrance where case worker angels and their assignments entered to begin the induction process. Straight ahead, a hallway branched off oddly in two different directions forming a v-shaped corridor. Down the right corridor was the entrance to the conference room with guarded double doors. Anjella explained that after a preliminary processing is completed, each case moves into the conference room for review. After their review, the angels and cases exit through a side door of the conference room into the hallway on the left side of the fork. Then they walk back toward the main room to the observation screen or turn right and continue down the hall to exit the building. She pointed out the observation screen that was twelve feet to their left. It was about six feet high and eight feet long. The screen was slanted on a forty five degree angle so that only the person or persons standing directly in front of it could see it. This area was roped off from the main area and could only be entered via the conference room.

An old man and his angel walked up to the screen. Matt moved over to the gold velvet ropes and stood on his toes in a futile effort to sneak a peak. He watched as the old man gestured and pointed to an area on the screen. The old man's shoulders raised and lowered and he let out a wonderful chuckle as he embraced his angel. The two turned and began walking down the left hallway past the conference room. The old man continued to talk excitedly and pat his angel on the back.

Matt turned toward Anjella to ask what the screen was. Enon went off into a booth for a moment.

"That's the eternity window. After your review, if you have led a good life on Earth and are deemed worthy by the Elders, you will receive your first reward in Heaven. This window allows you to see where you will be spending your next phase as a spirit. Usually, whatever your true passion was on Earth is the dream that comes true for you at the eternity window. Take Mr. Baxter, who just finished his viewing. He was a kind, decent man while living on Earth. His true passion was gardening, specifically working with roses. In the eternity window he saw that he would be working in one of our best gardens here in Heaven. He has been assigned the privilege of crossbreeding the next six hybrid roses for Earth. This is a dream come true for Mr. Baxter, as you can imagine. When you receive your eternal rewards here in Heaven for a good life on Earth, the emotional or physical sufferings you may have experienced while on Earth hardly seem any trouble at all."

Matt contemplated what his window would look like. He wondered how he would fare before the Elders. The thought suddenly occurred to him that you could not change the bad deeds you performed during your life. How often had he taken for granted the things that he had done without heeding the warnings given by his family regarding responsibility? Perhaps he was too young to believe in the frailty of life. He was beginning to dread his foolishness now.

Enon signaled to Anjella and Matt to come into the second booth. The booth was nicely furnished with a large dark wood desk and comfortable chairs. Enon was standing next to another male angel in a white robe who was seated behind the desk. This angel looked up at Matt and said, "Hi, my name is Stefan. Please have a seat. I have just a few items to go over with you, before you go in front of the Elders for your review." He turned to Enon and asked, "Have you adequately explained the review process to Matt?"

Anjella sat down in the chair next to Matt and responded, trying to gain some credit. "I explained the process to Matt, however, since he is a return case, I did not go into all the details of check in."

"Oh, a return case, how interesting." Stefan perused a screen on his desk. "Yes, I see here. It says an unscheduled racing accident. We don't see too many of these. Very well then, this curtails the interview process a bit. Matt, just for the record you are Matthew Stephen Bradley, born to Stephen Joseph and Janet Ashley on September 4, 1976?"

"Yes sir."

"Since you will be returning to Earth, I will not go into the details of your likes and dislikes at this time. I am going to leave you for a moment to arrange for your review. When I return, your case workers will escort you into the meeting. I know it seems a little intimidating, but the review is not as bad as most souls think. The Elders are very wise and kind. We will do our best to make it as comfortable as possible." With that, the young angel disappeared before their eyes.

"Hey, how come he gets to blink in and out and you don't?" Matt inquired to Enon.

Enon waved his hand. "They like to show off a little in processing. They don't get the attention most case worker angels do around here, so they feel left out."

Matt shook his head. "Too much like Earth if you ask me!" This whole process was overwhelming to his senses. Heaven was not what he expected and far from what he was taught. It seemed so physical to him sometimes and then he only had to look down at the floor and see his case worker's robes blending into the marble. Yet, their robes were made from fiber and their hair and skin seemed just like his. When he walked, they glided or was he gliding along with them? It was hard to distinguish what was illusion and what was real. Matt had become intrigued in this new world and he dreaded the idea of leaving it so soon.

Stefan's return was not as flashy. He spoke up from the door. "The Elders are ready to receive you Matthew."

Matt froze. He looked over at Anjella for comfort. She smiled softly and took his hand as they stood up. Enon placed his hands on Matt's shoulders and gently turned him toward the hallway. Matt thought he felt a slight squeeze. Enon's facial expression softened, too. "Let's go Matt." He said quietly.

They turned down the hallway and stopped at the guarded doors to the conference room. Two tall, sinewy angels in armored suits stood in front of the doors. Both angels acknowledged the case workers and stepped aside as the doors swung open on their own. The room appeared very bright and the three proceeded in. The room was small compared to the other areas Matt had seen. He noticed the rectangular shape of the room defied the triangular walls from the exterior hall and this subtle illusion amused him again. In the center of the room was a large table in the shape of a half circle. Twelve men were sitting on the curved side directly facing him. The table was made of a white iridescent material. The Elders wore robes of various colors and adornments. Each Elder emanated wisdom beyond human comprehension. Matt was directed by Enon to sit in the lone chair at the center of the table facing the twelve men. Two female and two male angels stood in attendance behind the Elders. They were dressed in sleeveless white full-length gowns with gold belts at their waists. Everyone exuded a positive attitude that somewhat allayed Matt's fears.

Matt surveyed the Elders. The scene before him was reminiscent of the Last Supper except that the men appeared older. Could they be the twelve apostles of Jesus Christ? He felt very intimidated as he sat down. The two men in the center appeared to run the meeting. They conferred quietly for a moment and then turned to Matt. The Elder on the left was the only one to speak.

"Welcome Matthew. We are pleased to see you." There was no attempt at introductions on their part.

Matt blushed. "I'm sorry sir, this is all very confusing to me."

"We are sure it is. Before we begin your review, we need to explain what has happened to you." The Elder sat back in his chair gathering his thoughts and allowed Matt to get comfortable before starting.

"When each soul incarnates on Earth, it leaves Heaven with a planned agenda. The agenda is designed to bring this soul closer to oneness with God, which is pure unconditional love. This is the ultimate goal of every soul. At a certain point, the soul advances to a state of being that does not require physical manifestation on Earth, but continues its work here in Heaven. These souls join the Illuminati. But until then, each soul, with the help of its guides, chooses the experiences necessary in the next Earth lifetime to help itself grow. In most cases, you even choose how long you will live and what illness or accident you will die from. Then, a carefully orchestrated plan is made between a group of souls all incarnating at the same time, who have agreed to help each other. From this group comes your parents, friends and other associates you encounter throughout your life. This does not mean that every soul you meet on Earth is part of your group. The souls that are a part of your group usually are the people that you bond with quickly or the ones that you are in conflict with the most."

Matt's eyebrows raised in surprise at the Elders last comment about conflict, thinking about his relationship with his dad.

The Elder smiled. "You expected that your avenues of growth would only come from pleasant encounters?" Before Matt could answer he went on. "It is surprising to many souls when they begin to remember these things upon their return. While in the physical state, it is hard to comprehend that the boss who drives you crazy, or the loved one who betrays you, or the friend who stabs you in the back had actually agreed to the circumstances *before* they went down to Earth." The Elder savored the concept with a glint of laughter in his eyes. "You grow by how you see yourself in each experience you have. Life on Earth will always have chaos. It is how you allow the chaos to affect you that determines your growth. Were you a victim or a martyr or a hero? Did you let that situation defeat you or did you step up and take charge of the situation? The souls who agree to play the aggressor in such events are actually giving you the greatest gift of love! Of course, not everything that happens to you is predestined. There are unfortunate occasions that happen more frequently than we would like, where a soul strays so far off course that his or her destructive actions affect innocent bystanders. And oh, what a frenzy that makes for those guardian angels! But, after some shifting around of plans, eventually everything is set back on course and life goes on. Now, in your case, Matt, *you* are that unfortunate strayed soul. This was not your time to come home. In fact, you were on the verge of an incredible breakthrough."

Matt was dumbfounded. Surely he was the victim in this tragic occurrence, he thought to himself. He moved over to let Jeff win the race. He was trying to help his buddy. How could he be the rogue that disturbed the delicate balance of whatever mission he was on?

The Elder knew his thoughts instantly and answered his questioning stare. "I know you do not understand this now, but you will see in time. Unfortunately for you, when you come back sooner than anticipated, and in your case by at least fifty years, your soul is in a state of shock. It takes some time to remember everything before the incarnation. If you were to stay here, your memory of whom you are, the entire *you* that has always existed, would come back to you. You see, when you are born all memory of Heaven and your goals are erased from your conscious memory. You simply forget. It is up to your soul, your higher self, to persuade your conscience to make choices that will help you remember your plan, or maybe calling is a more comfortable word to use. As your soul evolves through many lifetimes, you remember earlier and earlier of your connection with the Divine and consequently, you make the more perfect choices sooner, moving you closer to your true Godself experience.

Let me give you the bigger picture, if I may. The wisest leaders on Earth reconnect with their higher self early on. This gives them insights and capabilities beyond that of the normal man or woman. They are able to lead and inspire masses of souls. People in positions of power who become destructive forces on Earth experience the same awakening, but allow their human ego and attachment to the material world to overshadow their mission. The unparalleled joy, that is the birthright of each human being, is when they discover and act upon a calling that helps others. However, few souls are enlightened enough to come to Earth with such grand agendas. It takes an incredibly strong soul to withstand the test of the material world. That is why many will stray."

The Elder stopped talking. Matt noticed that his heart was throbbing, as he tried to take in the Elder's explanation. His mind spun off a dozen questions at one time. Even so, he remained in a strangely calm state. The Elders allowed him time to gather his thoughts.

"We know you have many questions. Are you clear about most of what I have told you?"

"Yes, I think so, but I would like to know about my own mission. What was it about and who is my guide, is it Enon?" Enon and Anjella exchanged amused glances.

"No, Matt, Enon is not your guide. Normally your guide would have greeted you and seeing him may have helped you remember. But in your case, special angels were assigned because of your untimely death and the need to send you right back. Although, your guide is always with you in spirit and can be summoned by your thoughts. Why don't you summon his presence and let him explain the nature of your mission."

Matt did a double take. "How can I do that, sir?"

"Just use your intention."

Matt shifted in his chair and began to call his guide forth, unsure of what to expect. Immediately, a gray mist appeared behind the Elder who was speaking and a form of a man appeared. To Matt's utter amazement, a small Indian medicine man stood holding a sacred pipe in his right hand. He looked about sixty years old with long salt and pepper hair tied in a ponytail. He wore a headband made of cloth with a feather hanging down over his left ear. He was dressed in a long, white shirt that was decorated with rust and dark blue ribbons and he wore buffalo skin pants laced down the sides with rawhide. What was most startling to Matt was that the Indian's face looked exactly like the face of a statue his mother had in the curio cabinet at the top of the second floor landing of their house. Matt used to get in trouble for borrowing it to play Cowboys and Indians in his bedroom. His mother said that it was a very special gift to her from Grandmother Anna. Matt was always drawn to the Indian's face whenever he ran up the stairs.

The Indian spoke in a deep, sagacious voice with a strikingly familiar tone. "Matthew, welcome back. Do you remember me?"

"Roaming Bear? Your name is Roaming Bear, isn't it? Yes, I remember you now!" Matt became excited as memories trickled into his mind. "I can remember a talk we had. Yes, you had your arm around me and we were walking somewhere. I was happy, but I can't remember why yet."

"Yes, that was our last conversation before you left here. I was wishing you good luck."

"Right, now I remember. I was going to a place to meditate. I think it was called the Preparation Tank." Matt clearly saw a picture of this as he talked. He felt like a trap door had been opened and everything became familiar again. He was with his dear friend whom he had known forever. He realized that this was not the first time they had shared this walk together.

"Good, Matthew, very good." Roaming Bear unfolded his arms and relaxed his posture. "I am glad it is coming back to you. I have missed you while you were gone. You had quite an interesting time in this life. Things looked very promising for you, until your unfortunate accident." The Indian squinted as he spoke. "You were very close to discovering your calling. It is a shame this had to happen to you."

"So I have heard, Roaming Bear. But I still don't remember what my calling was." Matt looked into his friend's eyes. He felt relieved to be making sense of everything. Until seeing Roaming Bear, he was afraid he was not dead, but going mad. He was afraid the calmness he was feeling was his own mind deceiving him. But now, he knew it was real.

"This was a very important life for you Matthew. You were so close to graduating onto the next level here. Had you completed your mission, you would have joined the Illuminati."

"The Illuminati, you mean I would stay here?"

"Yes, exactly." Roaming Bear gave Matt a sympathetic smile. "Your objective in this lifetime was to experience in the physical state the ultimate act of unconditional love which is forgiveness. Also, you had agreed to assist your mother and father in their goal of being involved in the very initial steps of harmonizing modern western medicine and traditional ancient medicine. This is something that must occur for human civilization to advance spiritually in the next millennium cycle on Earth."

The more Roaming Bear spoke, the more memories surfaced for Matt. Roaming Bear asked him if he remembered the gathering room where he joined a large group of souls and their guides to discuss the nature of their next visit to Earth. Matt recalled bits and pieces of this, but not the details. The gathering room was where souls would come to discuss the goals the group would focus on and each soul would select the circumstances necessary for their growth and enlist the help of other souls. Some souls would remain together as families or best friends, while others would meet for special events and move off in different directions. By the end of the meeting, the complete life cycles were established and the ultimate outcome displayed on a viewing screen. When the group was satisfied with the results, the meeting adjourned and each individual went to their preparation tank to prepare for their incarnation.

Matt grew flustered again by Roaming Bear's words. He couldn't see any connection between the goals he had had at the time of his death and his mission. Certainly, his mother had shown interest in Indian medicine but his father seemed indifferent. And since his dad was president of a pharmaceutical distributor, it seem impossible that either parent could outwardly become involved in such a revolution without jeopardizing his father's career. Besides, he knew his father too well to even entertain the idea that he would give up his almighty title even for his mother.

The Elder sensed Matt's frustrations, "Matt, perhaps it would be easier if we can illustrate this for you through your life review. The review is divided into several parts. We will show you all of the good deeds you have performed during your stay on Earth as well as all of your transgressions and how both affected your fellow souls. Do you have a preference for which you would like to see first?"

"Can we just skip the transgressions altogether?" Matt joked nervously.

The Elder smiled warmly, "No Matt, what's good for the goose is good for the gander." Several of the Elders chuckled softly. Matt looked deeply into their eyes. He saw no judgment or condemnation. They seemed to accept him as he was, regardless of what the review might reveal.

Matt relaxed. "Okay, let's go with the good deeds first." He hoped it would be the longer of the two reviews.

"Very well, let's begin." As the Elder said this, a four-foot screen appeared in the table directly in front of him. Several pictures began to flash before his eyes at great speeds, but he saw every detail.

The review was two-dimensional. Matt saw various events in his life flash by as still photos, yet he was aware of how each event affected the individuals involved. He knew instinctively the chain of events resulting from that particular action.

He was very surprised to see pictures of himself as early as six months old. In one picture, Matt was in a stroller in the park. An old woman walked by the stroller and stopped to look at him. She was very sad and lonely. Her husband and family had immigrated to America over thirty-five years ago from Poland. Her two children had grown up and moved to other states. She missed her grandchildren dearly. As she was looking at Matt, he reached up and grabbed her finger and began playing with the tip of her long painted nail. He smiled and cooed at her. This simple touch brought back the loving memory of holding her own children and grandchildren. The old woman's eyes filled with tears as she turned to Matt's mom and told her how special this little boy was. The old woman went home and told her husband how wonderful it felt to feel a child respond to her. The next day, she applied for a job at a local day care center and was hired. Her life became full again. Matt could not believe how this simple act of kindness from a seemingly unaware infant affected this woman.

Many of the events that flashed by brought great delight to Matt, as he remembered the good times he had had with his best friends, Charlie, Robbie and Stuart. He was fortunate to link up with a group of boys who liked to volunteer in school and neighborhood projects. He saw scenes of himself working at local car washes and carnivals with them to help raise money for school and church. The best time he ever recalled was when his boy scout troop went to West Virginia to help repair homes with the Appalachian Trinity Housing Project that helped people in the poorest mountain communities there. It was the first time that he ever painted a house and he managed to get as much paint on himself as he did on the wall. That experience seemed more like fun than work to him.

Pictures of his good deeds and kind acts continued to go by. Each time he saw how little acts of kindness made such a difference in so many people's lives. One good word created a ripple effect that spread from person to person.

When it came to good deeds, Matt had an uncanny sense of timing. He seemed to know exactly when someone would need cheering up. Matt's eyes defiantly filled with tears as he saw a picture of himself with his mother when he was eight, just a short time before Sarah's death. The memories came back at a slower pace and he could hear the whole conversation that went on. It was the day he had picked some buttercups for her on the way home from school and was about to surprise her.

"Hi, mom. I'm home!" he called out to her from the kitchen. He hid the flowers behind his back, as he entered the dining room. Janet was wiping her eyes with a tissue when he came in. She tried to act casual.

"Oh, hi Matt. I didn't hear you come in. I'm trying to clean off this table. It looks like a tornado came through here." Her voice was shaky.

Matt moved around the far side of the table, so she could not see the buttercups. "How's Sarah doing?"

"Just fine. She's getting better every day! I think she's asleep right now." Janet wiped her sweaty palms on her skirt.

"Will she have to go back to the hospital?"

Janet's response was harsh. "No! She won't!"

Matt was surprised at how she snapped at him. "Well, jeez, I was just asking. It's not like I want her to go!"

Janet realized what she had done and rushed around the table to hug him. "Oh, I'm so sorry, Matt. I didn't mean to snap at you. It's just, I'm tired. I haven't had much sleep and with your father out of town—it's been hard." Janet pulled him into her and started kissing his head.

"Okay, okay. You don't have to get mushy on me." Matt pulled away from her. "Anyway, I picked these for you!"

Janet gathered the half-crushed buttercups from his outstretched hand and began to cry, which turned into a river of tears. She pulled out a chair and slumped down into it. After a moment, she realized how overblown her reaction was. She wiped her eyes and nose and apologized. "I'm sorry. I'm not sad. I really love them. I guess I'm more tired than I thought," she laughed. "Thank you. Thank you sooo much! This was just what I needed."

Matt was not sure what was going on. "Is something else wrong, Mom?"

"No, no. I'm fine, sweetheart. Daddy will be home tonight and things will be better. I promise!"

Matt had no idea at the time what a toll Sarah's illness had taken on his mother or that his gesture had given her just enough strength to get through the rest of her day. However, he saw now that had he not done this good deed, his mother's current mood would have led to a big argument with his father over something trivial that night.

The pictures began to speed up again as the review scanned the rest of his life. In his early years before Sarah's death, his good deeds centered around his family, usually helping his father clean the garage or helping his mother with the groceries. However, he noticed that by the time he reached his teen years, his good deeds seldom went to his father. The absence of these pictures made him feel guilty.

As this part of the life review ended, Matt had a good feeling about the kind of person he was, but this feeling was contradicted in his heart by the absence of love towards his father. He began to feel apprehensive about what was to come next.

When the screen faded away, the Elder spoke.

"As you can see from your review, you led a good life on Earth. Considering how young you were when you left Earth, you learned very early on how to live as God wants us to live. Much of the credit goes to your parents. They raised you well. We know you have already noticed your lack of charity toward your father in your later years. This is such a shame, because the two of you would have shared a wonderful life together. You will soon learn that had you exercised a little more patience that the two of you would have worked out your differences."

"Sir, with all due respect, my father and I never agreed on anything and I don't see how that would change. He was wrapped up in his work and never had time for me." Matt became defensive.

The Elder shook his head. "Is that your opinion of your father?"

"Yes it is, sir." Matt replied sternly.

The Elder conferred with the others briefly and turned to Matt smiling. "We will allow you to see shortly how blind you became to your father's intentions. Yes, it is true that he spent a great deal of time away from your family, but that was necessary for the plan. It was his position at his company that would give your family the power to accomplish your mission. Before you get too defensive about this, I think it is necessary for you to get to know your family's backgrounds better, so you may understand their positions.

Matt moved around uncomfortably in his seat. He began to feel heat rise up the back of his neck. He tried to remain aloof as he responded. "I don't think that's necessary, sir. I feel I know them as good as any one can know them. I don't think there will be any surprises."

The Elder was amused. "Well, young man, that is a bold statement. So, you are telling me that you believe in your heart that it is possible to know everything there is to know about another person."

"Well, yes. I mean, they're my parents. I don't think it is possible to live together as a family and not know who they are. I saw them every day of my life."

The Elder nodded his head. "Very well. This should go quickly then. Let's start."

Matt tried to object but the screen appeared on the table. The first picture was of his father, Stephen, as a young boy studying. Matt sat fixed in his conviction as the screen revealed the truth.

Stephen came from an upper middle class family who lived in the prosperous community of Sterling, Pennsylvania. His parents, Bernard and Margaret Bradley were quite demanding of their three children. Early in their marriage, Margaret came into an unexpected inheritance. They used the money to advance both of their education, as well as their social status. Stephen attended the Scottsdale Farm Boys Preparatory School instead of public school, before attending the prestigious University of Pennsylvania Wharton Business School. He majored in Business Management for his undergraduate and graduate studies. His parents expected perfection from him and Stephen tried hard to deliver. He was a gifted athlete but his parents never allowed him to pursue sports. They drilled into him that power and status were the most important accomplishments in life. So he buried his head in his work and became an honor student throughout high school and college.

Matt glanced up at the Elder as the school picture faded. "I didn't know my dad even liked sports. My grandparents were never like that when they were around me." Matt felt bad for his father. *His* whole life centered on sports growing up, and he could not imagine life without them.

"Interesting, isn't it." The Elder motioned to continue and Matt looked down again.

The next picture was one of Stephen in college. Although he had been a bookworm in high school, the bookish, nerd reputation alluded him because of his charm and good looks. In college, he wore his hair short on the sides and slightly longer on top in a James Dean style. His intense blue eyes made girls swoon. His skin was fair but not pale. He had a square chin and strong cheekbones and could easily have been a male model. He became a real girl-chaser until he met Janet. Then everything changed.

The next picture was one of his young father and mother sitting together on a couch in his parent's living room. They were watching a movie and eating popcorn. Matt watched the scene come alive as Stephen began to nuzzle Janet's neck and she pretended to protest.

"Hey, you're getting greasy butter on my neck!" she laughed and tried to push him away.

Stephen caught her hands as she half-heartedly struggled. He was laughing, too. "You didn't complain the last time we watched a movie!"

"Ah, well, if you recall, we never finished that movie! Besides, I'm afraid you're beginning to think that all you have to do is butter my neck for a good time." She tried to sound serious, but laughed as he kissed her lips.

Stephen wrapped his one arm around her neck and she felt something rest on her shoulder.

"Well, maybe this will convince you of my intention." Stephen kissed her neck again. Janet strained to see what was in his hand and caught sight of a blue velvet box. She spun out of his embrace, surprised.

"What's this?"

He pulled his arm out from behind her back and straightened up. His eyes grew serious as he slid down off the couch in front of her and knelt with his forearms resting across her knees. Janet started shaking as the meaning of his gesture began to register.

"Janet, I wish I was more original, but I don't want to mess this up. Will you marry me?"

Janet gasped as he opened the velvet box. It had a simple round one-and-a-half carat diamond ring mounted on a plain thin gold band. It was a style she would have picked out herself—simple, but elegant. She was speechless. Stephen took it out of the box and slipped it on her finger. It was one size too big and he blushed at his mistake.

"We can have it fixed." He said awkwardly. He was dying inside to hear her answer. "So, how 'bout it?"

Janet had tears in her eyes. Though she had known him for a long time, they had only been dating a short while. "Stephen," she replied, as she wiped her eyes, "it's beautiful, but, are you sure you are ready? I mean, don't you have a few wild oats left to sew?"

He was surprised at her question. "No, I don't. Really, Janet, I love you."

Janet gasped. "Really Stephen?"

"Yes! I don't want to be with anyone else but you for the rest of my life."

Janet let out a nervous laugh. "Oh, I know about ten girls who'll be sorry to hear you say that."

Stephen got off his knees and sat as close to her as he could. He pulled her face into his. "Janet, you are my world now. The only thing I can think about any more is how much I want to spend my life with you. To raise a family and grow old together. All I know is that I can't even breathe without you!"

Her tears spilled onto her cheeks. "What's a girl suppose to say to something like that?" she whispered.

"I hope yes." Stephen answered while pulling back some loose strands of hair that had fallen across her face.

"Yes." She whispered back. "Yes, I'll marry you!"

The picture faded with Janet's words and Matt sat stunned by what he witnessed. The tenderness and passion his father demonstrated towards his mother was something he had never witnessed before. He dreaded admitting this in light of what he told the Elder.

He addressed the Elders. "I never saw that side of him. They barely held hands."

"Your father showed his affection often when you were young—even to you. As the years went by and the family dynamics changed, all of your affection towards each other suffered greatly."

"My father didn't show me much affection. He was never around. I don't remember any time that he went out of his way to show me he loved me."

"That's right, Matthew. You do not *remember* anything happening, but that does not mean that it did not happen. Look further."

The screen activated and stopped on a picture of Stephen and Janet posing with Matt holding a baseball bat when he was twelve. Matt knew instantly what this was about and was puzzled about how this applied to the Elder's point. The picture was taken right after the final game of the playoffs against the Bears. His team had won the league championship and it was his homerun in the eighth inning that clinched the victory. He remembered the conversation he had with his mother just before that last game.

Matt, Ellen and his mom were about to leave for the game and he was upset.

"Mom, is Dad going to make the game today?"

Janet was busy getting Ellen ready to leave. "Matt, we talked about this last night. He told you that he has a big presentation today that is very important. He's going to do his best to leave as early as possible."

Matt was punching his baseball glove. "So, that means no."

Janet stopped what she was doing. "I didn't say that. He promised he would get there as soon as possible."

"That's what he said the last three times and he never came. I'm gonna be the only guy on the team who's dad is a no-show!"

Janet felt sorry for Matt because it was the truth. She walked over to him and sat down to explain. "Matt, your father has felt so bad about missing those games. He did everything he could to try and come, but this proposal he's been working so hard on is really important to him, and to all of us. If they accept his proposal, it means that he will have a very secure future at work and that will benefit all of us. What he is working on is really, really important to me. It will benefit so many people."

Matt stared at her with a blank expression.

"I know you can't understand this right now, but you will some day. Anyway, Daddy said he would try as hard as he could to get out early, so let's not get ahead of ourselves."

Matt did not buy any of what she said, but did not want to argue with her. "Okay. Let's just go."

Stephen did arrive to see the ninth inning, but missed Matt's game-clinching homerun. Matt was so upset that he missed his moment of glory that he did not appreciate the fact that he showed up at all. His father tried to make it up to him by offering to take the team out to dinner to celebrate, but Matt sulked and refused to go. The coach handed Stephen the game-winning ball as they were leaving and he stuck it in his pocket and took it to work the next day.

What Matt did not know at the time was that Stephen's proposal to his company was to integrate a line of herbal and homeopathic remedies into their drug distribution channel. It was the early nineteen eighties and public interest in natural remedies was gaining momentum. Stephen's gut feelings told him that this was a new direction that medicine was taking. His company was already tracking the growth of health food stores across the country and he was sure it would be a big trend by the nineties. Already, a small number of main stream physicians and researchers were promoting the use of homeopathic and herbal treatments and the public was responding to their advice.

Janet had actually done the initial research and put him in touch with a well-known French homeopathic pharmaceutical company who was very interested in forming a partnership with his company. Stephen was more excited about his projected profits, but he also knew that he was taking a big risk with his career if the board of directors did not like it.

Although Stephen was nervous about how the officers would accept his proposal, he was troubled more about missing Matt's final game. His presentation was at two o'clock and expected to run at least two-and-a-half hours, depending on how many questions were asked. Matt's game would probably end by five o'clock. He hoped he could make the last few innings. To his delight, he ended his presentation slightly ahead of schedule. His heart sank, however, as a barrage of questions were thrown at him right away. Finally, at four-thirty the CEO said that he had another meeting to go to and thought it best if everyone went home and studied the proposal. They would resume with their questions the next morning. Stephen sped out of the office, without regard for protocol, and raced to the ball field.

He was so relieved when he made it in time to see Matt play in the last inning and was heartbroken that he had missed his son's big hit. When Matt rejected his offer to help the team celebrate, Stephen did not know how else to make it up to him and gave up. His proposal was accepted unanimously several weeks later and he was promoted to Vice President of Sales for the new product line. This promotion, however, seemed meaningless to him. He could not forget the look in Matt's eyes that said he was a failure as a father.

Matt woefully watched scenes of his father pulling the ball out of his desk drawer and massaging the leather stitching while gazing at his picture on the desk. Only now, did he realize how hard his father had tried to make him happy that day. Only now, did he see a small seed planted that would grow into their mission. Only now, did he realize that he never asked his mom what the presentation was about that day, and he never knew that his father was the driving force behind the division that brought so much success to his company.

Matt's eyes remained glued to the screen.

"Matthew. Do you understand now that your father did love you very much?"

Matt squeezed his eyes shut. "Yes, I do. I was wrong about him." Matt could relate now to what Gram had told him about how close-minded he was at times.

"It is important that you remain open to the truth in this review, no matter how painful it becomes. This review is an opportunity for you to gain understanding about the misconceptions that you have carried around for so long. Only then, will you be able to grasp the changes you must make to grow. Now you know a little more about your father. Let us move on to your mother. Are you ready to begin?"

At this time, Matt felt like a large boulder was crushing his heart and lungs. His breath grew shallow. He thought if he dared to exhale too long, the boulder would squeeze the last inch of existence out of him. He nodded his consent anyway.

As the pictures changed to Janet's life, Matt could only hope that he knew his mother as well as he thought he did. He knew that she came from a simpler middle class family in a farm town in Pennsylvania called Bakersville. She was naturally beautiful with a peaches and cream complexion, high cheekbones and full lips. Her dark brown hair framed her face angelically and accented her large, almond shaped brown eyes that always mirrored her emotions. The pictures showed that she seemed just as happy living in a small farmhouse in Bakersville as she was living in their current home in affluent Forrest Hills.

As her life flew by him on the screen, Matt was immediately drawn to a picture of his mother at the age of ten. She was sitting in Grandma Anna's kitchen eating freshly made gingersnap cookies with a glass of milk. Janet seemed anxious for Gram to finish cleaning up and sit with her.

"Gram! Tell me that story 'bout Naomi and her family. The one you wanted to tell me when Mom came last week."

Gram finished wiping her hands off and sat down across from Janet. She grabbed a cookie from the plate in between them.

"Oh, yes, that's right. Let's see! As I started telling you, Naomi was my grandmother on my mother's side of the family. That makes her your great, great grandmother! In fact, you remind me of her. You have her eyes. Anyway, she was a full-blooded Muskogee Indian. Her father, John Little Bear, and her mother, Star, were actually from a group of Indians that walked the famous Trail of Tears!"

"What's that?" Janet asked while reaching for another cookie.

Anna cringed when she thought about it. She tried to adjust the explanation for a ten-year-old to understand.

"Well, back in the eighteen hundred's, there was a President named Andrew Jackson. Have you heard of him at school?"

"Sure, but not very much."

"Okay, well, here's a history lesson for ya. This fellow signed a special order to evacuate the Indians that lived in the southeastern part of our country from their homes. They were moved to another part of the country that's now Oklahoma."

"For good?" Janet asked.

Anna sighed. "Yes, for good. No one had a choice. They just up and moved whole villages."

"You mean all the Muskga..."

"The Muskogees. And the Chickasaws, the Cherokees and a few others."

"Who are they?"

"The white men of that time. The men in charge of the government back then. They decided that the Indians didn't have a right to their own land. Imagine that! So they ordered them to pack up and leave immediately."

Janet was puzzled. "Wow. That doesn't sound fair."

"No it wasn't. And it wasn't the worst of it. Not only did the Indians have to leave their land, but these people made the journey so difficult that many Indians never made it to Oklahoma."

"Why not?" Janet asked completely engrossed in Anna's story.

"The Indians were herded like cattle across rough land in the wintertime. Many of the elderly and weak died along the way."

"But not John Little Bear." Janet surmised.

"No, he survived and so did Star, but they did loose a child she was carrying before they got to Oklahoma."

"Oh, no!" Janet exclaimed. "That's terrible. But everything was okay when they got to Oklahoma, right."

Anna shrugged her shoulders. "Things got a little better, but nothing could repair the damage of loosing your homeland and all those loved ones. They did make a home at a place called Fort Gibson and that's where Naomi grew up."

Janet thought about everything she had been told so far before asking her next question. "These men who did this. Were they evil Gram?"

"I wouldn't call them evil, Janet. I think they were just ignorant."

"I don't understand what that means."

"Ignorant is when you don't know enough about something and act anyway. The white men didn't take any time to try and understand the Indians. They made snap judgements about who the Indians were and labeled them savages. Ignorance made them fearful and it's natural to try to remove something that scares you from your surroundings. I think that's what happened."

"But what did the Indians do to the men that did this to them?"

Anna smiled. "Nothing."

"Nothing!" Janet was surprised. "Why didn't they try to get their land back?"

"They couldn't fight the white men. They had made treaties with the white men and the Indians believe fully that their word was their honor. Sometimes that honor cost them their lives."

"I can't believe people can be so cruel!" Janet replied. "I hope I never do anything like that to anyone."

"I'm sure you won't. You're not that kind of person." Anna consoled her.

Janet looked a little sullen. "But, I'm white. Maybe I'm ignorant, too."

Anna squeezed Janet's hand. "No you're not! And remember, you're part Muskogee! You have honor in your blood."

Janet felt better and that reminded her of the question she wanted to ask. "So, how did you get here, in Pennsylvania?"

"When Naomi was seventeen, she fell in love with a young Irish Catholic man named Jack McBride. He was a soldier at Fort Gibson. They married and when his duty was up, he brought her to his home here in Pennsylvania."

"Was she happy to be back here?"

"At first she was. She did have a romantic idea that if she came back to the East Coast that she would reconnect to her roots. But it wasn't like that at all."

"Why not?"

"Because she thought that there would be traces of her Indian ancestry around, when actually, it was like no Indian ever existed here. Her in-laws were all Catholics and they made her give up all of her traditions and celebrations. She had to raise her children according to their beliefs. They wouldn't even let her fix her husband a cup of herbal tea to cure his colds!"

Janet fidgeted in her seat. "That's awful. I mean, why didn't they want her to be herself? Everyone should be able to do what they want."

Gram patted her hand. "I know, I know. But…that's how some folks are. Naomi did manage to sneak a few things by them. Grandpa Jack helped, but it wasn't easy for them. That's why I'm able to pass some of our Indian ways on to you!"

Janet smiled. "Well, I'm never gonna let anyone tell me what to do! If I want to do something Indian, then I will!"

Anna smiled back. "I hope you can, Janet. I'm so glad you've taken an interest in our heritage. We should be proud to be part Indian. Your mother, she never wanted to know. I think she is embarrassed by it."

"Not me." Janet reconfirmed. "I love my Indian heritage."

For the first time, Matt saw how much his mother loved the private times she had with Gram and how drawn she was to her Indian heritage. Pictures of her life flashed by that told the whole story. He watched her vow to continue Anna's traditions herself. This was not as easy as she thought it would be. Janet's mother would reprimand her whenever she caught her singing an Indian song or speaking about what she was learning from Anna. When it became apparent that Anna was getting in trouble with her mother too, they both agreed to keep things between themselves.

Towards the end of Janet's high school years, she looked forward to the freedom college would bring to her. Janet had waited a long time to pursue her dream. She fantasized about learning all she could about the Indians, so she could work with them in some capacity. Janet found the courage to profess a desire to major in history and study Native American culture to her parents, who flat-out rejected the idea. They argued that she would be wasting her degree going after such a non-profitable field of study. After a long round of arguments, Janet finally gave in. She decided on a business major and landed a full scholarship to Penn. She received a degree in Health Care Management and Policy. Failing to keep her promise to herself left a void in her heart that grew larger as the years went by.

When Janet married Stephen, she hoped that she would finally be able to integrate some of the traditions Gram had taught her back into her life. Unfortunately, when Stephen's career skyrocketed at the Pharmaceutical Distributor, it became a problem again. Gram had remained close to her, which made it even worse for Janet. Her grandmother was a constant reminder of the broken promise that Janet had made to her years ago. Their relationship became tense at times. Janet tried to bury all of her feelings about the subject deep inside of her, which became her own trail of tears.

The vision of his mother's heartbreak was almost too much to watch and the screen melted away again.

Matt became accustomed to the dead silence that accompanied the fading pictures. He did not wait for the Elder to speak. "I didn't realize how much her heritage meant to her. She never told me about Naomi. She did give us special medicine for colds and other stuff when we were young, but a lot of that stopped after Sarah died. I just thought it was because we were getting older and could take regular medicine. I really didn't know about this!"

"You are right. Things happened that kept challenging your mother's beliefs. It was especially hard for her because there was no one other then her grandmother to support her. She was on her own, so to speak. This was a time when most people never even thought about what had happened to the Indians. Modern medicine was advancing so rapidly that doctors were completely ignoring the old knowledge. This has been the one mistake repeated time-and-time-again on Earth. Modern evolution is supposed to meld together the old and the new, not replace it. Together, old and new create wisdom. This is the missing link."

"That makes sense. My mom must have sensed this as a young girl. She's like a pioneer then."

"Yes, she is, but being a pioneer can be extremely difficult. We would like you to see one more example of the struggles your mother has endured. Please watch."

The screen showed a recent picture of Janet sitting in the kitchen crying. The look of sorrow on her face was almost more than Matt could handle. He sensed that it was right after he left her on the day he died. He remembered the horrible things he said to her. It was the first time that he ever brought up Sarah's death in one of their fights. He also had the feeling that this haunting memory that Janet was reliving in her mind was something that had been chasing her for a long time. He glanced up at the Elder to plead not to go into this dark place. He did not want to know the truth.

The Elder responded gently before he could speak. "It is necessary, Matthew. Please continue."

Janet's thoughts rolled onto the screen like a movie. Matt cast his eyes back down and watched again. Her first thought was about the accusations that Matt had just made against his father. She felt too helpless to tell him the truth about Sarah. She began thinking of that awful year her poor baby girl suffered so much. "How much of her suffering was my fault?" She wondered.

It had all started when Sarah developed a cough that would not go away. Sarah started taking naps in the afternoon again, which she had stopped doing the year before. In just a week, the naps became longer and longer and Sarah's fatigue grew worse instead of better. When she took Sarah to the doctor's office, he discovered swollen lymph nodes in her neck and her lungs were very congested. He suggested they get a chest x-ray to start. The x-ray showed several shadows in both lungs. He ordered a biopsy of both her neck and lungs immediately after that and sent it to an oncologist at Children's Hospital of Philadelphia for review. They confirmed his worst fears. Sarah had Non-Hodgkin's Lymphoma. Janet remembered how confused she was when Dr. Stockard sat them down to tell them the news. He said that Sarah had third stage aggressive lymphoma that was spreading rapidly. He guessed that she would require immediate chemotherapy and possibly radiation to stop the rapid growth. He referred them to an oncologist named Doctor Schmidt at Children's Hospital and his office set up the appointment for the next day. Janet refused to believe that his diagnosis was true. She kept shaking her head and telling him that there was some mistake. Sarah had a cough and swollen glands. Matt had those symptoms several times when he was her age and it was just a virus. All the way home in the car she kept thinking to herself that they needed a second opinion. Doctors are wrong all the time. This would never happen to one of my babies, she thought. God would never let it happen.

Unfortunately, no one in the family would listen to her request about a second opinion. Stephen got on the phone to his company and they put him in touch with a group of research doctors working on new chemotherapy drugs at one of their suppliers. The doctors were optimistic that these new experimental drugs would be the best treatment for Sarah. He pressured Janet to give up the idea of getting a second opinion, on the advice by these doctors that the disease was spreading too quickly and treatment must start right away. Stephen convinced her to let Sarah undergo the first round of the new drugs. The side effects were harsh and Sarah's hair fell out immediately. Nausea developed and Sarah lost her appetite, while sores in her mouth and throat made eating solid foods all the more difficult. Even cold drinks hurt going down. Janet remembered how Sarah's beautiful little face swelled up and how it upset Matt to see her that way. Then Sarah developed a shortness of breath and the cough she had before the treatments had gotten worse. Her weight dropped severely. After four weeks of drugs and radiation, the doctors were concerned about the first test results. The enlarged lymph nodes in her neck shrank less than five percent and the tumors in her lungs were slightly larger. Her white blood cell count was critically low and she was at high risk for infection. They gave her blood transfusions to try to build her count back up. Finally, the doctors released Sarah from the hospital to wait and see if she would improve, before the next round of treatments could begin. Sarah's health continued to decline at home.

Reliving this memory felt abhorrent, but Janet's mind wandered to the conversation she had with Gram after Sarah came home. Janet was standing at the foot of Sarah's bed studying her daughter's heavily sedated body. Gram walked over to stand next to Janet.

"The medicine is not working, Janet."

"She's a strong girl, Gram. She'll get better soon."

"She is growing weaker, dear." Anna rubbed her shoulder.

Janet repeated. "No! She's a strong girl."

"Janet, Sarah needs someone else to be strong for her now. She's too young to fight this alone."

Janet walked over and sat by Sarah on the bed. "There's a Dr. Wells in Springfield. He's a homeopathic doctor. Mary Gilbert told me about him when she stopped by this morning. Her sister has breast cancer and he is treating her without chemotherapy. She is in remission now. I think we should call him. The doctors have convinced Stephen to try the chemotherapy again, when Sarah is strong enough, but I think it is unnecessary."

Anna grew concerned. "Janet, breast cancer is much different than what Sarah has and she is so young. She needs healing from someone else."

Janet looked over her shoulder into her grandmother's eyes. She knew what she was about to say and did not want to hear it.

"Your kind of medicine won't work either. You've done all the rituals and prayers you could think of and it hasn't made a difference."

Anna spoke sternly. "I think the healing has to come from you."

Janet grew angry and defensive. "From me? What do you mean? I am the *only one* around here who seems to believe she *will* get better!"

"Janet, I hate to even say these words, but you are the only one who *refuses* to accept how ill Sarah is. Why do you think that is?"

Janet could not believe what Anna had just said. Even her grandmother was ganging up on her. "I know that Sarah is sick; but *I believe* she is going to get well soon. I think we should wait a little longer before giving her any more drugs. In fact, I think that the *drugs* are making her sicker. How do we know it's not the drugs that are making the tumors larger?"

"That makes no sense, Janet! Even herbal medicines that Indian medicine men use cause side effects in the body. Both medicines are attacking the poison in the body. It is a physical war going on inside, but it is the *spirit* that creates the miracle of recovery!"

Janet grew angrier with her grandmother. "Don't talk to me about miracles! Why do we have to rely on miracles? Why did God allow this to happen to my Sarah? What did she do to deserve this?"

Anna sat down on the other side of the bed. She wished she had an answer for her, but she did not. She reached across and held Janet's hand. "I don't know why it happens to innocent people. Only God knows. However, I do know that faith in your own spirit's abilities is needed to help the miracle along. What are you so afraid of? You come from a long line of healers. *You are a healer, dear!* Why does this scare you now?"

"Gram that is ridiculous! I am not a healer. I don't have the ability to heal anybody. Yes, I loved learning about the Indian ways when I was younger, but I am no medicine man. For Heaven sakes, I don't know anything about healing any kind of illness. Didn't you tell me that healers are taught all those things from childhood? They are born with special powers that I don't have."

"Child, everyone is born with these powers, but most people never know they have these abilities. It is not a coincidence that you were exposed to these concepts or that your heart is drawn to them! Medicine men are taught what herbs to use and what prayers to say, but they are just the dressings. What they are really taught is to *believe that they can heal!* And I *have* taught you that!"

"You believe this, Gram, and yet you haven't been able to heal Sarah!"

"I have prayed to The Great Spirit and I am being told that the healing must come from you. You must believe you can heal her, but first, you must accept that she is sick!"

Janet pulled away from Anna and straightened the covers under Sarah's arms. She ran her hand over her daughter's cheek. Her voice returned to her normal tone. "You're wrong, Grandma. I think I will contact Dr. Wells tomorrow. I'm sure I can convince Stephen to talk to him before we consider another chemotherapy treatment."

A tear that fell on Janet's knee, interrupted her daydreaming. She sighed and wiped her eyes as she thought about that conversation. She still would not believe that she could have done anything to save her daughter. Gram could not possibly be right. Only special people could heal in that way. She was just an ordinary person in an ordinary world. How could she consider this possibility in this day-and-age? How would Stephen and his family react to such an idea? Faith healers may have had their place before modern medicine took root, but today it would be unheard of that the wife of a high-powered pharmaceutical executive was going around healing people with chants and sage!

As Janet recalled, she never did contact Dr. Wells. That night Sarah could not breathe and they rushed her to the hospital. The doctors almost laughed at her suggestion about contacting Dr. Wells and after they talked to Stephen privately, she was never able to convince him to consider it anymore.

A chill ran down her back when she thought of the next two months that followed. Sarah developed pneumonia and became too weak to undergo additional chemotherapy. The lymphoma spread into her liver and stomach. Finally, Sarah's lungs failed. They put her in an oxygen tent and all Janet could do was reach under the plastic tent and hold her hand.

From then on, each second was marked by the shallow gasps of Sarah's breath. Janet sat by her daughter's side day and night, not even allowing Stephen to take a turn so she could go home to be with Matt and Ellen. She was afraid that she would not be there when Sarah woke up. As Sarah's breathing grew weaker and weaker, Janet began to pray to God, asking him to help change Stephen's mind about Dr. Wells. Then she prayed that God would save her daughter, sometimes crying out in anger and cursing Him, when nothing would change. Sarah drifted in and out of a deep sleep, but never recognized Janet when she opened her eyes.

Finally, the night before she died, Sarah did wake up and regained her lucidity. Her face was bright, her eyes were clear, and she sat up in bed for the first time in a month. Janet thought it was a miracle until the doctors explained to her that Sarah's lungs had filled with fluid and there was nothing left for them to do but keep her comfortable. A nurse gently explained that it was common for people to look like they were doing better just before they passed away. Janet called Stephen and when he arrived, they removed the oxygen tent from the bed and disconnected all of the monitors, except for a few. The two of them were able to hold Sarah in their arms one last time.

Sarah recognized her parents most of the time, however, she kept pointing toward the door and saying, *No me! No me!* Janet thought that Sarah was afraid that they were going to send her off to another painful test and tried to comfort her. "Oh, Sarah, my baby! Mommy's here! You're not going to have anymore tests. Don't worry! Daddy is here, too, and we love you. Just rest in our arms, baby! Mommy and Daddy won't let anyone hurt you."

Janet and Stephen took turns rocking Sarah and trying to comfort her as she continued to point to the door and repeat the same phrase. *No me! No me!* Her infant-like state alarmed both of them and they fought to understand what she meant. They were never able to understand what she was trying to tell them, but it was the last thing she said before she closed her little eyes and died.

Janet shook her head and brought herself back to the present moment. "No me, Sarah! I wish it were *me* instead of you!"

The screen faded away, leaving the haunting image of his mother's tear-stained face in Matt's mind.

It was awful for him to watch his mother's distress, especially now that he knew what Sarah was trying to tell her when she said *No me!* Matt could see on the screen that Sarah was pointing to an old woman that she saw standing in the doorway of her hospital room. The woman was smiling and holding out her hand to Sarah and Matt knew it was *Naomi*, Janet's great, great grandmother, who had come to take her home. How he wished he could tell his mother to help relieve her distress.

This last revelation left Matt too stunned to speak. Never in a million years would he have guessed that his mother harbored such an emotional wound; and, again, there was the tie to their mission together.

The Elder aroused him from his thoughts. "We know that this insight is very hard for you to deal with. We needed to show you that you are mistaken to think that you can know someone completely by outward appearances alone. Now you know what is behind each of your parents actions."

Matt blinked away tears that burned his eyes. "Yes, I do. Why couldn't I see it while I was with them?"

"You have your own past that influences your own behavior. It is this way for *every single soul* that walks the Earth! If everyone realized this on Earth, forgiveness would come naturally to all."

Matt thought about everyone that he loved in his life—his parents, his grandparents, his sister and aunts and uncles. He felt foolish when he recalled how he treated them.

The Elder used this thought to cue the screen. When Ellen's picture appeared, Matt hoped he could handle any surprises.

Matt's sister Ellen looked exactly like her mom but had her father's fairer complexion, giving her a fragile look. Ellen was too little to understand what was going on when Sarah passed away and had no real memories of that trying year, except through stories told by the family. The pictures told a story of how Ellen perceived her family life.

When Ellen was a young girl, she picked up on the tension that was silently festering between her parents and Matt. She felt like an outsider. Many times when she was alone with her mother, Janet responded to her questions as if she were answering Sarah. At other times, she felt that Janet's love was smothering her.

Ellen felt the overwhelming burden of trying to live in the shadow of a sister she never knew and who never had a chance to be anything but perfect in her short time on Earth. This caused Ellen to draw into herself and she became very shy. Unlike her competitive brother and father, she preferred blending into the background of life. She was studious and loved music, especially the piano. She used her music lessons as a means of escape from the family. In her music, she found a world of acceptance and contentment. Ellen became very skilled, but her shyness held her back from pursuing public recognition. Her parents, particularly Stephen, tried hard to coax her into competitions. Ellen was quite content playing for herself and her family. She did not need a spotlight to enjoy her gift. When she went to college, Stephen pressured her to pursue a degree in music, hoping to draw her out of her shyness so she would perform in public.

While Matt watched the pictures go by, he realized how often he had ignored her. He never knew that she secretly wished she were more outgoing like him. Now he wished he had known, so he could have told her how wrong she was. She should be proud of her accomplishments. He never noticed how talented she was until now. He should have been more sensitive to her. Matt looked up at the Elders but this time there was no need for words. He knew his failings already.

When Ellen's pictures faded away, Matt thought he was done with this part of the review, until he saw a picture of himself appear on the screen. He pondered what they could possibly reveal to him about himself that he did not already know.

The awesome truth came to him when he studied the only picture that appeared on the screen. It was a current photo of him taken this past summer. Next to his picture, a new picture of his father at about the same age appeared. Although Matt spent years vehemently denying it, the truth hit him like a hammer across his forehead that left him dazed. He saw, for the first time ever, that he was the spitting image of his father. The man he despised the most and swore he would never be like. The pictures said it all. He grew to the same height, had the same slender, yet muscular build and intense eyes as his father. The only difference in physical appearance was that Matt's hair was slightly darker brown. Matt had the same boyish charm and zest for competition; only he enjoyed the physical challenges of sports and motorcycle racing, while Stephen enjoyed the challenges of board room meetings in the business world. Both men were risk takers with incomparable intuition on how the games were supposed to be played in whatever they undertook. Matt saw that their similar strengths and competitiveness were part of the reasons that they clashed often. That is why their victories on either side were bittersweet. Furthermore, they shared an intense love for Janet that kept them together all of these years.

Matt stared at the two images without moving for a long time. Neither his mind nor his heart could process everything that he had seen. The images swirled together becoming a jumble of emotions almost too much for him to handle.

The Elder's voice broke his trance and the swirling images popped like a bubble from his mind. His mood lifted and he felt clear-headed again.

"Matthew, you will be alright. Nothing you see or hear can hurt you."

Matt looked at him with disbelief.

"The truth can be painful, but you must experience the pain to clear it away. That is how the truth will set you free. The memories, hereafter, will serve you as lessons learned. Hard lessons, we know. But lessons you will never forget, will you?"

"No, I will never forget." Matt felt like a reprimanded puppy with his tail between his legs, even though, the Elder's words were neither caustic nor admonishing.

"Very well, we must continue with the review. Now we will review your transgressions. Keep in mind what you know and try to see each example with your new perspective." Matt cast his eyes down at the screen. Anjella, who had been completely still up until this moment, moved forward to stand directly behind him. Her presence felt like a blanket of warmth that wrapped around him and held him up. He was grateful for her support.

♥ ♥ ♥ ♥ ♥ ♥ ♥

The beginning of the second review seemed trivial, at first. Many pictures showed Matt as a young child doing the typical kid sins. Although they had little impact on the individual Matt offended, it still made him wince. There were a few times that Matt felt terrible at how his teasing another child or name calling added to this individual's low self esteem that sent them on to bigger problems as adults.

The real pain came as Matt viewed scenes with his father, With his new knowledge, he could not believe how mean and insensitive he was to him at times. Matt saw the real struggles his father went through trying not to disappoint him. His father worked long hours to climb the corporate ladder.

70

Many events that were important to Matt came at crucial junctures in his father's career. It pained Stephen to have to choose between his children and work, but he believed it would only be for a short time longer and then he could devote time to his family. But the hard reality was that free time didn't come until the kids were grown. By that time, his son and daughter were busy doing other things and Matt, in particular, would not give him the time of day. Stephen suffered greatly during those years.

Matt winced at one incident that occurred when he was sixteen when he was dating a young girl named Susan. Matt was quite popular in school and could have any girl that he wanted. When he got a chance to go out with Jodi Donavon, the captain of the cheerleading squad, he abruptly stopped calling Susan. Susan was crushed and thought that she had done something wrong. The next time she became involved with another boy, she wanted so much to make sure this boy wouldn't leave her that she slept with him. The experience was horrible and the boy dumped her the next day. Susan got a reputation for being easy from that one incident and spent many years trying to correct her low self-esteem. Matt did not want to believe that he was part of her decision, but he knew now that he was.

In another picture, Matt was working in the Accounting Department for his dad's company during the summer break from school after his freshman year. Matt did not want to work in an office. He wanted to race motorcycles. His father went through great pains to get him this position. Stephen wanted to teach Matt responsibility. He also hoped that they would grow closer. Matt took the job as a means to help finance his racing expenses. He had just started racing with Jeff that summer. It was a costly sport, because his bike required constant maintenance and retrofits, as he advanced through the ranks. Each race required a new set of $200 tires. Matt's mind was on motorcycle racing alone and he never exhibited any commitment to his job. Because he was the President's son, his fellow office workers put up with his mistakes, rather than face possible retribution for their complaints against him. Matt saw how hard he made it for everyone working there and how he affected employee morale by creating dissension within the ranks. Some took it out on their families when they got home at night. Other people had difficult personal problems to deal with and Matt's actions only compounded their troubles.

The review began to weigh heavily on Matt. He could not imagine how the Elders could have told him a short time ago that he had led a good life on Earth. Time and time again, he saw the rejection he gave to his father, and indirectly to his mother and sister. He watched discussions between his parents over each incident. He felt the agony he caused his beloved mother by putting her in the middle of the feuds. By this time, Matt's father was so frustrated that he gave up trying. He had no idea how many times his parents argued about him. There were also several times that his sister suffered because of the tension between his father and himself.

Scenes of arguments with his father, which grew more frequent and vicious in the last two years, became harder to watch now that Matt could compassionately see both sides of the argument. The last fight they had was slowed down so Matt could absorb it entirely. Stephen had just stormed through the front door after work demanding to talk to Matt.

"Janet! Where is he? I want to talk to Matthew right now!" His voice bellowed through the two-story entranceway.

Janet came rushing into the hallway from the dining room. "He's upstairs. What on Earth is the matter?"

"Matthew!" Stephen called up the stairs. "Get down here this instant!"

Matthew saw himself walking slowly down the stairs with a cocky, defiant stride. One hand was in his jeans' pocket and the other held the banister. He did not attempt to address the issue that he knew his dad was raving about.

"How could you do this to me? I get back to my office at four and find three angry managers waiting outside my door, hopping mad because they claim not only did you not finish the report due today, but that you lost all the fiscal tax files reports on the computer! And that you had the nerve to tell them you didn't bother to back the reports up on disc! Oh, not to mention, your solution to all this was to *QUIT*! And to make matters even worse, you dare tell them that you *quit* the only job you have, to pursue some kind of motorcycle racing career! Do you know how badly you have embarrassed this family today?"

Janet turned to Matt who was standing on the sixth step with his arms folded. "Matt, is this true? You did all this?"

"Yeah, I did. I quit! I told them not to give me that project. I hate dealing with numbers."

"You hate numbers, for God's sake, it's an *accounting* department! What did you think you would be doing?" Stephen dropped his briefcase right where he was standing and began pacing back and forth, rubbing his chin. "Well, if you think you can just walk away from this mess, you are sadly mistaken. You will march into work tomorrow morning and fix this mess. I'll call Charlie in Systems and get someone in to help you retrieve your files and then you will finish the reports, if you have to stay there all weekend." Stephen picked up his briefcase as if the discussion was over.

"No! I'm not going to do it. I quit and that's that. I have a racing lesson all day tomorrow and I'm not going to miss it." Matt leaned against the banister and tightened his arms bracing for the fight.

"Oh, I disagree. No son of mine is a quitter! You will finish your summer working at my company, whether it's in accounting or the mailroom, I don't care, but *you are not quitting!*"

"Yes, I am and I'm not only quitting this job, I'm quitting school, too. I'm going to start racing in competitions next month and I'm not stopping until I win the championship."

"Oh, so now you're throwing away your education so you can hotrod all over town like some hippie! No. You can just get that thought out of your head right now! You are going to get an education and you are going to find a responsible line of employment, is that understood? No one in this family is going to act like an irresponsible maniac. When you graduate and get a decent job, then you can pursue whatever hobby you want, but for now you are getting an education."

Matt looked over at Janet who stood frozen in shock. "Mom, talk to him. He can't make me go to work or to school. I'm a grown man and I can do whatever I want with my life." Janet just shook her head and looked over at her husband.

"Well, okay! So how do you suppose that you are going to be able to afford this career of yours without working?"

"I'm going to use the money in my trust account that Grandma left me for now and when I start winning the bigger races, I'll earn the rest. I'm also going to work in Jeff's dad's cycle shop."

"Like hell you'll use that money. Your grandparents left it specifically for an education." Stephen thought he had Matt on this point.

"Learning to race *is* an education and besides I have half of the first disbursement left in the bank. I can pull out the rest in two years." Matt countered his father's point but was in for a surprise.

"Oh no you can't! That trust specifically states that after the initial payment to you at eighteen, all other payments will go directly to the university for your graduate studies. Your mother and I are the only ones who have the power to release any other expenses from that account until you are 30 years old. And I guarantee you, you will not see a penny of that money if you drop out of school now."

Matt looked over at Janet pleading not to take his father's side. "Mom, you won't let him do this, will you? All I want to do is race. It's in my blood."

Janet looked back and forth between the two men. "Matt, I have to agree with your father. Racing is too dangerous! You need a good education if you want to get anywhere in life. I couldn't bear to see you get hurt. I think your father is right. I know how upset you are, but in time, I think you'll see we were right about this."

"You have no idea how upset I am. Neither one of you even know me anymore. All you worry about is how things look to other people. Matt, get a responsible job! Ellen, play your music for everyone! Do either of you ever think about what we want in this house? Well, you can take your corporate job and shove it, Dad. I'm going to race bikes with or without your help." Matt stormed up the stairs towards his room.

"Matt, come back here! If you don't report to work tomorrow, you can find another place to live! You think you have it so hard, well, maybe you ought to go out on your own and find out just how good a life you have here. There's a million boys out there who would jump at the chance to get the education you can have." Stephen marched into the library for a drink.

Janet followed Matt up the stairs. "Matt wait, your father didn't mean what he said about you leaving. I'm sure we can work something out. Let's just wait a while and we'll discuss this after dinner, when everyone has had time to cool down."

"No Mom, go back down stairs. There's nothing to discuss. You're on his side again."

"What do you mean, I'm on his side? I'm not on anyone's side. I just think racing is too dangerous."

Matt turned toward his mother in the hallway just outside his door. "No, I mean it. Leave me alone. You can't change my mind this time. If he wants me to leave, I'm out-of-here." Matt slammed his bedroom door on his mother. It was the first time he ever lashed out at her during one of his fights with his father.

Panic rose in Janet's throat and she leaned against Matt's door with her palms and left cheek pressed hard against the painted wood. She wanted to say something but she couldn't. She squeezed tears out of her eyes and pushed herself off the door and wiped her eyes. She couldn't stand to see them fight anymore. She couldn't bear the thought of Matt leaving her. She had to protect him from himself and his father. Her family was not going to fall apart this way. "Don't worry Matt, you won't have to leave. Please, just stay. I can't bear the thought of you leaving now. I'll go talk to your father."

Matt held his breath listening to her walk down the stairs. Then he exhaled deeply. He didn't know how much longer he could stand living in this house.

Janet walked into the library where Stephen was drinking a brandy while staring out at the front lawn. He glanced over his shoulder as she approached him. He already knew what she was going to say.

"Stephen, Matt is staying in this house. I hate what he is doing with his life, but he needs me. He needs us. I won't let him leave and I want you to promise me you will never say those words to him again, no matter what happens. My family is going to stay together." Janet walked out without waiting for his response. Stephen swirled the last drops of brandy around in his glass. "Of course, Janet. Anything for you." He whispered and finished off his drink.

Matt was able to see what Stephen was thinking about when he said those words. It came to him as a complete surprise and left him speechless.

Stephen's thoughts flashed back to when Sarah was ill. It was the day they found out that Sarah had cancer. They had come home right before Matt was due home from school. Stephen's sister, Joyce, and Grandma Anna were waiting for them. Janet put Sarah up in her bed to rest and then everyone gathered in the living room and Stephen told them the news. Joyce started making calls to their mother and father and Grandma Anna went out back to call on the spirits or something like that. Janet and Stephen were left alone. He recalled their painful conversation. "Janet, Matt will be here any moment. We need to tell him what's going on."

"No, I don't want him to know. There is so much we are not sure of and this may be all a big mistake. I want to make an appointment with another doctor to get a second opinion."

"But we will be seeing the oncologist tomorrow. We can discuss your doubts with him."

"I want another family doctor's opinion, Stephen. He is just going to agree with Dr. Stockard. It's his job."

"Janet, be serious. Why would you say something like that about someone you don't even know? I'm sure that if he disagrees with Dr. Stockard's test results, he'll tell us. Either way, I think we should let Matt know what's going on."

"No, we are not going to tell him anything. I don't want him worrying. He's too young to be exposed to this. We'll tell him later when we know more."

Stephen was upset. "Janet, I think that's a mistake. I think Matt can handle it."

Janet began to cry. "No, Stephen, please, let's wait. I have enough to deal with right now."

Stephen wrapped his arms around her. He couldn't stand to see her cry. "Okay, we'll wait a while."

Matt was shocked at what he saw. He remembered that day so well. When he came home from school, the house was filled with relatives and friends. Some were crying and some took turns making phone calls to other people. Matt remembered asking his father what was going on. Stephen and Janet were in the library with Grandma and Grandpa Bradley and Matt was standing in the doorway. He could see his mom was crying. "Dad, what's going on? Is something wrong?" Stephen was at the doorway and turned toward Janet, begging her with his eyes to let him tell his son. Janet shook her head no emphatically.

Stephen looked down at Matt. "Don't worry about it son. It's nothing that concerns you. Why don't you go out back and play for a while? We're going to order pizza for dinner soon. Your mom and I need to talk to your grandparents right now."

Matt heard his mom say, "Close the door, Stephen." And he watched his father slowly close the door and then heard more crying inside. He remembered how hurt he was and later how bitter he became towards his father, thinking that Stephen had kept him from knowing about Sarah's illness. He even knew at that moment that it was Janet who wouldn't let him know that Sarah was dying the day he went to school and came home to hear the news. He remembered his father received a call early in the morning when it was still dark from his mother, who was at the hospital. He came down stairs later to find Gram making breakfast for him. She told him that his father had to go to the hospital to see Sarah and that he wanted Matt to go to school. Matt asked if everything was all right and Gram hesitantly told him that it was and that his father said he could go in to see Sarah after dinner. He never did get to see her again. He held so much anger against his father for denying him his last opportunity to see his sister. They never told him Sarah was dying and all along it was his mother who kept it from him. He also knew that she did it out of love, but this left him more shaken and confused.

♥ ♥ ♥ ♥ ♥ ♥ ♥ ♥

Finally, Matt saw the still frame of the last conversation he had with his mother the morning of his death. Knowing what he knew now about the circumstances around Sarah's death made him feel devastated and he could hardly keep his eyes on the screen. It started when Janet told him the week before that his father wanted the family to meet for dinner at his favorite restaurant, The Brandywine Grille, on Saturday for an important announcement. The family had gathered there before on more than one occasion for big announcements. Matt assumed his father was going to tell everyone that he was off to China to make the deal of a lifetime or he was hosting some ambassador again and he would give a list of events the family was required to attend. Matt sneered at the thought of another boring dinner with his father. Anyway, it was out of the question. Saturday was the grand opening race at Capitol View and his chance to race a 750CC Superbike for the first time. Matt brushed the idea off, but Janet pleaded with him to be there, for her sake.

Usually, Janet wouldn't push too hard, knowing that when she forced Stephen and Matt together, the experience was usually unpleasant, to say the least. But this time, Janet knew Stephen had been going through a tremendous re-evaluation of his life since his best friend's heart attack and had made new decisions in the direction he wanted his life to take. It was sort of a mid-life crisis. This announcement, whatever it was, would be a last chance effort to bring her family back together again. She feared Matt would be leaving home soon and it would become difficult to arrange interaction between the two of them. It was barely feasible now.

Matt was taken aback by his mother's insistence on this occasion and wondered if she knew more than she told him. He knew, however, that he was going to have to disappoint her this time. Saturday was the most important day of his life.

Even if he wanted to go, Saturday was impossible. Scouts from all of the professional teams would be there. He couldn't risk losing this opportunity to be noticed and a chance at some big money if he placed. Especially because his odds of placing in the top five was possible, since the top experienced racers would not be in the race. Bob White told Matt that he had been coaxing Ducari for months to take a look at Jeff and him. Everything he had been working so hard for this past year depended on this next race. Janet's request was out of the question.

There was nothing his mother could say to him to change his mind, he thought. But when he looked into her beautiful, pleading eyes, he could only manage to put her off by telling her that he would try to be there. Janet was truly disappointed because she knew Matt's answer was an obvious no, but left their conversation at that, hoping somehow during the week that he would change his mind.

Janet awoke at six o'clock Saturday morning and made a special effort to visit Matt hoping to find him asleep. She knew that if he were going to the racetrack, he would be out of the house early. She hadn't told Stephen that he probably wouldn't be there. Stephen had changed so much in the past few weeks. He shed his corporate persona and became the man she had married long ago. He was relaxed and attentive when he was home, which was earlier and earlier each day. The playful attitude he exhibited at night caught her off guard at first, since it had been so long since he had been so lighthearted. She did not want to spoil the change and so she decided somewhat selfishly to wait until the last moment to tell him, praying for a miracle.

It only took one look at her son that morning to know that he had already decided not to come. He was dressed in his racing outfit with his racing gloves and knee guards sitting beside him on the bed. Matt was

77

finishing lacing his boots when she entered his room. He told her that he had a big race in Harrisburg at the new stadium.

When Matt looked up at his mom's face, he knew he was in for a fight. Before she could say anything, he held his hand up to make his case. He started by telling her that this race was the most important race of his life, but Janet wouldn't buy it.

"What do you mean it's the most important race? I know your schedule and you don't have to be at your next race until next month."

"That's for dirt bike racing, Mom. This is different."

"How different?"

"This is a superbike race." Matt knew he opened a can of worms with his answer.

"A superbike race? You mean on one of those fast bikes! Matt, are you out of your mind? Bob put you up to this, didn't he? You're going to get yourself killed on one of those things! How long have you been training?"

"Relax Mom, I've been practicing for awhile. Probably six months in between dirt bike races. And don't worry, I know what I'm doing."

"You do? And what about your dirt bike racing? I thought you were doing well at that."

"I am! Not that anyone in this house cares, but I happen to be in first place right now. But after this season, I plan on moving over to track racing. It's where the real money is."

"Is money what this is all about?"

"No, not at all, but it doesn't hurt. I like racing, Mom. And just so you know, I'm damn good!"

Janet was close to tears. "So race your dirt bikes and next year you can see about track racing. You have family obligations tonight."

Matt became angry. He used a tone he had never used with his mother before. "*I can't wait until next year*! I need the money and I *want* to race on a professional team. Man, every scout will be there today. I can't afford to lose this opportunity."

"And what do you think your father's going to say when he hears this? First, you leave school to race dirt bikes, and now you're not even finished your dirt bike season and suddenly you're moving on to superbike racing. I'm beginning to think he's right when he says you don't know what's important in life."

"Who cares what he thinks about me. Just because you jump when he says jump, doesn't mean I have to."

Janet turned to face off her son. "How dare you speak to me like that! You have no idea what family loyalty is. You know, there are more important things in life than racing around on motorcycles and partying every weekend."

Matt lost his composure, as he jumped up from his bed and leaned in close to Janet's face and shouted. "And what would they be, Mom? Lying around like a rug while you watch your husband walk all over you? Or how about giving up your dreams, so the great corporate president can rise to stardom! I don't know how you put up with him!" It was an outburst that he never expected to make.

He immediately regretted every word he said, as he watched his mother re-coil away from him. Her bottom lip was quivering, as she tried to comprehend what he just said. Her hand came up over her mouth and she just stood there staring at him like he was a stranger.

"I'm sorry Mom. I didn't mean it! Please, I'm sorry!" Matt moved toward Janet to hug her but she pushed him away. Her voice was a whisper when she finally spoke.

"Is that what you think of me? That I'm some kind of a rug! And that your father is some kind of a monster? What on Earth would make you think that about us?" She began to cry.

"No, I don't. I mean, what I meant was that you've spent so many years letting Dad run this family and call the shots. And I know you had dreams of your own. You used to tell me about them when I was little. But when Sarah got sick, everything changed. You gave all that up for Dad's career. And you spend all your time making sure he's happy. What about you?"

"What about me? You think that I'm not happy with my life. Did it ever occur to you that you can find happiness in more than one way? Just because I didn't pursue my interests, doesn't mean I'm not happy. Did it ever occur to you that I may *like* being a president's wife? That I may *like* taking care of my family?"

"Well, yeah, but it's not fair that you had to give up your dreams for Dad!"

"I never gave up my dreams for your father! It was *my* choice not to pursue my own interests. Your father had nothing to do with it."

"But what about when Sarah died? You know, I used to listen at the top of the steps at night to you and Dad talking about Sarah's condition. I remember hearing you plead with Dad to stop the chemotherapy. I remember how sick it made Sarah. But he let them give it to her anyway. And she got worse and died. He never cared about what you felt. He didn't even care enough to tell *me* the truth."

Janet drew a sharp breath in, as if Matt's words stung her. "That's not true! He cared more than you could possibly know! He went through the same agony all of us did. Your father did what he thought was best for Sarah

79

at the time. No one is to blame for her death! No one, do you understand me!"

"Yeah, I do. See, even today you still won't admit that Dad failed us back then. He let them give Sarah that horrible medicine and radiation treatment and then left you alone with her care, while he went off on trips everywhere. He didn't even have the courage to tell me she was dying! Instead he sent me off to school and I didn't get to say goodbye to her! I hardly saw her the last two months she was alive! Does that sound like someone with the family's best interest in mind?"

"No Matt, you don't understand. You were too young to understand then. Things were a lot more complicated than you realize. I wish I could explain it to you, but I can't." Janet wanted to tell him the truth, but her mind would not allow her to share that dark place in her memories.

"Matt, please, let this go. Your father loves you more than you could possibly know. Don't disappoint him tonight. For me, please, just come to the dinner."

Matt was puzzled about what his mom was saying. "What was there to explain?" He thought to himself before answering her. "I can't promise anything, Mom! I don't know what time the races end, but I doubt I could get back by seven. Besides, Dad's surprises never involve me anyway. Just tell me tomorrow what happened. I'm sure he will not be that upset if I don't show up!"

"That is not true Matt! Your father specifically wanted all of us there. Your sister is coming home from school this afternoon. I know he wants to talk to you. This dinner is very important to him!" Her voice quivered slightly on the verge of tears again.

"Matt, please promise me you will be there. You know if you go to the raceway that you will not show up tonight. I promise that if you come to this dinner, things will be different this time. I cannot bear the heartbreak of you and your father continuing to be at odds with one another."

"Listen Mom, we know what excites Dad these days. He'll probably never miss me." Matt was gathering his keys and wallet.

It was always hard to resist his mother when she pleaded. No matter how hard she tried today, Matt was going to the raceway. Oddly, his heart was screaming for him to listen to her, but he decided he would deal with the repercussions later. His mother never stayed mad at him for long. He mumbled as he started to walk past her, careful not to look directly into those eyes. "I have to go, Mom. I'll see you later."

"Is that a *no* then?" Janet demanded with an angrier tone. "Please, Matt. Do this for me! I promise I will never ask you again." Realizing she hadn't convinced him, she threw in a desperate measure. "If you do this for me, I promise I'll release your trust fund to you."

Matt stopped dead in his tracks. He couldn't believe his ears. He was caught up in such a dilemma, he could hardly think. He had never lied to his mother before. He vowed he would never cause her any pain, and yet he just said such callous words to her that it made him wince. And now he stood peering into her tear-filled eyes that reflected back his own guilty conscience. He couldn't believe that she was so desperate that she would actually concede his trust fund over to him against his father's will. But even so, he would have to disappoint her. He couldn't take the chance of finding out later that his father could block her efforts. And besides, he couldn't give up a chance for the kind of exposure he would have today. Glancing at his alarm clock, he realized he was running late and had to leave.

"Okay, Mom, I'll try to be there on time, but that's all I can promise." To add to his betrayal, he kissed her cheek as he passed by.

Janet felt relieved, but also worried herself that she may have promised too much. Usually, she could have her way with Stephen when it came to matters involving Matt. But after he conceded to allow him to stay in the house after their last fight, she wasn't sure she could ever convince him to release the trust money and hoped that his new change of heart was enough to mend all wounds. She loved Matt so much and wanted him to be happy and she knew motorcycle racing was his passion, but it was such a dangerous sport, too. Janet did not know what she would do if she ever lost him. She watched her handsome son walk out of his room and down the stairs. From the upstairs banister she called down to him in a now cheerful tone. "I love you, Matt. You won't regret doing this!" Matt winced when he heard her response but kept on walking.

Watching these scenes knowing the outcome of his actions brought the realization to his heart of how horribly he intended to hurt her. The pain he felt for his own selfishness tore his heart in two and made him sob. Thank God, he thought, that Jeff was able to tell her that he had intended to be there after all; but it was hardly a consolation for his soul. Matt looked past the Elders to his guide. Roaming Bear's eyes conveyed a sympathetic understanding of the tormented feelings that Matt was having. He tried to console him.

"Now you understand more about the human experience. It is far more complex than most souls realize. You came here believing that your father was a sinner and your mother was a saint. The truth is that there is a very fine line between saint and sinner. Further, there is no right and wrong to either state. To be human is to imperfect. What is hard for many to understand is that there is no other way to be. You are meant to be both a saint and a sinner! No one can escape this reality."

The Elders perceived Matt's weariness and stopped the review. Matt glanced at each man, feeling condemned. Still the Elders held nothing but compassion in their eyes. There was no judgment or criticism to be made. "Matt," the Elder on the left began, "we know this is a very overwhelming experience. Please try not to judge yourself too harshly. Everyone living on Earth creates negative and positive effects on other souls. This is a natural process to growth. You may have some responsibility in a way a person experiences those moments in their life, but they make their own choices as to how they react to each circumstance. God has given everyone on Earth free will. Your entire experience on Earth is based on each choice you make. You chose early on to reject your father because you thought that he did not love you. Your mind reasoned that if you rejected him first, you wouldn't feel the pain of rejection yourself. Unfortunately, this leads to other feelings such as bitterness, resentment and jealousy. You chose to judge your father based on the amount of time he spent with you, so you blinded yourself from seeing the quality of time he was able to give. If you had allowed yourself this insight, you would not have experienced rejection, but experienced instead an overwhelming source of true love."

Matt silently sat contemplating what the Elder told him. The atmosphere surrounding him resounded with the truth the Elder spoke. Even the lilting music that seemed to swirl around him wrapped him in a strange confidence that this revelation could never be denied. Nor did he feel condemned for lack of this insight by anyone in the room. Still, his own feelings of guilt were overwhelming enough to cast his own sentence to burn in the pits of hell! Matt could only raise his head limply and nod in agreement.

The Elder realized his words were hard for Matt to comprehend, but continued. "Matt, the point I am really trying to make is that your father's repeated attempts to win your love were only viewed by you as inadequate or superficial. It is unfortunate that it often requires the experience of a serious tragedy to *awaken* us from the delusion of thought that traps us within the paradigm we've created. Only after experiencing these unanticipated events do we decide that the existing paradigm no longer fits our view of the world."

Matt was bewildered, "So I was the cause of my father's rejection of me in my later years?"

"No, Matt, your father chose to reject you, but only after he was worn down from your constant acts of rejection. He could have remained loving toward you. But do you see how much more difficult it was for him to remain in a loving state when his soul, which is also trying to experience unconditional love, was continually exposed to the negative energy you unknowingly projected?"

"Yes, sir, I can see that now." Matt wanted to crawl into a hole and die all over again. To think that this is how he treated the people he loved the most in the world. And now he was faced with the reality that his father would never know how much he loved him. He shuddered as he thought about how his death would effect his family now. Would losing another child destroy his parents?

The Elder spoke, "Occasionally during these reviews we show souls how things would have been if they had made a different choice, usually because this particular soul is very close to moving on to a higher level of existence. In your case, you were practically minutes away from a major breakthrough—one that would have changed the direction of your life completely and created the opportunities for your mission with your parents to succeed. More importantly, to have the physical experience of total unconditional love that is necessary to move into the Illuminati. It is the only way one can relinquish his need for the Earth experience. We would like to show you what would have happened if you had stayed home and gone to that dinner, so you can understand your mission completely. Is this okay with you?"

Matt felt he had no choice but to say yes and braced for the worst, again.

Chapter 4

Matt sat in a tranquil silence waiting for the screen to reappear. A slight breeze dried the beads of perspiration that had formed on his hairline. He was surprised, once again, that he could feel all of the sensations of the body even after death. The Elder who directed the review shuffled in his seat, as he began to speak.

"This will explain to you how you and your family would have successfully accomplished the mission we spoke about earlier."

Matt braced against the arms of his chair for the next battery of scenes, like a prisoner waiting for the first jolt of electricity in his execution. He felt like a broken man unsure of how he could survive much more. The screen appeared and began to flash its pictures. This time Matt saw the sequence of events from his parents' perspectives. It started a few weeks before the accident. His father was talking to his mother at breakfast before work about his best friend, Ted Davenport. Ted had just had a major heart attack at the age of forty-eight. Stephen was the same age as Ted and the news hit him hard. Matt saw his father telling his mother how difficult it was for Ted to recover from the shock of his heart attack. Ted had a very close family and even with their support, he was having difficulty dealing with his condition. Stephen thought about how broken his own family had become. Ellen was living on campus at the University of Pennsylvania and only came home on holidays. He wasn't even speaking to Matt anymore.

Stephen thought long and hard about the choices he had made over the last twenty years. Was his success worth losing his family? Would success mean anything if he had a stroke or a heart attack tomorrow? How much support would he get from Ellen and Matt? As Stephen began to review his life from the time he first became a father until now, he thought about the early years with Matt and how easy and satisfying his life was then. He was just getting started at Healthcare as a salesman. Although he traveled a good deal, he still spent a great amount of time with Janet and Matt. They lived a simple and joyous life in their small house in a quiet little neighborhood west of Philadelphia called Springton.

Stephen was a much different man then. The happiness he experienced back then was beyond description. He felt so lucky that Janet was his wife and Matt was such a healthy, happy baby boy. There were no late night meetings, budget reviews or clients to entertain. Back then, he had shared so much quality time with his family.

By the time Sarah came along, he had worked himself up to Assistant Regional Manager and his responsibilities had already doubled. It was at that time, he reflected, that he lost control of himself and turned into a workaholic. His goals changed, as he envisioned a shot at the company's presidency. Although he tried to remain an attentive husband and father, it was impossible to balance his time evenly between work and home. He got so caught up in the political fervor at work that it slowly changed his values and way of thinking. His desire to obtain his new goal not only changed his priorities where his family was concerned, it also led him to believe that his family must also conform to the protocol required by an up and coming executive in order for him to succeed.

So here he was today, President of one of the largest pharmaceutical distributors in the country. He was already pegged as one of the top five business leaders in the nation by a leading business magazine. Stephen was wealthy and prestigious, with his finger on the economy and the fluctuations of the market at every moment of the day. Dining with politicians and dignitaries had become an everyday occurrence and the steady stream of executive assistants and vice presidents through his office validated his prominence. Yet on any given day, to his present embarrassment, he could not tell a single soul what his wife, son or daughter was doing that day or any other day. Now all of his accomplishments became inappropriate answers when stacked up to the judgment day questions he had been asking himself. "What have I done for the people I love and whom have I helped with my success?" Sadly, Stephen drew a blank. It became a moment of complete and total humiliation, as the God-awful truth revealed itself from his soul that these successes did not amount to a hill of beans when compared to the larger meaning of life. Sitting behind his mahogany desk in his spacious office with a panoramic view of the valley that surrounded his dynasty, Stephen Bradley broke down and wept an ocean of tears for the first time since Sarah's death.

It took days for Stephen to collect his thoughts. First, he had to deal with the separation he now felt from the world that he had loved for so long, his work. Every meeting lingered endlessly and his detachment was quite obvious to those who worked with him. At home, he had difficulty sleeping, as he wrestled with his change of heart.

Breakfast with Janet became awkward. He felt so unworthy of her love and struggled to find the words to apologize for the demands that his own goals imposed on her. Never once had he considered what kind of life she may have wanted to pursue. And how could he ever make up for those agonizing days during Sarah's illness? To think that he had put his daughter through such painful procedures for the sake of his career was unbearable. He was so confused about what was best for Sarah. After the doctors took him aside, he was convinced that there were no other options, but what if he was wrong and Janet was right.

Stephen was able to shield himself from the torment of watching his little girl waste away before his eyes. Yet Janet handled it all with such loving fortitude to the very end. The most unbelievable thing that Stephen realized was that after all they went through, Janet never held this against him and had silently forgiven him for his erroneous judgment. All he could do at the present moment was sigh.

Janet knew Stephen was going through something very painful, but wisely decided to let Stephen come to her when he was ready.

For days he silently wandered through the torments of his soul, searching for the wisdom and strength to redirect his life and reclaim a loving relationship with his family. On that Friday, Stephen sat absentmindedly staring at a magazine left by a former passenger in the pocket of his first class airline seat. There before him in a small box at the bottom of page seven was a quote from Sheldon Kopp that spoke the words he needed to hear, "In the long run, we get no more than we have been willing to risk".

The words resounded, as an epiphany in his head, until every cell of his body rejoiced. There was no perfect way for Stephen to resolve his dilemma. He would have to come clean and throw himself at the mercy of his family. But more importantly, he knew he had to accept whatever reaction it spurred. The damage was done with his children. It would be up to them to either forgive him or reject his intent. He, too, would have to forgive them, if they chose to walk away. Stephen no longer felt confused but flooded with peace and hope. "It is a rare moment in a person's life," he thought, "when you receive an intuition so strong that it cannot be explained in human terms, but somehow you know it is the truth. Perhaps this is the seed from which wisdom is truly born." Stephen's body felt lighter and his heart felt freed from the guilt that had been weighing him down like an anchor. *Everything would be okay*, his heart told him and he felt a comforting touch of grace lull him to sleep for the rest of the trip home.

Stephen arrived home late that Friday night. Janet was already asleep. He tried to sleep but his mind raced through the events of the past week. Before he finally closed his eyes, he decided how he would approach his family. He kissed Janet gingerly on the cheek and stroked her silky hair, marveling at how fortunate he had been to have such a loving, loyal wife. Then he fell into a peaceful slumber.

On Saturday morning, Stephen confessed to Janet how ashamed he was for the way he had treated his family for such a long time. It was still difficult to put into words how he felt, but Janet's eyes told him she knew what he meant. They held hands that morning across the breakfast table for the first time in years. Janet was so relieved to finally hear what was bothering Stephen. He told her what had happened on the plane and that he planned to make amends to both her and the children. He told her that he wanted to gather the family together for dinner next Saturday at the Brandywine Grille to apologize and make a special announcement. He also asked her not to mention what she knew to the children because he felt it should come from him.

Janet happily made the dinner reservations and called Ellen at school. Next, she set off to find Matt before he left the house that morning. Matt had just finished getting dressed when she knocked on his bedroom door. She told him that Stephen had asked the family to gather at the Brandywine Grille for dinner the following Saturday at 7:00 p.m. He had a big announcement to make.

The scene with his mother was not much different from what had actually happened at the start. Matt still sneered at the thought of dinner with his dad. This time, however, Janet's persistence wore him down, even after he told her about how important racing at Capitol View was to him. Matt became aware of the gnawing feeling in his gut and gave in to her request, even though it made him sick inside to think of what he was about to give up. It was this act that changed the dynamics of their conversation and altered the direction of the outcome. Janet was still disappointed that Matt's interest in motorcycle racing had escalated to such a dangerous level, but she always knew deep down that he would not be able to let it go if it was his real dream. "Will you make this one exception for your father and me, Matt? I promise, I'll see what I can do about your trust fund, if you do this for me! This dinner is very important."

"Yeah, I'll be there, but you have no idea what I'm giving up for you, Mom. I'll probably live to regret this! I can't believe I'm giving up a chance like this!"

"I know this is important to you and I promise, if you do this for me, I will *never* ask you to give up another racing event again. I'll even go to see your next race, if you like. I promise, I'll stand by you on your decision to race professionally with your father." Janet's voice changed from a desperate plea to a coddling tone. "You know, you always told me I was your good luck charm!" Her smile and doe eyes melted Matt's defensive reasoning away. He reluctantly agreed to go and told Janet, again, that he was only doing this for her. She kissed him on the head and told him he wouldn't regret it. Matt asked her if she knew what the announcement was. Janet said no, but she was sure it was something special. When she left his room, Janet felt his indecision about his promise and prayed he wouldn't change his mind. She feared Jeff and Bob would talk him out of his decision before the week was up.

All week long, Matt did have second thoughts about passing up his chance to race. Bob White was livid when he talked to Matt on the phone. He called him back four times that week trying to convince him to go, reminding him of all the hard work he did for him with the Ducari people. Jeff silently thought that he was crazy, too, but was also relieved that he didn't have to compete against him. Matt could not comprehend why he was allowing himself to pass up a chance like this, but deep in his heart, he knew it was the right thing to do. This consolation did not relieve the ache in his heart or prevent the bad dreams that haunted his sleep and kept him in a state of constant indecision.

On the next Saturday, Matt awoke without an alarm at 5:45 a.m. This was the time he would have set his alarm clock for to get up for the race. He lay there staring at the time, fully wanting to jump out of bed and begin his usual routine. He looked over at his dresser and saw his helmet and racing gloves neatly laid out in a ceremonial stance. His mind screamed at him to spring out of bed and dress before anyone would know. He had withdrawn his name from the race, but they would still have his application on file. If he got to the track by nine o'clock, he could register again. The alarm clock now said six o'clock. There was not a moment to spare.

Matt sat up and threw his legs over the bed. He rubbed his eyes and cursed. "Damn, damn, damn!" He got up from the bed and walked over to the door and quietly opened it. He looked down the long hallway to the double doors of his parents' bedroom suite. The stairway was just past their doors. There was not a sound in the house. "Good." He thought. "I should be able to slip by without disturbing them." He closed his door and walked into the bathroom to shower and shave. He started the water running for the shower and left it lukewarm. He was groggy from the lack of sleep over the past week and needed a boost for the long drive ahead. Matt stepped into the shower and began to go over a checklist in his head. "Bob has the new tires I ordered. I can call him from the car to make sure he brings them. The racing papers are in my nightstand, I need to put them by my keys so I don't forget them. I have a full tank of gas so I shouldn't have to stop." Everything seemed to be in order. He turned the faucet to cold and felt the welcomed jolt the cold water sent through his body. His mind reeled off several scenarios of what would happen when he got back tonight with his mother and father. His mom would be mad, of course, but when they heard about how well he raced and hopefully interest from Ducari or some other team, they would see that this was not just a pipe dream and come to terms with it.

Matt had convinced himself that everything would be all right until he looked at himself in the mirror when he began to shave. He systematically smeared the shaving cream on the sides of his face and suddenly locked eyes with a stranger in the mirror. "What am I doing?" he asked his reflection. The eyes that looked back seemed hollow and cold. "You're going to be a winner, today. That's what you're doing." He did not recognize the frigid voice that spoke inside his head. It sounded too sinister to be his.

"But I'm going to lie to my mom. I told myself I would never hurt her." He continued this strange conversation.

His reflection spoke back. "So, she's a big girl, she'll get over it. Besides the dinner was your dad's idea and who cares what he thinks? This is your big chance! Are you going to let your old man ruin it for you? How long are you going to let him control your life? Would your old man give up a chance like this for you?" The face in the mirror made a strong argument.

Not strong enough, though, to override the memory of Janet's smile, when she thought Matt was coming to the dinner. It was a smile he rarely saw anymore. Not since Sarah died. Matt looked down into the sink and watched the water wash the shaving cream off the razor. He tried to empty his thoughts from his head and felt a wave of uncertainty twist in his stomach at the quandary he was in. Go! Don't go! Go! Don't go! As the battle went on in his head, the tightening of his belly expanded to constrict his heart. Matt looked up and locked eyes with the face again. He looked into the eyes, clenching his fists and leaned closer, as if he was in a staring match. He tried to see what was behind those devilish eyes. He warred with his conscience until finally the eyes softened and began to water. He smacked his hands on the sink counter and cursed again, "Jesus!" He tapped the razor on the side of the sink and placed it back in its holder. Then he left the bathroom and dressed. He wrote a note for his mom and left it on the dresser. He walked with an angry gait past his parent's bedroom door and left the house.

Janet rose at 6:30 before her husband. She looked over at him sleeping so peacefully with a contented look on his face. She sighed quietly as she thought about the possibility that this evening she may get her whole family back. It was never the same since Sarah's death. No one knew how to heal from their loss. They did the best they could. Maybe enough time had gone by and they could get on with their lives together. Janet hoped Matt would keep his word. She could not believe she had asked him so flagrantly to give up the race today. After all, he was twenty-two years old and he could do and should be able to do anything he wanted. Only a mother could get away with such a demand.

Unable to resist the temptation, Janet crept down the hall to glance into Matt's room, hoping not to disturb him. His door was already open and she knew this meant trouble. She looked over at his empty queen size bed with his comforter and sheets scrunched at the end of it. Her heart jumped when she scanned the bathroom door and found it open. Panic rose into her throat, as she continued to roam for signs of her son.

At last she saw the note Matt had placed neatly on the center of his dresser. She walked over to the note and carefully picked it up, handling it like it was a bomb about to go off. And surely it could be. The note was addressed to her and it read, "Mom, I went out to run a few errands. I'll meet you on time at the restaurant. Love, Matt." Janet breathed a sigh of relief and crumpled the paper into her chest with both hands. Into her teary view came the neatly folded racing gloves and helmet. Janet stroked the soft leather gloves and savored the love she felt from her son. She prayed to God to bless him with the greatest racing career he could ever achieve. She knew that she could no longer hold him back from achieving his dreams and would do anything she could to help him, regardless of the risk.

♥♥♥♥♥♥♥

That evening, Matt was the first to arrive at the restaurant. The Brandywine Grille was a four star restaurant that was part of an elaborate corporate conference center in Forrest Hills called The Sherwood Resort. The center included a resort hotel with three restaurants, nine conference rooms with state-of-the-art facilities and a golf and health club. Stephen's company had an executive membership and used the center regularly. Stephen held VIP status. There were three private dining rooms off the Brandywine Grille's main restaurant that very few people had access to. Stephen was one of them. In the lobby was an exclusive gift shop called Melody's.

Matt had left the house wearing a pair of khaki pants and a polo shirt and decided not to change for dinner. He knew that it would probably irritate his father but he did not want to talk to either parent before the dinner. His mood was still dark and he resented his mother for forcing his hand today. Matt decided to browse through the gift shop while he waited. Ellen's birthday was coming up next month and he wanted to check out the jewelry counter that was in the front of the shop. Here, he had full view of the main corridor that led to the restaurants. A pretty red-headed clerk appeared behind the counter almost out of nowhere. Matt was looking at a selection of gold and silver bracelets when she offered her help. Her voice was bubbly with sexy undertones and Matt noticed right away the large diamond engagement ring on her left hand. Too bad, he thought. It had been a while since he had dated anyone. Racing had filled his weekends for the last few months.

"Is this gift for a girlfriend?" she queried when she removed two stunning gold bracelets from the case for Matt to view.

"No actually, it's for my sister. It's her birthday next month."

"Oh," she said in a surprised tone and then raised her voice oddly in what appeared to be an empty shop, "Lucky sister!"

Matt caught her glancing over his shoulder while she spoke. There were two steps behind him that led to a second level of the store that displayed fashions and contained two dressing rooms. He turned in the direction the clerk was sending her voice and was briefly able to see the back of a young shapely girl in a light green floral dress ducking behind a tall display of sunglasses near the dressing room. Her sleeveless dress clung tightly at the waist and hips and draped softly down her legs in a swishing fashion. The brief glimpse at her profile was enough to see that she was an attractive girl and her mysterious departure left Matt intrigued. He turned back to the clerk.

"A friend of yours?" he flirted.

Before the clerk could answer him, a loud tap on the gift shop window interrupted them. There stood Ellen laughing and shaking her head through the window and signaling with her hand for Matt to come outside. Matt blushed slightly at the clerk and told her that she was his sister, and that he had better come back later.

Ellen was still laughing when he opened the door. "Boy, Matt, every time I turn around I find you flirting with some pretty girl! I hope you noticed that rock on her hand."

"Yeah, I noticed and I wasn't flirting with her!" Matt swung his sister around and gave her a big hug, while looking back into the gift shop to see if he could catch one last glimpse of the mystery girl, but she wasn't in sight. The clerk winked at him and mouthed, 'come back soon'. Matt smiled once more at her and decided to change the never-ending subject of his love life with Ellen.

"So, do you have any clue as to what the *big announcement* is tonight?"

"No, not at all. Mom just said that whatever it is, it is really important to Dad. They went ahead to the restaurant." Ellen began to walk down the corridor holding on to Matt's arm.

"Well, it better be damn good! He'll never appreciate what I gave up for him today." Matt ambled along side of Ellen casually. He was never in a hurry to meet his father.

"What was the big sacrifice this time? A date with a pretty girl?" Ellen asked enviously. She wished that she were as outgoing as Matt was with the opposite sex. Her dates were few and far between these days. She knew deep down that she was too selective about whom she dated and that reputation scared away potential courtiers. There was one guy at school named Shawn that she felt attracted to and thought that he might be interested also. But she was too reticent to approach him.

"No, I haven't seen anybody lately. I've been too busy racing. There are only two dirt bike races left and the big grand opening race at Capitol View today. That's where I was supposed to be. I don't know how I let Mom talk me into giving it all up, but it's too damn late to think about it. Bob White is going to ream my ass next week when I see him." This thought was beginning to make Matt hot under the collar again. He still couldn't believe that he actually caved in to his mom's demands.

"Well, if anyone can make you feel guilty enough to change your mind, it's our wonderful mother. She must have put a real guilt trip on you!" Ellen was totally surprised that Matt gave his chance up. She knew how important racing was to him. "I can't wait to get the whole routine tonight myself." Ellen began to mimic her mom. "Ellen, how are your studies going? Are you keeping up with your piano lessons? I heard Joan Billaby's son might be interested in you. Do you want me to try and set something up for you, after all, you're going to need a date for next month's charity gala. I hope you're not considering showing up alone again. You're so pretty and talented...and so on, and so on and so on!"

They both laughed. Ellen could mimic her mother's voice so perfectly.

"So, how *did* she manage to change your mind this time?"

Matt smiled at his quirky sister. She was really a very pretty girl, but she insisted on dressing conservatively and hiding her beautiful eyes behind thick-framed glasses. They had so little in common. He wondered if they would remain close, as they grew older and moved into different worlds.

He gestured with his hand to show his dismay, as he answered her. "It was so weird! She was so persistent and she started to get angry. It was the first time she wouldn't take no for an answer. This must be something really important. Besides, you know she hates the idea of me racing probably more than Dad does. She even went so far as to promise to help me get my trust fund money."

"Get out!" Ellen was stunned. "This dinner must be important. Well, I've got my own bomb to drop on them tonight, so I hope Dad's going to be in a good mood."

Matt's eyebrows raised at Ellen's unusually rebellious tone. "What could you possibly tell Dad that would rattle his cage?"

"I want to change my major from music to a teaching degree, which will add another year of school before graduating."

"Ouch—He's not going to like that!"

92

Ellen shrugged. "I know, but I really want to teach and I can't ignore it any longer. I don't want to pursue a music career or even teach it and if I don't quit now, I'm gonna end up hating the piano."

Matt put his arm around her shoulders. "I'm proud of you! I never thought you had it in you. You're okay."

Ellen laughed. "Yeah, you just like that I'm gonna divert the attention from you tonight."

Matt gave her a reassuring squeeze. "No! I'm serious. I'm really proud of you!"

The two walked silently the rest of the way to the restaurant perplexed by the whole situation.

Janet and Stephen were waiting for them by the small hallway that led to the private rooms. Matt noticed right off that his father was casually dressed tonight. They were even wearing the same Ralph Lauren polo shirt! They were seated in their usual room with a view overlooking the golf course. The table was elegantly set with candles and fresh flowers. Stephen ordered a bottle of Krug Grand Cuvee Reserve, Janet's favorite champagne and an assortment of appetizers to start the evening. He appeared slightly nervous. Matt was too preoccupied with thoughts of the race to notice his parents holding hands, which was not their normal behavior in public. Ellen could not contain her curiosity any longer. "Okay, Dad, what gives? The suspense is killing me."

As Stephen fumbled with his napkin and attempted to answer Ellen, the wine steward appeared with the champagne. Relieved, he tasted the champagne and nodded his approval. He waited for the waiter to leave the room before addressing Ellen again. Janet noticed that Matt was impatiently flipping his silverware, as the conversation grew scarce. She tried to divert everyone's attention by asking Ellen about school.

Ellen hesitantly took the opportunity to talk to her parents about changing her Liberal Arts major from Music to Elementary Education. She had already completed her junior year and this would mean adding another year of studies before graduating. She loved playing the piano, but she wanted to do something else with her life. Her parents had pressured her into majoring in music, with the hopes that she would finally agree to perform publicly. Her real passion was to teach young children. She braced herself for an onslaught of arguments on why teaching would not be right for her or the family. She imagined what they really wanted to say was that Sarah would have never disappointed them and that Sarah was a bright child and why aren't you more like Sarah! Perhaps, even worse, they would be thinking that she was becoming more like her brother and would someday give up school altogether, too.

Amazingly, both parents agreed instantly. Ellen was sure they would insist that she finish her music degree in her senior year. Even Matt found their reaction hard to believe.

The hors d'oeuvres arrived and the family chose their entrees. Stephen asked that the door to their room be closed. The odd chain of events began to intrigue both Ellen and Matt. Ellen looked at Matt with eyebrows raised, questioning him silently. Matt shrugged his shoulders back to her, unsure of where this was going.

Stephen decided he had to take the plunge. Still uncertain of what he would say, he straightened up in his chair and asked for everyone's attention. He hardly knew where to begin.

First, he gazed at his lovely wife, who looked more elegant than ever. His eyes then moved to Ellen. Her porcelain complexion made her seem so fragile, yet she had the same haunting beauty as her mother. He looked over at Matt and saw a handsome young man, who had a great lust for life and adventure. His eyes began to fill with tears, as he surveyed his great blessings. He cleared his throat and returned his gaze to Janet.

His voice cracked as a lump rose in his throat. "Never in my life did I dream I would be so fortunate to marry an angel in disguise. Janet, you have been the rock that has held this family together. You gave up your own dreams to allow me to achieve mine. And I will love you forever."

Stephen looked toward Ellen. "My little girl, you remind me of your mother more and more each day. I want to call you my little girl, but it's hard to ignore what a beautiful young woman you have grown into. I am proud of you. Still, you will always be my little girl."

Matt's eyes were cast down as he doodled pictures on the side of his water glass, slightly annoyed by the drama his father displayed.

"Matt," Stephen went on. "You are my only son and I know we have not been close. I always dreamed that I would be the perfect dad, but I know that I failed you. I'm sorry. I had to make choices and, at the time, I thought they were the best for everyone in this family, but they may not have been. I cannot erase the past, but I do mean to make amends in the future to all of you." Uncharacteristically, he wiped tears from his eyes.

Ellen and Matt grew uncomfortable at this uncharacteristic display of emotions. Stephen saw the questions in their eyes. "I know this sounds pretty unusual, coming from a guy who hasn't been around much in your life." Stephen took a deep breath and sighed. It was time to get it all out. "You know my best friend, Ted, had a heart attack last month. He is my age and I watched what a toll this took on him. Yet he had the luxury of being close to his family. I watched with envy at how his family stood by him and the overwhelming love that they shared together. I am convinced that it was only through their love and support that Ted recovered. It was their bond that gave him something to fight for, a reason to live. It hit me hard that if this happened to me today, I would not have the same support. This is more my fault than yours. I began to think of what success really means to someone, if it means losing his family." Stephen felt overwhelmed by emotion and lowered his eyes for a moment. He lifted his head and looked at each one of them tenderly. "Well, it's not worth it. And I have been a fool to think that I could make amends later in life when I was ready for it."

Matt finally looked up from his water glass, as his father was speaking, curious about what might be coming next. It was such a huge departure from his father's typical behavior. Could this really be his chance to finally have his father back in his life again? And did he want him?

Stephen paused to sip his champagne and continued. "So, I've decided to make a few changes in my life and I hope it's not too late." He looked toward Janet. "First off, Janet, I believe it is time you get a chance to pursue whatever interest that you desire. You have been the president's wife long enough. Whatever you would like to do...go back to school, travel, go to work, anything. It is time for us to focus on *your* interests." Janet's eyes filled with tears, as she grabbed her husband's hand and kissed it. Matt and Ellen looked at their father with surprise.

"Now, as for Ellen and Matt, I know I can't make up for all the years I was not around, but at least I can try. If you all agree, I have scheduled time off next month to take a family vacation. I thought maybe we could go to Europe, but if that interferes with any of your plans, we could do it over the Christmas holidays." Stephen looked directly at Matt and emphasized. "You do not have to go, if you don't want to. I just thought that this would be a good way for us to get reacquainted with each other. I understand if you feel this is too much, too soon. Just, please, do me a favor and think about it."

Ellen squealed with delight. "Oh, Daddy this is wonderful! I have always wanted to visit Italy and France. I'm sure I can work something out at school." Matt was certainly taken off guard. His only thoughts of seeing Europe were part of his ultimate dream of racing in the World Grand Prix Championship some day. He would love a chance to visit the tracks at Misano, Italy or Donnington Park, England or Hockenheimring, Germany. He thought it was a nice gesture on his dad's part, but he had already decided that when he suggested visiting a racing site that an argument would definitely ensue.

Stephen waited a moment, as Janet and Ellen exchanged ideas about the trip. "Matt, there is one more thing I would like to say." Matt began to brace himself for the inevitable contention until he registered a tone of sincerity in his father's voice. "I have given this a lot of thought the past few days. I know how much you like to race and I know my objection to this has been the source of our greatest conflicts. I realize that I have been wrong to try to stop you from fulfilling your own dreams. You have every right to follow your own destiny. If you want to pursue a racing career, then I will support you. I'm still not comfortable with the danger involved, but I know you are the best at everything you do, despite what I've said to you in the past."

Matt's eyes widened, as he allowed his father's words to sink in.

"You mean it? You're not just kidding?" he asked with a trace of skepticism lingering in his thoughts.

"Well, to show you how much I mean it, tomorrow we can go visit Bob White and he can explain to me where you are and what you need to become a world champion." He paused and watched Matt's eyebrows arch in surprise at his comment and laughed at the comical look on Matt's face. "I hope you know, I don't doubt you'll succeed at this dream of yours! You know, you are very much like me in this regard!" Stephen smiled and blushed at his own comment. "I know you will need a better racing bike, but I want to understand how the racing circuit works and what kind of training and money you will need." He looked over at Janet for a moment and smiled before adding, "And I think it is time that I come out and see you race."

Matt smiled at his father for the first time in a long time. "Wow, you don't know how much this means to me. I'm going to be number one someday. I just know it." Janet and Ellen wiped away tears, as they watched this incredible reunion take place. All four Bradleys were smiling together as a family. Stephen told them, again, how sorry he was and how much he loved them. The rest of the dinner was a joyful experience that ended after midnight.

Jubilation filled the conference room, as everyone savored the precious story ending.

"Stop!" Matt yelled and raised his hand to interrupt. He looked around at everyone's dismayed expressions, shaking his head.

"Is something wrong?" The Elder asked.

Matt shook his head emphatically. "Yes, something is wrong!" He pointed to the screen. "You're telling that this would have happened!"

The Elder nodded yes.

"You mean, if I had gone to this dinner, he would have said all those things."

"Yes, he would have."

"And just like that," Matt snapped his fingers, "we would've lived happily-ever-after."

The Elder chuckled. "Not every minute of the rest of your lives, of course, but, in time, your wounds would have healed."

Matt flashed the Elder a skeptical look. "So, my dad has this total change of heart and he supports my racing career and we become buddies for the rest of our lives together."

The Elder continued to be amused despite Matt's obvious disbelief. "Yes and no, Matt. Yes, your father would have met with Bob White and would have released your trust fund. Your parents would have attended your races, and it would have been harder to watch you than they thought. No matter how good you got, they would worry about you every race, but they would keep their word.

"You would be skeptical in the beginning and would test your father often. You would turn down the Europe vacation, just to see your father's reaction and he would have remained patient. In time, your skepticism would fade and real healing would have happened between the two of you. Would you like to hear more?"

Matt sat back in his chair too shocked to speak, so he nodded yes to the Elder.

"Very well. Your friend, Jeff, places first in the 750 race at Capitol View on opening day and Bob White convinces Ducari to give Jeff and you a tryout the next week. Ducari signs Bob up to manage both of you on a secondary superbike team with limited commitment until they see what you can do. You surprise the entire racing circuit by placing third in the U.S. Superbike Competition, while Jeff places fifth. You move up to Ducari's number one superbike team the next year and after winning the U.S. title, advance to their World Grand Prix team. It takes you three years, but finally in the fall of 2002, you stand on the podium in Misano, Italy, as the World Grand Prix Champion, with your mother and father cheering you on.

"All of this would have come true had you remained on Earth."

Matt nervously rubbed his right hand across the smooth tabletop, contemplating everything that the Elder had just said. He tried to imagine the feeling of becoming the World Grand Prix Champion. A smile crept on to his face, as he savored the idea. After a few minutes of daydreaming, he returned to the present moment and wondered out loud. "So what happens to my mom?"

"Oh, your mother's life becomes very busy. She tries some volunteer work, but eventually goes back to school to study psychology, in the hopes of becoming a family counselor. Psychology does not hold her interest for long and she stumbles onto information about the University of Lethbridge in Alberta, Canada. They have a whole department of Native American Studies that offer courses from a Native perspective. She is able to attend a short summer program in Alberta, where she finds out about a workshop in Sante Fe, New Mexico offered by the Association of American Indian Physicians on cross cultural medicine. The workshop provides physicians, medical students and others interested in the Native American people, a greater understanding of the role of traditional Indian healers. This experience helps her to realize her life's ambition to bring a greater awareness of the potential for using spiritual practices to help facilitate healing from numerous degrees of illness. Janet returns home and becomes the AAIP's coordinator for workshops on the East Coast. She begins the arduous task of educating the local medical community. Later, she studies Eastern Medicine, after meeting a local acupuncturist, Dr. Cheng, who has the same challenges as the Indian Physicians."

Matt nods his head, as the Elder finishes. "So that's how she fulfills the mission, but I don't see how I fit into all of this." He reasons to himself, which by this time he knows is like talking out loud to everyone in the room.

"It would have been just the beginning, Matt." The Elder tapped his fingers on the table and the screen appeared. "Why don't you let the rest of the story tell itself?"

A picture of Ellen on her wedding day appeared on the screen. Matt watched the story unfold.

In September 1999, Ellen married Shawn Gallagher from school. One year later a bouncing baby girl named Anna was born. When Anna turned two years old, she was diagnosed through DNA assessment to have the defective gene that caused the lymphoma cancer that killed Sarah. The early detection gave the family a few years to find a cure before the cancer began to manifest.

At first the family was devastated. Janet did not think she could tolerate seeing little Anna go through the same suffering her Sarah had gone through. Treatments had improved since Sarah's death, but there was no cure yet. At a family meeting to discuss their options, Anna's doctor suggested putting Anna in an experimental program at the University Hospital in Philadelphia that involved isolating the gene responsible for this illness and replacing it with a healthy one. This gene replacement program was in its infant years and there was no guarantee that it would work. Janet, Stephen, Ellen, Shawn and Shawn's mother, Julia, were in the doctor's conference room. Janet jumped up as soon as she heard the doctor mention the experimental program. She looked at Ellen. "No, don't do it, Ellen. At least, not yet. We don't know what this will do for Anna and neither do they. I just started working with The Institute for Enlightenment in Medicine (IEM) and they have several alternative treatments for cancer. I think we should investigate them first. There is a conference in Boston in six weeks that I am attending, where the idea of combining these treatments with standard medical treatments for cancer will be discussed. I think it will be of help. We have a little time."

Ellen did not question her mother's request. Anna was not even showing symptoms at this point. "Alright Mom, we'll wait." The family left the flustered pediatric oncologist's office together. Dr. Coltenbach cautioned them not to take too much time. He was eager to refer Anna to the program, because he thought her case would be perfect for them and like a lot of physicians, he held alternative medicine in contempt and couldn't conceive of any other approach.

When Janet went to the conference, she carried an entirely different agenda than she originally planned. Now that Matt was a celebrity, Janet had been going with him to visit various children's hospitals, as part of his PR work. The children were always excited to receive his signature-racing cap, but their hearts always broke when they saw the suffering of so many children. At every visit, there was always some child that reminded them of Sarah.

Janet was currently looking into various ways that alternative medicines could be used, at least, to help ease some of the side effects from present medical treatments for children. The upcoming conference in Boston was a symposium of traditionally trained medical doctors and the world's leading authorities of various alternative medicines, who were coming together for the first time to discuss this very subject. Stephen was able to arrange for Janet to address this group through a friend on the board of directors at Children's Hospital Medical Center in Boston, who was hosting this event. The news of Anna's situation changed this opportunity for Janet into a full-blown quest for information.

When Janet arrived at the conference, she was given the cold shoulder by both sides because of her lack of credentials. One quick call to Matt and a visit by a world racing legend the next day drew the attention of the press and gave Janet the forum to make her point. The press sensationalized the event and two top oncologists specializing in children's cancer volunteered to help Janet. Two highly respected homeopathic physicians from IEM, Dr. Peter Hughley and Dr. Elizabeth Lehman, along with the oncologists, Dr. Lodi Azemun and Dr. Lee Tsering, worked with Janet to devise a program for Anna. They combined high doses of vitamins, supplements and herbal treatments followed by small doses of chemotherapy when the first signs of cancer cells appeared. The supplements slowed the cancer process down by strengthening the body's immune system and that allowed the low dose of chemotherapy drugs to kill off the cancer with minimal side effects and complete success. The results were astonishing. What was more impressive was that the doctors cross-trained each other, so that they had an understanding and respect for each other's practices. After they decided on the right combination of herbs and vitamins to boost the immune system, they concocted several remedies to relieve the symptoms of the chemotherapy. They used high doses of vitamin E to boost Anna's immune system. Concentrated doses of green tea were used to protect against the promotion stages of the cancer. After close monitoring of Anna's condition, mild chemo treatments destroyed the cancer at the earliest stage possible. The treatment was so successful that the doctors refined the herbal cocktail and called it New Life Therapy. A trial study was developed and a new avenue for the early detection and treatment of cancer was established.

At age five, Anna's original physician pronounced her cancer-free. The new methods were not only successful in treating the cancer, but they also cut the medical costs in half. The main line medical authorities balked at the success as a fluke and played it down to the public. Drs. Azemun and Tsering were isolated from their medical community. However, it was a breakthrough in the alternative health society. Desperate parents of children with cancer sought Drs. Hughley and Lehman out for help. One by one, the cases were reviewed by the four doctors until they became so busy that they decided to form their own practice together. With Janet's organizational skills and Stephen's financial contacts, they were able to establish The Healing Touch Foundation. Soon other doctors and specialists in physical therapy, massage, Shiatsu, guided imagery hypnosis and Rieki came on board. The staff reviewed each case and a personal treatment plan was devised.

Matt used his celebrity status to continue to promote the results and made this an ongoing commitment for the rest of his life. Ellen even became involved and began to work with doctors and music therapists who specialized in the use of music to increase the body's healing potential. Ellen created several compositions of classical music and sounds that enhanced the body's immune system and targeted healing in specific areas. Over the next twenty years, the movement grew until a council of this nature treated nearly fifty percent of all serious illnesses. Matt's family joined many other individuals, each doing their small part to add to the raising of the global consciousness. Alone, they affected maybe a thousand individual lives, but as other centers sprung up with various versions of this type of healing philosophy, millions were healed. This first step helped to restructure the public's awareness that slowly helped to change other societal views.

As the last picture faded, the Elders watched Matt silently, allowing him more time to absorb everything.

Matt gulped hard and slumped in his chair while staring at the space on the table that was once a screen. This was all too incredible to comprehend.

To believe that his whole family would have accomplished all of this together, if not for one mistake—his mistake! How could a single mishap make such a world of difference in the lives of so many individuals? He became horrified by his irresponsibility toward his parents and toward God. He felt his spirit shrinking. He deserved hell as a punishment. It was hell just knowing what he ruined by one selfish act. All he could think about was his family and how much suffering he caused them.

"Matt," the Elder spoke softly. "We are not here today to condemn you for your actions on Earth. We are here to help you understand your wrongdoing, so you can learn from your mistakes."

"I don't deserve compassion, sir." Matt's eyes stung with salty tears, "I deserve hell for what I've done."

The Elder was amused, "What, pray tell, is hell to you?"

"You know, the fiery pit. Being damned there for all eternity." When he said it, he became fearful.

"It doesn't work that way here."

"It doesn't?" Matt was secretly relieved.

"No. You said it to yourself earlier, isn't it hell just knowing what you did?" The Elder shook his head and sat back in his chair and smiled. "Hell is not some burning damnation, but the knowledge of how far from God you have come. It is the absence of pure, unconditional love that your spirit knows exists. That is all hell is and I do believe that is quite enough."

"But I ruined the mission for my family and all the others in my group. I screwed up God's plan." Matt still could not shake his doomed feelings.

Most of the Elders chuckled. The Elder speaking to Matt stood and began to pace behind the table. He looked at Matt in a grandfatherly way, the look of one who already knows the lessons his little grandson needed to learn. "No, Matt. You *did not* screw up God's plan. It is impossible. It has never happened, ever." He continued his pacing with his hands folded behind his back.

"God's plan may have been delayed by your interpretation, however, here it is viewed only as changed. True, you have caused your family a great deal of sadness as they grieve your departure; but God is with them and they will go on without you. Your sister will still marry and give them a granddaughter and this will now be the vehicle for healing the loss of you and Sarah. She will still have the cancer that killed Sarah and she will still be saved by the same method. It has been arranged that instead of using your influence at the conference, your mother will meet the world's foremost authority in children's cancer, Dr. Jacob Feinstein, who would not have been there before. His heart will be called to go because of the experience he will have watching his own daughter die from a similar illness. He will bump into Janet before the conference begins and they will share their stories. Then, when your mother meets resistance from the conference members, he will jump in and take up her argument. His credentials cannot be disputed and the same thing will result, with a little less public fanfare. Then the plan will be back on the same course and the same results will be achieved. I hope that makes you feel better."

Matt was so relieved. "Great. So I am going back as the granddaughter? That is why I must return so quickly?"

The Elder shook his head no. "The spirit who will be Anna has been arranged for some time. This spirit has had a great deal of experience in helping others through her own suffering. It takes a brave soul to volunteer for such a blessed task. And in this case, *she* deserves to experience a healing on Earth."

It came to Matt instantly. A smile crept over his face. He looked at his guide, Roaming Bear, who was also smiling at Matt's correct assumption. "It will be Sarah, won't it? She is in preparation to go back to Earth."

"Yes Matt, it will be Sarah. And your mother will sense that it is her spirit. Your mother is a very wise soul."

"Damn, damn, damn!" Matt became startled at his obscene reaction. "I am so sorry, sir. I mean, wow."

The Elders laughed. It was not the first time they had heard that language. Matt was so happy that Sarah was getting a chance to go back to Earth on such a wonderful mission that he forgot about himself. The notion suddenly came to him. "So, if Sarah is going back as Anna, then why am I going back?"

"Because you have not experienced unconditional love through forgiveness in the physical realm."

"But I have! I have forgiven out of love. Didn't I let Jeff win the race?" Matt was confused and agitated. He wasn't ready to go back. He couldn't even consider the thought.

"And how is that forgiveness?"

"Because Jeff half blamed me for what his father did when he gave me the bike instead of him. I gave him the lead and sacrificed my own win. That has got to count as forgiveness!"

"You were giving Jeff the opportunity to pass you, to serve your own purpose of satisfying your guilty conscience. The reason that you fell was because you were not supposed to be there to begin with. The reality, Matt, is that Jeff was *supposed* to win the race! He would have ridden the new cycle and *he* would have won the race without your help."

Matt was stunned. He felt like an idiot. How smug his ego was to think that Jeff was not talented enough to win on his own. The Elder's words smarted. It took a moment to recover.

"Okay, you're right. I was wrong to think that it was because of me that Jeff won the race. But now I know what unconditional love is. Really! I feel it in every cell of my being." He began to pound his chest. "I know what a mistake I made with my father. How I hurt him. And with my mother, too. And with Jeff. I wouldn't feel so horrible if I didn't understand. There is no reason why I must go back!"

"Every soul must experience these revelations in the physical sense. It is the only way it is embedded forever in your soul. You also owe fifty years of service on Earth, as agreed to before this past life." The Elders tone remained calm and unobtrusive.

Matt looked over to Roaming Bear for help. His friend shook his head and spoke. "You must serve your time, my friend. There is no way out of this."

The Elder conferred with the man to his right and continued. "You will go through the entire process again until you have learned the lessons that merit you to stay here and move on to the Illuminati. You will select a new set of parents and a new situation that will allow you the opportunity to experience unconditional love through forgiveness. This is not uncommon, Matt. Many souls require numerous attempts on Earth before they can move on. Some souls have been going through this process since the dawn of time. You are fortunate because you have only one more lesson to learn. Hopefully you will be successful the next time. Your case workers will help you with this process." The Elders began to rise from their seats and the meeting seemed to have ended with that statement.

"No!" Matt exclaimed, "I can't go back!"

The Elders halted and looked with dismay at the bold, young man. Enon and Anjella flanked Matt and moved closer to whisper in his ears.

"Matt, what are you doing?" Enon was flabbergasted. "No one has ever talked to the Elders like this!"

Anjella grabbed his arm. "Matt, please, the meeting is over. No one gets to choose their course at the meeting. It is already decided by the Council."

"No," he exclaimed again, shaking Anjella off his arm. "Please, sirs, you can't send me back. I won't go!" The Elders paused and returned to their chairs. The Elder who convened the meeting began to speak again.

"Matt, exactly what is the problem with this arrangement? The Council has discussed the circumstances of your life and death at great length and deemed that the path we have mapped out for you is both fair and appropriate." Still the Elder's voice held no resentment.

"I am sorry for the outburst, sirs." Matt said humbly and recomposed himself. "But will you *please* listen to me?" He saw the Council seat themselves at the direction of the Elder and took that as a yes. The Elder nodded to go on. Matt took a deep breath and prayed for the right words, as he continued. "I know that I have learned my lesson about true love. I know because I am still carrying a knife in my heart from watching what I did to the people I loved most in the world. I can't imagine going back to live an entire lifetime over again. I can't imagine taking the chance of forgetting everything I have just learned and possibly hurting my new family the same way. There must be a way to prove to you that I have learned this lesson once and for all without sending me back for another fifty years to live another life." His voice changed to a pleading tone. "I *want* to stay in Heaven, sirs. I don't want to go back to Earth. I am grieving deeply for my sins. Isn't that proof that I have learned from this experience?"

Seldom did any soul gain an opportunity to address the Council in this way. Even in Heaven, Matt had a way of charming the most enlightened souls. Anjella and Enon stood frozen beside Matt, as if waiting for a bolt of lightning to strike them all. Roaming Bear almost wept for his friend. They all held their breath waiting for the Council's response. The Council conferred amongst themselves. Because they had a telepathic block on the conversation, Matt and his guides could only watch. Enon was astonished at what was taking place. Anjella looked over at Enon to see if he knew what would happen next. They conferred silently to themselves also. Enon told her that he never, ever saw the Council reconsider a judgment before. The two of them became as nervous as Matt.

The Elder in charge looked up at Matt and grinned in amusement. "Matt, you are quite a different soul than we are used to here. We have not had a soul object to a judgment verbally in a million years. Since you are adamant that you have learned your lesson, we are going to challenge this. We will give you one opportunity to prove it. This is highly unusual and *you will be given only one chance*! If you fail, you will go back to Earth and begin the process again. And you will add an additional twenty years to the fifty of that lifetime. Are you sure you want to do this?"

Matt nodded enthusiastically, although he had no idea what he must do to appease the Council. The Elder continued. "We will allow you the opportunity to make one rescue attempt on Earth for a soul that has been sent to learn the same lesson about which you now claim to be enlightened. You will not go back to Earth as a new soul. Rather, you will use another being to orchestrate this rescue. Your caseworker angels will explain the rules to you that you must obey. I am warning you that you *must* obey all of the rules! If you succeed, we will grant you admission to the Illuminati. Before you get too excited, Matt, the success rate of such assignments is fifty-fifty. I would normally ask you if this is acceptable terms, but this time, you do not have a choice." The Elder chuckled.

Matt was filled with elation. "Thank you sirs, thank you. I won't let you down!" The Council rose again from their seats and began to leave the room through their private door on the far wall. This time the gentlemen were chatting away about what just happened. Matt turned to Anjella and Enon with a grin from ear to ear. Enon was not happy at all. Anjella looked very concerned. "Cheer up, guys," Matt said, "This is going to be a piece of cake." He patted Enon on the back.

Enon looked in utter dismay and replied "Matt, you have no idea how big a piece of cake you just asked for." He shook his head and told them both to follow him. Anjella just shrugged her shoulders at Matt. Her lack of experience in this type of case left her with no clue as to what Enon was talking about.

Roaming Bear came over to the three of them. He looked straight into Matt's eyes to convey his concern. "Well, my friend, I wish you luck. You certainly have a way about you. This will not be as easy as you think. I am not allowed to help you this time. Enon and Anjella will watch over you. When you return next time, I hope we will get a chance to talk. Peace be with you." Roaming Bear squeezed Matt's shoulders and turned to exit the door the Council used. Before he made it to the door, his figure became translucent light and shrank away, just like his great-grandmother.

Enon, Anjella and Matt left the conference room by the side door and headed to the right to exit the building. From there, they headed to a special processing center tucked away from the normal activities. Matt's excitement began to fade, as he thought about Roaming Bear's words of warning, although he promised himself that he would make this work. After this rescue mission, he was never going back to Earth again!

Chapter 5

The corridor exiting the building was plain. There was no door. Instead, a simple archway led onto a path just outside lined with two hedges of tall rose bushes. The pink, white and lavender buds gave off a sweet fragrance and reached nine feet in the air. The flowers reminded Matt of Mr. Baxter from the eternity window. The path was about twenty feet long and veered to the right. At the end of the path the walkway split into two opposite directions.

The angels led a silent march taking the right walkway with Matt trailing behind. Matt noticed that both angels' attitudes were different now. Enon was more than annoyed at the turn of events. Anjella seemed to be silently cautious, unsure of what was to follow. As Matt walked to where the pathway split in opposite directions, he glanced to the left and halted with a gasp. He looked to his right where Anjella and Enon were headed and saw a group of buildings resembling the one they just left. They appeared to be made of white stone. They looked very much like a modern office complex, only without any windows. Gazing to the left, Matt saw an entirely different vista. Before him was a spectacular kingdom of crystal palaces dotting lush green valleys as far as the eye could see. The walkway that appeared to be smooth marble turned into a golden highway leading to the first splendid city set behind crystal walls. Matt squatted down and touched the smooth gold bricks that butted up against the marble walkway he was standing on. He realized the road was made up of real gold bricks. He couldn't imagine what the total value the gold walkway would amount to on Earth. Lush foliage lined the roads, mixed with colorful masses of flowers and fruit trees. Lakes fed into streams that ran through the valleys. The waters were intense shades of blue and crystal clear. Matt suddenly yearned to run and dive into the fresh lake by the first palace to feel the cool water. It was calling to him in a song it made on its own. "Everything is so alive here!" Matt whispered to himself. "I can't go back to Earth, I just can't!"

Anjella rushed back to Matt. She wanted to give him more time to drink in the beautiful picture before him, but she knew it would only make things worse. "Matt, you must come with us, now. We have to go." Matt looked at Anjella with saddened eyes.

"This is really Heaven, isn't it? Nothing could be more beautiful!"

"Yes, it is beautiful and someday you will be here forever and can explore every one of those cities. But now you must go back to Earth and complete your mission to make this possible."

Matt peered out at the magnificence before him one more time and turned to walk with Anjella. "I'm glad God makes you forget this place when you go down to Earth. It would be hell for all of us if we could remember." Anjella grew concerned at Matt's disheartening statement and tried to cheer him up.

"There are many beautiful things about Earth, too. Only as a human can you experience love in the physical sense. You know, I will never know what it is like to feel a mother's touch or fall in love. There are many of us here who would love to have a chance to experience what you take for granted in the physical world." Her words had a soothing tone and eased his mind.

Enon's pace quickened down the pathway. Anjella and Matt both knew it was a sign to get moving. "We are right behind you, Enon." Anjella chimed and they both picked up the pace. Matt glanced over his shoulder a few more times, trying to burn the memory into his heart so he wouldn't forget.

They entered the building adjacent to the one they had just left. The decor was much like Human Affairs. Anjella and Enon escorted Matt down a hallway to another room. When they entered the room, it appeared to be set up much like the conference room where Matt spoke to the Elders, but with a straight table in the middle of the room. Angels were hurrying left and right, conferring with each other and then leaving quickly. It seemed more like a command post. There was a large screen behind the table in the center of the wall, about ten feet high by fifteen feet long. Enon was greeted by a male angel named Sage. He was tall and well built with a square jaw and broad, square shoulders. He held his posture like a military man. Enon signaled for Anjella and Matt to be seated at the center of the table. Enon went around to the other side and seated himself beside Sage. Matt could tell that Sage and Enon were talking telepathically, although he was not privy to the content.

Enon began to explain the case assignment to Matt. His tone was authoritarian and dead serious. "Matthew, I want you to pay close attention to everything I say. It is critical that the assignment be followed as planned, to avoid complications. Just like the Elder warned you, there are very specific rules we are required to follow that cannot be changed." Enon tapped his hand on a manual that appeared instantaneously under his hand on the table. Matt did a double take and then smiled. He began to think of how incredible it must be to stay here in Heaven. Just to think that one can go from fairly drab buildings to crystal cities in a blink of the eye astounded him. He thought it was so cool watching the angels flitting back and forth in a scene that resembled the stock exchange floor on a Friday morning. He marveled at this Universal mind that created the intricate laws of give and take. He pictured the lake by the first crystal city in his mind and wondered if the lake was the "living waters" the bible talked about. Anjella saw Matt's mind drifting and nudged his back.

"Hey, listen up. You can not miss what is being said here. It is too important." Matt sat up in his seat and apologized. Enon continued speaking.

"Your assignment is as follows: Please focus on the screen behind me, as we review." The blank screen filled with a panoramic shot of a farm field and zoomed to the side of a road. There lay a girl in her early twenties. She was lying on her stomach on the roadside with most of her face buried in grass. The girl was moaning and beginning to stir. Enon went on.

"This is Elizabeth Harris, known as Beth to her family and friends. She went through a very rough experience last night and was thrown from a car and abandoned. Beth has an estranged relationship with her father and is about to make a terrible and fatal mistake by running away from her family for good. This decision will lead her onto a desperate path and permanently alienate her from her family. Your mission, Matt, is to prevent her from leaving her family and convince her to reconcile with her father." Enon's words sounded like they came right out of a James Bond movie script.

Matt was surprised at such an easy assignment. All he had to do is go down and convince her not to leave and make up with her dad. It never occurred to him how he would have responded to such an attempt in his life. It didn't seem like such a challenge. "Is that all I have to do?" he asked Enon.

"Do you think this is an easy task, young man?" Enon grew frustrated. "You have not been told the rules to this escapade yet. Would you like to hear them?"

"Yes, quite frankly, I'm curious as to how I get back to Earth this time, if I can't use my body." Matt felt like an A-student getting a C-student assignment at school.

The screen panned back and Matt saw a priest in his sixties walking leisurely down the side of the road. "This is Father Patrick O'Donnell. He likes to be called Father Pat. We have made arrangements for you to use him to accomplish this mission. You will go down to Earth and assume his body. He will allow you to use his mind, although this is involuntary on his part. Your thoughts will become his actions. All of the knowledge you need to perform his duties will be automatically incorporated into your intelligence. It sounds strange, but I assure you it should be an effortless coordination between the two of you. As long as you relax and do not fight the flow of thoughts, you will operate through him smoothly. When you leave his body, he will have no memory of your existence. He will believe that he had been operating of his own accord. You will help Beth recover physically and at the same time help her to see her errors and reunite her with her father. Both individuals in this case are very strong minded characters, much like you and your father, so do not think this will be an easy task."

Matt still felt rather confident. "Well, now that I know the errors I made with my own father, I am sure I can convince her to change her way of thinking."

Enon looked across at Matt and drew his eyebrows together. "Let's hope it will be that easy, young man, for your sake. There are a few rules that you must, and I mean *must*, follow while on Earth this time.

"First, you can only work with this girl to successfully complete this mission. You must heal her way of thinking. You cannot try to change others around her. Any attempts will fail and also violate the rules. So, for example, you cannot try to convince her father directly to change his way of thinking and reunite them that way. This reunification must come from Beth's heart. *She* must see the light. It is the only way her soul can be saved.

"Second, you may call on our assistance two times during your stay on Earth. After that, you are on your own.

"Third, once you have taken on a physical form, you cannot change into another form. You must work through Father Pat alone and no other person or thing.

"Fourth, you cannot appear as yourself to anyone while on Earth. So, if you're thinking of looking up your family or friends while you're down there, forget it. They cannot see you and will not believe you are residing in Father Pat. It will only bring them pain if you try.

"These rules are very critical, Matt, do you understand what I am saying?"

Matt was still busy watching the screen. He saw the priest drawing closer to the girl lying on the ground. He wondered how it would feel to enter Father Pat's body. His mind was racing and scattered, thinking about everything but the specific rules at this time. Anjella nudged him again, only harder.

"Oh yeah, Enon, right, right. A piece of cake! I can't wait to start so I can get back here. How long do you think I'll be down there? A few days or maybe a week?"

Enon shook his head in defeat, "I hope long enough to make this happen for your sake and hers." He turned to look at the poor girl and wondered if she would be better off with or without Matt's help.

"So, how do I get down there? Let's burn some rubber."

Anjella spoke up. "I think you are really going to like this ride. Follow me."

The three of them walked over to the viewing screen. The scene panned back and it looked like they were viewing the Earth from a distance of about two hundred feet in the air. The priest was about twenty yards away from Beth's body. All of a sudden, the screen transformed into a hole in the sky and the view became three-dimensional. Matt was asked to stand on a platform at the edge of the screen. When he stepped in front of the screen, Matt felt like he was losing his balance, as he teetered on the edge. Enon told him that all he had to do was lean forward when he said go and his spirit would travel down and assume Father Pat's body, by using his own intention. Matt was only to think about assuming the form as he got closer, and he would go right into the body of the priest. It would only take a few seconds. Everything had been carefully arranged so that Father Pat would stroll by Beth's body at this exact time. No other person would be around to witness the event or to create any problems. Angels had worked frantically, diverting other humans and pets away from the road. It took a great deal of coordination to make such a plan work, but everything was set to go.

Matt was awestruck by the whole process. What a thrill this will be, he thought. He looked back to take in the contrast of the operation going on behind him, as he stood at the split of two worlds. He was about to fly down to Earth from Heaven! Oh, if Jeff could see him now.

To his own surprise, Matt suddenly began to feel dizzy, as his gaze returned to the scene below. He suddenly lost courage in his ability to fly. Enon asked if he was ready and Matt turned and abruptly said no, he couldn't jump.

"Why do we have to do it this way? Can't you just blink me down there?"

Enon explained that there was no choice. "We have limited vehicles to use on a soul that is between two dimensions. What happened to the daredevil racer? I thought you would enjoy it this way!"

Matt looked down at the tiny figures below him that resembled little ants on the ground. The tall trees were no larger than a dime from where he stood. He felt like he needed a parachute or, better yet, a plane! Enon lost his patience, which angels rarely do. "You must go *now* or everything will be ruined." Enon instructed Sage to keep the angels on alert. There may be a delay.

Anjella calmed Enon down and asked if she could try. She walked up and onto the platform with Matt and put her arm around him. "Matt, you keep forgetting that you are a spirit now. You do not have a physical body to harm. You will not feel like you are falling at all. It will be over in less time than you think, trust me." He didn't seem convinced at all. "I know what you need," Anjella tapped her head, as if it were such an obvious solution. She placed her two hands on the center of his shoulders.

Matt felt a tightness develop between his shoulder blades. His muscles were drawing together in a ball. Out of the ball grew full-sized angel wings made of soft white feathers. Strangely, it felt like they had always been there. Matt moved his shoulders slightly and the wings spread out about eight feet wide. His delight shone on his face in a brilliant gleaming smile. "Will these work?"

"Of course, silly, now you should have no problem flying. But you must go now!" Anjella squeezed him around the waist and stepped back down. Matt looked at Enon, who was now fit to be tied, and smiled. "Ready when you are!" Enon checked with Sage and looked down at the scene. With all the Earth time that passed, Father Pat was still moments away from Beth's body. Enon held his hand up like a flagman in a race and said "Now, go!"

With that, Matt gulped hard, closed his eyes and leaned forward. He felt the wind catch his wings and his body soar weightlessly through the sky. He opened his eyes and realized that he was, indeed, flying. It was a wonderfully exhilarating feeling.

Meanwhile, Enon gestured to Anjella to come over for a private conference. "I don't think we needed to go to such flamboyant extremes as giving Matt wings for such an easy trip to Earth!" Enon scolded Anjella. Anjella drew her hands on her hips in complete and utter frustration. "Well, how did you think we were going to get him down there without them? He obviously needed a boost of confidence and it worked!"

Enon twitched his nose and looked reminiscently at the platform. "I could have given him a push. I think it would have done us both some good!"

"Oh, Enon," Anjella retorted, "If you keep this up, you are going to end up in the Time Out Ward polishing those tarnished wings you've been wearing. I think we better get back to work." and she turned toward the screen to watch Matt's progress.

Matt was soaring straight to Earth with a weightlessness that defied gravity. His wings made it easy to glide. He raised his head for a moment and felt himself swooping back up toward Heaven like a fighter jet maneuver in a dogfight. "Damn, damn, damn! This is incredible," he thought. Matt leaned left and right, creating new flight paths in the air. He began doing loops and dives in various combinations. The feeling of flying was even more rewarding than racing at top speeds. Matt was so distracted by the fun he was having that he almost forgot about the mission.

Anjella cringed, as she watched Matt's aerial aerobic display, knowing Enon would blame her because she had given him the wings. She reasoned with herself that knowing Matt, he would have done this with or without those wings. And she was probably right. Once he left Heaven, however, she could not communicate with him unless he called on her. He was on his own and she could only watch and hope for the best.

Enon, meanwhile, did not have time to lecture Anjella about her rookie mistake. Matt was throwing the whole timing off again and this could mean disaster. Sage was alerting all angels on the case that the mission was delayed again. Angels were running left and right, issuing new directions. It was early enough in the morning on Earth that most people and animals were still sleeping. This would be the saving grace, Enon thought.

As Matt looped and spun for the fifth time, Father Pat came into clear view, which jolted his memory back to the important mission he was supposed to be on. He straightened his flight path and relaxed, as he looked left and right and saw no one else around. Father Pat was a few yards away from Beth and it looked like Matt would arrive just in the nick of time.

Father Pat stopped and turned to Beth's body. Matt readied himself as he approached the back of the pastor. Anjella and Enon both held their breath, as they watched the apparent success before their eyes.

Matt began to make his intention to enter Father Pat. Just that second, Father Pat bent down and rolled Beth over to check her condition. As Matt focused on the head of Father Pat, it disappeared and was replaced by a tiny ruby-throated hummingbird that was wandering over to his favorite patch of day lilies that edged the farm field for his morning breakfast. Matt had already begun his intention, and was saying the words to himself, as he saw the little bird. "I intend to assume the body of...a hummingbird?" He did not mean to say it, but the bird registered in his mind before he could say Father Pat. Matt's spirit was sucked into the little body of the hummingbird, sending the bird's body into an aerial aerobic dance of its own. Matt's mind raced to gain composure as the Earth spun around and around. He felt out of control, as the little bird's heart raced at over twelve hundred beats per minute. He tried to remember what Enon said would happen when the two minds met.

Matt could feel the little bird's mind fighting to gain control, as it spun toward the ground. Matt beat the bird's wings frantically trying to level himself off. He felt the bird's mind plead for control and he allowed the bird to take over. The bird increased his wing speed, spread his tail feathers forcing itself into a hover and landed gingerly on the edge of the fence just ten feet from Father Pat and Beth.

It took Matt a few long seconds to relax and get used to the bird's accelerated metabolism. The bird sat on the fence long enough to regain its composure and headed straight for the day lilies. The sweet nectar was the only source of energy that would instantly recover the tired bird's body. The little bird visited the day lilies and drank twice as much nectar as it usually would, until it felt fully recovered. As the bird settled on the fencing for a final rest, Matt watched Father Pat lift the almost lifeless body of Beth in his arms and turn toward the rectory at the end of the road, about a half a mile away. Matt saw his chance for redemption fade helplessly into the bright sun and called meekly for his angels.

Chapter 6

In a flash, Matt was seated as himself in the control room, across from a very unhappy Enon and a shocked, wide-eyed Anjella. On the screen behind them was a frozen picture of Father Pat carrying Beth down the road. Enon turned, first, to Sage and demanded to know how the hummingbird got into the picture. Sage said that the angels in charge of nature had their hands full holding back a flock of geese, who ventured into the area unexpectedly. The little hummingbird slipped by them unnoticed. Enon requested a meeting with those angels before he gave his report to the Council. He turned then to Matt and folded his arms.

The look of frustration on Enon's face said more than words could at that moment. Matt shrank down in his seat and prepared for the forthcoming lecture. "Well, Matt, I hope you're happy. Do you know what a mess you have made of this mission now? What happened to the boy who learned his lesson? If you really understood what was at stake here, you would have never engaged in such a selfish, childish act that we saw out there. And what about Beth? Were you thinking of her? And the Council, what about the Council? Do you realize that I am supposed to give them a report in a short while?" Enon went on and on. His lecture seemed to last an eternity. Anjella thought everyone in the room had had enough and interrupted.

"Enon, I think Matt understands what kind of mess he is in by now, and so does everyone else. I think we need to discuss how we are going to change this situation, so Matt can continue on."

Enon threw his hands in the air and rolled his eyes, "Continue on, continue on did you say? This mission will have to be canceled and Matt will have to go on to a new life, as originally planned by the Council." His tone was final.

Matt sat straight up when he heard the news. Anjella could not believe what she was hearing. "What do you mean cancel the mission? We can't do this to Matt, he needs our help."

"Well, it is too late for help, Anjella." Enon began to pace, "How do you suppose Matt will be able to work with Beth now that he is a hummingbird?"

"Why can't we start over? Hasn't that been done before?" It was clear Anjella had no experience with this type of return case.

"No!" Enon exclaimed, "Didn't you both hear me when I stated the rules? You cannot change subjects once you have assumed a physical form on Earth. It doesn't matter if it's a mistake or not. The rules were intended as a challenge, to see if the soul granted this opportunity was indeed ready to move on. I'm afraid Matt has shown poor judgment already. It is too late."

"Okay then," Anjella went on in Matt's defense. "Matt will just have to complete the mission as a hummingbird." Matt and Enon both looked at her as if she were crazy.

"Impossible." Enon snickered.

"Why not?" Anjella did not want to give up on Matt. He looked so broken-hearted sitting in the chair listening to the great debate. "I may not know much about these cases, but clearly other souls have accomplished their mission in animal forms."

"Yes, but they went as dogs or cats or other animals that humans relate to easily. I don't recall any human ever relating to a hummingbird before." Enon was resigned to accepting this mission as a complete failure.

"But," Anjella grasped for a straw, "has there ever been a case where a soul has failed as a hummingbird?" It was her final attempt to reason with Enon.

"No, since this appears to be the first hummingbird mission, I don't suppose we have record of a failure." Enon saw where this was going and didn't like it one bit.

"So, then, I think we should give Matt a chance to see if he can pull it off. The worst thing that will happen is that the mission will end up as a failure. But, I know how persuasive Matt can be. If he could win over the Council, I bet he can pull this off, too." Anjella winked at Matt, knowing her reasoning was sound.

Enon looked at both of them for a moment and rubbed his eyebrows. "Okay, Anjella, you win. I hope, for your sake, Matt is as charming as you believe he is." He walked over to his manual and flipped through several pages and then looked over at Matt.

"Since we are going to give this another try, I suppose we should go over the rules again. Are you ready to listen to them seriously this time?"

Matt nodded his head and gave a sheepish smile. "Don't worry, Enon, I think I have learned my lesson."

Enon was slightly amused, "You don't say!" He began repeating the same rules, but emphasized that he could only call on the angels one more time and added a new rule. "I did not see a need to mention this rule the last time, since you were supposed to be a human, but now that you are a hummingbird, this rule is quite important." He paused a moment and peered at Matt over the rim of his glasses. "Since you have assumed a hummingbird's body, you must obey the natural laws of that species. You must maintain the natural eating and sleeping habits of this bird to keep it alive and healthy. It is important to know that hummingbirds migrate south every year sometime between August and September in that area of the United States you will be in. If the hummingbird does not go south before the cold weather sets in, his body will not be able to tolerate the temperature and lack of food supply and will die. If the hummingbird dies, you will be forced to return to Heaven, regardless of where you are in your mission. So, not only do you have to follow the rules of simply being a bird, Matt, you also have a new time constraint. You have approximately four to six weeks to complete this mission. Considering the challenges you face, that is very little time."

Matt knew his chances were slim to none right now. Anjella stood over him and placed her hands on his shoulders as he sat in the chair. She saw the look of defeat in his eyes, but felt his strong desire to stay in Heaven in his heart. She knew he was a special soul and had the strength and determination to succeed, if he believed in himself. She searched for words to bring him strength. Her purple eyes grew in intensity as they looked into his puzzled expression. "Matt, I know you feel badly about what happened and rightly so. You have been trying all your life to be a champion. But not for the reasons you think. It is not because you desired to win your father's approval or to satisfy your own ego. It is because your soul has been seeking all this time to become a champion of God's love. And you have missed the mark repeatedly, because you do not believe that it is possible that God, the greatest champion of all, is a part of you! *This mission* is your opportunity to prove *you are a champion* by trusting your oneness with the Almighty and using God's strength that resides in you. You can do this! I have the utmost faith in your abilities because I know what is in your heart and that is God's love. Just as it is in each and every one of us." She squeezed his shoulders firmly. "Remember, everything is possible in God's world and you are a part of that world. You know about Heaven and its beauty and you have the luxury on this mission to be able to remember this anytime you want. Use this knowledge to give you the strength to accomplish this mission. God will never give up on you. God loves you and made you as you are now, perfect in every way. Keep the faith and you can do anything." Anjella looked over at Enon and signaled for him to respond as she said, "Enon and I will be with you every step of the way, won't we Enon?"

Enon tapped his fingers on the manual as he looked into Matt's helpless eyes. For some reason beyond his wildest imaginings, he knew Anjella was right. If anyone could pull this mission off, it would be Matt. "Yes, Matt, we will be with you every step of the way."

Matt felt his spirits lift and the pain in his heart easing as he looked at his two caseworkers. Tears filled his eyes and he turned toward the screen. The screen was still frozen on Father Pat carrying Beth toward the old house

at the end of the field. Beth's light brown hair cascaded down over Father
Pat's arm and her face was buried in his chest. She looked tiny and frail in
the priest's large arms and she reminded Matt briefly of his sister Ellen.
Anjella's words echoed in his mind. Matt realized that he had to give this
mission all he had, not only for his sake, but also for the girl whose future
rested in his hands.

"Okay, guys, it's now or never. I'll give it a try. Do I have to go back
down through the screen again?" Matt was hoping he wouldn't have to fly
down to Earth.

Anjella smiled as she clasped her hands together and looked over at
Enon for guidance. "No, Matt, now that you have assumed a form, we
simply send you back to the exact moment you left Earth. That is why the
screen is frozen. We do not interrupt Earth time coming and going."

Matt was relieved. Anjella hugged him and gave him some final words
of encouragement. Enon issued a final warning in a stern, fatherly tone.
"Remember, you only have one more opportunity to call on us. Use this
wisely. Once you use it up, you are on your own until the mission succeeds
or fails." And then in a more friendly tone he added, "Good luck, Matt, I
wish you well." Anjella squeezed his arm and asked Matt if he was ready.
Matt gave the thumbs up and in less than a second he was sitting on the
fence in the little bird's body watching the priest carry his assignment home.
Matt felt the bird's racing heart, but this time he made a conscious effort to
relax and settled into the bird's body. As the priest walked up the road, Matt
flitted from one bush to the next, keeping a safe distance behind him for
surveillance, forgetting that no one would possibly be suspicious of a
hummingbird. He watched the priest turn and walk through the backyard of
the first house he came to and enter the kitchen. Matt peered into the kitchen
window and watched an older woman help Father Pat carry the young girl
up to a bedroom on the second floor. The bedroom was directly above the
kitchen window. He watched as the old woman brought in a wet cloth.
Father Pat began to wipe the dirt off Beth's face and arms while the older
woman began to examine her wounds. Matt felt secure knowing that the girl
would be there for a little while.

The bird's mind was straining to remain in charge of its body and Matt
decided to let the bird take over for a short time so he could learn its feeding
habits. The bird raced over to a patch of red salvia in the front yard of the
rectory and lapped up the nectar with its long, tube shaped tongue. Then it
flew to a nearby oak tree and perched for about fifteen minutes. It returned
to the flowers again and repeated the same pattern. Matt realized that
frequent feedings were essential in order to keep the bird's racing
metabolism going. Flying was a lot more work than walking and Matt
practiced taking over the bird's body to get the hang of it. When he was sure

he knew the basics, he thanked the little bird and asked if he could take charge.

Chapter 7

Matt flew to one of the bedroom windows where Beth was sleeping and hid in the corner to listen to the conversation inside. The curtains on the window acted as camouflage shielding him from view. He could hear everything clearly.

Father Pat and the woman had just finished making Beth comfortable. Beth began to stir and moan before opening her eyes. She was groggy when she regained consciousness and saw the two strangers standing above her. At first, Beth panicked as she looked around the room. It was plain and sparsely decorated but definitely not a hospital room. There was a small dresser on the wall across from the bed with a lace doily, a crucifix and a small empty green vase on it. A picture of the Blessed Mother with the Baby Jesus hung over the dresser. The wall to Beth's left had two large windows with white lace curtains. Beth could see a large oak tree just outside the window across from her. The walls were covered with pink and green floral wallpaper that had faded with time. There was a small nightstand to her left and a chair in the corner on her right next to the bed.

"Where am I?" she asked the two strangers at her side.

Father Pat answered, "You are at St. Bartholomew's Rectory in Briarsville. Do you know our area?

"Sure, I do," Beth replied as she pulled herself up in bed, "I'm from this area."

Father Pat gingerly approached the next set of questions. He had a lot of experience dealing with runaways and young people on drugs and he could tell by Beth's dilated eyes that she was recovering from a bad night. "I'm Father Pat and this is Mrs. Gladys McCafferty, my secretary, housekeeper and all around good friend."

Mrs. McCafferty chimed in. "Everyone calls me Mrs. McC. What is your name, dear?"

Beth had a bad headache and strained to think for a moment. "My name is Beth, Beth Harris."

"Nice to meet you Beth." Father went on. "You're pretty banged up. The bruises on your arms and left cheek are bad, but I don't think anything is broken. You have a few deep cuts on your right calf. There was a lot of broken glass on the side of the road where I found you." Father Pat felt it was too soon to ask her how she got there. "Mrs. McC will finish cleaning them up for you, but you probably should go to the hospital for a complete checkup. Some of those cuts might require stitches." Beth noticed a basin with water, towels and bandages had appeared on the dresser next to the

119

green vase and was confused, but was distracted by the priest's last comment.

"No hospital or doctors!" Beth stammered. "I'm fine. I don't need special attention." Beth curled up into a tight ball on the bed.

Father Pat could see the fright in Beth's eyes. He was afraid to push her too hard. He knew she would leave the first chance she got, if she felt threatened. It would be better to leave her alone for a while until she felt safe enough to open up.

"Okay, Beth, no doctors for now, unless we find something serious, is that a deal?" Father Pat smiled and touched her hand. Beth flinched and pulled her hand under the covers.

"Alright." Beth was exhausted and every inch of her body hurt. She closed her eyes tightly, trying to force away the memories of what had happened to her. "I feel really tired, can I just close my eyes for a little while?" Her voice sounded far away. She was having trouble staying focused.

"Sure you can." Father Pat carefully asked the next question. "Who can we contact to let them know where you are and that you are okay?"

"No one!" Beth sat up straight holding on tight to the sheet that was clenched in her fists and realized her reaction was too abrupt. "I'm sorry, really. There's no one to call right now."

Mrs. McCafferty moved to the top of the bed and fluffed Beth's pillow. "Okay, dear, it's alright. We are not going to cause you any trouble. Maybe you need to rest some. Why don't you take a nice nap and afterwards I will help you with a shower and we'll find something clean for you to wear, while I wash your clothes. Father Pat presides over the ten o'clock mass now, so he will need to leave. I'll be downstairs if you need anything, just give me a call." Mrs. McCafferty reminded Beth of the perfect grandmother type. Although her hands looked weathered from years of labor, they were still soft. Her smile was nurturing. She had pure white hair pulled up neatly into a tight bun on her head that exaggerated her wrinkled face, but added to her natural charm as a caregiver.

Mrs. McCafferty was a special person indeed. She was one of those people who caught you by surprise with their hidden, yet magnetic charm. There was no one way to describe her. She was quiet, yet uplifting; modest and unassuming, yet boldly confident in her convictions; and highly intuitive, yet unobtrusive. Her joyous smile softened the hardest hearts and her delicate touch eased the fiercest tension right out of your body. What was most interesting was that all her good works were done without a spoken word, which left the recipient wondering if the change came from her or something else.

Before she came to work at the rectory, Mrs. McCafferty lived with her husband on a farm at the edge of the parish, about a forty-minute ride from the church. She and her husband, Edgar, kept to themselves, usually attending the 8:00 a.m. service on Sundays that was sparsely attended and then hurrying back to the farm. Edgar worked the farm alone, receiving an occasional hand during harvest time from some stranded individual who needed sheltering or a temporary job.

When she started working at the rectory, mysterious events began to happen at the church and were linked to her arrival. Rumors floated around the parish that she was a fortuneteller in her younger years and that she had psychic powers because of the way she always appeared ready to aid whatever crisis came about. If someone showed up at the rectory looking for food at ten o'clock at night, a casserole would be warming in the oven and a loaf of fresh baked bread would be wrapped in a bag ready to go. If someone were short of money in a grocery line, she would pull the exact change needed from her coat pocket. If Father received an emergency call from one of his parishioners during a winter storm at two in the morning, his coat, scarf, gloves and boots would be neatly piled by the hat rack in the livingroom waiting for him. Father Pat had grown so accustomed to her unique sense of timing that he hardly noticed it anymore.

When someone was bold enough to ask her about her *intuitiveness*, she would laugh it off and tell him or her, "you never know when God will send an angel your way, so I try to stay prepared!" Then she would quickly change the subject without that person realizing what just happened. But without a doubt, it was her wonderful, down-to-earth cooking that cast a spell over your tired, weary taste buds.

Her dishes were simple, but she could turn a hum-drum meal of meatloaf and mashed potatoes into a blissful, culinary experience, when she smothered them in her secret recipe brown gravy. Forget your waistline—second helpings were always a must and her desserts sent you on a trip straight to Heaven. All of the ladies in the parish who were the culinary wannabes, with their blue ribbon apple pies and strawberry jams, bristled at the compliments sent her way and whispered their own nasty rumors that her food had to be laced with an illegal substance. What else could explain how that simple brown gravy could make a person feel so good? Perhaps they weren't specks of thyme after all, they surmised. Their greatest source of frustration was that no one else who attended the church suppers seemed to care if that were true!

All Beth knew was that Mrs. McCafferty didn't know her at all, and yet she extended only warm feelings of acceptance. It made her feel a little more comfortable with finding herself in a strange place with people she didn't know. Beth was apprehensive about what would happen next, but she could not fight the wave of sleepiness that overcame her and she closed her heavy eyelids and slept for several hours.

Father Pat and Mrs. McCafferty left Beth and went downstairs to continue their morning schedule. They talked briefly about Beth. She wasn't the first stray they had taken in and certainly would not be the last. Matt listened in at the living room window.

"Poor thing," Mrs. McCafferty began. "Such a beautiful girl. How do these poor souls get so lost these days, Father?"

"Lord only knows! She doesn't look like the type of girl who would get involved in drugs, but then, they never do, do they? First, we'll need to find out what happened to her and how she ended up on the side of the road. Then we'll do our best to help her." He smiled and patted Mrs. McCafferty's shoulder, "Just like we always do, Mrs. McC."

Mrs. McCafferty grabbed the priest's black fedora that he always wore on Sunday and sent him off to the church, which was directly across from the rectory. The hat belonged to his father, Henry, and held special meaning to him. Pat never liked wearing hats, but he wore this hat to church, rain or shine, in hot or cold weather, since the day of his father's funeral twelve years ago. It was not an expensive hat, but his father wore it with as much pride as if it came from the finest hat shop in the world. Despite his modest background, Henry insisted that to be a gentleman, you must wear a hat and constantly admonished Pat for leaving the house without one. Every morning he would walk down the street and tip his hat to anyone he passed by and bid them good morning. Henry gave up trying to persuade Pat to wear a hat and admitted that a sign of a true gentleman was not the hat he wore, but how *gentle* the man was. Pat grew up to be a kind and generous young man and that made him proud. Becoming a priest was just the icing on the cake for his father. Henry's old hat made Pat feel like his father was still close to him. He missed him very much.

St. Bartholomew's was a small country church surrounded mostly by farms. There were several horse and cattle farms, but most of the local farmers grew corn, rye and alfalfa. The church sat on the edge of the town called Briarsville. Briarsville was halfway between the Pennsylvania Amish country and Philadelphia, about an hour in each direction. Thirty miles to the east of Briarsville was the growing high tech corporate community called Forrest Hills. Briarsville and neighboring towns were becoming the new hot spots for housing developments to support the increasing number of people working for the affluent corporations in Forrest Hills.

Farmers were jumping at the opportunity to sell off small parcels of their land for enormous profits in a year when crop yields were poor because of the summer's drought. As the number of families at St. Bartholomew's increased, Father Pat grew concerned that he would have to start adding more masses to handle the growing number of churchgoers. Father Pat had come to this church seven years ago in 1991, hoping to spend his last ten years before retirement in a quieter rural setting. He had served the church for over thirty years already and his entire career, except for the time he served in the Vietnam War, was spent working with lower income families in West Philadelphia, close to where he was brought up as a child. He looked forward to an easier assignment for his final ten years serving a small, modest community of people. He liked living in the rural atmosphere where life was much simpler. Or that, at least, was how it used to be. With the lack of priests available in the Church, he knew he would have to shoulder the new growth and the increasing number of problems that went with it.

Father Pat said mass and gave a warm sermon on patience. Although it was not planned, he placed special emphasis on patience within the parent/child relationship. He stressed that both adults and children needed to work extra hard to develop respect for each other. He knew this was especially difficult for parents, who were the authority figures of the family. He reminded the congregation to be more like Jesus, the good shepherd, who gently watched over his flock with love and understanding. This point was not relevant to the gospel's message today—he had written his homily on being patient with God's answers, but he felt compelled to address it anyway. Discovering a young girl abandoned on the side of the road would not be surprising in his old parish in Philadelphia, but to see this happening in his quaint little town was very disturbing. His own experience taught him that violence and drugs stemmed from the disintegration of the family unit. He wondered if society was ever going to come to terms with this reality before the problems saturated the entire country.

When the service was over, Father Pat stood outside of church and greeted everyone with a warm handshake or a friendly kiss. It was a beautiful, bright morning that already showed signs of heading towards a hot afternoon. The summer had been unseasonably hot and dry and everyone cursed the dreaded El Niño weather pattern that created the record-breaking temperatures in this area all summer long. One just had to look at the dried, brown lawns and the wilting flowers to know it was so. The church had a few ceiling fans that helped circulate the air, just enough to keep the weak from fainting. This community was used to hard summers and winters.

Father Pat's parishioners loved him dearly and thanked him for the wonderful homily, as they left the church. His sermons were always well done. He had a great sense of humor and would often weave it into heavy subjects just to lighten them up. Several people told him that they appreciated the comments he made concerning patience in regards to their children and would try to remember what he said. Father Pat smiled and thought of Beth. He wondered if she was a runaway. Her reaction when he questioned her about contacting her family certainly gave him that impression. However, she looked old enough to be on her own, too.

The gregarious Gloria McQuail's ardent greeting interrupted his thoughts and he quickly inquired about her husband, Sam's, arthritis problem. He had heard earlier in the week that Sam was having problems at work. Gloria updated him on her husband's latest doctor's visit and then extended Father Pat an invitation to her monthly get-together, as she called it. Father Pat graciously declined; remembering how unruly the last party had become. He usually tried to steer clear of that type of parishioner activity. He chatted with Gloria a few minutes longer while the last few stragglers bid their good-byes and walked back into the vestibule to speak with the altar boys.

When the parking lot cleared, Father Pat closed up the church and headed for the rectory. He knew Mrs. McCafferty would have a wonderful Sunday brunch prepared for him when he arrived. It would be a treat this morning, because she always cooked something special whenever a guest would be attending. He could smell sausages, pancakes and the delightful scent of cinnamon wafting through the air, as he came up to the kitchen door.

Matt sat in the oak tree and watched the priest walk into the kitchen. He flew down to a lilac bush that was directly under the window at the kitchen sink and listened in. Matt had no clue how he could help Beth better than Father Pat and Mrs. McCafferty.

Mrs. McCafferty was just pulling her prize winning cinnamon buns out of the oven.

"Why is it, dear woman, that I have to wait for company to get a taste of those heavenly cinnamon buns?" Father Pat teased her.

Mrs. McCafferty shooed him away from the hot pan as he tried to sneak a bite and said, "If I let you eat these every week, Father, you wouldn't make it to retirement."

Father Pat laughed, "Oh, but what a way to go my dear." After she put the pan down on the counter he added, "So has our little patient gotten up yet?"

"Oh, yes, but I think she should stay in bed for a few days." Mrs. McCafferty gave him a look of concern and continued, "While you were at mass, Beth asked me to help her with her shower Father and I noticed she had a great deal of difficulty walking. It was an accident of timing, but I saw that her thighs are severely bruised and I fear this is far more serious than we'd imagined. I think she was physically abused, if you know what I mean." Mrs. McCafferty blushed at the thought. Father Pat had a good deal of experience with sexual abuse and rape. He was no stranger to the subject.

"Hmm, does she know you saw the bruises?"

"No, Father, I don't think she knew I was in the room at the time and I didn't see the marks until after her shower. It was then that it made sense to me why I heard her crying so hard as she washed herself. She was in there for at least a half-hour! Shouldn't we inform the authorities anyway? I didn't know what to do at the time." Mrs. McCafferty frowned as she began to fix a tray for Beth.

"No, Mrs. McCafferty, you did the right thing. From my experience, if she was raped and it was by a stranger, she would probably have told us right off. Unfortunately, most girls who get into this kind of trouble with someone they know are too afraid to do anything about it. They think they did something to provoke it or are being punished for doing something bad. Even if we did report it, she probably wouldn't press charges anyway. You saw how upset she was when we mentioned taking her to the hospital." Father Pat squeezed Mrs. McCafferty's shoulder.

Matt listened intently to the conversation. He couldn't believe what he heard. "Beth was raped!" He thought in amazement. Now he felt more lost than ever. This was not a simple case of a girl passing out on the street from a night of partying with her friends. Beth had been in real trouble. She may have been beaten and raped. Matt watched Mrs. McCafferty bring a tray with a large stack of pancakes, sausage, cinnamon bun, maple syrup and orange juice up to Beth. He flew immediately up to the bedroom sill. Beth was sitting up in bed and combing her hair. Her hair was much longer than he expected. She looked so much better since she showered. Beth had the classic girl next door beauty, just like his mother. Her skin was creamy beige and she had wide hazel eyes. Her cheekbones were high and her nose thin and long with a slight curl on the end. Her eyes were very expressive and right now they revealed the deep sadness she was feeling.

Matt had taken the opportunity while Beth showered to search for food. He already knew about the day lilies up the road, but wanted to be sure he had other sources. The red salvia flowers in the front of the house did not hold as much nectar as the lilies and it would not be long before he used the nectar up. He had no idea if flowers replenished their nectar or how often it would be. Fortunately, the house next to the church had a beautiful, small flower garden and a great trumpet vine climbing the side of the house. Many of the flowers were wilting in the summer heat and Matt knew this was not a good sign. When he got back to the house he rested on a branch of the oak tree. A small gnat landed beside him and he began to watch it crawl away. Before he knew what he was doing he flicked his long tongue and snatched the gnat up and swallowed it whole. Matt thought he would be grossed out, but was surprised that he liked the taste. It seemed like an entirely natural process. "Oh wow, I eat bugs!" This was a relief because Matt felt safer knowing he had an alternate food source, if he needed it. The sweet, sugary nectar tasted much better and gave him instant energy, though, and he hoped it would last.

Mrs. McCafferty greeted Beth with a friendly hello. Beth smelled the scrumptious breakfast way before she entered the room. The strong aroma upset her stomach. Mrs. McCafferty set the tray over her legs on the bed and straightened out her pillows. "Beth," she said briskly, "I wasn't sure how hungry you are, so I gave you a little of everything. Eat as much as you want if you're up to it. There's plenty more down stairs, if Father Pat doesn't eat it all before I get back. Father Pat would like to visit you after breakfast, would that be okay?"

Beth avoided making eye contact with her and tried to change the subject. "This smells good but I'm not sure I can eat much right now." Beth continued to ignore Mrs. McCafferty's question, as she poured syrup on the cakes and took a small bite to try and appease her hostess.

Mrs. McCafferty opted not to pursue the matter. Beth was wearing one of her sleeveless summer nightgowns that was obviously too big on her. "Just so you know, I put your purse in this top drawer. I'll put your clothes there after I wash them." She was trying to hold off washing them in case Father was able to talk Beth into going to the police. She fussed around the room for a minute longer, so it wouldn't seem like she was abandoning her. "You look a lot better, but you still need to take it easy, dear. Would you like something to read?"

"Not right now, thank you." Beth answered while staring out the window. Seeing how preoccupied Beth was, Mrs. McCafferty excused herself to go eat with Father Pat. Beth managed a faint smile as she left the room. Mrs. McCafferty's fussing reminded her of how her own mother used to take care of her when she was sick as a little girl. Then, sadly, she remembered her own little girl, Emmy, and thought about how much she missed her. She moved the tray of untouched food aside and settled back onto the pillow and closed her eyes again. Surprisingly, the small taste of pancake made her feel better, but she was too tired to eat anymore. Sleeping seemed like the only means of escape from the memories of what had occurred the night before.

Matt saw Beth close her eyes and went down to the kitchen window. He felt terrible listening in on private conversations, but he had no choice.

He watched Mrs. McCafferty return to the kitchen and pour herself a cup of tea. She sat down across from Father Pat. Father Pat was working on his second cinnamon bun and looked happy as a kitten with a ball of yarn.

Without looking at the pan on the stove, Mrs. McCafferty admonished him. "Father Pat, don't think I don't know you're working on your second bun there!" She knew him almost as well as she had known her husband.

Mrs. McCafferty came on board as housekeeper and secretary for the rectory when Father Pat first came to the parish. Her husband had died four months earlier and she felt too lonely living by herself with no one to take care of. They were never able to have children and she was left with a 50-acre farm that was too big to care for and a house that was too lonely to live in. She had worked hard as a farmer's wife but had no other job experience. Taking care of her husband and her home and whomever else God sent her way was what she loved doing the most. She wanted to continue to help others for however long she had left here on earth. When she heard there was an opening for a housekeeper for the new parish priest at the rectory, she knew it was the answer to her prayers. The two of them bonded instantly and Father Pat offered her the job on the spot. She sold her farm, which gave her a fair income to draw on in her later years and took up a room at the rectory. They were dear friends ever since.

When Father Pat graduated from the Seminary in 1958, he was assigned to Our Lady of Hope, one of the larger parishes in a low-income section on the west side of Philadelphia. His gentle nature and no-nonsense approach eventually earned him the acceptance and trust of the children and parents in the projects. Father Pat was a large man of six foot two inches and had a muscular build. He had been a strapping young man with sandy brown hair and deep blue eyes. His skin was light and freckled and that added to his charm. He had large hands and a strong stride that gave him a rock solid presence, but his extremely gentle nature and great sense of humor balanced this. His greatest strength was his ability to listen to his parishioners' troubles without judging them. Most of the families in the projects just wanted someone to hear their story and offer them hope through acceptance, which restored their own sense of dignity. They were tired of receiving canned lectures and literature on how they could change their lives in a neighborhood with impossible barriers to break through.

Father Pat could relate to their troubles. He grew up a few neighborhoods over in a low-income section just outside Center City. Unlike the South section of town that was predominantly Italian, this small neighborhood was a mixed bag of Irish, Italian, Black and Hispanic, sandwiched between the industrial port and the main city where everyone got along. His father owned a corner grocery store that supported most of the neighborhood. Few people owned cars and the larger supermarkets were too far away to walk to. Most families couldn't afford to take buses. The store's profits were barely enough to make ends meet. Henry was a good man with a soft heart and was constantly chastised by his accountant, Mr. Berstein, for extending too much credit. But Henry wasn't interested in making a lot of money. He knew every family that used his store and could never turn them away when they were in desperate times and needed help. Henry believed emphatically that God always provides for his children and if God wanted him to be materially rich, he would be. He loved his wife, Mary, and two children, Pat and Dorothy, and knew he was already spiritually blessed and that suited him just fine. Everyone in the neighborhood loved and respected Henry for his generosity. And everyone to whom he extended credit eventually paid him back, even if it took ten years.

Father Pat's own father had instilled in him the belief that everyone had a right to their dignity, regardless of whether they were homeless, a hooker, a drug user or a beggar. The working girls on the corner of 60th and Market, down the street from Our Lady nicknamed him "Big Jesus" and the name stuck with him. Although he felt uncomfortable with the comparison, he allowed them to call him that since it was a sign of acceptance. He worked unceasingly to bring a sense of optimism to his parish family and he created many programs for children and families in need to provide as much safety and security as possible to those who wanted it.

Presiding over Our Lady of Hope was like a war zone all of its own. So when Father Pat was recruited to be an Army chaplain and medic during the last two years of the Vietnam War, he had little adjustment to make on the front line. He was used to the ugliness of war and was already street wise enough to survive. When the troops were finally pulled out from the senseless military campaign, Father Pat went back to his parish and took up the battle in the inner city again. When he had seen enough violence and degradation to last a lifetime, he asked to be transferred to a rural area far from the action.

Father Pat and Mrs. McCafferty became very close, but their relationship remained completely platonic. Because they were so close in age, he was sixty-two and she was sixty-five, they kept the formality of proper names. This made their relationship more comfortable and kept the parish gossip quiet.

Both of them had a soft spot for strays of all sorts. Mrs. McCafferty had always befriended a lost dog or cat and even a lost soul from time to time on the farm. So it remained quite natural when Father Pat began bringing home stray kids to house temporarily until they could help them on their way. Mrs.

McCafferty enjoyed the opportunity to take care of children. It was a chance to fill an empty space in her heart.

The two of them sat and ate in silence for a few moments. Father Pat began to speak as he mopped up the maple syrup with the last of his pancake. "So, did you ask Beth if I could visit her this afternoon?"

"Yes, I did, but she ignored the question altogether." Mrs. McCafferty took a sip of tea and continued, "I'll ask her again when I get her tray."

"No need, Mrs. McC, I think I'll go get her tray myself and see if she's willing to talk." Father Pat knew the pattern most young people took when they were scared and unsure of whom to trust. First they ignore you, then they talk, but say very little and eventually, they either talk or walk. It was a gamble every time. He walked to the base of the stairway and looked up to the top of the stairs. The first conversation was always the toughest and hardest to guess the outcome. He grabbed the handrail for support, made the sign of the cross and said a little prayer. It was a simple prayer "Lord, help me to say the right words and bless her with the courage to respond." After that, he walked briskly up the steps and turned toward Beth's room. An afternoon thunderstorm was brewing and the sky became dark. Father hoped it would cool things down a little as he knocked on Beth's door. There was no answer.

Chapter 8

Father Pat tapped several more times on Beth's door. After a few minutes he quietly turned the knob and opened the door three or four inches. He could see the tray sitting on the right side of the bed. The sheet was neatly pulled down where Beth had been laying and the pillow sat upright against the headboard. He wondered if she would have been able to walk down the stairs and slip by them in her present condition. He never thought of keeping watch over her. Beth seemed too weak and tired to try an escape.

Father Pat opened the door wide and called out Beth's name. As the room came into full view, he breathed a sigh of relief when he saw Beth standing at the foot of the bed staring at the picture of Mary and the Baby Jesus. She was holding onto the dresser for support and she was crying. "Beth," Father Pat sighed, "You should be in bed right now." He walked over to her and guided her toward the bed.

"I'm okay, Father, I heard the storm coming and went over to lower the windows, but this one was stuck." Beth eased herself down on the bed and pulled her legs up under the sheet. As she did this, she groaned from the intense pain that shot through her pelvic area. Father Pat went over to the window and closed it halfway. He walked around the room and pulled the chair up next to her bed and sat down.

Matt had just arrived on the windowsill across from Beth as the rain began to fall. There was no shelter against the pounding rain, so he crouched into the corner against the window trim. He was beginning to grow frustrated and fatigued at the same time. He was having a hard time deciding when to leave to eat and when to stay. Moving from window to window, he was afraid of missing any of the conversations, hoping for a clue as to how he could help Beth. He first wanted to know how long she would be staying at the rectory. If he was sure it would be for a while, he could relax a little and leave to eat more often. The bird's energy level fluctuated dramatically when he didn't feed regularly and he was concerned about the long-term effects this would have on its body. He listened carefully now as Father Pat began to speak.

"Beth, I know you are not feeling very well, but I need to ask you a few things in order to help you. Are you sure you don't want me to call a doctor to check on you? I know of a very reliable and discreet doctor who would come by here to examine you. He wouldn't tell the police or anyone."

Beth was emphatic, "No, Father, I'm okay. I just need to rest."

Father Pat smiled, "I think you will be needing more than a little rest to recover, Beth. You have some pretty big cuts. Mrs. McC said the gash on your ankle could use more than a butterfly bandage."

He tried to probe deeper. "We would feel better to know we haven't missed anything serious. Just as a precaution."

Beth just repeated that she would be fine.

"Is there anyone you would like me to contact? Any family member or a friend perhaps?" Father Pat watched her reaction carefully. Her eyes resisted the thought immediately. She shook her head no.

"No, I don't want my family to know and the only friend I really have is in California. I thought I had other friends, but I was wrong." Beth was obviously making an implication about someone she knew.

"Do you want to tell me what happened last night? Anything you say will be kept in the strictest confidence. I only want to help." Father Pat placed his hand on her hand and patted it lightly. Beth pulled her hand away and drew the sheet high up over her chest as a shield.

"I don't think I can tell anyone what happened. I don't want to remember." She looked away from Father Pat to the window. She did not notice Matt.

Father sat for a moment to gather his thoughts before speaking. "I know this is difficult. You probably don't know who to trust right now, do you?"

She turned back and looked him straight in the eyes. Her eyes reflected the abandonment she was experiencing. "I don't think I can ever trust anyone again, Father. My life is a mess and there is no hope for me."

Father Pat leaned toward her and took her hand firmly. "Beth, listen to me. There is always hope. You just have to work through your anger and fears to get to it." Beth looked back at the window and remained silent.

Father thought of another approach. "Beth, I have been living for sixty-two years now and I have witnessed more sorrow and pain in my lifetime than I ever could believe possible. And I have learned one great lesson in all of it. Life will always have chaos. My dear mother, God rest her soul, used to tell me that you can't have a joyous life until you know what joy is. She said every sad experience we go through is just one more opportunity to know joy, by knowing what isn't joy. It's how we learn right from wrong, love from hate, generosity from greed. Do you understand what I am saying?"

Beth ran her finger over the bumps in the crumpled sheet for a minute before responding sarcastically. "Well then Father, I should be an expert on joy by now!"

Father Pat smiled. At least he was getting her to speak. "My mother also used to tell me that when your life takes a turn for the worse and you find yourself standing in the middle of chaos, if you listen very carefully, you can hear the rustling of angels all around you. She said that they are constantly working with you to see you through the hard times, so you can know joy! I have always found that a comforting thought."

She flipped her hair over her left ear. "So, Father, have you ever heard angels rustling when you've been in trouble?" Her words were dry.

"Me?" Father Pat sat up in his chair. "Well, once or twice, I believe so. Yes, I believe they are around us."

"I don't hear anything, Father. I would love to, but I don't even know how to listen right now." Beth's eyes softened as tears rolled down her face and she brushed them away with her hand.

Father Pat placed his warm, strong hand on her shoulder. "Maybe we can learn to hear the angels together! Would you be willing to answer a few questions for me?"

Beth bit her lip as she mulled over his question. "I'll try."

Father squeezed her shoulder and let out a sigh of relief. "That a girl! We'll take it slow, okay? Just do the best you can."

When she appeared ready, he continued. "Are you living at home with your parents?"

Beth pushed her hair behind her left ear again. It was something she did when she was nervous. "I lived with them until about three months ago and then I moved out."

"You live on your own?" Father Pat continued the questions, hoping she would keep answering.

"No, I moved into an apartment with a girl I know at work. We work at an insurance agency as secretaries. But I won't be going back to live with her."

"Would she know about what happened or did she have anything to do with last night?" Father Pat was pleased he had gotten this far. ·

"Yes," Beth hesitated, "And no, it wasn't her fault directly." She became agitated and curled up her feet under her legs, "Father I am really tired, I don't think I want to talk anymore."

Father Pat smiled and rose from his chair. He placed the chair back in the corner. "Okay I'll take your tray downstairs. Mrs. McC will check in on you before dinner. Are you allergic to any foods that I should tell her about?"

Beth smiled at his concern, "No, anything will be fine."

Father Pat picked up the tray and walked into the hallway. Beth lay back on the pillow and stared out the window. She could not see Matt, but he saw her look less anxious than she had all day. She closed her eyes and drifted off to sleep. Matt raced for cover in the middle of the oak tree in the front yard. He was pleased to know that birds can fly with their wings soaking wet, although it does take more effort. He was wet and tired, so he took advantage of the break by closing his eyes and falling asleep, too.

Father Pat took Beth's tray into the kitchen and then went into his office to catch up on some paperwork. Mrs. McCafferty cleaned the kitchen and settled down in the living room with a new needlework project. The passing thunderstorm sent a cool breeze through the living room windows that brought some relief to the muggy day. Mrs. McCafferty wondered if Beth was comfortable, but thought that it was too soon to check in on her. Later on she would bring her a glass of lemonade.

At about three thirty, Father Pat received a call from Roberta Smith, one of his parishioners, telling him that her husband was in the hospital with a heart attack. Dennis Smith was a local farmer who lived about twenty miles out of town. He was nearing seventy, but appeared no older than sixty. Father Pat was surprised at the news and told Roberta he was on his way to the hospital. He told Mrs. McCafferty not to hold dinner. Roberta and Dennis' family was scattered across several states and he assured Roberta that he would stay with her until someone arrived. Father Pat told Mrs. McCafferty that Dennis appeared to be stabilized but the next eight hours would tell for sure. Mrs. McCafferty said she would be saying prayers and asked Father to give Roberta her best. She remembered how lonely and confusing it was in the hospital when her husband was rushed in with his fatal heart attack. After seeing Father off, she said her rosary and returned to her needlework.

At five o'clock Mrs. McCafferty brought Beth the glass of lemonade. Beth was awake but motionless. Mrs. McCafferty cleared her throat as she opened the door. It was her way of announcing herself. Beth smiled at her and pulled herself up higher on the pillow. Mrs. McCafferty smiled back and sat on the edge of the bed and handed Beth the glass. "Well, dear, you are looking much better. I thought you could use a cool drink. How are you feeling?" You would never know Mrs. McCafferty didn't have children, she was a real natural.

"I feel better, Mrs. McC," Beth looped her hair over her left ear again, "but I have a really bad headache. Do you have any aspirin I could take?"

"Why, of course, Beth, I'll be right back." Mrs. McCafferty rushed into her bedroom murmuring to herself that she must be slipping to overlook such an obvious thing and returned a minute later with two pills. Beth took the medicine and swallowed hard. "I should have thought about it earlier, Beth, I am sorry. It's been a long time since I had a patient to take care of." Mrs. McCafferty tidied up the sheet and the folded cover at the bottom of the bed. She began to tell Beth about dinner plans.

"Father Pat will not be here for dinner tonight. He had an emergency at the hospital. One of the local farmers had a heart attack and he went to be with his wife."

"I'm sorry to hear that." Beth admired how Father Pat and Mrs. McCafferty could drop everything to go help others. They were special people. "Mrs. McCafferty, does Father do this kind of thing often?"

"What, go to the hospital? It is pretty routine when you are a priest, dear."

"No, I'm sure it is. I mean take in strangers like me and nurse them back to health. You both act like this is just an ordinary thing you do." Beth trembled a little as she realized what a helpless state she had been in when she arrived. Who knows what would have happened to her if Father had not come along? If the police had found her, they would have brought her to the hospital and contacted her family. That would have been a nightmare. If someone else found her, they could have done anything to her and she would have been helpless to save herself.

"Oh, we have had a few visitors stay with us until they could sort things through. No one has come here physically hurt like you are, but many have been very hurt in other ways. We just do our best to help any way we can." Mrs. McCafferty was glad Beth was opening up, she took this opportunity to plant a seed. "It is really up to you to decide how much help you allow us to give you. You must realize by now that Father Pat is only concerned about your welfare and will protect you in whatever way he can. He has nice broad shoulders to lean on." She patted Beth's leg and changed to a lighter topic. "Since it is just the two of us dear, I was wondering if you wouldn't mind some leftover stew and a salad?"

"Sure," Beth replied. "I love stew."

"Good," Mrs. McCafferty rose to go downstairs. "If you would like, I could set up a small table here and eat with you. No sense us both staring at walls while we eat. Would that be okay?"

Beth was glad for the company. "Yes, I would like that."

Mrs. McCafferty walked to the doorway. "I'll be back in a few minutes. There are several paperback stories in the nightstand next to your bed if you would like some reading material. I'm not sure they will interest you, but you're welcome to them." With that, she was gone and moments later the smell of savory stew rose up the stairway into Beth's room. Beth's appetite was returning and she looked forward to her dinner companion's return.

In the meantime, Matt woke from his afternoon slumber, recharged at his favorite day lily patch and returned to Beth's window. He felt much better physically, but emotionally he still felt lost. Maybe Enon was right. Maybe it would be impossible to succeed as a hummingbird. Doubts floated across his mind as he watched his subject reading a small paperback book. Well, he thought, there was nothing else to do but keep listening and hope he could find out that special piece of information that would make the light bulb go off in his head. He wondered if Enon and Anjella were watching him. He thought about cheerful Anjella and how he missed her encouragement right now.

Mrs. McCafferty entered the room carrying a large tray. She placed it down on the dresser and brought a small folding table in and set it up next to Beth's bed. The aroma of stew filled the bedroom and drifted through the windows. It triggered a yearning in Matt that brought back memories of his mother's cooking. The conversation between the two women broke his trance and he listened in.

"There was just enough for both of us." She began. "I brought some bread and a salad, too. Now, don't be polite, Beth, dig in. It will make me happy. I know you don't feel very hungry, but if you take a few bites that just might change." Mrs. McCafferty loved to watch people enjoy her cooking. Cooking was her pride and joy. The first bite of stew that Beth took was really hot, but was deliciously rich and comforting.

"Oh, Mrs. McC, this is so good." Beth reached for a piece of Italian bread to sop up the gravy. The bread was warm and every bit as good as the stew. Mrs. McCafferty beamed at her obvious success. She decided to let Beth lead the conversation, if she wanted to talk. The two women ate quietly for a while.

Beth smiled as she began nibbling at her salad. She was surprised at how hungry she suddenly felt. "You know, I haven't had a meal like this since Christmas."

"Was that meal with your family, dear?"

"Yes, my mom went all out and made a turkey dinner with stuffing and sweet potatoes and the works. Everything was homemade, even the cranberry sauce." Beth washed a piece of bread down with ice tea and continued. "It was one of the happiest dinners I can remember." She almost wished she hadn't said that, but it did feel good remembering some of the good times.

Mrs. McCafferty tried to be very careful during her interrogation. "Was your whole family there, Beth?"

"Yes," Beth hesitated, but continued, "It was my mother, my father and my little girl, Emmy." She knew she was opening herself up to a lot of questions about her family and her home life, but almost welcomed the opportunity to tell someone who may be sympathetic.

"You have a little girl? How old is she?"

Beth had a trace of tears in her eyes. "Emmy will be four in October." She didn't care to add anything else.

135

"Is she still with your mom and dad?" Mrs. McCafferty was surprised at Emmy's age. This would mean Beth had given birth probably in high school or right after.

"Yes, my mom is taking care of her until I can send for her. Emmy is really close to her Grandmom and PopPop."

"What about you dear? Are you close to your parents?"

"My mom, yes, but my dad, no way." Beth looked past Mrs. McCafferty to the wall. "My dad and I have been at odds since I was twelve. I don't know why, but I never was able to do anything right growing up. He's never trusted me." She placed the salad bowl on top of her empty dinner plate and sipped some more tea.

"Do you want to talk about this? Is that why you left home?" Mrs. McCafferty usually left the grilling up to Father Pat, but she sensed that Beth might be ready to talk right now.

"Well, there is not much to talk about, really." Beth thought a moment about how she could sum up the last nine years living with her father. "You see, when I was a little girl, I remember having a lot of fun with my dad. I guess it was when I was about five or six years old. We used to go to the park and have picnics or family barbecues like a normal family. But when I got a little older, it was like my father suddenly turned on me. I still can't figure out what I did wrong." Beth tried to change the subject a little. "Did you get along with your mom and dad growing up, Mrs. McC?"

Mrs. McCafferty blushed. Rarely did anyone bother to ask her about her own life. "Oh, I guess I had a regular relationship with my parents growing up. You see back in the depression days life was a lot simpler than now. My dad worked on the farm from five o'clock in the morning until sundown. I would usually see him at dinner and afterwards he would sit on the porch and read the paper or have an evening cup of coffee with my mother. We loved each other but we didn't do much bonding back then. There was never time for recreation on a farm. Crops and cattle needed tending every day. My father died when I was eighteen, so if there was bonding to be done, I didn't get the chance. My mother and I were close, though. She was close to all her children. I came from a family of seven children."

Beth looked at Mrs. McC as she reminisced. She saw a strong woman filled with gentleness and understanding ways. Her eyes seemed to smile all the time. Beth's mother was a lot like her, but Mrs. McCafferty seemed a bit wiser than her mother did. Maybe it was just the age difference, but something told Beth if she met Mrs. McC when she was thirty, she would have the same sense of wisdom.

Beth decided to go on. "When I was in junior high school, I got into a few scrapes, but nothing really serious. One time, I remember, I got a D in math on my report card. I knew my father would be really upset with me, so I tried to forge it and make it a B, but I did a really bad job. When my mother showed my father he was furious. He screamed at me and accused me of being a liar. I had just tried out and was accepted in the school choir and for a punishment, he forbid me to sing in the choir. I thought that was an extreme punishment, since he knew how much singing meant to me. I tried to get my mom to talk to him, but she wouldn't. Even the music director tried to change his mind. He told him that I had a real undeveloped talent, but my father wouldn't budge. I couldn't believe that he would take away the one thing that made me happy, but he did. I never did anything bad before that, but from then on, he never believed a word I said. I told him I was sorry and I would never do it again, but it was like it was too late. So after a while, I started lying just because I knew he would think I was anyway." Beth stared into her ice tea glass for a moment. Mrs. McCafferty remained silent. Matt strained intently for her next words.

"And then the real crisis happened that drove a wall between us forever." Beth choked up a little but swallowed hard and continued. "When I was seventeen, at the end of my senior year, I started dating this really good looking boy named David. He was two years older than I was and in college. I thought I was really in love. He told me stories of how he was going to marry me and take me all over the world. We spent the whole summer together. I was going to go to Swarthmore College for a nursing degree the next fall. I assumed it was just a matter of time before I became his wife, so when he asked me to sleep with him, I did. I couldn't believe I got pregnant. When I told him, he was furious and accused me of trying to trap him into marriage. His parents sent him to Europe to finish school and told me that they would have nothing to do with the child and denied it was their son's. I didn't know what to do.

"I told my parents when I couldn't hide it anymore, but my father immediately accused me of being a tramp. I was crushed and if I could have, I would have left the house right then and there. But I didn't have a job or a place to go, so I stayed with them and got a job as a secretary after Emmy was born. The only thing that has kept me there all this time was that my father was so good to Emmy. He was the father she never had. But a day didn't go by that he didn't remind me of how I threw my life away. Finally, I couldn't take it anymore and I decided I had to move out of the house. One of the secretaries I worked with, Rachel, offered to put me up at her place for a while. We had just become friends. I only planned on staying with her until I could save enough to get an apartment for Emmy and me." Beth thought about the sequence of events that happened in just three short months and began to cry. Mrs. McCafferty moved the table away from the bed and sat beside her. She put her arms around Beth and let her cry on her shoulder. Beth began to sob harder and harder, releasing all of the pent up frustration and sadness. It was a good cry; the kind that left you exhausted. Mrs. McCafferty just rocked her back and forth, and encouraged her to let it all out.

Beth pulled away finally and Mrs. McCafferty handed her a box of tissues that Beth had never seen before. After Beth cleared her head she fell back onto her pillow. "I'm sorry, I didn't mean to get so carried away." Beth looked embarrassed. "It just seems like I keep making one mistake after another and life is getting so hard. The more I try to prove to my father that I am not the person he thinks I am, the more I am becoming that person. Not that Emmy was ever a mistake." Beth blew into the tissue again. "She means the world to me and I miss her so much. I really thought leaving her with my mom and dad was the best thing for her, while I tried to get my life together. But now I fear I have made a terrible mistake. Who knows what my father will do if he finds out what's happened to me? Oh, he can't find out what a mess I'm in, he just can't."

"There, there Beth, everything will be alright." Mrs. McCafferty fixed the sheet and smiled. "You just have to take things one step at a time. Let's concentrate first on getting you better and then we will work on solving your other problems. Trust me, child, everything can work out in the end, if you have a little faith." Mrs. McCafferty stood and leaned over Beth and kissed her forehead. "And faith is what we're here to give you." She smiled and gathered the dishes on the tray. "Why don't you rest a while, Beth, and if you want to talk later, I'll be more than happy to. But if you want to call it a night, we can talk tomorrow." Before she went downstairs she turned to Beth and added, "You said you work at an insurance firm, will you need to call them tomorrow to let them know you aren't coming in?"

Beth grimaced when she realized her job was now in jeopardy. "Oh, I forgot. I don't know what to tell them. What can I say? I don't even know how long I will be out."

"Why don't you just tell them you have a family emergency. It isn't a lie at all. Father Pat may be able to help you here. Why don't you talk to him tomorrow? I'll show you where the phone is when you are ready." Mrs. McCafferty cleared the tray and table from her room and handed her the clean nightgown. Beth told Mrs. McCafferty that she would like to take another shower and go to bed. She thanked Mrs. McC again for her help.

Matt flew away at the end of their conversation and found shelter in the oak tree for the night. He thought about everything Beth said and felt overwhelming sympathy for her. Beth had more problems than just a strained relationship with her father. There was Emmy, her four-year-old daughter, and her job and her wounds to deal with. This was not the simple case Matt thought he was getting into. There were a lot of mysteries to solve. Like why has her father been so hard on her all these years? What really happened last night? And how can he help her? Matt wondered about these questions and many more, until he drifted off to sleep.

Chapter 9

$\mathbf{F}$ather Pat came home a little past midnight. He stepped into the kitchen to make himself a nightcap and rummaged through the refrigerator for a snack. He enjoyed an occasional Manhattan in the evenings. There was a block of cheddar cheese and some wheat crackers that would do for a midnight snack. It was a long evening, but, thankfully, Dennis would be okay. Roberta's sister arrived at the hospital at about eleven o'clock. Father Pat prayed over Dennis, who was still in intensive care, and told Roberta to call him if there were any changes. He anointed Dennis with holy oil, but did not need to give him the formal last rites since he had improved considerably.

Father wandered into the living room and set his drink down on a small table by the rocking chair. As he lowered himself into the rocker, he wondered how the dinner went between Mrs. McCafferty and Beth. He thought about everything that happened to Beth and prayed he made the right call, not getting her to a doctor. It was such a sensitive subject. His experience told him that forcing her might have caused her to leave the first chance she got. At least this way, he could prove himself trustworthy and hopefully she would open up. If he only knew whether or not she was raped. Of course, there would be many folks who would adamantly disagree with his tactics, but he had enough experience to trust his intuition. Father Pat sipped the last of his cocktail, placed his plate in the sink and headed for bed.

Monday morning started off hotter than any day so far this summer. The thermometer on the front porch of the house read 78 degrees before seven o'clock. The steamy day promised to reach near one hundred degrees. Mrs. McCafferty was up with the birds and by seven thirty, Father Pat joined her for a cup of coffee out on the front porch. The house did not have air conditioning. They used a few window fans when the weather got unbearable.

The rectory was an old farmhouse donated to the Diocese by Eli Stoltzfus upon his death in 1967. A neighboring farmer bought the land to the west of the house. The land to the east was sold to developers and, in a few short years, suburban homes dotted the landscape. Mass was offered in the rectory up until 1972, when the parish had enough money to build St. Bartholomew's church.

The house had a large covered front porch. It had a main foyer with the living room off to the left and formal dining room on the right. Behind the living room and dining room and across the entire length of the back of the house was the kitchen. It was big enough to hold a large kitchen table and chairs, a walk in pantry and a laundry room. The door to the back yard was between the kitchen cabinets and the laundry area. The back steps were wooden and led directly down into the back yard. There was a handrail on each side of the steps with a wide plank on the rail of the top step to set flowerpots on, though none were currently there. A large lilac bush grew directly under the kitchen window. On the other side of the steps a bed was filled with half choked rose bushes. Large oak trees surrounded the front and sides of the house. Lining the backyard was a row of evergreens that blocked most of the view of the alfalfa field behind it. There was a six-foot fence separating the only neighbor's yard from the rectory.

The backyard was in dire need of attention. Mrs. McCafferty never had much of a gardener's thumb that was Jenny Stoltzfus' gift. All of the flowerbeds were overgrown with weeds. Mrs. McCafferty was grateful that few people saw the sorry state of the garden. As usual, she felt guilty that she had let Mrs. Stoltzfus' beautiful garden go. The only regular attention it got was a weekly mowing by an altar boy.

Mrs. McCafferty filled Father in on her conversation with Beth the night before. She was upset by what Beth told her. Father Pat wasn't surprised by what he heard. It was a typical scenario that he had heard many times before, when a mother or a father was openly hostile to one or more of their children. The children, who want more than anything in the world to have their parent's approval, feel rejected and develop low self-esteem, which leads them down endless paths of destruction. He couldn't fathom why Beth's father became so hostile to her, but he knew there were always a number of reasons that might attribute to the breakdown of trust within a family. Her father could be an alcoholic, or have trouble at work, or suffer from his own low self-esteem. Parents usually don't fully understand why they are so hard on their children. There are so many emotions that some people have learned to bury deep inside rather than cope with as they happen. When these individuals have their own children, many times the children stir up feelings in the adult that have been suppressed for years. Father Pat couldn't blame half the kids who ran away from their horrible family environments. Sometimes it is the parents who needed the counseling, and not the children. In those cases, the parents hardly ever seek help and the children rarely stick around. Father Pat sighed. "We can't judge these things Mrs. McCafferty. We don't even know the whole story. I'm glad you were able to get that much out of her so soon. It is a good sign."

Mrs. McCafferty thought she heard movement on the second floor and excused herself to check on Beth. Father Pat smiled at her. She reminded him of an old mother hen whenever they had visitors. He could tell she was becoming fond of Beth already and he hoped that between the two of them, they could help her.

Beth, indeed, was awake. Once the initial fatigue had worn off, she hardly slept all night. She was haunted by a constant stream of nightmares that she had every time she closed her eyes. Mrs. McCafferty found her working her way down the hall towards the bathroom. The tiny steps she took told Mrs. McCafferty that she still needed another day of bed rest. "Beth, good morning, do you need any help?"

"No, Mrs. McC, I'm fine. I was just going to clean up before I came downstairs for breakfast. I woke up to that great smell of coffee. It sure does help get you out of bed." Beth put on a brave act, despite the pain she felt with every step.

"No, Beth, I think it's too soon for you to try the stairs out." Mrs. McCafferty was not going to take no for an answer and you could hear it in her voice. "Why don't I start by bringing you some coffee before I fix us all something to eat. You can practice moving around up here today. If you make out okay, we can try the stairs tomorrow. It's better not to rush these things, you know."

Beth wanted to object, but she felt her strength fading as she made her way to the bathroom door. "Okay, you win, but just today. Tomorrow I am sure I will be well enough to go downstairs." Mrs. McCafferty just smiled and left to get the coffee. When Beth returned from the bathroom, a tray with coffee, sugar and cream was already on the dresser.

Beth picked up the hot coffee and savored the first sip. She settled back on her pillow and let her legs hang off the bed. She imagined Emmy running into her room like she always did immediately when she woke up and climbing into bed with her. Emmy would have a million questions for Beth about anything and everything. She was a real chatterbox. They would lie in bed for a half-hour before going down stairs for breakfast. Beth grew angry with herself for leaving Emmy with her parents. She wanted to be with her so much that her heart physically ached every time she thought about her. Mrs. McCafferty must think I am a terrible mother for leaving her like I did, she thought to herself. As she finished her coffee, Beth became more determined than ever to find a place to live and bring Emmy home for good. She saw no other way to deal with the situation.

Mrs. McCafferty brought Beth's breakfast up to her a few minutes later. She made scrambled eggs, toast and bacon and added a glass of orange juice to the tray. "You are spoiling me rotten, Mrs. McC. It's like you know what all my favorite foods are. Thank you." Mrs. McCafferty blushed at Beth's gratitude.

"It is a real pleasure, Beth. I love taking care of people this way. I feel that God gives each of us a unique talent that allows us to help other people. Father Pat knows how to reach people through their souls. I, on the other hand, know how to reach them through their stomachs!" Beth giggled at her analogy.

"I bet you've saved a lot of souls!"

"Well, I don't know about that, dear, but I try." Mrs. McCafferty went over to her window and opened it all the way. She picked up the fan that was propped against the dresser and placed it in the window across from Beth. "It's going to be a real scorcher today. I hope this room isn't too stuffy for you." She said as she turned it on.

"I never grew up with air conditioning, so I'm used to the heat. I'll just keep the sheet off me when I am in bed." Beth planned on moving around as much as she could to begin loosening up her stiff muscles. She didn't want to stay in bed any longer. She had too many things to do.

"Don't push it Beth." Mrs. McCafferty walked over to the doorway. "I'll be back in a bit. Enjoy your breakfast." Beth marveled at Mrs. McCafferty's perkiness. It was really contagious. Beth thought it was sad that she never got to enjoy grandchildren. She would have been the perfect grandmother. "When I get settled in my own place with Emmy, I will invite her to visit. Emmy will love her, too." She thought.

Everyone spent that morning taking it easy. Father Pat reserved Mondays as his official day off, save for an emergency. When he finished breakfast, he went on his daily walk past the fields in back of the rectory. He used to walk into town, but was stopped too often by his parishioners. What would often start off as a simple hello often ended up in a lengthy conversation about this or that. Not only did he fail to get any exercise, but also he never got a break from his work. Inevitably the conversation would change to discussions about a problem they were having and they expected him to attend to it immediately. The road past the farm fields was quiet and hardly traveled by anyone on foot.

When Father Pat returned from his walk, he spent an hour reading the weekend newspaper and then placed a call to his friend, Father Lawrence Massey. Father Massey was not only his closest friend, but also has been his spiritual advisor for the last twenty years. He is the Vicar for Priestly Spirituality at the Archdiocese of Philadelphia, but before that he was the Pastor of Our Lady of Hope when Father Pat was first assigned there. Father Pat took over his position when Father Massey moved over to the Chancery.

They normally met once a month on his day off for lunch or a round of golf. They were scheduled to golf at 11:00 this morning, but Father Pat hesitated to leave Beth alone. He knew Mrs. McCafferty needed to run a few errands.

Father Massey knew by the timing of the phone call that his date was about to be canceled. Pat had been canceling their meetings a lot lately, since his congregation started to grow. "Good morning, Pat! This must mean golf is off today."

"You know me so well, Larry. Yes, it does. How are you doing?"

"Can't complain. So what's happening this time? If you keep this up, I'm going to have to find a new golf partner!"

Father Pat laughed. "Maybe you can find someone to give you some competition! Anyway, I did have a very interesting walk yesterday morning. I wasn't a quarter-of-a-mile up the road and I found a young girl lying half-unconscious. She was pretty banged up."

"Did you call the police?" Father Massey asked, keeping his fingers crossed.

"No, she's upstairs in the guest room sleeping."

Father Massey was exasperated. "Pat, don't tell me you're doing it again! You can't keep taking these stray kids in. Remember what happened the last time? You were robbed!"

"Oh, you exaggerate, Larry. It was just a watch and a few dollars. Besides this girl is different."

"How so?"

"Well, she's having a little trouble getting around, so I don't see her running off with our valuables just yet."

"What? Why didn't you take her to the hospital if she's that bad?" Father Massey almost did not want to know the answer.

"Because, she didn't want to and she was scared. I was afraid that she would run away the first chance she got, if we pushed her."

"Well, if she can run away then how badly hurt is she exactly?"

Father Pat took a little delight in stringing his old friend along. He knew how they hated to hear about this kind of thing down at the Chancery. "Oh, she has a bruised face and some cuts on her legs from the glass I found her lying in, but nothing looks too serious right now."

Father Massey felt a little better. "If that's all, then I guess it isn't too bad, but you need to find her parents or call the police. You can't keep getting involved in these situations."

"Who better than a priest, Larry? Besides, she won't tell us where she's from and she'll have nothing to do with the police. They may only make matters worse."

"Do you think she's done something wrong, Pat?"

"No, I doubt it, but Mrs. McC thinks she may have been assaulted or possibly raped."

"Raped! For God sakes, Pat, are you out of your mind! The Bishop will have your head if he ever finds out. She needs to go to the hospital so that the police can collect the evidence and locate her family. What if it was a serial rapist who attacked her? Whoever did it could be miles away by now. If anything happens to this girl, Pat, *we're sure* to see a lawsuit. You need to take her right away!" Father Massey's tone of voice changed from friendly advice to an order. His job wasn't an easy one. The Bishop created his position at the Chancery when he recognized his priests needed someone to talk to about the personal problems they were experiencing on a completely confidential basis. Father Massey was well liked by his peers and the obvious man for the job. But it was a disturbing task for him personally sometimes, when he realized these men were in over their head and needed outside assistance. They did not always take his advice.

"Larry, you are getting too upset about this. I know what I'm doing. From what we know so far, her family ties have been severed and, apparently, she doesn't have anyone else to trust. We don't know for sure if she was actually raped and I feel she'll confide in us soon, if we can get her to trust us. Mrs. McC didn't come across this possibility until after she showered, so there is no evidence. If her physical condition gets worse, I'll get her to the hospital and I already told her that. For now, I want to just wait and see what happens."

"Pat, you're bound and determined to put me in my grave before my time! It's not like the old days when priests could get involved in their communities like this. We don't have the time anymore. That's what the police and social services are for."

"Larry, do you hear what you just said? Maybe it's changed in your neck-of-the-woods, but I don't *ever* plan on changing how I do my job. They'll have to retire me first!"

"They just may do that if this becomes a problem for them, Pat!" Father Massey rubbed his forehead. "Okay, just *promise me* you will not let this situation get out of hand."

"You got it! I'll call you next week."

"Or *sooner*, if things change!"

"Sure, I'll talk to you later." Father Pat hung up the phone and sat back in his chair to mull over his conversation. The priesthood *had changed* so much in the last ten years. He shook his head at the thought that even priests had to worry about being sued for trying to help someone nowadays and returned to reading the newspaper.

Mrs. McCafferty ran her errands in town and stopped by the church second hand store to pick up some shorts, tops and undergarments for Beth. If she planned on coming downstairs tomorrow, she would need appropriate clothes, she thought and she guessed that Beth was about a size eight. She was able to pick up a nice sundress, too. The church had an emergency fund for this type of need. After that she went grocery shopping and returned home to prepare lunch.

Matt flitted by Beth's window several times that morning and observed her reading or walking around the bed. So far, no one had discovered him, to his relief. He used his free time exploring the area and practicing flying. He was amazed at how unique hummingbirds were compared to other types of birds. Hummingbirds' wings had only one movable joint in the shoulder. Most birds have several movable joints in their wings. When a hummingbird hovers, he moves his wings forward and then rotates them backward nearly 180 degrees. During this movement the wing tips trace a horizontal figure eight in the air. The wings beat about 78 times per second during normal flight and up to 200 times per second during a display dive. Even at rest, a hummingbird takes 250 breaths per minute. All of this accelerated activity requires the little bird to eat half its weight in sugar each day to maintain its strength. This was no small task. Matt discovered he needed to stock up on sugar whenever he could. He required feedings about every fifteen minutes and sometimes that interfered with listening in on conversations at the rectory. He began experimenting with varying eating intervals to see the effect it would have on his body. He found that if he ate twice as much in one feeding and did not fly too much, that he could stretch the next feeding to thirty or forty minutes. His biggest concern was finding a suitable sugar supply. The flowers were wilting in the intense heat and his food source did not look promising.

Matt returned to the rectory about midday. He arrived just in time to hear the lunch conversation between Mrs. McCafferty and Father Pat. He learned that Father Pat would speak to Beth around two o'clock and see if he could find out more about what happened the night she was left on the road side and determine what the next best step would be. Mrs. McCafferty told Father Pat about Beth's job and that she left a message that she was sick today but she needed to call them back and explain that she would not be coming in this week. He said he would take care of that, too.

"Great," Matt thought. "That gives me a couple hours to feed." He flew away in search of more food sources. Matt wandered toward the center of town looking for any kind of flower garden. About one mile away from the rectory was a beautiful flower garden on the side of a large Victorian style home. It was a gold mine of nectar, filled with white begonias, red turtlehead snapdragons, scarlet bee balm and red cardinal flowers. Honeysuckle climbed a border fence about thirty feet long. Matt could hardly believe the buffet of flowers laid out before him.

He started with the begonias and moved over to the large patch of bee balm, which, he discovered, had the largest source of nectar of all the flowers. Before he knew what was happening, he was broadsided by something that sent him spinning in the air. After he regained his composure and assumed a hovering stance, the unseen attacker hit him again from behind. His mind raced and he hovered again, turning around searching for the source until he came eye to eye with his opponent. To his shock, another ruby-throated hummingbird was staring him down about five feet away. Matt backed up a few feet and watched his opponent for a minute. The other hummingbird swooped toward Matt in a U pattern. He twittered and spread his tail in a fan shape, as if to give Matt some kind of message. The hummingbird's eyes were colder than ice. Matt assumed it was a warning. He decided to test the waters and moved over to the honeysuckle flowers. Again the male hummingbird dove at Matt and pecked his head with his long, sharp beak as he passed by. The beak really hurt Matt's head for a moment. He heard the twitter once again behind him to his left and moved down to another flower. This time the little bird attacked with a vengeance and locked beaks with Matt, as he turned to ward off his enemy. The two birds fell to the ground and rolled around for a moment, until Matt could free his beak from his opponent's grip. Matt flew away back toward the rectory. The other bird followed him for about three blocks, then watched Matt continue on. Matt turned and hovered, wondering why the bird did not continue his chase. It appeared to be guarding its territory. Matt didn't know how big a hummingbird's territory was, but he knew two things: One, hummingbirds were vicious fighters; and two, don't cross into their territory unless you are up for the fight of your life. Matt returned to the rectory with both his ego and head a little bruised.

The afternoon proved to be a real steam bath. Matt rested in the oak tree before heading for the salvia patch out back. He drained the first flower and moved on to the second. He became paranoid and stopped often to look around for a possible attacker. He hoped he was right about the other bird's territory. If this were what he was up against on an everyday basis, he would never last. He tried to drink fast so he could return to the rectory. After he had filled himself up, he returned to Beth's room and was nearly sucked into the screen by the whirring fan that he forgot was sitting in the window across from Beth. He was forced to land on the window ledge at the foot of her bed. He could see Beth from where he perched, but he didn't know if he would be able to hear her speak. His breath was faster than normal and he felt an incredible wave of fatigue. Matt hoped the rest on the ledge would help him recover from his latest adventure. Father was not in the room yet and Beth was reading, so he closed his eyes and rested his weary body.

Father Pat climbed the stairs to Beth's room at exactly two o'clock. Beth's door was open, so he walked straight in. She looked up from her book and placed it face down on the bed, so she wouldn't loose her page. "You look better, Beth. I see Mrs. McC is taking good care of you." Matt could hear Father Pat's voice without straining.

"She is really great Father. She makes me feel so good with all her fussing."

"I know, I have to show a lot of will power around her cinnamon buns. It really isn't that hard, since she slaps my hand every time I reach for one. It's funny, she'll fuss if you don't eat everything she makes, and she'll slap my hand if I do!" he chuckled and pulled the chair from the corner.

"I'm glad to hear every thing is okay with the farmer. Did you stay at the hospital all night?"

"Now who's sounding like a mother hen?" Father Pat teased Beth. "No, I was home before one o'clock. Both of you were asleep, lucky you."

Beth seemed pleased to have the casual conversation. She knew the serious questions would be coming soon. She didn't know how much she wanted to tell Father, so she decided to take it one question at a time.

"Mrs. McCafferty told me you needed to call work and arrange for time off. Did you speak to anyone directly this morning?"

"No, I left a message on my boss' voice mail that I would be out sick today. He has management meetings on Monday mornings."

"What is his name?"

"Mr. Manley. He is a really nice man, but I don't want him to know what happened to me. He might say something to my mom if she calls for me at work. I don't know what to tell him." Beth flipped her hair behind her left ear. Mr. Manley was the only boss she ever had. She had been working for him for four years, since she started at General Life Insurance Company.

"Why don't I call him and explain that you have a personal emergency. I will vouch for you and tell him you need this week off. Do you think he will have a problem with that?"

Beth thought a moment, "He probably will not, but he may be concerned about contacting me for questions. I left a few things pending."

"Okay, we'll just give him our number here. Sound like a plan?"

"Yes, it's better than anything I can think of." Father handed Beth a piece of paper and a pen. She wrote down her boss' telephone number. Father Pat left the room and made the phone call in his room. He had the only phone on the second floor. He returned smiling about fifteen minutes later. He told Beth that he had a good conversation with her boss and that he seemed, indeed, to be a very nice man. Her boss was concerned and suspicious, at first, and asked Father Pat several questions regarding his relationship with Beth. She was a hard working, reliable employee and having a strange person call her out sick for a whole week was totally out of character for her, even if he was a priest. Father Pat assured him that Beth was alright and she would call him during the week to let him know how she was doing. Mr. Manley said Beth had two weeks of sick time and vacation accrued. If she needed more time off, then they would have to put her on temporary leave. Beth was relieved, but nervous about how she was ever going to explain this to him.

"What kind of problem did you say I was having? Did he want details?" She chewed on her lip.

"Oh, I said you had injured yourself and that the incident was of a personal nature that you would rather keep confidential and that I was helping you. He asked if it was serious. I said I thought a few weeks at the most would be an appropriate time frame to heal, but if you needed more, you would give him fair notice. He was a little wary at first, until I convinced him that I was legitimate. I asked him to keep our discussion confidential and he said he would for the time being."

"Good." Beth said assuring herself, "Good. But two weeks is hardly enough time to work through all of my problems. I need to find a place to live on my salary. That will be almost an impossible feat in itself."

Father Pat leaned forward and rested his chin in his right hand. "Have you thought about going home to your parents and trying to work things out? I hope you don't mind, Mrs. McCafferty filled me in on your troubles at home."

Beth choked and laughed at the same time. "Ha, you don't know my father. I have tried to talk to him for years but no matter what I say, he thinks I'm a liar. I don't even know what I could have ever done that was bad enough for him to think that. I mean, I told a few fibs and cheated on a report card once, but isn't that pretty normal? And when I got pregnant with Emmy, he wouldn't believe that David told me that he was planning on marrying me. My father insisted that I was lying. How could he think such a thing? He's basing everything on a few minor mishaps from my junior high days. What ever happened to forgive and forget? The thing that really ticks me off, Father is that he never judges anyone else that way. Not my mother or his friends, or even Emmy. Just me!" Beth's frustration and hurt were apparent. What was the point of another scene like the one they had that drove her to leave?

Father Pat shook his head a little, "I know it's hard; but sometimes the person who is right has to be the one to forgive the other for their blind spots. If you can show compassion for your father, I guess you could say turn the other cheek, in time, he may come around." Beth sat up straight in the bed poised and ready to voice her opposition. He held up his hand to silence her protest. "Listen to me for a minute, and think. I want you to really think. Mrs. McCafferty told me you have a four-year-old daughter. You are twenty-two, maybe twenty three years old? You need a safe place to raise your daughter and you need to be with her. Before you give up entirely on your father, ask yourself what you would want him to do, if the shoe were on the other foot?" He squeezed her hand a moment and spoke gently. "You have not told me what happened to you the night you were left on the side of the road, but looking back on the three months you were away from home, can you honestly say to yourself that you have a safer place to raise your daughter than at your parents' home?"

Father looked at Beth's tear-filled eyes but knew he must continue to push. "Will you tell me what happened to you that night you were left on the road? I need to know the whole story. I can't help you unless I understand where you're coming from. You see, you can only see things through the one way mirror, which is your point of view. The same can be said for your father. But I can see both sides and help you to uncover your blind spots, too. Maybe you don't have any. It's possible. But that doesn't mean we can't repair this relationship you have with your father."

Beth looked at him for a moment. She asked herself why she felt so defensive. How much should she share with this stranger who took her in and was caring for her? Would he use her mistakes against her to make her wrong in this situation? What did she have to lose? What did she have to gain? Being on her own without the ability to support herself properly was scary. Depending on others for help did not always guarantee success either. Every man she loved or trusted had hurt her. What did she want to happen in her heart of hearts? Beth sat on the bed with her knees drawn up under her nightgown and rocked back and forth. She looked over at Father Pat, who sat patiently waiting for a response. He wasn't intimidated by her silence, but showed a look of concern as he waited. If she didn't take this opportunity to get help, it would probably be a mistake. How many people would go out of their way to help her like Father and Mrs. McC have?

"Okay, Father, I'll tell you what happened, but you have to promise me you will not tell a soul, even Mrs. McC about this." She looked up at him with a cautious glare in her eyes.

"Beth, you have my word. Consider this a confession. I am obliged under sacred oath to hold what you say secret. Even if you murdered someone, I could not, and would not tell anyone. This is really between you and God. It will feel good to get it all off your chest, trust me."

Beth sat up and pushed her hair behind her left ear again. Matt and Father Pat sat there silently, as Beth gathered her thoughts for a moment and began.

"I left home the first week of May. The Sunday before, my dad and I had a really bad argument. I started telling my mom at dinner that there was a chance that I would be able to start night school and get reimbursed by my company. My father laughed at me and told me there was no way in hell that an insurance company was going to pay for me to take nursing classes. I told him that the first couple of years courses were general subjects that could apply to any degree. I would begin taking nursing subjects after I had completed all of my mandatory classes. Besides, insurance companies did use nurses to help evaluate insurance claims. He slammed his glass down and said, but you're planning to work at a hospital, so you're going to lie again to get your way. I told him it wasn't a lie and my boss already knew what my major was. He thought it was great that I wanted to go into nursing and he didn't have a problem with it. It will take me probably six years of night school to complete my degree. There was no threat of my leaving the job any time soon, so what was the big deal?

"My father got so angry when I said that and started his usual lecture about how I can't go through life lying about everything to get my way and someday it will catch up with me. He told me I already ruined my life and it wouldn't be likely that I'd ever get a husband now that I had a child. He even said that I ruined his and my mother's life by saddling them with the financial responsibility of taking care of Emmy and me. He said that he had planned on selling the house by now and going into early retirement.

"The argument went back and forth. I told him I paid them plenty of board to cover expenses. He said it wasn't enough. After a half hour of arguing, I got up and left the table and told them I would leave and find a place to live and take Emmy away from them, if she was so much trouble and my mother became upset and began yelling at both of us. Emmy started crying and I don't remember all of what Mom said, because I ran to my room and shut my door.

"At work the next morning, I mentioned the fight to my new friend Rachel at lunch. She started working at my office about four months ago and offered to share her apartment with me until I could find something suitable. She couldn't take Emmy, but she convinced me that it was a good idea to get out of the house and go back later for Emmy. I would be living ten minutes away, so I could see her on the weekends and after work, before my dad came home. It sounded like a great idea.

"Well, Rachel and I got along great, even though most of my girlfriends at work didn't like her at all. You see, she is gorgeous and she comes from Texas and has that southern accent. Most of the girls think it's fake or at least exaggerated, but I know it is real." What Beth wasn't about to tell Father Pat was that Rachel had a knock-out figure and she dressed in sexy outfits that included short skirts and low-cut blouses. All of the men in the office drooled over her constantly and everyone thought she got the position of secretary to the Comptroller because of her looks. What really made the girls jealous is that she was asked out on a date by the dreamy blonde Express Delivery driver on her first day of work. Every single girl had been vying for a date with him for the last six months, when he started delivering at the office.

"From the very first day that I moved in with her, I felt like things were finally coming together. We had very different backgrounds, but it was like we clicked the minute we met. Normally, I would have never tried to be her friend, because I wasn't very outgoing and I never had all the attention she gets from men, but something made me go up and introduce myself to her. She joked that we might be some kind of cosmic soul sisters!

"A couple of weeks after I moved in, she started bringing Rick, the delivery guy, around. She had been seeing him steadily, even on the nights she worked overtime. They seemed to be getting close and not much later, he started bringing his friends around. He lived in a house with three other guys. They all were nice to me. Two of the guys, Jack and Brian, are sort of computer nerds. They're really shy and they always have their laptops with them. They are always looking up something on the Internet. The other guy, Mark, is really nice looking and didn't seem interested in computers, but he used to shout 'show me the numbers!' every time Brian or Jack would look something up on the computer. I could tell it really annoyed Brian when he did that. Rick and Mark really don't seem like the kind of guys who would hang around Jack and Brian, but I thought it was like Rachel and my relationship—opposites attract sometimes. It helped me feel like I fit in. Mark teased me a lot, too. More like a kid-sister kind of thing than I would have liked." Beth realized she had spoke too candidly with this priest and blushed.

"It's okay dear, go on."

"Okay, well, Rachel told me that Rick and his friends were having a big party and that all kinds of neat people were going to be there. She wanted me to come along. I told her I wasn't much of a partier, but she said that she would help me find something to wear and that it would be fun. Beth remembered their conversation in her head, "Beth, you need to loosen up a bit, honey! You're such a pretty girl. I'll fix up your hair real nice and do your makeup and, oh, I have a really great denim skirt and top you could wear. When I get done with you, girl, you're gonna knock'em dead at the party. We'll make Mark notice you, for sure. It's time he knew you were interested in him. You gotta let your hair down and live a little!" When Beth began to protest about approaching Mark, Rachel wouldn't hear it. "You can't stay a wallflower forever. I'm gonna show you what living is all about this weekend and you'll thank me for it."

Beth's conversation with Father Pat faded in and out as her mind went over the last three months, but he sat there patiently and waited without a word. She resumed talking to him. "I thought it would be a really great chance to get to know Mark, so I said yes."

Again, her mind wandered and she thought about what an awful mistake that was. And then she remembered the conversation she had with her friend, Katie, at work when she told her about the party. They were supposed to go out to the movies that night with one of their other girlfriends after she got off of work. Katie was mad that she was canceling out on them. Beth thought Katie was jealous when she complained that she was spending less and less time with her old friends now that she moved in with Rachel, but it was true. She liked hanging out with someone as pretty as Rachel and getting attention from the guys. Having freedom and fun were something she never had a chance to experience before, because she had Emmy right out of high school.

Beth brought her knees up to her chest and hugged her legs. She grew anxious as the memories of the party drew near. It was hard to explain what happened next, since a lot of it was so unclear to her. She took a deep breath and continued out loud. "On Saturday, Rachel helped me get ready and it was like I was transformed into a princess." Rachel made Beth look glamorous with the skill of a Hollywood makeup artist. She was wearing the short skirt that Rachel had suggested, but went with one of her own tops. She wasn't comfortable in the low cut sleeveless blouse that Rachel offered, but she still looked great.

"I felt so good about myself when we walked into the living room of Rick's house and everyone turned to look at us. I could tell that the guys were admiring both of us. I know it sounds vain, but it was the first time something like that every happened to me. Rick came over and introduced us to the people sitting on the sofa. His house is awesome! It is a very plain brick townhouse on the outside, but the living room looked like something from *lifestyles of the rich and famous*. He has one of those *big* TV screens against the far wall, with a large sectional sofa and marble coffee table in front of it. There are tall plants in the corner and paintings with lights above them. He has a great stereo system with speakers all through the house. The dining room is more like an office and has two large mahogany desks with computers and several printers. The kitchen is a gourmet cook's delight. I couldn't believe a delivery guy could afford such nice stuff. Rachel explained to me that the guys were heavy investors and had hit the jackpot more than once."

"We sat down in the living room and Rick brought us champagne. It was *Dom Perignon!* Everyone was real friendly, but I did notice that there weren't many girls at the party. Rachel didn't find that unusual. We were there for a couple of hours. I guess it was about 11 o'clock when Rick pulled Rachel away and she came back and told me she was going out to get some more ice with Rick. I was nervous about being left alone, but I was having a nice conversation with one of the girls, but I can't remember her name now. Anyway, Rachel left and after a few minutes Mark came over and sat down next to me."

Beth grew quiet again. How could she explain to this priest what happened next, without making herself look like she asked for trouble? Closing her eyes, she continued her story. Her words were laced with regret. It started as a dream come true.

"When Mark sat down, I grew so nervous that I could hardly talk. He put his arm around my shoulder and gave me a squeeze." She grew silent as she relived what happened next in her mind.

"Having a good time, Beth?"

"Yes, I am. Rick has a really nice place."

"It's pretty nice, but not as nice as the house we plan on building next year."

"You're gonna build a house together?"

"Yeah, it's gonna have a swimming pool and a hot tub with lots of land for privacy." Mark was rubbing her arm while he talked.

"That sounds great. I can't wait to see it!" Beth was at a loss for words. She was praying that he would ask her out, so she wouldn't have to try. Her heart began racing when he suddenly put his hand on her knee.

"Can I ask you something?"

Beth's throat was so dry that her voiced cracked when she answered. "Sure, anything."

Mark leaned over to whisper in her ear. She could feel his moist breath on her neck. She closed her eyes and waited with breathless anticipation. "Brian wants to know if you would go out with him sometime? He's a little shy around girls, as you probably can tell, but he *really* likes you!"

She was shell-shocked! Her heart sank into the pit of her stomach, while her mind raced to come up with an answer. It came out a little stronger than she meant. "No! Tell him thanks, but I'm not interested right now."

Mark gave her an angry look at her response. "Why not? He's a nice guy. Isn't he good enough for you?"

"No, I mean, I didn't mean it that way. It's just that I am kind of interested in someone else right now." Oh gees, she thought, why did I go and say that.

"Oh, I see. Well, I guess I'll have to tell him that. You know, he's a great guy and he doesn't often get the courage to tell a girl he's interested. It wouldn't hurt you to just go out with him once."

"No, I'm sorry, I just don't want to."

Mark looked at her strangely. She wasn't sure what he was thinking. "It's not because he's not good enough for you then?"

"No, not at all."

He shook his head. "Okay, well, it doesn't hurt to ask." He looked down at her empty champagne glass. "Would you like me to get you a refill?"

Beth was afraid to say no to him again. The strange way he was acting suddenly made her feel very uneasy. "Yes, thanks."

Mark walked into the kitchen and was there for a few minutes. She turned to the girl sitting next to her, but found herself staring at an empty seat. Beth hadn't noticed that the girl had risen and was standing in the dining room. She looked over at the kitchen entrance just as Brian and Jack walked out, avoiding eye contact. They sat down at the computers and typed away. Mark walked out of the kitchen with a full glass of champagne and almost spilled some of it when someone backed into him as he came through the dining room. He cursed at the guy, but was smiling and back to his old self by the time he reached her. "Almost lost it! Here...to your health, drink up!" Beth took the glass and took a sip.

"Drink up! There's plenty more where that came from."

She smiled and took a big gulp and placed the glass down on the coffee table. "Let me know if you need anything else," was the last thing she heard Mark say.

Five minutes later the room began to spin and she felt like she was going to be sick. She looked around for Rachel, wondering what was taking her so long. The nausea grew worse and she stood up to find the bathroom. The room spun faster and faster and she remembered falling back into somebody's arms. She heard voices around her but they were muffled and then everything went black.

Beth kept staring straightforward, watching the horrific scene play out again in her memory. She suddenly realized that Father Pat was waiting to hear what happened after Mark sat down. She told him an abbreviated story about how Mark asked her if she would go out with Brian and she said no and that Mark asked if he could refill her champagne glass. She also told him that Mark seemed angry that she said no, but then was okay when he got back with her drink. She remembered very little of what happened next, but she told him everything she could.

"I felt like I was floating. I kept coming to but was unable to move my arms or legs and then I would pass out again, so I only know bits and pieces. I remember walking outside with someone holding me up. I could hear two voices. I must have been thrown onto the floor of a van because my face hit the edge of a box and the pain brought me out of the trance that I was in. I remember the sound of the doors closing.

Beth cried into her arms that were resting on her coiled legs. Father Pat moved over to the bed and held her gently. She looked up and wiped her eyes with the back of her right hand. She tried to calm down and continued in a quiet voice. "I know I continued to fade in and out of consciousness during it. I remember feeling the hem of my skirt bunched up under my arms and I heard noises and grunting and felt a terrible pain between my legs one time. I know there were two guys in the van, but I don't know who was on me. I was afraid to look and let them know I was awake, but I think one was Brian and maybe the other guy was Jack. He has a blue van. Someone opened the door just then and saw my eyes were open and cursed. I don't know who that was. The next thing I remember was my head being jerked around and beer was being poured down my throat and I started choking and passed out again. The next time I woke up, I was still lying in the back of the van and I realized that we were moving, because I could feel the vibration of the tires going over the road. I remember I knew I'd been raped by at least one of them and thought I was going to die. I really wanted to die. I passed out again and that's all I remember until I woke up here." Beth covered her head in shame. Father Pat gently ran his hand over her hair.

"It's okay, Beth. You will be alright. It's all over now, just a memory, child." His eyebrows drew together, as his anger rose in his throat and he forced back his unchristian thoughts of revenge on these animals Beth had described. "It wasn't your fault, Beth. You did not do anything wrong. *You were a victim.* It's possible that this fellow, Mark, gave you a type of drug that leaves a person helpless to defend themselves. I don't know much about it but it sounds like it could be a date-rape drug. They should be damned for such a cowardly act! We need to go to the police and report this."

Beth looked up at Father Pat through her tears. "No! No one can ever know, Father. I just want to forget it ever happened. Promise me, Father Pat."

"But Beth, what if they do it again?"

"I can't prove anything Father. Who's going to believe me? I'm not even sure it was Brian and Jack! It could have been anybody at the party! I never saw their faces. People will just think I asked for it. I know my father will. It will only make matters worse. The police can't do anything!"

"What about Rachel? Do you think she was a part of it?"

"I don't know! I can't believe she would do something like this, but I really don't know her very well. Maybe she's not the person I thought she was. Katie and the other girls didn't trust her. Maybe they sensed that she was trouble."

Father Pat nodded and rocked Beth until her crying stopped. He sat there in silence with her, knowing there wasn't much he could say right now to make the pain go away.

Matt sat in total disbelief and shock. He couldn't comprehend how any man could treat a woman like that. He looked at Beth still shaking from sobs in Father Pat's arms. She looked so innocent and frail. Matt grew angry inside. He wanted to hurt the guys who did this to her. He couldn't believe the injustice. He thought about what he was here to do. "How does someone recover from something like this? And how does someone go home to face a bad relationship with another man after all this has happened? Oh God, how am I going to be able to help her?"

Chapter 10

For the next few days, Father Pat and Mrs. McCafferty did their best to help Beth both physically and emotionally. The hand print bruises on Beth's arms were no longer recognizable and the deep cut on her calf was healing nicely. The bruise on her face at the jawbone was still pretty dark. Father Pat counseled Beth on her options regarding the rape. He reminded her that she could still go to the police and press charges against these men and that she needed to get herself checked out by a doctor. He delicately approached the subjects of pregnancy and HIV and how important it was to put these concerns to rest. Beth insisted that she was fine and that she was sure that she wasn't pregnant. She didn't tell Father, but she was presently experiencing cramps and that was a sure sign that her period was coming. Her period had been so erratic lately that she couldn't keep track of a due date.

Beth was adamant that she wanted nothing to do with the police. She told Father Pat that she knew how hard it would be to convict anyone and prove that they slipped a drug into her drink. She also knew that having a child out of wedlock would be used against her in court and that the whole experience would hurt Emmy. The conversation began to upset her and Father decided not to push her any harder for the time being.

Mrs. McCafferty tended to Beth's physical well being. By Tuesday, Beth was able to make it down the stairs. She sat on the front porch for a few hours in a comfortable wooden rocker and spent the time daydreaming about life with Emmy. Her daughter was the only thing that mattered in this world to her and she knew she could make it if she kept Emmy in mind. How she was going to make it was another thought altogether. It felt good to be outside breathing in the summer air, even if it was a bit stifling.

Matt sat on the oak tree branch looking down at Beth. He thought about how he was going to approach her and began practicing his lines. "Beth, I am Matt sent by God!" He thought to himself, "No, that sounds too heavy. How about, "Hey there Beth, how are you? I'm Matt the hummingbird and I have a message for you!" Matt frowned, "I sound like an idiot! I can just see her response. Hi Matt, how are you? Why don't you sit down and take a load off." Or maybe I can say, "Beth, go home to your father and make amends, God says it will be okay." Matt began to peck at the bark on the branch where he rested and thought, "Damn, this is not going to be easy. What if she doesn't hear me? Is my voice tiny or do I sound like my old voice? How will I know?" He decided the best thing to do was just to get her to notice him first. Then, when she was comfortable with him, he would talk. He looked at her gently rocking on the porch. Her eyes were dark from crying and lack of sleep. She had been through so much, reliving her experience with Father Pat. He decided that today was not the day. I'll wait two more days. Yes, that was a better idea, he thought. This would give him time to practice what he was going to say. Really, he was hoping this would give him time to get up the nerve, although he would not admit that to himself. "Funny," he thought ruefully, "I've never been shy around a pretty girl before."

Mrs. McCafferty noticed Beth holding her stomach and wincing every once in a while. She asked Beth if there was something wrong, but Beth insisted she was just fine. She said that it was almost her time of the month and she usually experienced a few cramps. She assured Mrs. McCafferty it was nothing serious. Beth wondered herself what this pain could be. It would come three or four times a day with different intensities. She was determined that she would put off medical treatment until this whole experience was far behind her.

Father Pat talked to Beth for a short time on Tuesday. He had meetings to attend most of the morning and visited the home bound in the afternoon. They talked only about plans for the future. Father would bring up formal counseling for the rape later, after Beth felt more in control of her life. Beth said she wanted to get back to work as quickly as possible. Father asked her if she felt she would be in any kind of danger working so close to Rachel. Beth said if she did, she would look for another job. Maybe she would find one with better pay. In the meantime, Father Pat suggested she rest often and even if she decided not to go home to live with her parents, he hoped she would think about working things out with her father. It would mean more to Emmy in the future than she could possibly know. He gave her some food for thought. "There is only one way a relationship can go if it doesn't grow closer—it will grow further apart. You owe it to yourself to keep trying while it's still salvageable."

"Father, I'm sorry if I've been difficult. I really appreciate everything you are doing for me. I don't know what I would've done, if you hadn't found me. But, I'm fine about what's happened and I can handle it. I know what I'm doing!"

"Beth, you're still in shock about what happened. As time goes by, you may feel differently. We're here to help you and I want you *always* to remember that. There are a lot of ways that you can find help in dealing with your situation. I hope you will keep an open mind about them."

"I will. In the meantime, I would like to find a way to repay you for your kindness. I'm feeling much better, so if there's something I can do around here to help you or Mrs. McC out, I'd really like to!"

Father Pat chuckled softly, but it was really to cover up the sadness he felt about Beth's denial of her pain. "Well, the only kind of help we've been missing lately is with the gardening, if you can even call those beds out back a garden anymore!"

Beth's eyes lit up. "It's been a while since I helped my mother with our flower beds, but I can pull out weeds. Only, I'm not much of a green thumb and I may pull a few flowers out at the same time."

"Oh, don't worry about that, I'm pretty sure that's all we have out there." They laughed together. They shared the same sense of humor and that made Beth feel close to him. It also made her realize what she did not share with her father. Father Pat was becoming a grandfatherly figure to her and they both enjoyed it.

Tuesday evening, Beth made the call she had been dreading to her mother, Mary. Beth's parents were taking Emmy to visit her great aunt in Baltimore over the weekend. They were going to spend the weekend at the harbor, visiting the Baltimore Aquarium. They were supposed to return late Sunday evening, so her mom did not expect to hear from her until Monday evening. Beth was so exhausted Monday evening that she didn't have the strength or courage to call her mom. Now she prayed that her mom didn't try calling her at Rachel's apartment and was thankful when her mother told her she went shopping after dinner and didn't get home until after Emmy went to bed. When she found out Beth had not called, she made up an excuse to Beth's dad, so that there wouldn't be trouble, but was a little worried since it was the first time this had ever happened.

Beth told her mother she had come down with a severe stomach virus and slept through last night. Mary was concerned but Beth said she would be fine, although she wouldn't be able to see Emmy this week. Beth knew this would look suspicious to her mom, but she needed time for the bruises to heal. She told her mom that work was really busy and she would have to work nights and the next weekend to make up for the time she was out. Her mother thought it was odd that she wouldn't make time to see Emmy even once that week, but she let it go when Beth told her that she would call Emmy every night and asked her to put Emmy on the phone.

The conversation with Emmy was short, but sweet. Emmy was such a precious child with the sunniest disposition anyone had ever seen. She would burst into a room and light up everyone in it with her contagious smile. She had soft curly brown tresses that framed her cherub-cheeked face. Her hazel eyes were large and round and were more expressive than seemed humanly possible. She had a cute little nose dotted with freckles and her lips were thin. Her top lip was flat and this overemphasized her bottom lip when she smiled. Along with her deep dimples, it made her smile form almost a half circle, like you see on a smiley face sticker.

Beth fought back tears as she spoke to Emmy. "Hi, angel! How's Mommy's little girl?"

"I'm fine, Mommy. When are ya coming home?"

"Oh, Mommy's sick right now baby. I have a real bad tummy ache, so I won't be able to see you for a few days." She squeezed tears out of her eyes as she tried to change the subject.

"How was Baltimore? Can you tell me all about it?"

"Oh, Mommy, I saw dolphins and we got *splashed*!"

"You did! How did that happen?"

"We went to a show and they had words on the empty seats by the big pool that said *splash zoon* and Grandmom said we would get wet if we sat there, but I wanted to see the dolphins real good and PopPop said okay, so they swim over to us and made a big wave and we got *soaked* but PopPop got mostly wet, cause he tried to cover me up!" Emmy giggled. "Oh, and Aunt Marie bought me a new pink dress with *two* pockets and she gave me a bunch of pennies to put in them and PopPop gave me a bunch, too."

Emmy loved to wear pretty little dresses and jumpers with big pockets in the front. She would fill them with her latest stash of pennies that she managed to finagle from Pop Pop or some other softhearted person. You could always hear her coming because she loved to reach both hands deep into her pockets and jingle her treasure. To Emmy, pennies were worth more than silver or gold because they seemed to be readily available almost all of the time.

"Grandmom made me stop wearing the dress so she could wash it, so I put the pennies in my purse." She held up her kitty-cat purse to the phone and shook it so Beth could hear how many pennies she collected.

"Sounds like you hit the jackpot this time! I can't wait to see your new dress. I bet you look like a little princess in it!"

"When are you coming home, Mommy? I miss you!"

"Soon, baby! But this week I have to work late, so I'll call you every night before you go to bed and I promise we'll do something special together next week!"

"Okay, Mommy. I love you!"

"I love you, too, Emmy!"

Emmy seemed quite content with Beth's reasoning. She blew her mom kisses and was about to hang up the phone and Beth added. *"I promise, we'll be together soon and I'll never leave you again, angel!"* Beth hung up the phone and burst into tears.

♥♥♥♥♥♥♥

On Wednesday morning, Beth spent the whole day downstairs, but did not visit the backyard. She stayed on the front porch during the afternoon heat reading magazines and checked the newspaper for jobs and apartments. Both listings were disappointing. Most insurance jobs were for data entry or clerical work and there were no two-bedroom apartments that she could afford. She thought about getting a one-bedroom apartment, but that would be taking Emmy from a large house with her own bedroom to a cramped living area. Beth wasn't sure how Emmy would react to moving away from her grandparents. If she couldn't offer her at least a decent living environment, Emmy was no better off than the arrangement she had now. There was only one other option she could see possible at this point. Her best friend, Karen Ross, lived in Berkeley, California. She was going to school there. Whenever Beth and Karen talked together, they would fantasize about Beth moving out there with Karen and starting their own business. Karen lived in a small cottage outside of the campus. It had two bedrooms and a loft that would be ideal for her and Emmy. Beth was always afraid of making such a big transition. She relied heavily on her mother for Emmy's care. The thought of adding daycare fees to her weekly expenses was scary. It would stretch her budget way too far. Karen said that she wouldn't have to pay rent until she could afford it, so that would help. Beth could go out to Berkeley first, and when she was settled in, she would come and get Emmy and their things. They could take a great car adventure across the United States. It almost seemed like the only real option at this time.

Beth joined Father Pat and Mrs. McCafferty for dinner on Wednesday. She was wearing the pink sundress that Mrs. McCafferty brought her and it fit her perfectly. Her color was returning and she looked very pretty this evening. Most of the conversation was casual and pleasant to start. Beth told them she was discouraged by the paper and would have to rethink her plans. Father Pat asked if that meant she was considering going home. Beth shook her head no, as she took a bite of Mrs. McCafferty's delicious tuna casserole. When she swallowed, she added, "I don't think I will ever be able to go back home, Father. I've thought a lot about it, and I don't believe that will help improve our relationship. I think a little distance may work better for us."

"Well, what do you plan to do, Beth?" Father Pat was saddened that she wouldn't listen to his reasoning.

"I don't know yet. Maybe I can find an efficiency apartment that will allow me to save a little money and I can bring Emmy there on the weekends to stay with me. If I don't find an apartment here soon, maybe I'll move in with my best friend in California. I know I can trust her. Maybe

California is just what I need in my life. It would put some distance between me and everything that has happened here."

"Did you see any such apartments in the paper, dear?" Mrs. McCafferty asked, as she passed the rolls around. She did not want to see Beth run away from her problems.

"No, not even one. They must be hard to come by around here." Beth could see this conversation had the potential of turning into a lecture, so she decided to cut it off. She wiped her mouth with a napkin and began to excuse herself. "Please forgive me, I think I'm getting tired. If you don't mind, I would like to go to my room now."

Father Pat could see the wall Beth was beginning to build around herself. He had seen it many times before when young people bare their souls and are looking for immediate support for their cause. When they don't get it, they turn back into themselves and refuse to listen anymore. Everyone expects immediate results. "Sure, Beth. Call us if you need anything." He added. "I will check around town tomorrow and see if there are any apartments available that weren't in the paper."

"Thank you. I think that tomorrow I will start working on the backyard. I could use some fresh air." Beth said good night and thanked Mrs. McCafferty for a wonderful dinner. She asked Father Pat if she could use his phone to call Emmy and say good night. She went up into his room and this time closed the door. Father Pat and Mrs. McCafferty heard the door close. They returned to eating in silence.

Matt arrived just as Beth started talking about working in the backyard. Several small kitchen appliances camouflaged the lower half of the kitchen window. Matt sat comfortably on a branch of the lilac bush without a need to hide. He did not hear Beth tell Father Pat she was considering moving to California, nor did he notice Beth's change of attitude. He was just grateful to hear Beth would be outside tomorrow. This was a perfect opportunity to try out step one of his plan. As he watched her the last few days, he noticed that she seemed to be handling what had happened to her very well. Maybe this wouldn't be as hard as he thought. He could wait until she started weeding and swoop in to the rescue. It was a perfect plan. Matt couldn't be happier at that moment. He knew what he was going to do.

He imagined the scene as it took place before his eyes. Beth would be gardening and he would hover in front of her about four feet away. She would look up and he would dart around and fly away. A few minutes later he would return and hover a little closer to her. When she became curious, he would move even closer and make eye contact. Then he would speak to her and take it from there. It was a perfect plan.

Matt was so full of himself that he did a little victory dance along the lilac bush. As he moved along the branch savoring his pending success, he noticed his reflection in the toaster that was on top of the radiator cover that sat directly under the window. He was amazed to see how brilliant and iridescent the sun's reflection made his feathers appear. His ruby red throat sparkled, sending out a prism of color when he turned his body towards the sun. He had a thick black ring on his neck just below his red throat that formed a striking collar over his dazzling green wings. Matt spread his wings out full length for a better view. The iridescent feathers reminded him of Anjella's beautiful wings. He wrapped the wings around himself and admired his regal cape. Then he drew one wing over his beak to show just his eyes and pretended he was a vampire leering at his reflection. The colors of his wings were too impressive for such a dark character. Upon further study, his long, tapered beak reminded him of a sword and quickly he transformed his image into a gallant, swashbuckling Musketeer dueling to save the life of a fair maiden. He skillfully lunged forward at an invisible foe, making graceful figure eights with his mighty sword. His imagination ran wild as he quickly disarmed his inept sparring partner and saved the damsel in distress.

His admiration for himself gave him the boost of confidence his ego needed. Unfortunately, his imagined chivalry distracted him from his unsafe environment and he didn't register the imminent danger lurking a few feet away. He hopped along the branch humming the tune from one of his favorite movies, Rocky, and feeling as powerful as a locomotive. He was sure his plan would work fast, because after all, most people would take the sign of a talking hummingbird as something extraordinary. Surely a sign from God! Beth would be so shocked that God would send such a messenger to her rescue that she would eagerly make amends with her father and return to her parents' house to live happily ever after.

Matt was still facing the house as he hopped along the bending lilac branch. He was close to the steps by the time he noticed a large shadow looming over his shoulders. He froze on the branch for a moment and adrenaline raced through his little body, as he realized what the outline of the shadow was. He turned his head slowly and confirmed his worst nightmare. Only inches away on the top rail of the steps sat the biggest, ugliest, meanest street cat a bird could ever imagine. The rusty colored tabby with mangy, matted fur sat poised for the kill. His rear end was coiled up and his back feet were moving in eager anticipation. His ears were flattened. Half of his left ear was missing and he had a chunk of fur missing from his head. The tail swished excitedly as the deep black eyes calculated the proper pouncing time.

Matt spread his wings and began to flap frantically. He was only inches off the branch when the great tabby sprang through the air. Matt moved backward as the cat clawed at him. The cat struck the end of his left wing, slashing the tip off. Matt fell straight down behind the lilac bush as the cat fell into the bush after him, clawing and hissing down through the foliage. Matt landed on his back just inches from the base of the bush. The tabby became tangled in the branches and began thrashing to escape. Matt could not roll over on his stomach to run. He watched in horror as the cat caught a glimpse of him. The tabby abandoned his attempt to free himself from the bush and began to swipe at Matt using both front paws. The first strike brought the cat's claws within a half-inch of Matt's body. The cat's body sunk deeper into the bush towards him and Matt knew his time was up. He watched the furry beast raise his right paw in the air for his victory slash. As the curly daggers sliced through the air towards him, Matt closed his eyes and said his last prayer. It was all over. He thought for a second about Beth and how close he had come to fulfilling his mission. Then he breathed his last breath of hope. "Angels!" he shouted. He felt the claws tear into his little body and send him rolling across the ground. He opened his eyes to a familiar white mist swirling around him and felt a warm sensation envelop him. He closed his eyes again and smiled, feeling peace flood his body and mind. He was delighted to think he was going to his heavenly home again. Maybe only for a short time, but Heaven felt so good.

When Matt opened his eyes, he was sitting in the control room across from Enon, Sage and Anjella. All three angels had a look of concern on their faces. Matt looked down at himself and saw his human body form again. It felt good to be out of the hummingbird's high-strung body. Matt smiled nervously at his angels. "Damn, I guess I really screwed up this time, huh?"

Anjella reached across the table and squeezed his hands. "You had us worried there for a minute. I thought you were never going to call for us. If you waited one more second, the bird's body would have failed and it would have been too late."

"It's hard to think straight, when a cat fifty times bigger than you is about to eat you for supper!" Matt felt better that it was not over. "I never thought I would run into so many problems down there."

Enon surprised himself by feeling equally relieved that Matt had called them in time, but returned to the matter at hand. "I told you Matt, you must obey the natural laws of the species. A hummingbird is prey for a variety of insects and animals, including other birds. We would have thought that your run in with the other hummingbird would have given you a clue."

Matt was flustered, "It did, Enon, but I have a lot to think about down there. Like how I'm going to talk to Beth. Or will there be enough food to survive and now, I got a giant tabby to worry about. And I was getting so close to talking to Beth!"

"You were?" Enon asked sarcastically. "You're awfully sure of yourself these days, despite the experiences you've gone through." Enon rose from the table and walked back and forth behind the two other angels. "I have a little advice for you, Matt. *Never* assume you are in control down there! You don't know everything that's going on." He paused for a moment, "If you think you know everything, then you can't see the truth that sits right under your nose."

Matt was thoroughly confused. "I don't follow you! Do you mean you know things that are going on that I don't? How is that supposed to help me?" Enon made no attempt to answer. Matt grew more perplexed. "So, are you going to tell me or do I have to guess?"

Anjella leaned forward, "We can't tell you that kind of information, Matt. You are supposed to figure it out on your own." She saw his shoulders shrink as he buried his face in his hands. "Don't worry, you'll do fine. We're fairly impressed by what you have accomplished in such a short time!"

"Like what?" Matt slammed his hands down on the table. "So far, I've almost gotten clobbered by another bird, and if it weren't for you guys, I would have been the tabby's dinner. Now I find out I have missed important information. And, I don't have the faintest idea how I am going to complete this mission. *If* I ever do get a chance to speak to Beth!"

Anjella smiled, "Matt, so far you have survived! If you think that is a small feat, you're fooling yourself. Most human souls wouldn't have been able to figure out how to fly or eat as a hummingbird. But you were smart enough to let the bird teach you. So now you have to be smart about the cat and find a way to outsmart it!"

Matt jumped to attention with Anjella's last words, "What do you mean outsmart it?" Can't you guys get rid of it?"

Enon scoffed, "No, Matt, we can not change nature. We can restore the bird's body and send you back down, but we can not tamper with anything else in nature. It is against the law."

"So, I have to go back down and find a way to outwit a twenty pound cat so I can get to Beth? Damn, could the Council have made this any harder for me?"

Enon began to feel a little sorry for Matt, but was amused at Matt's naivete at the same time. "Yes Matt, if the cat is still around, you will have to find a way around it yourself."

"And this time, you can't help me if I get in trouble!" Matt prayed the answer would be different than he knew it would be.

"No, we can not assist you any further. You are on your own." Enon closed the manual he was scanning to be sure he hadn't missed anything.

"Damn," Matt exclaimed. "So when do I go back?"

Anjella and Sage rose from the table. Anjella looked empathetically into Matt's sad eyes. "You must go back now. The bird's body has been restored and you will awaken in the oak tree at the side of the house. The next time we will see you is *after* you complete your mission." Anjella made sure she emphasized to Matt that she expected him to succeed, even though she was beginning to wonder how he could beat the odds.

Matt rose from the table. "Well, let's get the show on the road. No sense standing around here chit-chatting. I've got a soul to save."

"That's the spirit, Matt!" Anjella knew he was putting on a good face, but thought it would help if he didn't know she could tell.

There was no need to move to the screen. Matt knew the routine by now. He shook Sage and Enon's hands and hugged Anjella. Before he finished the hug, he was sitting on a branch of the oak tree. He looked up and saw the light in Beth's room go out. Hopefully, tomorrow would be a better day, he thought, and turned his head down under his wing and fell asleep.

Chapter 11

Thursday morning started with a light rain shower that headed a small cold front from the northwest. It promised temporary relief from the intense humidity for a few days. The air was crisp and much cooler. Beth awoke early to the sound of the last few raindrops, as they pattered against the window. The window was cracked a few inches and the cool breeze caressed Beth's arms and legs that hung out from under the sheets. Mrs. McCafferty must have been in already and closed the window some. Beth felt strange that she didn't hear her come in, since, once again, she had hardly slept. As she pulled herself up in bed, she noticed just a slight stiffness in her thighs and stomach area. She wondered if she would get the sharp pain in her abdomen today. Maybe everything was healing now and it would go away.

Beth swung her legs over the bed and sat for a moment. She thought about all of her options, which were few, and made a decision. She appreciated everything Father Pat and Mrs. McCafferty had done for her, but they did not realize how difficult it would be to return to live with her parents. She decided to place a collect call to Karen this evening and see if her offer was still open. She had enough money to travel by bus to California. The drive across the country alone was too intimidating. She would tell her mother she had a wonderful promotion opportunity in Berkeley and had to go right away. When she was settled, she would come back to get Emmy and their things and drive back to California using her own car. Her mother would be upset about losing Emmy, but she would feel better knowing Beth would be living with Karen. Beth's parents always liked Karen. Yes, this would be best for everyone. She would not have to face her father, or Rachel, or ever run into those guys again. Beth could forget all of the terrible pain she had gone through and get on with her life. She would be with Emmy and that was the most important objective. Together, they could make a new life for themselves. Beth felt sure that this was the right thing to do. This time, she would not let anyone stop her. It was a done deal.

Beth dressed and went downstairs for breakfast. Mrs. McCafferty was making pancakes. Father Pat had already left for his morning walk. Beth passed on a big breakfast and ate an English muffin quickly. She was anxious to get out of the house and into the backyard. Gardening would help the day go by faster and get her outside into the fresh air. She was pale and hoped to get enough sun to bring color back into her face. Maybe it would help make the bruise on her face less noticeable.

Matt was sitting on the tall fence post between the two backyards surveying the property. There was no sign of the cat so far, but he decided he would be very cautious this morning. He couldn't chance another run in with it. Hopefully, it was a stray cat passing through and not a local resident. Matt heard the back door open and saw Beth step out onto the landing. She was carrying some gardening tools.

Beth looked lovely today. She was wearing a pale blue denim blouse and white denim shorts. She was barefoot and reminded Matt of a country girl on a farm. Her hair was pulled back into a loose ponytail with a few strands framing her face. Her paleness did not subtract from the natural beauty of her face. She radiated softness in her demeanor. She was petite but had a model's body, with long slender legs and arms, a trim waist and long neck. She stepped into the yard as gracefully as a princess entering a ballroom.

Beth stepped on the cool, wet grass in the yard and surveyed the territory, looking for a place to begin. The flowerbeds closest to the house required the most work. Beth decided to begin with the beds over by the rose bushes. She found a large wooden bucket that was dry enough to use as a bench until the heat from the sun dried the grass. She sat down and began pulling weeds between the rose bushes. The rain from the night before made some of the weeds a little slippery, but made the earth more pliable. Pulling out all of the weeds would not be very difficult. The smell of the earth was soothing and it felt good to be busy, she thought. It allowed her a chance to stop thinking about problems that she could not solve and gave her one that she could.

Matt watched Beth from the fence with great intensity. He looked around for the cat again. A knot grew in his stomach as he anticipated his first approach. "Was it too soon?" he asked himself. Should he just do it and get it over with? He surveyed the yard one more time. Yes, he decided. It was now or never. Beth rose and walked over to the trash can that was right next to the steps with the first pile of weeds in her hand. The trash can was the old metal type and the lid had been severely bent from being thrown around by trash collectors. The can was still round, so Beth had to balance the lid on top carefully, so it didn't slip into the can. Matt held his breath and made his first attempt. He flew over to the can as she was putting the lid on. Beth heard a buzzing sound from behind her and swished her hand over her head to ward off the impending insect. She missed Matt's body by a few inches. Matt dove toward the ground and flew back over to the fence. He knew he was never in real danger by her waving hands, but hadn't thought about what he sounded like to a human. He never encountered a hummingbird before himself. He heard the hum of his wings when he flew but never noticed that it sounded like a buzzing bug until now. He decided he would have to approach her from the front.

Beth moved over to the rose bushes and returned to her weeding. She was singing softly to herself. Matt was surprised by her melodious voice. Even though she was singing very quietly, he could tell her voice had incredible range and was impressed that such a provocative voice could come from such a petite body. Beth was singing a jazzed up version of the old gospel hymn, Amazing Grace, which was her favorite song growing up. She used to sing it all the time as a young girl, especially when she was feeling low and somehow turned the bluesy lyrics into a jazz beat along the way. It was as if she was born to sing jazz and she was drawn to it naturally. None of the kids in school even knew what jazz was, but that didn't stop her from singing jazz songs in front of them. Her voice was so good that her friends in the playground enjoyed listening to her belt out her latest memorized song or a short little scat ditty that she created, even if they didn't understand what she was singing. Her father had a collection of jazz records hidden in his closet that she would drag out and play when he was at work, until he found out and forbid her to listen to his records anymore. This didn't stop Beth. She found a jazz station on the radio and by the age of twelve, had memorized almost all of the hits from the legendary Ella Fitzgerald and even some of Billie Holiday's.

Ella was Beth's idol and she especially admired her scat singing. Beth enjoyed singing Ella's upbeat tunes like *Lady Be Good* and *A-Tisket, A-Tasket*, but really shone when she sang scat with the same perfect pitch and clarity that would have made her idol proud. Later, when Beth was a little older, she worked on the more sensual songs of Billie Holiday, Lena Horne, and Sarah Vaughn.

With Beth's attractive looks and great voice, Matt imagined she could become an incredible jazz singer if she wanted to. He compared her voice to his favorite up-and-coming singer, Nancy Kelly. Beth's voice was far superior to any of the local singers he used to listen to at Roxy's Jazz House on the Main Line. He closed his eyes to concentrate on each silky, rich note and moved to the entrancing rhythm of the song. What a coincidence that she would be interested in the same music he was, he thought. Most of the girls he dated had no interest in jazz or the blues or appreciated music of any kind. This added dimension of Beth's persona was quite intriguing and Matt felt a genuine attraction to her developing. Normally, he was drawn to a more aggressive and sexy type of girl, like the voluptuous girls that hung out at the racing events, but Beth had a purity and sophistication about her that the other girls never had. Matt shook his head to snap out of the daydream state he was in. How could he be thinking such thoughts when he was sitting on a fence in a bird's body?

Matt refocused on the task at hand and looked around the yard before trying his next attempt. This time he approached Beth from her right side, moving in along the back of the house. He stopped close to the wall of the house and hovered about four feet away to Beth's right, well out of arms reach. Beth glanced toward the buzzing sound to see what kind of bug was approaching, but only caught a flash of Matt, as her attention was turned to the noise of the trash can lid falling into the can. The rusty colored tabby came out from between the trash can and the house to the left of Beth and knocked the can as he sprang toward his target hovering twelve feet away. The cat never noticed Beth on his approach and she startled him as he came out from behind the can, breaking his concentration.

Matt saw his stalker in plenty of time to zoom back to the high fence and then up to the telephone wires that stretched between the two houses. He was not going to take any chances. Beth walked over to the can and balanced the lid back on top. He heard her talking to the cat. "Hey fat cat, what do you think you're doing? Trying to catch a big fat bug for breakfast." Beth brushed her hands together to clean off the dirt and went over to the frustrated feline who was now cleaning his paws by the rose bushes. Beth leaned over to pet the tabby. She looked for a collar, although she was sure it was a stray by the shape it was in. "Oh, poor baby, are you hungry?" The cat began to rub against her legs and meowed faintly. He knew how to get attention from a friendly stranger. "Why don't I go in the house and get you some milk. I'll see if Mrs. McC has some leftovers to feed you." Beth walked up the steps and opened the screen door. She looked back at the scruffy cat, feeling sorry for the poor thing. "Now don't go anywhere, I'll be right back."

Beth returned with a bowl of milk and some hard cheese. It was all she could scrounge up in the kitchen. She placed the milk down on the top step and let the cat jump up into her lap. She broke off a piece of cheese and hand fed the cat, whispering words of encouragement. She felt an instant bond with the orphan, who was a little beaten up and looking for some tender-loving-care much like herself. "Maybe I'll take you with me when I go." She said. Matt was relieved. He thought she was figuring out how to move home.

Matt sat on the high wire feeling overwhelmed at his predicament. He watched Beth cuddle the cat and stroke its back. The feline glanced at the high wire and gave Matt a smirk, which he took as a challenge. There was no time to feel sorry for himself. He had come this far and a mangy alley cat was not going to get the best of him. He started to get angry and he could feel his adrenaline rushing through him. "Oh yeah, you ugly beast?" He remarked to himself. "You may have won round one and two, but I will get you on round three." Matt watched from the high wire in between his feedings for the rest of the day, trying to figure out how to outsmart the crafty cat.

By dinnertime, the scruffy cat had won over Beth and Mrs. McCafferty's hearts and was invited inside for the night. Matt was able to listen to dinner conversation at the window in peace. Father Pat told Beth he did not have any luck locating an apartment for her, but he would keep on trying. Beth told him it was alright. She didn't seem bothered by the news.

Father Pat and Mrs. McCafferty exchanged a glance. Mrs. McCafferty asked Beth leading questions about Emmy and her parents to focus on the good times she shared with her family. She was hoping that if Beth talked about the good times enough, she would think about how much she missed them and see the possibilities of reuniting with her family. It was a very difficult task to try to take on the world and raise a daughter at the same time. It didn't make sense to either of them that she would consider trying to do it all on her own, when she had a safe place to be. The world was not as safe as it used to be. Children fell prey to the most sinister villains these days. To live in a house where you didn't get along all the time with your father was still far better than facing the dangers of living alone. Family structure was important, especially for Emmy. Too many children were being raised without the stability of a family unit and it was hurting society. Beth did not see it that way at all.

Beth was sharp enough to know where the conversation was headed again, so she politely excused herself early from the table. Once again, she asked Father Pat if she could make a few calls upstairs using his phone. When she went upstairs this time, she grabbed her phone directory from her purse and went into Father Pat's room and closed his door. Her first call was collect to Karen. It was only about eight o'clock on the East Coast; she hoped she wasn't calling too early. She sighed with relief as she heard Karen's voice on the other end accepting the call.

Karen was thrilled to hear of Beth's decision. She had been living alone for four years now and was considering getting a roommate. Beth told Karen about her father and her terrible experience at the party. They cried together for a while. Karen insisted she come as soon as possible. She told Beth to call her tomorrow evening about the same time and she would have bus information. Karen asked Beth how soon she was planning to come. Beth said immediately. As much as she loved and appreciated the help Father Pat and Mrs. McCafferty gave her, she could see that they were committed to reuniting her with her father and she just couldn't handle that again. Beth told Karen about how big Emmy had gotten and what a delightful girl she was. She assured Karen that Emmy would not be a problem. Karen loved children and couldn't wait to see Emmy. Beth had sent her pictures each year, but the last time she saw her in person was when she was just weeks old and Karen was leaving for California. When Beth hung up she was certain that this was the perfect answer to her prayers.

Her next call was to Emmy. Beth was so excited to tell Emmy that they would be together soon. She did not go into the details, but told Emmy to keep it their little secret. Emmy loved keeping secrets.

She talked to her mom and said she would be over on Sunday for a visit. She decided to wait and tell her mom and dad in person. She did not know how they would react but she didn't care. Her father could rant and rave all he wanted. She wouldn't be around to hear his grief anymore. She felt bad about leaving her mom, though. They had always been so close. And Beth knew how much her mother loved Emmy. It would break her heart, but Beth didn't feel she had any other choice. Although she felt close to her mother, Beth never understood why her mom never stood up to her father when he would pick a fight with her. She could tell her mother thought he was over-reacting many times. This disturbed Beth, but she felt deep down that her mother had her own reasons. She could not imagine what they could be, but she thought her mother always looked torn—or maybe trapped was a better word—when she and her dad would argue. Still Beth resented that she would not support her. When she hung up the phone, Beth felt more scared than relieved. It was normal to be scared, she justified to herself. At that moment a fiery pain shot across her abdomen and she rushed to her bedroom to lie down.

Matt heard every word of both conversations. He couldn't believe his ears. Beth was leaving for California. He wasn't sure if Sunday would be her last day at the rectory or just the day that she would visit and tell her parents. He would have to find out. He moved to her bedroom window and saw Beth rocking on the bed clutching her stomach. After several minutes, she pulled herself under the sheet and fell asleep. Once again, his mission was falling apart. He sat on the window ledge staring helplessly at the sleeping figure. What could he do now? Maybe Father Pat could convince Beth it was a big mistake. And then he grew more depressed when he thought about the tone of Beth's conversation. Would she even tell him she was leaving? Probably not, he thought. Beth didn't want any confrontation, that was why she was running away. "What can I do now?" he thought. He watched Beth for a half-hour until he was sure she was sleeping for the night. He foraged for food out at the day lilies and returned to the protection of the old oak tree to sleep. He was surprised to find out that even hummingbirds had nightmares and his mind played out a string of the worst nightmares imaginable, waking him several times during the long night. He dreamt of angry tabby cats chasing him every time he tried to approach Beth and other dreams of waking up in the morning to discover Beth had slipped out of the house while he was sleeping and he didn't know how to find her. Matt became paranoid and tried to stay awake, looking for signs of movement in the house, but he couldn't fight his fatigue and finally closed his eyes to continue the battle with his conscience.

Chapter 12

Friday was another beautiful day with plenty of sunshine throughout the day. Beth continued to work on the weeding in the backyard. Unfortunately for Matt, the tabby spent the entire day hovering around Beth. Matt could see the cat studying the yard, looking for the hummingbird. The cat sat on the top step stretching out in the hot sun. Occasionally, he would jump down and rub up against Beth for some attention. Matt didn't bother making any attempt to approach Beth. The cat was too alert and too close and Matt had not figured out how he could hover long enough for Beth to notice him without the cat interfering.

The weather was comfortable enough for Beth to take short breaks sitting in the shade of the poplar trees at the back of the yard. She tired frequently, which surprised her because she was always in good shape. She cringed as she briefly thought about what had really happened to her the other night and hoped she would never remember. She sipped a bottle of water and let her mind wander to the time in her life when she enjoyed gardening with her mother. It was when she was in high school and just beginning to experience the turmoil with her father.

Like every other girl her age, Beth was in the throes of becoming a woman and her emotions and hormones were spinning out of control on a daily basis. The distractions of boys and dating, along with the constant flow of crises shared among her equally emotionally charged girlfriends, created a time of stress and anxiety for her that appeared to be the end of the world one day; only to turn around the next day, and experience some marvelous occurrence that would put her right back on cloud nine.

Beth relied on her close relationship with her mother to keep herself anchored during those topsy-turvy times. She remembered how she used to sneak up behind her mother and watch her jump as she sprinkled a handful of grass clippings down her back. Although her mother loved her flowers, she was particularly fearful of bugs. Mary would initially shriek with panic but always ended up laughing at how many times Beth was able to pull that practical joke off on her.

Beth would then pull up a paper bag to kneel on and join in her mother's search for the smallest sign of a weed. She remembered teasing her mother one time by bringing a magnifying glass to assist her search for weeds, which made them both laugh for the longest time. It was in the midst of all of their fun that Beth would get to ask her mom a question about something that was bothering her, like something about boy troubles, or what to do about Jennifer Whales, who was spreading more rumors about her or more often, why was Dad so grumpy all the time. Her mother did not always have great answers, but it was the security of being able to ask her anything, that made Beth feel so close to her.

Several conversations stood out in her memories. Beth began pulling dry, brown grass out of the ground and rocking back and forth as she replayed them in her mind. Beth remembered one time plopping down next to her mother by the red Lincoln rosebush where she was planting begonias. Before Mary could say a good morning, Beth blurted out her latest dilemma.

"Mom, this creep in my class, Jimmy Mitchell, called me a surfboard in front of the whole school today! I have never been so humiliated in my life!"

Mary was unfamiliar with the latest slang that kids were using. "Why on earth would he call you a surfboard?"

Beth rolled her eyes at her mom's ignorance and sounded demoralized as she tried to explain to her mother the crisis at hand. "*Because* I'm tall and skinny and flat as a board!"

"You're not skinny and for Heaven's sake, you just turned fifiteen. A lot of girls don't develop that way for another year." Mary was never comfortable discussing issues of a sexual nature with Beth.

"You've got to be kidding! There's only one other girl in my class still wearing training bras. Karen is an A-cup and Jennifer Whales is a B-cup already!"

"Must you be so blunt about these things?"

Beth was almost jamming the delicate begonia seedlings into the holes that Mary had made. "I've never been so embarrassed about anything in my whole life! I'll never be able to go to school on Monday and face everyone. All I'm gonna hear is hey, surfboard, can I get a ride on you!"

"Now I don't think that because one rude young man called you that means the whole school will join in. And watch what you're doing with those plants or you're gonna break the flowers off at the base!"

"He's not a young man—he's a jerk and I'm never gonna get a date now!"

Mary stopped digging and gave Beth her full attention. "You listen to me. You are a beautiful, smart and wonderful girl! There are a lot of boys out there that will like you for more than how your body looks."

"Oh yeah, well I doubt that any boy's paying attention to my personality. If I have to rely on that, I'm in big trouble."

"What's wrong with your personality? You've got a lot of girlfriends, don't you?"

"But boys are different, Mom. Besides, how can I expect a boy to like me, when my own father doesn't."

"*That is not true!* You're father likes you."

"No he doesn't!"

"*Yes*, he does. He just has trouble showing you sometimes. He works very hard to give you a good home and nice clothes."

"But that doesn't mean he likes me. He *has* to do those things—he's my father."

"He does them because he loves you!"

"But that still doesn't mean he likes me."

Mary was exasperated. "I think the problem is that you're just as stubborn as he is sometimes. You are more like him than you think."

Beth huffed. "*I am not at all like Dad!* We are like night and day."

"No, you both are equally bull-headed and think that you know everything."

Beth exclaimed, "You're wrong!" Then broke into laughter as she realized what she just said. Mary joined in.

But like everything else in her life, even those cherished times in the garden had grown sour. When Beth was in her senior year, she spent less time at home and the gardening get-togethers became sparse. It happened only when Beth was in trouble or at her wits end about something. She remembered the time they talked just before her graduation.

Once again, she snuck up on her mother. "Hi, Mom!"

Mary jumped. "Stop doing that! One of these days you're gonna give me a heart attack. I'm getting too old for your jokes. It's been a while since you have helped me out here. Hand me the peat moss, please." Mary smiled at her daughter as she opened the bag and started sprinkling it around the rose bushes. "Is something wrong?"

"No, no. Everything's cool." Beth began tracing heart shapes in the peat moss as she tried to muster the courage to ask her question. "Mom."

"Yes."

"How do you know when you're in love?"

Mary continued spreading the moss. "In love! You're too young to know what love is."

"But how do you know if you are?"

Mary stopped her work and brushed off her hands. She could sense there was something behind Beth's question and maybe it was time to talk. "Well, I guess, there's different kinds of love and you have to be careful which kind you're in before you do something about it."

"I don't get it."

"Well, for starters, there's puppy love, when you think you're in love because everything feels so wonderful and you've never felt that way before, but that never lasts. And then there's a sort of love that, well, is a physical attraction to someone who's the total opposite of you and it hits you fast and hard and hard is usually how you fall when it's over. And then there's what I think is real love."

"What's real love?"

Mary took Beth's hands into hers and squeezed them hard to make her point. "Real love is when you can just as easily be a friend to that person as you can a partner and nothing that happens between you could ruin what you have together, because you only want what's best for each other—that to me is real love!"

Beth was stunned by her mother's passionate answer. "Is that what you and Daddy have?"

"Yes it is. We knew each other as friends a long time before we fell in love."

"Is that why you let him make all the decisions around here?"

"What do you mean?"

"Is that why you don't say anything when he makes decisions…about what happens to me?"

"No, Beth. He's your father and he feels strongly about how you should be raised."

"And you don't have an opinion?"

Mary was startled. "Of course I do. But your father believes it's his duty to make the rules."

Beth was flustered at Mary's answers. "That doesn't make sense! Especially if you both supposedly care about what each other thinks."

Mary was taken aback by how the conversation strayed to this subject. "Beth, it's hard to explain. It's just more complicated than you realize."

Beth cringed as she remembered those last words. It seemed to be the only answer her mother came up with whenever they talked about her problems from then on. *Life is more complicated than you realize!* It was what her mom told her when she came to her totally devastated when David abandoned her and her father believed his family's accusations regarding her pregancy. It was an answer that answered nothing! It did not give a real reason why others reacted as they did and it was not consoling at all. Beth wanted to be consoled. She wanted to be believed and supported. She wanted her mother to stand up for her!

The last thought was so gripping that it made her whole body flinch and brought her back to the present where she saw clumps of dried brown grass strewn around a one foot hole that she had made on each side of where she was sitting.

"You're right mother…life *is* more complicated than I ever imagined. But why? First Daddy abandons me, then David, then Brandon…No! Don't even go there Beth!" She thought to herself, but she couldn't help it. She had not let herself think about him for a long time. "Brandon, why?" she said outloud. "Why did you have to go and prove my mother right?" Tears began to roll down her cheek as she remembered thinking that nothing in her life could ever get worse than losing Brandon, but she was wrong. "Maybe this is all my life will ever be like. The only love I can count on is from Emmy and look how complicated I've made that now!" Beth whispered to herself. She decided she had had enough of gardening and memories for one day, so she gathered up the clumps of grass to throw away and went into the house to take a nap. She felt a fiery headache coming on.

The dinner routine that night was the same. Father Pat and Mrs. McCafferty tried to subtly engage Beth in conversation. Beth skirted the issues long enough to finish dinner. She felt bad that she had to treat them in such a way, but her mind was made up. She did not tell them about her plans either. When she excused herself, she went upstairs to make her two important calls. Matt was already waiting at Father Pat's bedroom window.

First she called Karen, who had all the information for her trip. The bus would leave on Monday morning at eleven o'clock sharp. A two-way ticket cost three hundred and twenty five dollars. It would take four days and require two transfers. Karen checked out airfare and it would be over a thousand dollars on such short notice. Beth had no choice but to ride the bus. That left her with just enough money for food and expenses for the four-day trip. Beth would leave the rectory Sunday morning while Father Pat and Mrs. McCafferty were at church. She would leave them a good bye note that thanked them and apologized for the way she had to go, but she would not tell them exactly where she was going. Sunday she would spend at her family's house. She would tell her parents about her transfer and future plans. Beth had only taken about half her belongings to Rachel's apartment, so she would have enough clothes to take with her. She decided it was best not to get her things from Rachel's apartment. There was nothing there that couldn't be replaced and she wanted to avoid seeing or speaking to Rachel completely. God forbid, the guys might still hang out there. As for work, she would call Mr. Manley's voice mail on Monday morning while he was in his management meeting and leave a message that she would not be coming back. Beth felt horrible for having to treat him this way, after he showed so much concern for her; but she felt she had no choice. On Monday, she could stop at the bank and close her account before leaving. She couldn't think of a way to get her car from Rachel's yet, but she'd think about that later.

Karen told Beth that she had several pages of classified ads waiting for her when she arrived. Beth would get a job and come back to get Emmy. It was a perfect plan. When Beth hung up the phone, she assured herself that she was not running away, but starting a new life. It bothered her for a moment that she would even have to do that. She placed a quick call to Emmy and told her that she could not wait to see her on Sunday. Emmy was excited, too.

Matt returned to the oak tree out front. He sat there for hours until the stars began to appear in the darkened sky. His heart grew heavy as he remembered Beth's conversation with Karen. Now he realized he only had Saturday to contact Beth and convince her not to leave. He knew the cat would again be close to her and he would probably have one shot to make this work. There must be a way to outsmart the tabby. Matt gathered together the pros and cons of the situation. He knew he was faster than the cat. That was one for the pros. He also knew the cat was determined to get him and would stay alert. That was one for the cons. Beth was almost finished with the weeding, that was another con. He tried to think of another pro but went blank. "It really doesn't matter how many cons, I come up with." he thought, "I don't have a choice at this point. I'm either going to get squashed again by that ugly beast or get Beth's attention long enough to speak with her. Since there is no guarantee she'll even believe what she's hearing, it doesn't matter."

He thought about what Enon told to him would happen, if she went off to California. Something about if she ran away, she would never come back. It didn't make sense to him, knowing now how much Emmy meant to Beth. He wished he had asked Enon what he meant by that statement. Matt grew more determined than ever. "I am the only one who can save her now. I won't let a flea bitten furball keep me from helping Beth!" As he said these words to himself he remembered Anjella's counsel just before he came to Earth the second time, "Remember, everything is possible in God's world and you are a part of that world." Matt began to feel stronger. He knew she was right. How he missed her loving support. She always knew exactly what to say to give him inspiration and courage. He looked up into the night sky that was filled with hundreds of shining stars and imagined her beautiful face smiling down on him. For a moment, he thought he saw a star winking at him. He knew Anjella was there and he thanked her and winked back. He closed his eyes, hoping that his dreams would give him some answers to help him tomorrow.

♥♥♥♥♥♥♥

Matt woke Saturday morning hardly rested. Rain was falling steadily and promised to continue for a long time. Nothing could be worse at this moment, he thought. Beth would not be working in the back yard today. His mission was inevitably failing him. Tomorrow morning she would be leaving the rectory for good. He couldn't speak to Father Pat to warn him and even if he could, Father Pat could not keep her against her will. Now, he would surely have only one chance left to stop her. How could he convince her in one moment to abandon her plans, when he knew she was determined to leave everything that had caused her pain behind to start a new life? How was he going to outsmart the cat? It looked hopeless.

To make matters worse, he had hoped Anjella or Enon could send him some guidance during his dreams that could tell him a way to outsmart the cat, but instead, he spent the entire night dreaming the same dream over and over, probably ten times. The scene of his second attempt to contact Beth played out in exact detail. He watched himself fly to Beth's right side by the house. Beth tilted her head up towards him for just a second before looking quickly in the other direction. He saw the trash can lid fall to the bottom of the can with a crashing sound at the same time. The cat came out from behind the clattering can and ran past Beth. The cat sprang through the air toward him. It ended the same way every time with him flying over to the fence and up to the wires. He replayed the scene through his mind as he flew to the lily patch up the street. "Maybe there was a message in the dream. But what?" He thought.

Matt flew back to the kitchen window just in time to hear Mrs. McCafferty and Father Pat speak to Beth. Beth was in an exceptionally good mood this morning. She asked Father Pat what time the mass was tomorrow. He told her that a visiting priest said the eight o'clock mass on Sunday morning and he said the ten o'clock mass, but there was also a mass at five o'clock on Saturday evening. She asked if Mrs. McCafferty would be attending his mass. They both looked at each other for a second and then at Beth. Father asked, "Were you thinking about coming to mass tomorrow?" He was delighted at the thought.

"No," Beth said politely, "I just wanted to make sure Mrs. McC didn't miss mass on my account. I know she didn't go last week because of me, but I am feeling fine now." Mrs. McCafferty smiled at Beth's concern.

"Well, that is very considerate of you. I was planning to attend the ten o'clock mass already. You're surely capable of looking after yourself now. Since you brought up the subject, I usually do not cook breakfast until after the service. There's always fresh fruit to hold you over until then. Is that alright with you?"

Beth smiled, "That's perfect." And she added, "Oh, by the way, I think I will visit Emmy tomorrow afternoon and probably stay for dinner."

Father Pat and Mrs. McCafferty were both very pleased at the news. Father finished a sip of coffee and then put his hand on Beth's, "I think that is a great idea. Will you be coming back here for the night?"

"I don't know, Father, I'll have to see how it goes." Beth felt bad telling a half lie. Of course, she knew she would never be coming back.

Father Pat asked her if he could give her a ride to her folks after brunch. Beth felt obliged to go along and say yes. By the time they got back from church, she would be gone. She never gave them her parent's address and they probably wouldn't try contacting her there anyway. Her letter would lead them to believe she was leaving town immediately.

Beth helped Mrs. McCafferty clear the breakfast table and returned to her room. She wrote her goodbye letter and tucked it into her pillowcase when she was done. She made her bed and went into the living room to read. The cat jumped into her lap and slept contentedly while she stroked his back. Mrs. McCafferty had fallen for the orphan already and Beth decided the rectory would be a great home for the little guy. It made her feel like she was leaving a little reminder of herself with them. It was all she had to give. The hours went by slowly the rest of the day. Beth napped that afternoon and listened to the steady beat of the rain as she daydreamed of her new life in California with Emmy.

Matt spent the rest of the day between the front and the back yards of the rectory. He was determined to come up with a plan for tomorrow morning. He wasn't sure which door Beth would use to leave. He had a hunch it would be the back door. He figured that by leaving through the front door, it might draw attention from someone. In either case, he had to be prepared and needed a plan to divert the cat. If she decided to leave through the front door, there was no railing on the front porch or anything high enough for the cat to use to leap from. This would be the ideal setting for Matt to grab Beth's attention. He could hover at Beth's eye level and could respond to the cat's attacks much easier. But the backyard would be much more difficult. It was filled with items for the cat to use, especially the steps, the flowerbeds and the trash can. Matt studied the back door for hours. He went over the dream in his head a hundred times. He hoped the dream was telling him something. He looked at the steps, the trash can and the flowerbed again. He began to say the words out loud over and over, "Steps, trash can, flowerbed. Steps, trash can, flowerbed." Finally the light bulb went off in his head. "Of course!" he exclaimed, "It could work, it could work!" Matt was excited. He finally understood what the dream was telling him. By now he was soaking wet, but he surveyed the area over and over again to make sure his idea would work.

When Matt went to sleep that night he was exhausted but ready for tomorrow morning. Before he closed his eyes, he thought to himself, "Cat, get ready, the mouse has come out to play!"

Chapter 13

Everyone rose early on Sunday morning. Matt was awake at sunrise and spent the first hour of the day eating as much nectar as he could possibly find. Father Pat left about seven o'clock for his morning walk. Beth was up by six thirty, but lay in bed nervously thinking about the day ahead of her. Mrs. McCafferty rose with the birds, as usual, and made a special fruit salad for everyone to munch on before church.

Father Pat returned from his walk to find the women dressed and eating fruit salad at the kitchen table. Beth tried not to appear nervous as she struck up a conversation. She was anxious for them to leave so she could be on her way. It was difficult deceiving such wonderful people. She wouldn't blame them if they hated her for what she was about to do. She knew they never would, though. They were far too forgiving and understanding for that. Rather, they would probably be heartbroken instead. She decided she would write to them when she settled in California and tell them how great her life was going. When she returned to get Emmy, she would visit with them. Beth was sure they would be happy for her when they saw how well she was doing.

Father Pat picked up on Beth's nervousness. He noticed that she flipped her hair behind her left ear often, just like she did the day she told him about her terrible experience. He figured she was anxious about the meeting with her parents. "Beth, you look nervous. Are you worried about this afternoon?"

Beth stammered as she flipped her hair again. "Well yes, a little. I'm not sure what I'm going to say to my dad. It is a little nerve wracking, I guess."

Father Pat reassured her, "Relax and just be yourself. It's not going to be easy and all the answers won't come right away. Just take it step by step. And remember, if you need me or Mrs. McC, we would be happy to help in any way we can. We are just so pleased to see you taking this first step on your own. You're doing the right thing, my child." After he placed his coffee cup down on the saucer, he reached over and gently squeezed her shoulder and added, "I think a special blessing always helps in these cases." He bowed his head and began to pray, "Father, thank you for bringing Beth into our lives. She is a fine young lady with wonderful courage like your son, Jesus. Bless her as she returns home this afternoon. Bring to her the words that will help heal the wounds between her and her father. May you send an angel to guide her always. For this we pray, amen."

Beth was overwhelmed with tears. His prayer not only touched her heart but also slowly twisted a knife of guilt that lay deep in her soul. She wiped her eyes and thanked him for the beautiful blessing, before excusing herself. This was going to be the most difficult thing she had ever done. She felt confused and selfish and guilty about leaving. It wasn't supposed to feel like this, she thought to herself. I need to go to California and start my life over again. There is nothing left for me here. When she reached the second floor, she ran to her room and threw herself on the bed, trying to muffle her sobs. Mrs. McCafferty and Father Pat wondered why she took the blessing so emotionally. They knew she had been under incredible strain. Maybe it was time to bring up formal counseling, Father Pat thought. He would speak to her about it after church. It was almost nine forty-five. Father Pat rose to prepare for mass. At nine fifty, Mrs. McCafferty yelled up the steps to Beth that they were leaving. Beth watched them walk across the street from the bathroom window. They cheerfully greeted their friends at the church entrance and proceeded inside.

Beth swallowed hard and went to the sink to splash water on her face. Her face was blotchy and her eyes were puffy. She decided to wait ten minutes before leaving. She wanted to be sure the mass was well underway and everyone was inside. The tabby was lying on Beth's bed and he stretched when he saw Beth come back in. He watched her remove the note from inside the pillow and place it in the center of the pillow after she made the bed. She sat on the edge of the bed and scratched the cat's back for a few minutes. "Well, tabby, it's time to go. I guess I should leave you outside until Mrs. McC comes back. Now you take good care of Mrs. McC, you hear? She needs someone to fuss over and I think you will do just fine." Beth picked up the cat and left the bedroom. She looked around at the room she had grown so comfortable in. When she left, she decided to leave the door open so they would see the note more easily. There was nothing to take with her. She had nothing with her when she arrived but the clothes on her back and a small purse. That was all that she would leave with. The clothes Mrs. McC had bought for her were neatly folded on the chair in the corner of the room.

Beth went downstairs, clutching the cat to her chest and fighting back more tears. When she reached the bottom step, she looked around the living room and at the front door. "Come on tabby, I guess we should go out the back way!" Beth headed for the kitchen with the cat.

Matt was in a frenzy trying to keep up with her. He raced from window to window, making sure she did not slip from his sight. When Beth stepped onto the first floor and looked at the front door, Matt held his breath, hoping she would leave that way. But when he heard her tell the cat she should leave by the back door, he raced ahead of them and sat on the fence until they came out. Matt surveyed the area one more time, hoping everything would work as he had planned.

Beth opened the back door with the cat in her arms and stepped out onto the landing. She put the cat down beside her and put a hand on each hip to think for a second. She leaned over and scratched the cat's head and told him to wait there for a moment. Beth reopened the door and stepped into the kitchen leaving the cat behind. The morning was already hot and she had at least two hours of walking to do. Beth decided to find a container to bring some water with her for the long walk ahead. The abandoned feline seemed annoyed and began swishing its tail back and forth in an aggravated fashion.

Matt held his breath before taking flight. He knew this was the perfect moment to get the cat out of his way. Every move must be timed perfectly in order for this to work. First, he flew high above the back steps chirping all the way and swooped down in front of the cat to get its attention. Matt stayed about four feet out of the cat's reach and headed back up into the air and hovered in the middle of the yard.

The tabby was delighted to see his nemesis return and hunched down into an attack position. Matt saw the cat's back paws moving in a steady pace just like the last attack and knew he had a few seconds before the cat would begin his approach. Quickly, he flew straight at the cat and veered off to the right, hovering vertically about five feet over the trash can that leaned up against the steps. The cat's back paws quickened and his tail slashed through the air. His ears went back flat against his head and his eyes narrowed into black slits as he calculated his timing against his winged prey.

Matt moved slightly closer and a few feet higher, hovering about five feet above the top railing. This forced the tabby to look straight up into the bright sun that silhouetted Matt's body, making it hard to judge how far away the little bird really was. Matt glared back at the mangy critter and taunted him further, "Here kitty, kitty!" The enraged cat hunkered down on its hind legs and sprang up onto the railing, then off the railing five feet straight up into the air at the little hummingbird. Matt zoomed two feet higher as the cat's paws stretched up into the sun at him, slashing through the air. He missed Matt by at least one and a half feet and began his descent. Matt held his breath and his heart raced while he watched to see if his own calculations were correct. One inch off and his plan would be foiled. The cat looked down toward the ground and realized where he was headed. Matt felt a wave of excitement fill his entire body as he saw the tabby land on the gingerly placed trash can lid. The cat was far enough to the right side to cause the lid to flip over and deposit the furball neatly at the bottom of the can. The lid kindly followed the tabby into the trash can, hitting the cat's head just hard enough to daze the poor thing for a while.

Matt did not anticipate the cat being harmed by the trash can lid and cautiously swooped down to check on his condition. He landed on the edge of the can and watched the cat's tail move slowly back and forth underneath the lid. The cat was alright and Matt flew over to the lilac bush to check in on Beth, hoping she didn't decide to go out the front door.

Beth was inside filling an empty soda bottle with cold water. When she was finished, she grabbed a banana off the counter. She placed the fruit into her small shoulder bag and turned toward the door. She didn't seem to notice the ruckus outside. Matt's excitement about the victory over the cat diminished as he saw Beth walk to the door. He never really finalized what he would do to get Beth's attention and he now froze in fear, as he watched the kitchen door open and Beth step out on the landing. She looked around for the cat without noticing the trash can and shrugged to herself. "How do you like that? I didn't even get to say a real goodbye to the little guy". Beth turned and took one more look at the house, feeling awful about how she was leaving and then started down the stairs.

Something jolted Matt back to his senses. He left the lilac bush and slowly flew over to Beth. Beth. heard the buzzing sound around her and walked toward the middle of the yard. She had planned to go behind the trees and follow the farmer's field down a few houses before cutting through to get back on to Main Street out of view of the church and the rectory. Matt followed behind for a few steps and then flew around her a little more than an arm's length to her right. Beth was looking down at the ground and swished at the buzzing noise without looking. Matt easily avoided her flailing hand and moved a little higher and straight ahead of her. He swallowed hard and began to talk in a hoarse voice. "Heh, Beth stop for a moment."

Beth slowed down and surveyed the area. There appeared to be no one around. She was sure she heard a male voice say her name and turned toward the house. Everything was quiet and so she shrugged her shoulders and continued on. Her nerves were beginning to get the best of her, she thought.

Matt realized he was so nervous that his own voice sounded as quiet as a mouse. Beth was almost across the yard and he decided to take stronger action this time. He swooped down to greet her at eye level and was about to speak when Beth swatted at him with her right hand and told the bug to leave her alone. Beth never did like bees and was a little scared of them. Matt dodged her hand and renewed his approach. This time he was able to get into her sight, but she still swatted at him without really looking at her intruder. She brushed at Matt's wing almost sending him tumbling through the air. Matt began to grow a little aggravated at the situation. He let her get ahead of him by about a foot and then yelled at the top of his voice, "Heh, Beth! Stop!"

Beth froze in her tracks. The voice was loud enough to be someone standing right behind her. She was sure it wasn't Father Pat's voice. There wasn't anyone else in this area that would know her. She looked to her left and then to her right but no one was there. She cautiously turned around expecting to see someone standing in the yard, but the yard was empty. "It must be the stress I'm under," she thought to herself. But when she turned to continue on, the voice yelled out again. "Turn around, Beth, I'm right behind you."

Beth turned looking back toward the house and stared at the empty yard. Slowly Matt dropped back down to eye level about five feet away. He was so small she almost did not see him against the bright sunlight, but heard the buzzing of his wings. Matt spoke a little more quietly this time. "Beth, don't be afraid, I won't hurt you, I'm not a bug."

Beth dropped her soda bottle and it rolled a few feet away. She looked at Matt for a minute and squinted her eyes to see better against the sun. The hummingbird moved another foot closer and hovered in silence. Beth put her hand over her eyebrows to shield the sun and saw a hummingbird. She had never been so close to one before, but recognized it instantly. Her eyes began to tear from the glare of the sun, causing her vision to blur. "I see a hummingbird in front of me, but I can't see you whoever you are!" Beth was amazed that the little bird remained so close to her.

"I *am* the hummingbird!" Matt assured her. His assurance was not what she wanted to hear.

"A hummingbird," Beth exclaimed, "You mean I'm talking to a bird?"

"Yes, you are," Matt laughed softly, "I can hardly believe it myself." He hoped that might help her see the humor in the situation.

Beth put her hands on her cheeks in amazement. She began to feel lightheaded. "Oh, I don't believe this, it can't be!" She thought she might be suffering from after-effects of the drug she was given at the party. She turned toward the farm field, picked up her bottle and started walking away, determined to leave as planned.

Matt raced ahead of her, staying clear out of reach, "Beth, wait, we have to talk!" He continued to hover backwards staying ahead of her. "I know this is a bit unbelievable, but you can't go to California! We have to talk!"

Beth kept walking. She hoped that if she ignored the bird it would just disappear like a bad dream, but when she heard it speak about California it halted her in her tracks. "How do you know about California? No one except my best friend knows about that."

187

Matt took a deep breath; this was the perfect opportunity to convince her to listen. "It's a long story Beth, but I have been listening at your window for the last week since you got here. I was sent by God to help you."

"God sent a hummingbird to help me?" Beth could hardly believe the irony of the situation. For the first time in her life she really could use God's intervention and to think He would send her a hummingbird! Beth continued walking to the end of the yard, determined to ignore this hallucination.

Matt scrambled to stay ahead of her. It was difficult to hover and fly backwards at the same time. It took a lot more concentration than he could give it at this moment. "Yes! I mean no. God didn't send you a hummingbird, he sent me. I mean, I was supposed to come down and enter Father Pat's body to help you, but I screwed up the timing and accidentally went into a hummingbird's body." Matt was flying erratically as he became breathless.

Beth stopped and stared at the little bird that was flitting about. The beautiful little bird looked normal except for the eyes. When she made eye contact, it felt as if she was looking into human eyes. The two of them remained deeply connected and speechless. This can't be, she thought to herself. The little bird moved closer until there was only two feet between them. He began to speak and Beth saw his long slender beak move with his words. She felt like she was in some kind of animated dream state and shook her head to wake up but the bird remained hovering before her. She closed her eyes and opened them again and he was still there—hallucinating was the last straw. Beth felt her knees give out and she crumpled to the ground. Matt lowered his body down to her eye level again.

"I know this is difficult, Beth, after all you have been through, but I really have come to help." Being in an altered state, as it were, he felt deep, mysterious feelings inside when they made eye contact that rendered him speechless for a moment. It was as if her spirit connected with his on a deeper level. He hoped this would help him convince her to stay.

Beth regained her wits and said to Matt, "So, God sent me a screw-up angel or whatever you are to help me out. That doesn't make me feel any better." She was nervously flipping her hair.

"No, Beth, I am not a screw-up angel, I am a screw-up human." Matt knew he didn't have time to explain everything right now. "I was alive on Earth till recently and got killed in a motorcycle accident. When I got to Heaven there was this life review in front of this council of Elders and, well, to make a long story short, they told me I had to come back and start over. Only, I didn't want to live another lifetime over again. You see Heaven is this amazing place and I didn't want to leave it. So I asked them if there was some way I could prove to them that I had learned my lesson and could stay in Heaven. They told me that if I saved a soul on Earth, I could return to Heaven forever. So, I got assigned to you. And, well, I know I made a few mistakes getting here, but I'm sure I can help you." Matt knew he sounded like he was babbling and wasn't sure he convinced even himself with that story.

"Oh, so what was the big lesson you needed to learn?" Beth couldn't believe she was carrying on a conversation with a little two-inch bird.

"My lesson was the meaning of true love."

"And so you're an expert at that now and can help me with my problems, right? What does this have to do with my problems?"

"Your problem is that you need to learn the same lesson, I mean about true love." Matt was getting tired, "Do you mind if I set down on your knee for a moment? I won't hurt you."

Beth laughed as she tried to clear her head that was beginning to ache. "Sure, what the heck! But I don't have all day. I have to leave before church is out."

"No, Beth, please don't leave. Just give me a few minutes of your time and hear me out." Matt gently landed on the top of her left knee. "Look, I know things haven't been going that well for you here, but from what I've been told, you shouldn't go to California."

"Why not?" Beth was curious. She was beginning to question her decision again.

"I don't know the specifics, just that you won't come back here if you do."

Now Beth was irritated. Here was a bird sitting on her knee, supposedly sent by God to help her but he could only tell her that if she goes to California that she wouldn't come back. "That's impossible!" Now she was growing more skeptical. "And tell me what is here for me if I stay?"

"Well for starters, Emmy. And don't forget your family and a safe place to live."

"Oh, so God wants me to go back to my parents and live with a father who doesn't even like me much less trust me and probably will never love me."

"No, it's not that way at all! God wants you to go back to your father and help him discover the true meaning of love, too." Matt buzzed into the air back to eye level with Beth. He really wanted to convince her to stay. "I know it doesn't make sense right now, but you've got to believe me. I was a lot like your father before I died. My father tried to reach me so many times and I wouldn't listen. It's a long story, but my father gave up on me, just like you're giving up on your father. Then one day he discovered he had made some decision early in life that allowed our family's relationship to fall apart. He didn't do anything wrong at that time, he just thought what he was doing was in everyone's best interest. When he decided that family was more important and tried again, I screwed up and got myself killed. If I had not been so selfish, we would be together right now and everyone would be happier than they ever could imagine. I don't know what has caused your father to mistrust you so much, but I know it's not your fault. Maybe if you go back and try again, something will happen this time that will open your father's eyes."

Matt landed back on Beth's left knee. He looked pleadingly into her eyes. "Beth, what's the worst that can happen if you fail again? You can go to California as you planned, but maybe you will be able to take Emmy with you, instead of running away and hoping to come up with a plan to bring Emmy out to California with you. How easy do you think that will be when you get out there? Even if you get a job right away, how long will it take for you to save enough money to come back for Emmy? What if it's too expensive to live out there? What if you can't get time off right away to come get her? At least, at your parent's home you will have time to think through your decision."

Beth's headache pounded at her temples. She rubbed them to try to ease the pain. She had already thought about these questions, but had chosen to push them out of her mind. She decided that her plan would just have to work. She would *make* it work. But now she wondered if the little bird was right. Could she be asking for more trouble? She shook her head and pondered everything that was happening. Time was running out. Father Pat would be back from church soon. She needed to leave now, before it was too late. She began to weep softly into her hands. Matt sat quietly on her knee. He didn't know what else to say. He just hoped and prayed he said enough. He looked into the sky in desperation, hoping Enon and Anjella would give him a clue. There was no special sign this morning. He felt very alone and helpless.

Beth straightened up and wiped her eyes. Her stomach turned over and her heart was pounding. She wondered again why her life had gotten so complicated. It seemed like she went from one heartache to another during the last five years. She looked down at the hummingbird through blurring eyes and tried to focus. How could this little creature or person or whatever it was supposed to be, help her regain her father's love?

"How are you going to help me, little bird?" Her voice sounded tired. "Do you have some heavenly plan?"

Matt grew nervous as he contemplated his answer. This could be the turning point in her decision, but if he lied and told her he had a plan, he could risk losing her trust. She had been let down my so many people in her life. He didn't want to be included in that list. If he told her the truth, she may still leave, because he could not give her a real solution. He decided to trust his instincts and go with honesty.

"Beth, I don't have a plan. I wish I did. I had a hard enough time figuring out how to dodge the cat all week. I think you just have to go home and be honest with your father and mother and take it one step at a time. I'm not sure how much help I can offer. But I will be there to support you. You have to do this on your own. It's the only way you are going to find real peace. Maybe together we can figure out what is behind your father's behavior. The one thing I have learned is that we are really blind to the sufferings of the people around us. I couldn't believe how much hardship my father endured when I rejected him while growing up. I caused a lot of pain and I didn't even notice it because I was too busy feeling sorry for myself. Now, I don't know if this goes for you, too, but isn't it worth one more shot? Wouldn't you like it better if you could stay close to your family? I guess you have to ask yourself honestly, why are you really going to California? Are you running away or trying to start a new life? If you are trying to start a new life, why can't that be with your own family?" Matt lowered his head and waited for Beth's answer. He felt like his own life hung in the balance. If she got up and walked away, he would know he failed and would probably be pulled back into Heaven and placed before the council in a flash.

Beth sat and rocked back and forth for a long time. Matt decided to give her some space and flew over to a clay pot that was turned over on its side by the poplar trees. He watched her rock. Tears were running down her face. Church would be out in a few minutes. It seemed like everything in the yard grew intensely silent. There was no wind, or rustling trees or buzzing flies or bees. Matt's breath caught in his throat as he watched Beth rise from the ground and brush off the grass from her denim skirt. She looked ahead to the farm field for a moment and then turned and looked back at the rectory. She picked up the soda bottle and opened it for a drink. When she glanced over at Matt, she smiled.

"So what did you do to the cat, little bird?" Beth turned back to the rectory and walked toward the steps. Matt jumped off the clay pot and buzzed over to Beth's right side. He told her what happened as they wandered toward the trash can. She tried to picture the tabby being outsmarted by a little bird, and laughed. Matt assured her the cat was alright and flew onto a branch of the lilac bush while Beth retrieved the dazed cat. She checked him over and he began to stir in her arms. There were no cuts or lumps; he just appeared sleepy. Beth sat on the steps and pet the cat's head while he came to. She would have to watch him closely for a concussion. She rocked the cat on the back stairs waiting for Father Pat to come home. She felt more unnerved now than she ever did before and wondered what the old priest would say. She hoped that this new development wouldn't cause more problems in her life than she already had. Beth looked over at the hummingbird and smiled. Life was about to get even crazier, she was sure.

Chapter 14

Father Pat and Mrs. McCafferty walked in the front door of the rectory after mass. The day promised to be another scorcher and Mrs. McCafferty went upstairs to put on a lighter dress. Father Pat took off his hat and placed it on a hook by the door. As he went into the kitchen and poured himself a glass of ice tea, he heard Beth's voice out back and went over to the window to see whom she was talking to.

To his surprise he saw no one in the area except Beth. She was sitting on the step rocking with the cat on her lap. At first he thought she was probably talking to the tabby, but it sounded more like a two-way conversation. He listened more intently to her words. It sounded like she had been crying as she sniffled between sentences. Her hands waved in the air occasionally. Father scanned the backyard, but still no one was in sight.

Mrs. McCafferty came bursting into the kitchen. Her face was white as a ghost and she could hardly speak. "Beth's gone, Father, she's gone. Here is a note she left for us. It sounds as if she has gone to see that best friend of hers. Oh Lord be with her!"

Father Pat held his hand up to quiet her. He took the note from her and signaled her not to speak. He pointed to the back steps and Mrs. McCafferty bent down to see out the window. She saw Beth rocking on the steps with the cat and let out a great sigh of relief. "Thank God!" She whispered as she wiped the tears from her eyes and turned back to Father Pat. "I wonder what made her change her mind?"

Father Pat finished reading the note and looked out at Beth again. "I'm not sure Mrs. McC, but I am worried about her. When I came into the kitchen she appeared to be talking to herself. She was even waving her hands in the air. We obviously misread Beth this morning and I hope we haven't overlooked signs of a breakdown. It's hard to say how long a person can hide their stress. I thought Beth was doing quite well." He looked at Mrs. McCafferty and gave her hand a squeeze. "Maybe we're getting too old for this type of work!"

"Nonsense Father," Mrs. McCafferty continued to look out the window, "You're never too old to save a wandering soul!" She smiled and poured herself a glass of tea. "So, should one of us see if she is alright?"

Father Pat frowned, "I'm not sure. Let's make a little noise and see if she notices we're here."

Mrs. McCafferty pulled a large skillet from the cabinet and clanked it onto the stove. She began to speak a little louder than necessary and Father

Pat chuckled as she practically yelled at him, "So, how do you want your eggs today, Father?"

Father Pat could hardly keep a straight face as he responded in his normal tone, "Anyway you would like to prepare them."

Beth heard the commotion in the kitchen. She looked at Matt closely one more time, trying to convince herself that this was real and not some dream. They had been talking mostly about Heaven. Matt told her more details of his experience and Beth was in total shock. She never thought much about the afterlife. Her family wasn't religious. She never contemplated having a Creator, or Heaven or angels. She was raised to focus on life as it was, which was very hard. You lived day to day and made the best of it. It was hard to dream of a future on Earth, much less in Heaven.

She placed the slightly dazed cat down on the landing and whispered softly to Matt, "So what do you think I should tell them?"

Matt smiled to himself. He was the last one to give such advice from his past experience but he knew it was true. "Tell them the truth."

"What if they think I'm crazy?"

"With their faith in God, I don't think that either of them will disbelieve you."

"Can I show you to them?" Beth knew that would be the easiest way to prove her story.

Matt wasn't certain that it was a good idea. "No, not yet anyway. No one can hear me but you. The most you can do is show them a trained hummingbird. Go talk to Father Pat and let me know what you're going to do. I will be in the front oak tree." Matt added one more thing before Beth left. "Oh, by the way, it will help a lot if you keep the cat inside when you plan on seeing me. I don't think I'm going to get another chance to fool it!"

Beth smiled. "Okay, I'll try to remember."

"Don't worry," Matt said, "I'll remind you!" Matt watched Beth straighten her clothes and wiped her eyes before she opened the kitchen door. As soon as she was inside, he flew away to find his long overdue lunch. He suddenly felt very tired.

Beth walked into the kitchen and startled Mrs. McCafferty. It was more a case of nerves for Mrs. McCafferty than anything else. She wasn't good at pretending. "Oh Beth, dear, there you are! I was just starting breakfast. I thought I'd make fried potatoes and scrambled eggs, is that okay with you?"

Beth could tell Mrs. McCafferty was nervous. She suddenly remembered the note she left on the pillow. Mrs. McCafferty looked like she had been crying. Beth wondered if her father or mother had shed any tears when she left them. She gave Mrs. McCafferty an unexpected hug. "Anything you fix is just fine!"

Mrs. McCafferty blushed. "Oh don't let me get you all greasy with my hands. Why don't you go in and freshen up before lunch?" She knew Father Pat was waiting for Beth in the living room.

Beth agreed and headed for the second floor. Father Pat was sitting in the rocking chair when she walked into the living room. He smiled and sat up on the edge of his seat. "Beth, can I talk to you for a moment?"

Beth saw by the look in his eyes that he already knew. She glanced at the small table beside the rocker and saw her note. It was a relief that she didn't have to find a way to bring it up to him. She sat on the sofa on the end closest to the rocker.

Father Pat nodded toward the note, as he began to speak, "We were glad to see you had a change of heart this morning. We would have hated to see you run off without a real goodbye. Do you want to tell me why you didn't leave as planned? I am sorry if I didn't realize you were more upset than you seemed. Maybe we should have had this talk earlier."

"It's not your fault Father, really." Beth began to flip her hair as she explained. "I'm just really tired of trying anymore. Life seems like one big problem. I wanted to leave and get a fresh start somewhere new. There are so many bad memories for me here. I didn't see and maybe I still don't see why I have to deal with them. I just want to forget the last three months ever happened. And, as for my father, well, I think I have tried enough. I mean I wouldn't be the first child that wasn't close to a parent during their life. Is there some rule that says I have to keep trying when my father doesn't want to try himself? I guess I just thought it would be easier to remove myself from the situation for good. It seemed like the best solution for everyone." Beth folded her hands in her lap and lowered her head like a child waiting for her reprimand.

Father Pat was curious. She had a good argument. It was true. You could have a productive life and an estranged relationship with a parent. But Beth had several issues to deal with before she could make her life productive. She had to deal with the rape. No one can bury that type of experience forever. It was bound to affect her life as she grew older. And then there was being an unwed mother. Society still looked down in many ways on women who found themselves in this situation. And there was the issue of trusting men. So far Beth had four or five men who had injured her emotionally. At least two of them had also harmed her physically. Beth would find it difficult to trust any man in the future without resolving these past experiences. Right now, all she wanted was some peace in her life and who could blame her? But you don't find peace when you bury or run from your problems. Father knew you could only find peace when you face your problems head on and forgive yourself and everyone involved. "So what made you change your mind and stay?" He finally asked her.

Beth knew this question was going to be a tough one. She smiled to herself when she thought about her answer. She placed her face in her hands and began to rub her temples. They still throbbed slightly from the headache. She decided to tell him the truth. If he thought she was crazy, then she would leave and continue with her original plan. She knew that with all the anguish she could be facing by returning home that she needed his support. Hummingbird or no hummingbird, she could not go through this alone.

"Well, Father, you may not believe this." She stood up and paced the floor while wringing her hands together. "I had every intention of leaving this morning. I got as far as the backyard." Beth proceeded to tell her incredible story about meeting the little hummingbird. She glanced over at Father Pat who sat motionless, listening intently to her every word. When she told him the part about finding the cat in the trash can, he even laughed. At best it made the story a little more plausible. It was a good chuckle that set her more at ease. Beth sat back down and rubbed her eyes. She looked over at him as she concluded her story. "So I decided not to leave until I could either make sense of this or confirm that I'm going insane. I sat down on the steps and the hummingbird began to tell me about what he saw in Heaven. If what he says is true, I don't blame him for trying to stay there." She looked up at Father who stroked his chin quizzically. "So Father, am I crazy or could God be talking to me through a hummingbird?"

Father Pat sat back in the rocker and scratched his head with his right hand. He thought about everything he had heard and looked over at Beth. She sat back down on the sofa with the look of anticipation of a child waiting by the radio to hear if there was a snow day before school. If the radio said yes, she would be jumping for joy, but if it said no, she would be devastated by the news. It was his turn to stand and pace for a while.

"Beth," he began, "I want to tell you a story that I have never shared with another soul. But I think you will appreciate it. I was a chaplain and medic during the Vietnam excursion. I saw many things that could be classified as miracles and have been commonly reported, only by word of mouth, mind you, in nearly every war fought around the world. Such as soldiers seeing angels taking the spirits of the dead into the skies and sightings of the Blessed Mother. But there was one story I witnessed that was different from those events. There was a young man named Danny whose platoon was under siege and hit hard by the Vietcong. He was in a foxhole with a buddy and shells were dropping all around them. Danny covered his buddy as he jumped out of the foxhole and moved to the next one. He was about to follow when a man in a Hawaiian print shirt and shorts appeared out of thin air next to him. The man told Danny he was his companion angel and to stay in the foxhole for five more minutes. He did and two minutes later a grenade blew up in the next hole killing his friend. When he got back to camp, he told a few of the guys and they laughed and said he was losing it. They said it was just battle fatigue. He became very embarrassed and never spoke about it again.

A few weeks later, his platoon was in the same situation again. He was alone in a foxhole and his commander signaled to advance. The angel appeared to Danny again with the same advice. This time Danny was afraid to believe him and left the hole. A bomb went off beside him and blew his right leg off. By the time I got to him, he could not be helped. He held on to me and told me what had happened. As he spoke he said that the angel was standing right behind me. He told me the angel said it was time to go. Danny asked the angel where he was going and smiled as he shook his head. Before he closed his eyes for the last time, I asked him what the angel said. "He said it's time for me to go on a vacation. You see, it has always been my dream to go to Hawaii." Father Pat stopped pacing and sat on the sofa next to Beth. She turned to him and wiped tears from her eyes that she had shed during his story.

"Beth, that experience has led me to believe that God can come to us in any form he desires, even if in your case, things weren't planned exactly to end up this way. Maybe this is the angel that I prayed would go with you to face your father. My advice to you is to take this as a very special sign from God. Who knows how many chances you will get to listen. Unlike Danny, you may only get one chance."

He pondered Beth's story for a few minutes longer and a mischievous smile crept onto his face. "Maybe you're hearing the rustling of angels!"

Beth sank back into the sofa and continued to massage her temples. "Father, I hope that you're right."

Mrs. McCafferty interrupted by announcing that lunch was ready. They went into the kitchen for lunch. As usual, everything was scrumptious. Father Pat and Beth continued their conversation, while Mrs. McCafferty sat politely silent, seemingly unperturbed by the exclusion.

Father Pat asked Beth what she was going to do now.

"I think I would like to visit Emmy today, as planned." She let them know that she had already intended to see her before leaving. "While I'm there, I will talk to my parents about coming home, but not tonight, if you don't mind." She looked at both of them for approval to return to the rectory this evening. They both insisted she stay as long as she liked. Beth continued, "If things go okay, I will go back home this week and give it a shot. But, if my father isn't willing to try and get along, I will stay only as long as it takes to save enough money to take Emmy to California." She thought for a moment and then added, "If God wants me to make amends with my father, I hope he's sent my father an angel, too. And it better be an angel with a lot of patience!" Mrs. McCafferty smiled and squeezed her hand.

When they finished lunch, Father Pat asked Beth if she still wanted a ride to her folks. Beth was grateful for the offer and accepted eagerly. Having Father Pat drop her off would give her the extra incentive to see this all the way through. She still could not believe she was going to ask her parents if she could come home. She wasn't sure she would even be able to say the words. Beth asked him to be ready by 2:00. She would call him after dinner, when she was ready to come home. Beth excused herself from the table and went outside to see the hummingbird. She made sure that the cat was in the house. The tabby was extremely annoyed by his incarceration and made it known by pacing and whining at the front door.

Beth sat down on the front porch steps and whistled for the bird. Matt zoomed down from the center of the tree and hovered about two feet away from her. "Did everything go alright?"

"Well, I think Father Pat actually believed me. He told me an interesting story that happened to him while he was in Vietnam, or do you already know this?" She chided him. "I keep forgetting you've been spying on us."

Matt blushed to himself, but, of course, it was not obvious, "No, I didn't listen in. I was busy getting my own lunch. I don't think I've told you how hard it is being a hummingbird. It's one experience I will never forget, no matter how many lifetimes I live!"

Beth continued, "Well anyway, to make a long story short, his story revealed that God sends angels in different forms and he thinks I should listen to you."

"Great!" Matt did a quick twirl in the air. "So, what is your plan for today? Are you going to visit your folks?"

"Yes, I'll be seeing them this afternoon and will probably stay for dinner. I'll be coming back here for the night. If all goes well, I will move back in sometime this week." All of a sudden, those words sounded very comforting to her.

Matt was grateful everything seemed to be moving along. He was concerned that her talk with Father Pat wouldn't turn out as well as it had. The whole day began to take its toll on him and he looked around for a bush to rest on, but the front was pretty bare by the porch. He asked Beth hesitantly, "Do you mind if I rest on your knee again? The more I hover, the more food I require and supplies around here are very limited."

Beth was amused by his politeness. "No, not at all. Go right ahead." She watched him gently lower his body down onto her knee. It was fascinating to watch this little creature move so gracefully. Beth thought it was one of the most beautiful birds she had ever seen. The tiny green feathers appeared iridescent as they glimmered in the sunlight. His rich ruby colored throat gave him a majestic look. But what fascinated Beth most of all was his tiny feet that she couldn't even feel resting on her knee. She became curious about how a human spirit fit into such a little body. "So, since you were a person before you became a bird, you must have had a name. What should I call you?"

"Oh, I'm sorry. I didn't realize I never introduced myself in all the excitement. My name is Matt Bradley."

"Matt Bradley," Beth teased, "Such a big name for a little bird! I guess I'll just call you Matt the hummingbird."

Matt opened his wings like he was throwing up his hands in the air. "Very cute. How about just calling me Matt?" They continued to banter back and forth for a few more minutes, neither realizing the bond they were creating.

"So, I heard you singing the other day while you were weeding. You have a great voice! Better than any jazz singer I have heard. I'm a big fan of jazz and the blues. Not many people our age are interested in jazz. I bet you could be famous if you sang professionally." Matt flew up to Beth's face while he talked. He began to perform shallow aerial dives, twittering at the bottom of the arch he outlined in the air. Little did he know that he was performing a male hummingbird mating display.

Beth blushed at such a compliment. For a while, she did nothing but dream about singing on stage with Ella, of course, and many of today's top performers like Dizzy Gillespie, The Yellowjackets, Special EFX, and Les McCann. "Sure I did. At one time it was all I dreamt of." Beth brought her knees up to her chest and wrapped her arms around her legs and began to rock. Matt rested on her right knee again.

"What happened?"

"Well, my father was completely opposed to me singing, even around the house. He told me I had to be more realistic about life and that show business wasn't all it was made out to be. He said that it was a hard way to make a living and corrupted most people who tried. I thought I had a pretty good voice, but he gave me the impression that I wasn't good enough to succeed."

"Good, hell, you're great! I could listen to you all night. Sing something for me now."

"Now!" Beth was really embarrassed. "I don't know, I feel funny singing out here. People will think I'm crazy if they see me."

"Can't be any crazier than sitting here talking to a hummingbird. Please...it would make me feel like I was home again." Matt twittered and spun around in the air. "Pretty please!" He continued coaxing Beth. He could see she was on the verge of smiling.

"I can't!" She exclaimed.

"Oh come on! You know you want to. By any chance do you sing scat?" Matt saw he struck a nerve with her.

"Well, yes, I can. It's my favorite."

"Then sing something. I would love to hear." Matt wore Beth down. A smile crept over her face and she began to laugh freely.

"Okay, I'll sing something! But just a short song I made up."

Beth straightened up and Matt flew down onto the top step next to her. She began singing her scat song. Matt listened to her melodious voice belting out a series of shobedodo, shobedodo, bopbops with such clear, mesmerizing notes that he began moving his tiny head to the melody. His wings began moving up and down to the beat and his tiny left foot moved back and forth like he was tapping his foot on the floor. When Beth looked down and saw the little bird bopping to her tune, she burst out laughing. Matt realized what she was laughing at and joined in. For a moment, both of them felt worlds away from their troubles and it felt really good. After their chuckles melted into relaxed thoughts, they agreed that they would meet on the porch tomorrow morning. Matt wished Beth luck and flew away to look for more food sources.

Father Pat's curiosity got the best of him and he peaked out the living room window. Beth appeared to be holding a grand conversation with the hummingbird. It was hard to see the little bird perched on her knee from his angle, but a rare glimpse allowed Father Pat to see Matt's beak moving as if he was speaking rather than chirping like a bird. He was certain it was real even though he could not hear a sound coming from the little bird. Father Pat left the window marveling at the scene he just witnessed. He went up to his room to freshen up before driving Beth to her parents, humming away. His steps were lighter and his mood a little merrier. It was wonderful, he thought, to receive the opportunity to see God's great works first hand. This experience he would surely never forget.

Beth watched Matt fly off down the street and got up to change for her visit, still stunned about the whole experience. Mrs. McC had given her a cotton shirt with sleeves down to the elbow that would cover the bruises on her arms and a pair of jeans that would cover the cut on her calf. The only bruise she couldn't cover up was the one on her face. It was greenish-yellow and too big to cover with makeup. Beth tried to think of how she could explain it away. The conversation with Matt seemed to take the edge off her nerves and she felt better about herself. "How nice of him to pay me such a great compliment about my singing," she thought. It felt good to be appreciated. Now it was time to face the one person who didn't seem to appreciate her at all.

Chapter 15

Father walked with Beth out to the front curb where the car was parked. His car was one of the few toys he had. It was a 1979 Delta 88 Oldsmobile. The car was his pride and joy and he babied it like it was a part of him. Except for a few scratches, it was in mint condition. It had a shiny copper penny exterior with cream-colored leather seats. Of course, it was a bit flamboyant for a man-of-the-cloth and certainly overstated for the sleepy town of Briarsville, but to Father Pat it was the only extravagance he could get away with in his vocational life. Mrs. McCafferty refused to drive it because its long front end made it difficult to see at intersections. The engine had been replaced several years ago and it purred like a kitten. He parked it under a large awning off the back door of the church when it rained and covered the car during snow to save the paint job. He was proud of the shape he kept it in. Beth loved the color particularly because it reminded her of how much Emmy loved new copper pennies.

The ride to Beth's house only took twenty-five minutes. She was hoping it would take longer. Father Pat tried to keep her distracted by telling her some other interesting war stories. She appreciated his efforts, but her mind was spinning with anticipation of her upcoming visit. She directed Father Pat through the back streets to her house. Beth apologized for not taking a more direct route to the house, but Father Pat was certain he could find her tonight. They pulled up in front of a small, red brick colonial house. The plantings around the yard were modest, but the lawn was a lush green color and meticulously manicured. Beth told Father the lawn had always been a hobby for her dad. Every spring he would prepare the lawn and all summer he would mow it and groom it for show. It gave him real joy.

Father Pat put the car in park and turned to Beth. He gave her the warmest smile of encouragement. "Beth, I know this is a very difficult step for you to take. But think about how you have come to this moment. You have been privileged to have someone from Heaven, God's house, bring you words of encouragement. I'm sure God just wants you to do your best and everything will fall into place. Remember to be honest with your father and mother. Tell them what is in your heart and how deeply you hurt inside because of your estranged relationship. And please remember, dear, no matter what happens today, you have Mrs. McCafferty and me and that little hummingbird of yours to come back to." He patted her knee in a grandfatherly fashion.

Beth turned to him with a slightly teary smile, "Father, thank you for everything you've done. I am so sorry for how I've acted these past few days. I don't know or fully comprehend everything that is happening to me, but I think I'm beginning to realize that going home may be the best solution. To be honest with you, I had a lot of doubts this morning when I was leaving to go to California. I'll do my best." Just then Emmy ran out the front door yelling for her mommy. "Well, there's my cue, I'll call you tonight."

She closed the car door and they exchanged smiles one more time. Father Pat drove off and Beth turned to greet her beautiful daughter who nearly tackled her with a great big hug. Beth knelt down and kissed her little girl over and over. She studied Emmy's angelic face that she had cupped between her hands. Emmy was the first to speak, "Mommy, you're home! I missed you sooo much. I have so much to tell you." She grabbed Beth's hand and began to pull her toward the front door. "Come inside. I have a big surprise for you!" Beth laughed and let her daughter drag her along the front walk. She had a much better feeling about this visit and being with Emmy renewed her resolve to change her life for the better. Emmy was worth any amount of sacrifice.

Beth and Emmy burst into the house. Only then did Beth realize she was really home. Standing in the foyer that was so familiar to her, she felt a sense of belonging to the surroundings. Emmy pulled her into the living room where her mother, Mary, sat waiting. Mary rose from her chair, a little shocked at Beth's gaunt appearance. She thought Beth looked frail and immediately noticed the bruise on her cheek. "Beth, look at you. Are you alright? What happened to your face? I didn't realize how sick you were when you called last week. I would have come and taken care of you." Mary had been having bad dreams for the last two weeks on and off. She usually had the same dream that Beth was hurt and it was dark and she was scared and calling out for her mother to help her. Mary would run through the darkness yelling Beth's name and trying to pinpoint where she was. She always woke before she found Beth. Mary could not shake this dream no matter how hard she tried. She studied the bruise closely and then put her arms around her daughter and hugged her tightly. It felt so good to both of them and they held on tight.

When they released their hug, Beth reached up and touched her tender jaw. "It was a silly accident. I slipped on the bathroom floor and came down on my knees and hit my face on the sink on the way down."

"You're lucky you didn't break your jaw! Did you see a doctor about it?"

"No Mom, I'm okay. I'm just glad to be home." Suddenly Emmy rushed in between them to separate them for attention.

"Mommy look what I have for you!" Emmy took Beth by the hand and led her to a small end table next to the sofa. There was a tiny vase filled with buttercups, which were Emmy's favorite flower, and a picture she drew for her mom. The picture was a crafty stick person drawing that showed her Grandmom and PopPop, her mom and herself standing inside a great big heart. "Do you like them Mommy?" Emmy looked up at Beth so innocently that it made her mom cry.

"Oh, Emmy, they're wonderful. I really love them. Where did you get the buttercups?"

"Grandmom and I went to the park this morning and we fed the ducks and I found a whole bunch of buttercups and dandelions and some blue flowers that I'll pick for you next time."

"Well, maybe the three of us can go together sometime and bring back a bunch." Beth tickled Emmy and made her drop to the floor. Her mother watched Beth curiously. Something was wrong with Beth, she sensed. She was different. It was so apparent to her, something only a mother could pick up. Beth always loved Emmy, that hadn't changed at all. But Beth never stayed away from Emmy as long as she had this past week. Mary wished now that she had found out earlier what was really going on. She seemed more mature and sensitive but she also looked stressed and worn. Something happened to her that wasn't good. Maybe her recent illness was worse than she let on. Mary wished she had never let her leave the house. She hoped that during Beth's visit, she could bring up having her come home.

Mary smiled at the two of them. She loved both her girls. "Beth, would you like some ice tea? I just made a fresh batch. Come into the kitchen and see the new ice tea maker your father bought for us." Beth and Emmy followed Mary into the kitchen walking hand and hand. Emmy didn't want to let her mom's hand go. Beth noticed how much she clung to her.

"Speaking of Dad, where is he?" Beth was hoping he went out for a little while so she could talk to her mom first about coming home before she approached him.

"Oh, your dad is over at Tom's house. He needed a hand with a deck he's building. He should be back any minute."

"Oh good, that's great!" Beth forced a smile. Her mother proceeded to show her how the new instant ice tea maker worked. She poured them each a glass and they went out back to the screened porch. Beth commented that the tea was delicious. Their house did not have air conditioning, but each room had a ceiling fan that moved the air enough to get some relief during the heat waves. The back screen room had two ceiling fans and was the most popular spot in the house during the summer. This room brought back many memories for Beth and she smiled as she recalled the usual routine. Beth's mom would work on a quilt at one end of the picnic table, while her father would read the newspaper at the other end. Beth would usually sit in a chaise lounge in the corner of the room and read if she was around. She liked to read romantic novels about the civil war and would daydream about the young captain who would come for her on his white horse. She bought the video of *Gone With The Wind* and watched it a hundred times.

Beth went straight for the chaise lounge and Emmy climbed up on her lap. Emmy laid her head down on her mother's shoulder and snuggled in close. Beth went to sip her tea and one of those awful pains shot through her abdomen. She winced as she sipped the tea. Mary noticed what was happening and immediately jumped up from the picnic bench. "Beth, are you okay?" She walked over to where Beth was sitting.

"Oh, yes, its nothing," Beth was able to respond more confidently than she actually felt. "It's just that time of the month." She fibbed.

"Are you sure? You looked like you were in a lot of pain." Mary knew she was lying.

"No, I'm okay really, please don't fuss." Beth quickly changed the subject. "What are we having for dinner? Is there something I can help with?"

Mary decided not to push her luck. She wanted everything to go well tonight. "We're having a chicken and rice casserole and a salad. Everything is all done. I just have to heat up the casserole. I wanted to have everything ready before you arrived so we could spend more time together."

Beth was surprised and delighted. She had never seen her mother so attentive before. Hopefully things would go this well with her father. "So Mom, what have you been up to lately?"

Mary filled Beth in on the latest quilting project the quilting club had begun and caught her up on all the local gossip. Emmy fell asleep on Beth's lap. Beth unconsciously stroked her little girl's hair as she chatted with her mother. When her mother asked Beth what had been happening with her, she fabricated a few stories not too far off the truth. She told her mom she went to a great big party and that work was hectic and she appreciated her boss' patience with her sick leave. She didn't bring up Rachel at all in the conversation, which her mom thought was odd. They both heard her father walk into the kitchen and the conversation stopped mid-sentence.

"Frank, we're on the porch. Beth is here!" They could hear him in the refrigerator and heard the familiar sound of a beer can pop open. Frank walked into the porch. Beth cradled Emmy close to her as her father came into the room. The silence was awkward and Mary began to get up to let Frank slide over on the picnic bench. He waved for her to stay seated. Frank took a sip of his beer and looked at Beth for a long moment.

"Hello, Beth." was all he said. His tone was matter-of-fact, neither aggressive nor happy.

Beth didn't know how to respond, but she did anyway. "Hi, Dad, how are you?"

Mary was not sure what Frank was going to do this visit. He used Beth's absence the last few days as another notch against her.

"Fine." He was surprised to see how sickly she looked. He was sure she was using it as an excuse. He felt a little guilty for not believing her. Then he noticed the bruise on her face. "What happened to your face?"

"I slipped in the bathroom. You know what a klutz I can be." Beth gulped hard waiting for his reaction but there was none.

Just then Emmy stirred and saw her PopPop. "PopPop!" She exclaimed, as she jumped off Beth and ran into his big burly arms. Frank Harris was a big man at six foot three. He worked as a manual laborer most of his life until his most recent promotion to foreman and it showed in his strong physique. But his large size and strong build melted every time his granddaughter ran into his arms. "PopPop, Mommy is home! Isn't that wonderful?" Emmy wrapped her arms in a bear hug around his thick neck.

"Yes, it's very nice." he commented and glanced at Mary. "Did you and Grandmom have a good time at the park this morning?"

Emmy's eyes grew wide with excitement. "Oh, yes, we did and I brought back a whole bunch of buttercups for Mommy, too!"

"Well, as long as those buttercups stay in the house and don't end up on my lawn little girl, that is fine with me." Frank was like a little kid himself around Emmy. Mary remembered him acting this way with Beth when she was a little girl, too, and she felt very sad for her daughter.

Emmy wiggled out of her PopPop's grasp and returned to the chaise lounge. This time she sat at the bottom with legs folded under her facing her mom. "Mommy wait until you see how many pennies I have collected! I bet I have at least a thousand!" Emmy spread her arms out wide to emphasize her treasure.

"A thousand, oh boy! I can't wait to see your collection!" Beth was delighted that Emmy was such a happy child. It made her feel less guilty for abandoning her like she did.

"Do you want to go count them with me, Mommy?"

How could anyone say no to such a sweet request? Beth thought. "Okay, that sounds like a great idea." Beth looked over at her mother. "Do you mind if we go treasure hunting?"

"No, that sounds fine. Maybe you and Emmy can take a little nap before dinner while you're up there, if you feel tired, that is." Her mother thought Beth looked a little sleepy.

"Well, I don't know about a real nap, but laying down might not be a bad idea. What do you think Emmy?" Beth pulled at Emmy's hands to help her stand up.

"Okay, Mommy, as long as we're together." Emmy began to run past her PopPop, yelling, "Last one upstairs is a rotten egg!"

"Hey, no fair!" Yelled Beth as she sprang off the lounge, "You didn't tell me we were going to race, rug rat!" Beth smiled at her mom and dad and ran past them in direct pursuit of her feisty daughter.

Mary turned toward Frank after watching the two girls scurry back into the house. "You could have given a warmer greeting than that, honestly Frank. Didn't you notice how sick Beth looks? It's obvious that there's something really wrong. In fact, I don't believe she has told me everything and I'm worried. Her face looks too drawn and pale to have been just a virus and I don't know about that bruise."

"Well, you know that's part of Beth's problem, she never tells us the real truth." Frank plopped down on the chaise lounge and sipped his beer.

Mary became annoyed at Frank's unconcerned attitude. "I don't think I blame her. You don't even act like her father anymore. Why would she tell us anything? I'm warning you Frank, if you don't come around and start acting like a concerned father, we are going to lose her and Emmy, too!" Mary slammed her hand down on the picnic table as she said this and she turned to go into the house.

"Hey, wait a minute!" Frank barked back. "Where is all this coming from, anyway?" Mary had never shown Frank such a temper before. He was used to her backing down.

"Frank, I just have a bad feeling that something more serious is wrong with Beth. Lately, when I hear Emmy talking about how much she misses her mother and daydreaming about us being a real family, I just wish I never let Beth leave in the first place. It breaks my heart to see the two of them separated like this. You better reconsider your holier-than-though attitude against your daughter and remember we are not so perfect in the lies department either." Mary hung her head, a little embarrassed about bringing up the subject.

"Now don't start talking about that again. We have been through this a hundred times and I told you it's in the past and let's leave it there. I don't want to talk about that anymore, Mary. Do you understand?" Frank looked away from her and stared at his beer can for a few minutes.

"Well, I'm going to ask Beth tonight to come back home and I don't want any arguments from you. And furthermore, you better find a way to deal with that situation and leave it in the past. And stop taking it out on your daughter. She isn't responsible for what happened and hasn't turned out to be the unscrupulous liar you think she is. She's just a girl making normal mistakes as she grows up and you continue to transfer problems from your past onto her, Frank." Mary walked over behind the chaise lounge and rubbed Frank's shoulders speaking softly. "Frank, Beth is your little girl. And I think she needs us. And Emmy needs us, too. Don't lie to yourself; you love having Emmy live with us. I should have stood up for Beth years ago. I think we made a mistake not telling her the truth. What's done is done and I agree it may be too late to tell her, but Frank, please take a look at your daughter and see how much she has grown. Please, Frank, for me." Mary kissed his head and walked into the kitchen.

Frank sat staring at his beer can. He ran his finger around the rim of the can and thought about a time long ago when he was so hurt and angry that he thought he could never love again. And then Mary came to him and rescued him from a terrible situation. He wasn't in love with her then, but he grew to love her in a much deeper way than he ever thought possible. He looked toward the kitchen. Mary had never reacted like this before. She always sat back quietly and tried not to get too involved in the fights between Beth and him. She was never this worried about Beth before either. He knew she loved Beth more than anything in the world and he decided to take her advice and give Beth a closer look. He rose from the chaise and went upstairs to take a shower before dinner.

Frank walked down the hallway and stopped abruptly at Emmy's room. Her bed was to the right of the doorway and along the far wall, so the two girls could not see him standing outside the door. He listened in on their conversation for a few minutes.

Beth had dumped Emmy's big purple dinosaur bank on the bed, creating a mountain of pennies. There were no silver coins in the bank. Emmy kept them in a separate bank. She did not care at all about the silver or how much it was worth. All she loved was pennies; especially the shiny new, bright copper ones. First, Emmy wanted Beth to help separate the old pennies from the shiny ones, so she could see how many new coins she had. They made two piles on the bed until all were separated.

Frank overheard Emmy talking to Beth. "Mommy, are you still sick?"

"No baby, I'm fine now." Beth began tickling Emmy on the bed, "Now that I'm with my favorite little girl!"

Emmy had a contagious giggle and both girls began to laugh together. "Stop, Mommy, before I have to go!"

"Emmy! We wouldn't want that now would we." Beth sat back against the wall and continued to make piles of one hundred pennies.

"Mommy?" Emmy asked a little more seriously, "Remember on the phone when we talked about our little secret? Are we still going to be together soon?"

Beth remembered the conversation. "Well, Emmy, if everything goes okay tonight, I hope that it will be this week. You know you are all I think about anymore. And I promise you, we are never going to be separated again." Emmy climbed into Beth's arms and Beth stroked her hair.

"Mommy, how come we can't stay here and live with Grandmom and PopPop and be a real family? I know Grandmom misses you, too. We have good talks together about us being a family, but it's not the same when you're not here."

Beth squeezed Emmy tightly, "I know it has been hard on you. I want more than anything to be a family again. But a family has to be able to live together and get along, and well, PopPop and I have not done a very good job have we?" Emmy nodded, remembering the fights they used to have. Beth continued, "I promise I am going to try as hard as I can to make it work. But if it doesn't, you and I will have to go someplace else and make our own family, okay?"

"Okay, just as long as we're together." Emmy snuggled down next to her mom and the two of them closed their eyes.

Frank realized they must have fallen asleep and looked in on them. The two of them lay side by side sleeping contentedly. For a moment, Beth looked like a little girl herself. Her hair had gently fallen across her eyes, hiding her age. It brought back memories of Beth as a little girl, sleeping snugly in his arms. How many times he had reminded himself then how she was worth all the pain he had gone through. He turned and continued to his room. As he showered, he thought about the conversation he heard, and how mature Beth sounded to him. He didn't know what she meant by going someplace else, but it was apparent she wanted to come home and try again. As he scrubbed the dirt off his arms he thought about what Mary had said. Had he misjudged Beth all these years? Did he really exaggerate Beth's mistakes?

Well, he was not sure about that but the least he could do was look at Beth closely now and see if she really had changed or maybe discover he had been wrong all along. He thought about his little granddaughter and how much he loved having her around. He would try for Emmy's sake and for Mary, too. As he finished his shower, it never occurred to him that he did not think about trying for Beth or for himself.

Beth and Emmy slept for an hour and awoke to the smell of the casserole baking in the oven. It was almost five o'clock. They ran downstairs and offered to set the table. The two of them worked side by side. Emmy showed Beth how she had learned to set the table all by herself. Frank and Mary both watched the two of them. They were two peas in a pod and were so joyful together. Mary knew Beth had to be suffering terribly from being separated from Emmy these past few months. She admired

Beth's courage to leave and try to find her own way. Mary knew she would never have had the courage to leave home under such distressing circumstances. Beth had such a strong will and great determination. If only Frank could see these qualities in his daughter, she thought. Then he would understand her actions so much better. Frank watched all three of them very carefully as he read his newspaper waiting for dinner.

Dinner went remarkably well. Emmy kept them all entertained with her wide-eyed stories and unending list of questions. Everyone ate heartily. Mary began to hope that they could work things out. Frank seemed more relaxed, too. He even asked Beth a few casual questions directly. When Mary served coffee, she decided that now was the time to move to a more serious subject.

"Beth, you haven't said a word of your roommate, Rachel."

Beth was taken off guard by the comment, "Oh, well, there is nothing much to tell. Rachel and I are really very different, so other than sharing living space, we don't do much together."

"That must be a little uncomfortable for you, I would think." Her mother saw her golden opportunity and seized it.

"Well, yes, it is a little strange. I was hoping to have saved enough for a down payment on my own place by now." Beth began to sweat a little. She wondered if this would be a perfect opportunity to ask to come home, but couldn't get the words to form in her mouth. Her mouth felt parched and she reached for her coffee.

"I see." Her mother said and looked over at Frank, "I was wondering if you would consider coming home for a while. Just until you've saved enough money for your own place. It seems silly having to arrange time to stop by and visit Emmy, when you could live here with her instead. I know you left because you and your father had trouble getting along, but we can work that out." Mary turned and gave Frank a penetrating look. "Can't we Frank?"

Frank looked bewildered for a moment. He looked over at Beth who sat there as nervous as he was and nodded his head. "I'm sure we can work something out."

Emmy jumped out of her chair and ran to her mother. "Oh, Mommy, please come back home, pleeease?"

Beth was speechless. She may have never had the courage to ask them to come back tonight on her own. She looked over at her mother and marveled at how she had changed. Maybe it would not be so hard after all. This was surely a sign from God. She looked at her father and thought she saw his expression soften a bit. She lifted her daughter up into her lap. "Sure Emmy, I would love to come home!"

Her mother walked over to her, too, and kissed her on the head. She glanced over at Frank with tears in her eyes and mouthed "I love you". The scene had become a little too uncomfortable for him and he politely excused himself from the table.

Beth and her mom talked about when she would come home and they decided that Tuesday would be best for everyone. Beth had to figure out how to get her things from Rachel's place, which included her car, and she had to return to work tomorrow. But it didn't matter how complex everything seemed tonight; she would get through all of it and come home on Tuesday evening.

The girls cleaned up the dishes and Beth called Father Pat to tell him to pick her up about eight o'clock. She spoke very softly on the phone so her mother could not hear and explained to her mother that her car was in the shop and a friend was picking her up. Beth felt bad about lying again to her mother but she put it behind her. This was the last time she would have to lie about anything to her parents.

Beth spent the rest of the night reading stories to Emmy and tucked her in bed. Emmy said her prayers and told God she was so grateful that her mommy was coming home. Beth added her thanks to the prayer. When Father Pat arrived, Beth quickly kissed her mother goodbye and rushed out the door before her parents could question who was picking her up. Everything worked out better than she could have ever hoped and she almost danced her way to the car. On the way home, she excitedly told Father Pat about the entire visit. She talked to him about how she could get her things and her car back from Rachel and he offered to help in any way, even if he was needed to go and retrieve the goods himself. Beth felt like her life was moving forward for the first time in a long time.

Chapter 16

Beth woke up Monday morning feeling happier than she had been in years. The sun cast dancing rays of sunshine through the oak leaves into her bedroom, as the wind gently tossed them about. She stretched and thought about the day ahead. She couldn't wait to tell Matt the good news about going home. Going to work would be difficult, but she chose to be optimistic today. She decided to avoid a confrontation with Rachel and concentrate on her work. Beth liked to avoid things. It made everything easier. She convinced herself that if she got to work early and stayed seated at her desk all day, most of her coworkers wouldn't see her bruised face. She reasoned that Mr. Manley never pried into her personal life and he probably was satisfied with the vague explanation Father Pat gave him. And, as for Rachel, well, she would just ask her for her car keys and send Father to get her things. There was no sense making a scene and she just didn't want to know that Rachel had anything to do with what happened. That would only confirm her poor judgment of the entire situation.

Beth showered and dressed in the long sleeve shirt and jeans for work. Her workplace dressed casually during the summer and the air conditioning was always run on high, so no one would think her outfit was odd. She rushed down stairs and greeted Mrs. McCafferty with a big hug and kiss. Mrs. McCafferty remarked how pleased she was that everything was working out so well for her. Between sniffles she added that things would be lonely around the rectory when Beth was gone. Beth assured her that she would bring Emmy to visit soon.

Beth's stomach was tied in knots despite her optimistic attitude and she ate very little before heading to the front porch. She checked to see if the cat was still in the house and found the lazy thing curled up on the rocker in the living room. Beth walked onto the front porch and sat on the top step. Matt was hovering in front of her before she could blink her eyes.

"So how did it go last night?" Matt had watched Beth come home with Father Pat and saw her chattering excitedly to the priest. He assumed from their light banter that the day was a success. He decided not to bother her until morning. Partially because he didn't want to find out that he could have been wrong about the reconciliation and that new complications could have developed. Matt wanted to be done with this mission so he could go home. It was lonely being a hummingbird. Both male and female hummingbirds live a very solitary life. A male will approach a female for a brief encounter to mate and then leave her territory right away. Females

The Rustling of Angels

occasionally share their area with another female and concentrate on raising their hatchlings. After mating season, males are left on their own. Matt knew he wasn't here to socialize and certainly not with other birds, but he found it difficult being on his own so much. He was used to a lot of attention. Something else was beginning to happen to him. He felt the little bird inside him urging him to head south. A few times during the night he had to fight the urge to take off and fly away. This driving force inside him continuously beckoned him to leave. He had to fight it constantly.

Beth's smile said more than words could right then. She had a small tear rolling down the side of her delicate nose. She wiped it away, trying not to smear her makeup. "It went really well, Matt. You won't believe this, but I didn't even have to ask to come home. My mother asked me! She said that it would all work out between my dad and me. My dad even agreed to give it a try. So I'll be leaving tomorrow, after work."

Matt was thrilled. "That is terrific! Damn, and to think that this mission seemed so hard at the beginning. You and your father have made up and I can go home!" Matt did a loop in the air.

Beth realized Matt misunderstood what she said. "Hold on a minute. My father and I didn't make up. In fact, we barely talked. All he said was that he was willing to try and make it work. I don't even know if I'll be able to last two weeks in that house if he doesn't change, but at least I'm going to try. You don't know my dad; he is really stubborn. I think he agreed just to appease my mother. She seemed really different yesterday. She was acting strange, in a good way, that is. She seemed really worried about me. It was nice to see her worrying more about me than about what my dad wants."

Matt tried to hide his disappointment. "Well, it's a good sign isn't it? It's just a matter of time. Right?"

"I really hope so! I was never so glad to see Emmy. I didn't realize how much I missed her. With everything that has happened, I forgot what a large hole I have in my heart from being separated from her." Beth clasped her hands together. "But now, we will be together and nothing will ever separate us again. If I leave this time, I am not leaving without her."

Matt thought about the news. Beth would be leaving the rectory tomorrow. Now there was a new problem. "So, how will we be able to talk once you move back home? Will you be coming here to visit or something?"

Beth looked at Matt, surprised. "Some angel you are!" she exclaimed, "No, you're coming with me!"

"How can I do that? I have all my food sources here." Matt hadn't given much thought past her returning home. He was sure that if she went back home, his mission would be done.

"Well, we have flowers around my house, too. I'm not going back there without you! You said you were here to help me make amends with my father and I'm counting on you. You know, if my mother hadn't asked me to come home, I don't think I would have had the courage to approach the subject last night. I can't do it alone! We'll just have to figure out how to bring you with me. Maybe I can put you in an old shoebox. I'll think of something angel, don't worry."

"I told you before, Beth, I'm not an angel!" Matt felt a new ball and chain weighing him down. The thought of looking for new food sources and fighting off new predators didn't appeal to him. He would miss the protection of the oak tree. He felt very vulnerable again.

Beth jumped up and straightened out her clothes. "Well, I have to go to work now. I have a big mess to clean up there with my work that's probably piled up. And I have to get my things back from Rachel." Beth grew flustered as she filled Matt in on her dilemma of not knowing how to approach Rachel to get her things back today.

Matt realized that he was the one who should be encouraging Beth, not the other way around. But he didn't have an answer for her. "I know you'll work it out Beth. You'll think of something!"

Beth headed back to the front door. "Matt, you better work on your angel skills while I'm gone. Even I could have told myself that. I'll talk to you tonight." She laughed and went back inside.

♥♥♥♥♥♥♥

The copper sedan rolled away from the curb and left Beth staring at her sullen image in the glass door of the General Life Insurance office building. She glanced up at the four story brick building wishing a miracle earthquake would send a shower of bricks down to bury her in one quick instant. All of the confidence she felt this morning completely dissolved as she contemplated facing her coworkers, her boss and worst of all Rachel, with a horrible bruise across her jaw and not a hint of an excuse for her sudden disappearance. She couldn't possibly avoid everyone today. She arrived thirty minutes early, as planned, hoping to pass by the unavoidable long line of secretaries' desks in Mahogany Row unnoticed. That was where the President and Vice Presidents' secretaries sat and where most of the company rumors began. She was sure that she couldn't slip by the Row at the normal starting time without Madge Cromwell or Betty DuPree noticing her face and jumping at her like two starving hyenas after an injured lamb. Of course, they would feign concern, but what they really would be after is every detail they could get, so that they could hit the gossip line before she made it to her desk.

Beth swallowed hard and squeezed the stinging tears out of her eyes. She had no choice but to go in and get it over with. The lobby was empty when she opened the door and she proceeded to the stairs and walked up to the third floor. She opened the door to the third floor and took a quick look at the Row. No one was there. She rushed through the room and walked past the empty cubicles in the main office area to her desk along the back wall where the managers' offices were. The only one that was in on the floor so far was Phil Buckman, who was busy pecking on his calculator keys. Beth sat down at her desk and let out a deep breath. She realized she had been holding her breath almost the whole time since she entered the building. Her hands were shaking and her knees knocked together. Beth surveyed her desk and saw a mountain of unopened mail in her inbox and the unfinished sales reports still where she had left them. As she turned on her computer her eyes made contact with Rachel's desk and her heart stopped. Beads of sweat formed on her forehead, as she tried to imagine what would happen when Rachel arrived. Her deep thoughts were suddenly interrupted when she heard her name being called from behind, startling her enough to make her jump as she spun around. Mr. Manley was standing in his office doorway looking surprised at her reaction. "I'm sorry. I didn't mean to scare you. Please, come into my office. I need to speak with you before I go to the managers meeting this morning." He sounded serious.

Beth followed him in and sat down in the first chair facing him. The idea that he was satisfied with Father Pat's explanation dissolved in her mind when she saw the look of concern he gave her. He sat back in his chair with his hands folded together on his desk before he spoke. "Beth, I'm glad you came back so soon. I was worried about you." Beth tried to sit on an angle so he couldn't see the bruise, but he noticed it right away. "I know the priest said you had a personal injury, but what happened to you?"

"Mr. Manley, I really appreciate your concern, but I can't talk about it. It's too personal. I hope you understand. I appreciate your keeping this to yourself. It really helped more than you could ever know. I just want to get back to work and put it behind me." He sat up and leaned on the desk studying the bruise. "Well, I understand, but I'm still concerned. So many things are a mystery right now. I would love to know what's going on."

"You can be sure, I'm fine and I won't be missing any more work. I can work through my breaks and lunches this week to catch up."

"Well, Shirley typed all of the cover letters I needed for the quotes last week, but I need those sales reports finished this morning. You can bring them into the meeting as soon as they're ready."

"Great, I was almost done with them. They should take me about an hour." Beth was relieved that this went so smoothly. Mr. Manley was such a nice boss to work for. She got up to go to her desk.

"Before you go, I think you should know that I told everyone that you took an unscheduled vacation last week. I didn't know how else to handle your sudden absence. Luckily there were a lot of people out on vacation, too. But now that you're back with that bruise on your face, they may be a little suspicious about your sudden disappearance, especially with Rachel resigning last Monday."

"Rachel resigned?" Beth was totally caught off guard and sunk back into her seat.

"Yes. You didn't know that? Beth, I'm concerned. You and Rachel aren't in trouble with the law are you?"

"No, no! It's nothing like that. Did she say why she left?"

"From what I heard, she told Stan she had a family emergency at home in Texas and she had to leave right away. Something concerning her mother's health."

"Oh God!" Beth exclaimed half out loud. She thought about her things that she left at the apartment. There was nothing that couldn't be replaced, but she did leave her car keys on her dresser the last night she was there. Beth wondered if her car would still be there. She immediately assumed Rachel made up the story about why she left and now she wondered if this meant she really was a part of what happened.

As if Mr. Manley was reading her mind, he opened up the top drawer of his desk and brought out a small manila envelope addressed to her. "I almost forgot, Rachel had asked me to give you this." He slid the envelope over to Beth.

Beth stammered. "Thank you. I guess I better get to work on those reports you need." She picked up the envelope and stood to leave, again.

"Beth, whatever happened, I'd be glad to help you in any way I can."

"Thanks, you already have. I'll be fine." Mr. Manley watched Beth leave his office. He shook his head with concern and returned to his notes for this morning's meeting.

Meanwhile, Beth returned to her desk and stared down at the envelope. There was a bulge in it that felt like keys. She opened the envelope and emptied the contents on her desk. Her car keys tumbled out first and two folded pieces of pink notepaper with her name on it fell on top of the keys.

Beth lifted the paper and held it with both hands, staring at it for a few minutes before opening it. She guessed it contained an explanation about what happened and whether Rachel was involved or not. It would probably answer whether her judgment had gone so astray about leaving her parents and whether all of this was somehow her fault. She flipped it open, took a deep breath, and began to read.

Dear Beth, Please forgive me. I am so sorry. I swear I had nothing to do with whatever happened Saturday night. Rick betrayed me. I thought I knew him better. He convinced me to stop by my place to be alone for a while. We got a little carried away and took longer than we planned. When we got back to the party, you were gone. No one would tell me where you went. I thought that maybe you had gone someplace with Mark, until I found him in the kitchen half drunk. He said he didn't know where you were. Everyone was acting funny. Finally a girl pulled me to the side and told me what she saw. She said that you passed out on the sofa and Brian and Jack took you outside. They were gone a long time and came back a half-hour before I did and said they took you home. I knew that was a lie because I would have been there when they brought you home. I asked Rick to find out what was going on.

After he spoke to them privately, he looked nervous, but assured me you were alright. He said that there was a big misunderstanding between you and them and that they decided to teach you a lesson, but the joke got out of hand. I insisted that we go back to my place to see you, but when we arrived you weren't there. Rick waited up all night with me until six o'clock in the morning when I decided to call the police. He cut me off and I knew something terrible had happened to you. Then he told me everything. I tried to call the police again, but he cut me off again and told me why I couldn't. I don't know if he was a part of what happened to you, but he sure has screwed me. They have something awful on me. I was such a fool not to see it coming. I can't believe these guys are so devious. I think you're right. No man can be trusted. What they did to you and what they've done to me is unbelievable. I can't tell you anything, but I knew if I went to the police, my life would be ruined.

When I came in this morning and heard you called in sick, I was so relieved to hear you were alive, but I still have to go. I could never face you and I'm afraid of what will happen if you press charges. I swear I had nothing to do with it! If you hate me, I understand. I already hate myself. I hope you are okay. I'm not going home like I told everyone. Please don't look for me. I'm sorry. Rachel.

There was a p.s. at the bottom of the page that told Beth her things were locked in her car in the parking garage.

Beth folded the pink paper several times and tucked it in her purse. Her emotions at that moment ranged from relief to pity for Rachel. Surprisingly, she didn't feel anger toward her at all. Perhaps Rachel would fair worse than she in this situation. Carrying around the guilt of what she unknowingly did and the fear of being tracked down by the police was punishment enough. "What could they possibly have on her?" she wondered. At least now, Beth had enough information to answer any questions she would be asked today.

She could go along with Rachel's story about her ill mother and she could tell everyone she injured her face falling off a jet ski at the shore. How fortunate for her that Mr. Manley told everyone she was on vacation. It would be a lie, of course, but after this, she vowed she would never lie again. Rachel's leaving would explain why she was moving back home, so every issue was taken care of in a tidy fashion. Maybe Matt had used some kind of angelic intervention, because these problems could not have been resolved any better.

Beth felt another burden lifted from her shoulders. This was a sign to her that everything would work out now. All she had to do was get Father Pat to drive her to the apartment complex after work and tomorrow she would move back home. Beth spent the rest of the day trying to catch up on her backlog and dreaming about being home again. The mystery pain came twice that day and she began to spot. Since her monthly cycle was due within a week, she didn't think much of the bleeding.

Beth told Father Pat that evening of her plan to take Matt with her. She would stop by after work on Tuesday to say goodbye and get Matt. Father Pat chuckled at the idea. He would have thought that Matt could have blinked himself over to Beth's house. Beth explained the rules that Matt had to follow when he assumed the bird's body. Father Pat wondered what would have happened if Matt had entered his body, as was planned. Would he have known that another spirit was within him? Would he have any recollection of what he did after the spirit had left him? He almost wished that Matt hadn't foiled the angels' plan to find out. Imagine, he thought to himself, God wanted to use me as a vessel for another human soul. He felt very privileged for this entire experience. He knew he would miss Beth a great deal and hoped that they would be able to stay in touch.

Tuesday evening came quickly. Matt waited for Beth in the oak tree. She pulled up in her dark blue compact car. Matt saw that the back seat was piled with clothes. She went into the rectory carrying something in her hand. It was a box and the first thing she did was poke large holes in it so Matt could have some air. The cat was at the back door and Beth let him in. She picked him up and hugged his scruffy body. "You be a good boy for Mrs. McC you hear?" She put the cat down by his water bowl. He rubbed up against her legs, giving her a final goodbye.

Mrs. McCafferty came down from upstairs. They smiled nervously at each other. "I don't know how to ever thank you for all you've done." Beth ran into her arms and held her tight. Both women made futile attempts to fight back the tears, but they poured out like the River Jordan. They laughed as they tried to compose themselves before Father saw them.

"It's been a real pleasure helping you, dear. Now, you come and visit us and bring that little angel, Emmy here like you promised."

"Oh, you can be sure of that, Mrs. McC, just as soon as I get settled in."

Father Pat walked in the front door just then. He shook his head and gave a good chuckle as he watched the women try to clean up their faces to hide the tears. "If the two of you thought that I wouldn't expect to find you crying, you don't know me very well!" Everyone laughed and the embarrassment lifted.

Father Pat walked Beth to the front door with his arm around her. "Now, I want you to keep in touch with me and let me know how everything is going. And remember, if I can be of assistance in any way, you just give a holler." He kissed Beth lightly on the head and squeezed her tight. There was a small tear forming in his eye that he quickly wiped away before either lady noticed.

"Thanks Father, I will never forget what you've done for me." Beth stood on her tiptoes and kissed him on the forehead. Then she walked onto the porch and opened the box. She walked down the steps and whistled. Matt was watching her the whole time, but hesitated to leave his safe oak tree. Father Pat and Mrs. McCafferty watched silently at the front door, keeping a respectful distance from the little hummingbird. They watched Matt zoom straight down from the oak tree. He hovered in front of Beth and they began to talk. Neither could hear their conversation.

Beth smiled at Matt and held the little box out in front of her. "In you go, angel."

Matt looked at her with dumbfounded eyes. "You're kidding me, right? I thought you were joking about the shoe box."

"Well, I wasn't. Get in the box unless you can find your way to my house yourself." Beth was amused at Matt's hesitance.

"I told you before, I don't have those kind of powers. But why a box? Can't I just sit on the front seat?"

"You can, I guess, but I just thought the box would be safer. That way no one will see you at the house. I can check out the backyard and make sure there aren't any stray cats around. Or would you like to do that yourself?" She gave Matt a smirk.

"Ha, ha, very funny. That's the last time I tell you about my weak spots. Okay, I'll go, but are you sure there are enough air holes in here?"

"There are plenty!"

Matt buzzed over the open box. "Doesn't look like it to me."

"Just get in the box already!" Beth exclaimed. She couldn't believe he was being such a chicken. She would have expected him to be brave and valiant like all the other heroes that come to rescue the fair maidens. Instead she stood there trying to coax him into the box. "The sooner you get in, the sooner you will get out, if you know what I mean."

"Okay, okay, I'm going. But you better talk to me the whole way. You know I was very afraid of the dark when I was little." The last words were muffled as Beth quickly placed the lid on the box as Matt settled in.

Beth got into the car and put the shoebox down on the seat beside her. She even buckled it in to keep it from moving. Matt heard the muffled sound of the car starting as he sat in his dark coffin, feeling terribly vulnerable. He heard her tap the top of the box a few times asking if he was alright.

The ride was over much faster than he anticipated. He was relieved when he felt the box being lifted from the seat as he slid across the floor of the box into one side. Beth walked around the house, scanning for predators. There was an apple tree in the corner of the yard that seemed safe and she lifted the box lid so Matt could fly out. Matt lay still in the corner of the box motionless. Beth began to panic as she checked the air holes. She put at least twelve large holes in the sides and that many in the lid. She was sure he would get enough air. She gently placed her fingers around the little bird's body and Matt lifted his head up and looked at her. "Fooled you!" He teased.

Beth nearly dropped the box. "Don't do that to me!" she exclaimed. "I really thought I hurt you!"

Matt began to laugh. "Well, you could have in that coffin you put me in."

"You were perfectly safe and you know it! Now that I know you're such a chicken I'll let you fend for yourself next time."

Matt started to check out the back yard. "No thanks! There better not be a next time for me." He flew up into the apple tree. It was lower than the oak tree and didn't give him a clear view of the house, but he could see the yards that connected very well. At least he would have a clear view of predators from there. Beth told Matt she needed to go back out front before she drew any suspicion. No one had heard her pull up yet. She walked quietly around the house and Matt settled into his new home. He would have to canvas the area for food. As he started to fly away, he hoped this would be an uneventful exploration.

Beth grabbed a few things from the car and walked toward the house. Emmy looked out the window and squealed when she saw her mommy. She opened the front door and nearly knocked her down when she entered the foyer.

"She's here, she's here, Grandmom," Emmy was jumping up and down. "Let me help you, Mommy." Emmy grabbed a small bag and ran ahead of

Beth to the stairs. "I'll take this up to your room, okay?" Mary walked out of the kitchen, smiling as she wiped her hands on her apron.

"Well, there you are, just in time. I thought I was going to have to tie Emmy down to keep her from hurting herself. She has been bouncing off the walls waiting for you."

"I'm glad to be here, too, Mom." She kissed her mother on the cheek. "How long until dinner?"

"Oh, about thirty minutes. Your father is working late and will be home soon. Can I help you with anything?"

"No, I think I will unload the car and get settled in my room, if you don't mind."

Mary hugged Beth again. "Not at all. I'm sure Emmy will be a big help to you." Mary went back into the kitchen to finish preparing supper. When she got to the sink, she breathed a sigh of relief. She had worried all day that Beth would change her mind. Now she prayed Frank would be cooperative, so she could get her family back together.

It took four trips to unload the car. Beth was exhausted by the time she lugged the last of her clothes and belongings upstairs. She collapsed on her bed, feeling the familiar soft quilt caress her face. The smell of the linens reminded her that she was home. The awful pain returned as she curled up on the bed. This time it lasted twice as long as usual. Emmy ran into the room to let Beth know PopPop was home and Grandmom said it was dinnertime.

Beth sat on the side of the bed to compose herself. The pain was so bad it drained all the color from her face. She ran to the bathroom and splashed cold water on her face and freshened up her makeup. When she was convinced she looked better, she headed downstairs.

Frank was sitting at the head of the table when Beth entered the dining room. He glanced briefly over at her as she sat down and said hello to him. His only reply was a nod. Beth looked at Mary who smiled nervously at her and started passing the dinner. The conversation was light and the dinner went quickly. Everyone was in a hurry to end the awkward first night. All in all, it went better than most had in the past. There was no arguing or bantering, which was a dramatic improvement. Beth and Mary were satisfied that it was at least a start.

Beth played with Emmy the rest of the evening until she put her to bed. Afterwards, she told her mother that she was going to sit outside for a while. Matt was in the apple tree watching the back door. He was so excited at the treasure he found that he couldn't wait to tell her. He zoomed over to the azalea bushes that lined the screen room as soon as he saw Beth come onto the porch. She sat in the chaise lounge, hoping to appear inconspicuous. "Matt," she whispered, "Is that you?" It was hard to tell through the screen.

221

"Yes, it's me," He whispered back. "Why are we being so secretive, all of a sudden?"

"I don't want to arouse any questions right now, okay! Did you find some food?"

"Did I find food! I found a gold mine. About two blocks over, a lady has three hummingbird feeders in her backyard." Matt was so excited he blurted out his story. "At first, I didn't know what they were, but I was attracted to some red flowers in her garden. Then a hummingbird zoomed past me and began drinking the red stuff in the feeders. Well, I thought I would be in for another fight, but this time there were two female hummingbirds. They tried to chase me a couple of times, but with three feeders and two birds, well, there was no point in that. The red stuff tasted a little sweeter than flower nectar but does the same thing. I feel great." He started to do a couple loops in the air, but he realized Beth would never see him through the screen. "So, how did your dinner go?"

Beth relaxed back in the chaise lounge. "I think I would call it pretty good. My dad didn't say too much, but we didn't argue either. I don't know what it will take to get a real dialogue going with him."

"How about if *you* start the conversation and tell him how *you* feel!" Matt emphasized the word "you" to get his point across. He was feeling frustrated by his lack of control in the situation and also feeling that time was short.

"Okay, touché! It's your turn to get the zingers in. I will, soon. I just need a little time to settle in." Beth flipped her hair behind her left ear.

"Beth, you are going to have to do it soon. I don't know how much time I will have here. I am already dealing with fighting off the bird's natural urge to migrate, I think. It's hard to concentrate on flying and eating and warding off predators. I want to be here for you, but I can't risk killing this bird in the process. You know you have to do it soon anyway. The more you put if off, the harder it will be later. Don't wait too long. Okay?"

"Okay, I promise." Beth heard her mother in the kitchen. "I better go. I'll talk to you around the same time tomorrow."

"Sure, same time." Matt watched Beth leave him in the blackness of the night. It was a cloud-covered sky that hid the moon and stars from him. Without the stars, he could not feel Anjella's presence and he felt very alone again. "Please Beth," he whispered, "please don't wait too long! I don't know how much more I can take." He flew into the center of the apple tree and slept the night away. He was very tired from the move.

Chapter 17

The next two weeks went by in a blink of an eye. Everything was going great for Beth, except for the occasional nightmare that left her in a cold sweat and recurring pains that she was beginning to be concerned about. Emmy and Beth were together every minute they could possibly squeeze out of the day. Mary was happy having a peaceful house again. Even Frank had become more responsive during dinner conversations. He watched Beth very closely and was slowly developing a change of heart.

Matt's situation, however, was a whole other issue. He was struggling constantly against the little bird's voice inside. He spent much of his time observing Beth, too. One Saturday afternoon, Beth and Emmy spread a blanket out in the backyard and laid in the sun. He watched as they laughed and played together with tears in his eyes. His emotions continued to betray him. It reminded him so much of his own childhood memories. Beth's hair was much like his mother's and it shimmered in the sunlight as it fell across her soft features. Her body was long and graceful and the way she was laying on her side emphasized her curvy shape.

One especially poignant moment occurred when Beth held buttercups under Emmy's chin to see if she liked butter. It was the same game his mother used to play with him and Ellen when they were young. Beth looked so beautiful stretched out on the blanket playing with Emmy. She emanated the perfect combination of youthfulness and motherly love. He felt very drawn to her and soon realized there was more to his relationship with her than just a misguided soul sent to rescue another. He was falling in love with her. Matt was bewildered by his revelation. Beth was not his type at all, he thought. She was more like..*his mother.* And one thing he swore to himself was that he would never fall in love with anyone like his mother. He loved his mother with all his might, of course, but there were so many things he didn't like about her. Like his mother, Beth could be vulnerable and too trusting one day and turn around and be stubborn, willful and determined the next.

Since he got to know her, however, her vulnerability did not seem like a flaw to him. It was rather attractive now. It gave her personality depth, unlike the straightforward, almost plastic personalities he usually dated. Beth represented a full-range of emotions that Matt had never allowed himself to experience and feeling them through her made something inside him come alive. He would do anything for her. Whatever she wanted—whatever made her happy. Here was a girl who had been knocked down time and time again but kept on fighting. Not for herself, but for her daughter. She may not always make the best decision, but she would try anything, even gamble with life, if she had to, for Emmy's sake. Matt realized that there was an almost heroic nature to a mother's love.

Suddenly, Matt understood why his father gave in to his mother's insistence to shelter their children from the truth many times. His father was not weak, but incredibly in love with his mother. So much in love that he would let his only son think that he was responsible for the grief their family went through when Sarah died, the grief that had torn the fabric of their unity apart. "What a fool I've been." He thought. Then, returning to his own feelings about Beth, he felt like a bigger fool. "Damn my luck! I'm finally with the most incredible girl I've ever met in my life and I can't do anything about it. If this isn't hell, I don't know what is."

During their evening rendezvous, Matt spent more time learning about Beth than encouraging her to speak to her father. One night, when Mary and Frank had gone to see a movie and Emmy was asleep in bed, they were able to talk freely. Beth had brought a radio out with her and they listened to a jazz station. Matt was able to come into the screen room and sit on the arm of the chaise lounge next to Beth. He loved being close to her. He missed the companionship of another person that he had taken for granted while he was alive.

Beth began to talk about her dreams for the future. She was telling him about her plans to go back to school and finish her nursing degree. "I figure I have about three more years to go if I include the summer semesters. That's really not too long."

"No, not at all. And by that time Emmy will be in school, so you won't have to worry about day care as much, if your mom isn't watching her by that time."

"Why would you say that? I'll probably still be here, if all goes well with my dad. I don't see any reason to leave here otherwise."

Matt had been doing his own bit of daydreaming while Beth was talking. He studied her features while she spoke, noticing how large her lovely hazel eyes were for the first time and how her thick, long eyelashes couldn't hide the wear and tear life had already brought her, even when she smiled. But, in contrast, her full lips deceived her eyes by looking softer than velvety rose petals and beckoning to be shown sweet affection. He wondered what it would feel like to kiss them. How could any man resist their invitation, he thought. The distraction had caused him to speak without thinking. "Oh, I'm sure, but I was thinking that in three years, you'll probably have found the man of your dreams and be married."

Beth was shocked at the suggestion. "No. I don't think so."

"Why not? You're too pretty and too nice to go unnoticed."

Beth was a little embarrassed by the compliment. "Well thanks, but, that hasn't been my experience. If you'll recall, I haven't had much luck in that area."

"I'd love to go out with you!" Matt spoke before he realized what he was saying. He said it so eagerly and with such little boy charm that he couldn't believe his own ears.

"You would!" Beth blushed. "Just my luck! My latest admirer is a two and a half-inch hummingbird. I bet you we would turn a lot of heads when we walked into a restaurant!" Beth laughed at the thought. "Thanks for saying that, but I'll have to pass."

Matt was mortified by his childish outburst, but even more wounded by her flat-out rejection. It was the first time that he had ever felt the sting from being dismissed so casually and he tried to salvage his ego. "*I meant,* if I were my old self, I would ask you out."

Beth curled her legs up and turned to face him on the lounge. "Really. Are you saying that if we had met before you died, you would have found me interesting?"

Matt thought for a moment about who he was before all this happened and realized he wouldn't have. Her looks would have sparked a glimmer of interest that would have faded once he realized what kind of girl she was—a nice girl, and he would have brushed her off like road dust on a leather jacket.

"To be honest, no. I wouldn't have. I was just another one of those jerks who was looking for a quick roll-in-the-hay with no strings attached."

Beth looked disappointed and turned her head away. "I see."

Matt flew in front of her face and saw a tear forming in her eye. He waited until their eyes met. "It would have been my loss, Beth. You're the most beautiful, bright, loving girl I have ever met. Any guy would be crazy to pass up a chance to be with you." Matt forgot what a sensitive subject this was for her.

As she wiped the tear that rolled down her cheek, he could see the depth of sadness in her eyes. "No, Matt. It doesn't matter. No matter who says they love me, even if they really do, one way or another, they leave me." The conversation became too uncomfortable for her, so she called it a night and let him out into the yard.

Matt flew over to the apple tree and thought about what she had said. He kicked himself over and over for being so insensitive. How could he be such an idiot and say he had feelings for her? Even if she took him seriously, he was a spirit and would be leaving her soon. Still, her reaction was so extreme. The way she was talking about being abandoned. He didn't say he loved her. He just said he would go out with her. There was something strange about what she said. Unless…she had feelings for him! No! How

225

ridiculous that seemed. He decided he should try and forget it happened and hoped that she would, too.

The next time they talked, Beth was distant and withdrawn and they only spoke for a few minutes. It took a few days for the awkwardness to fade away and to return to their normal selves, both pretending that nothing ever happened. There was no change with her father and Matt vowed that he would have to get her to do something soon, because he was running out of time.

♥♥♥♥♥♥♥

On the Monday before Labor Day weekend, Beth asked her parents at dinner if they had made any plans for the holiday. Her mother said that she thought a barbecue would be a nice idea. Beth asked if they would mind if she invited a few friends to visit. Her dad immediately stiffened at the thought of Beth's delinquent friends until he heard it was a priest and his housekeeper.

"How on earth did you end up with a priest and his housekeeper for friends?" Mary asked, puzzled.

"Oh, I met Father Pat a few weeks ago and we hit it off right away. He's a really nice person." Beth cringed as she realized she was lying again. She had promised herself that the lying would stop.

Mary looked at Frank who shrugged his shoulders. He was not thrilled at the idea of spending the day with a priest, but he was curious as to how Beth could have become a friend to one. It was another mystery surrounding his daughter.

"Well, I don't see why not. Do you think they would be comfortable with us? You know we're not really church folk."

"Why wouldn't they be? I'm sure they would like to meet you and they are dying to meet Emmy." Beth squeezed her mother's hand. "Thanks, Mom. It means a lot to me." Beth excused herself from the table to avoid any more questions. She couldn't believe that she even asked them—much less that they said yes.

After dinner, Beth called the rectory and extended the invitation. She was grateful they had not made plans. Beth wanted to show them how great everything was working out. Mrs. McCafferty offered to bring a dessert. Beth told them to come at two o'clock on Labor Day.

When Beth talked to Matt, he felt much better when he heard that this was part of her plan to get her father to see how she had changed and then talk to him about resolving their past differences once and for all. It was a perfect plan, they both thought. Matt went to sleep that night feeling relieved and yet surprisingly sad. Finally, his mission was coming to a conclusion, but that would mean that he would not be with Beth anymore. He wondered if they would be reunited in Heaven someday.

♥ ♥ ♥ ♥ ♥ ♥ ♥ ♥

Labor Day was a sunny day. The day promised to be hot, but not as humid as usual. Mary had the fans going on the porch and chairs set out for the guests. Frank was nervous about having a priest with him all day. He told Mary that he was not going to watch what he said just because a priest was there. She laughed at him and told him that a priest was a human being and she was sure that he had heard a few hard words in his day. Frank didn't really use much profanity but had a blunt way of talking to people. Beth played with Emmy in the backyard while waiting for her guests to arrive. She hoped that everything would go perfectly today. She knew Matt was right. If she wanted to stay with her parents, they had to do more than just exist together. They had to act like a family instead of walking around on eggshells all the time. It was not fair to any of them—especially Emmy.

Father Pat and Mrs. McCafferty arrived at two o'clock sharp. Beth ran inside to greet them at the door. Emmy stood behind her mother smiling at the pleasant looking people. She was always shy for about ten seconds when she met someone new. Beth was pleased to finally have an opportunity for them to meet Emmy. Mrs. McCafferty gave her a big hug and handed her a huge lollipop. It was six inches wide with rainbow colors that twisted around towards the center and looked big enough to be a paddle to Emmy. The look on her face made everyone smile.

Mary and Frank walked into the living room and introductions were made. Father Pat was dressed casually without his priest's collar. Mrs. McCafferty's dress was almost exactly the same as Mary's and it got a big laugh that broke the ice. After the introductions were over, Mary suggested that everyone retreat to the porch. She apologized for not having air conditioning, but Father Pat assured her that they did not have that luxury either. Both Mary and Frank were surprised to hear they lived together, but neither thought it was appropriate to ask questions. Frank offered to get drinks and was pleasantly surprised when Father Pat asked for a scotch on the rocks. He had a special bottle that he rarely had a chance to share with anyone. Mrs. McCafferty asked for an ice tea.

When everyone settled on the porch, Frank inquired as to how they had come to know Beth. There was such an age difference that it was hard to believe they shared much in common. Father Pat fielded the question expertly. "I met Beth on one of my walks."

Beth jumped in nervously. "I was in his area, over in Briarsville, visiting a friend and was lost. I asked him for directions and Father was kind enough to show me the way." Father Pat shot Beth an amused look. He was careful not to let the story telling go too far.

"You never mentioned you knew anyone in Briarsville, Beth!" Mary exclaimed.

"Oh, she's new at work. I guess I forgot to tell you."

Father Pat continued, "Beth is such a nice girl. I had a really enjoyable time talking with her. She told me so much about Emmy that I just had to see this little angel myself."

Once the conversation focused on Emmy, the original subject was forgotten. Emmy loved the attention and put on a great performance for her new admirers.

At about four thirty, Frank lit the grill and Mary went inside to make final dinner preparations. Mrs. McCafferty had brought a homemade peach pie that looked scrumptious. Beth set the table and sent her mother back outside to be with Mrs. McCafferty. The two women got along well together and Mrs. McCafferty reminisced about her days on the farm. Father Pat and Frank were die-hard baseball fans and they talked about their love for the game and their guesses on who would make it to the World Series. As usual, the Phillies had had a bad season and they commiserated about better teams in the past. Matt watched everyone from the apple tree. Everything was running smoothly.

When the coals were ready, Frank brought out a large London broil and placed it on the grill. It had been marinating overnight and sizzled when it hit the hot grill, sending light smoke and a terrific aroma throughout the screened porch. Everyone savored the wonderful smell of summer that whet their appetite for the upcoming feast. Mary was serving a pasta salad, a cold green bean and vinaigrette salad, fresh rolls and corn on the cob. Before Frank had the meat carved, everyone was already seated and anxiously waiting to eat. Father Pat gave a blessing and they all dug in.

The wonderful food did not slow down the dinner conversations. Mrs. McCafferty had a great interest in learning to quilt and Mary offered to show her the basic steps. Frank and Father Pat continued their talk on sports and even politics. Both were Republicans with very similar views. Emmy continued her charming antics making faces on her plate with her pasta salad and balancing a spoon on her nose. Beth savored every moment. She was so filled with joy that her face glowed with happiness. At the end of the meal, Mary put on a pot of coffee and everyone retired to the porch for a rest before dessert. Beth and Mary were left in the kitchen together and Mary hugged her daughter. "They are very nice people, Beth. This is such a lovely surprise." She brushed her daughter's hair from her face. "You are just full of surprises these days. I'm so glad you have come home. I really missed my little girl."

"I've missed you, too, Mom. This dinner has meant so much to me. I really like Father Pat and Mrs. McCafferty and I'm so relieved that Dad is getting along with Father Pat so well. I hope we can continue to see them." Beth felt so contented and peaceful that even the sharp pains that came more frequently didn't bother her as much. She resolved to make an appointment to get herself checked out this week.

The coffee maker bubbled and hissed as the last few drops of water percolated through the filter, signaling the coffee was ready. Mary sliced the peach pie and Beth began to bring the pieces out while Mary served the coffee. Beth gave her dad and Father Pat the first two pieces and went into the kitchen for the next round. She found Emmy using her finger to scrape peach filling from the pie pan. "Scat, rug rat, go wait with PopPop while I bring in the rest of the pie." Emmy shot out of the kitchen marching and Beth heard her chanting, "I want pie, I want pie."

Beth walked onto the porch balancing the four plates of pie on her arms like a waitress. She bent her knees to lower herself in front of Mrs. McCafferty, so she could take one of the plates resting on her arms. Frank commented that Beth looked like a professional waitress and everyone laughed. Beth moved around the table to her mother's side and started bending down the same way. The room began to spin and an excruciating pain shot through her entire abdomen, burning like a knife wound. Beth felt chills go up her spine and hot, wet liquid began running down the inside of her thighs. The room spun around until her eyes rolled back and she fainted falling backwards. She landed halfway on the chaise lounge with the pie plates splattering on top of her in her arms.

Mary screamed as she lunged for her daughter's arm, too late to stop her fall. Beth lay unconscious on the floor. Frank and Father Pat scrambled from their seats and Emmy screamed in panic along with her grandmother. The two men straightened Beth out on the floor, while Mary tried to clean up the pie that was crushed into Beth's clothes. Her face that was glowing pink only seconds ago was now pale and clammy. Father Pat instructed Mrs. McCafferty to call 911. As Mary brushed off the pieces of pie, she gasped as she saw Beth was bleeding heavily between the legs.

Frank was patting Beth's face trying to revive her. She was breathing, but would not wake up. "She's bleeding Frank, why is she bleeding?" Mary's mind filled with fear, as she realized how serious this was.

"I don't know, Mary. I don't know. I thought she looked much better since she's been home. Have you noticed anything lately?"

229

Mrs. McCafferty interrupted to tell them that the ambulance was on the way and went over to Emmy to hold the frightened child. "What's wrong with my mommy?" Emmy cried. "Mommy, Mommy!" Mrs. McCafferty put Emmy on her lap and shielded her from the sight of her mother, lying helplessly on the floor. Mary answered Frank's question, "I saw her flinch from a pain she was having a few weeks ago, but she said that it was her period and she was fine." Mary shook her head with regret. "I knew something was wrong with her!"

Father Pat brushed Beth's hair from her face. He checked her pulse, which was weak. Unbeknownst to him, she was also bleeding internally and there was nothing he could do to help her. "Good Lord, help her," he thought. He was full of regret that he did not make her see a doctor when she first arrived at the rectory. He had sworn to her that her confession about the rape would stay between them and for now, he had to remain silent.

The ambulance finally came a few minutes later. The paramedics put down their equipment next to Beth. Both men worked together like a well-oiled machine. They executed their duty with meticulous attention that had saved countless lives in their care and their medical knowledge was as good as any doctor's.

Frank and Father Pat moved the chaise lounge out of the way, so that the paramedic named Justin had more room to work at Beth's left side. He worked at a ferocious pace to evaluate her condition while Mike, the other paramedic, directed questions to Mary, who was still trying to clean up bits of pie from Beth's clothes.

"How old is she?"

"She's twenty-two."

"Can you tell me what happened, Ma'am?"

Mary began to ramble on; speaking so fast it was hard to understand her. Her voice and hands were shaking. "Yes, um, she was serving pie and had to stoop down to hand me a plate, when all of a sudden she cried out and fell backwards onto the chair. I thought the pain was in her stomach, but then I noticed she was bleeding between her legs and we called for help because she wouldn't wake up."

While Mary was speaking, Justin was calling out numbers to Mike, who was able to hear both conversations at the same time. "Her airway's clear." He checked her pulse at the carotid artery in her neck and then took her radial pulse at her wrist. "Pulse is rapid and weak."

Mike turned back to Mary. "Okay, Ma'am. I want you to take your time answering my questions, okay? Now, do you know if your daughter's pregnant?"

The room seemed to grow still with his question. Father Pat shot Mrs. McCafferty a look over everyone huddled around Beth. His eyes grew wide with fear and indecision. Mrs. McCafferty shared his fear and her eyes locked on to his quandary. She sent him back a questioning look that said, "What should we do?"

Mary and Frank shared the same fearful glance, too, unable to believe it was possible.

"Ma'am, do you know if she's pregnant?"

"No, she can't be!" Mary was adamant, but Frank interrupted.

"We don't know that, Mary." He looked at Mike. "We don't know."

"Okay. Do you know if she has had a fall recently or has been assaulted in any way?"

Mary remembered what Beth had told her about the bruise on her face. "Oh yes. A few weeks ago, she told me that she had slipped in the bathroom and hit her face on the sink! Maybe she hurt more than her face and didn't tell me." Mary prayed the paramedic would agree, but he showed no reaction to her answer and went on with other questions.

"Is she allergic to any medications?"

"Not that I know of."

"Does she have any allergies?"

"No."

"Does she have any past history of high blood pressure or use of blood thinners?"

"No."

The whole time Mike was asking Mary questions, Father Pat watched Justin work on Beth. The scene brought him back to his medic days in Vietnam and he understood everything that they were doing. The only thing missing was the sound of bullets flying over their heads. Justin had placed an oxygen mask on Beth's face and put a pad between her legs to catch the flow of blood. He checked her vitals and called out to Mike. "BP's low at 70 palp." Then he started a saline IV in her left elbow with a fluid bolus, open wide. Father Pat knew that her blood pressure was dangerously low and that he was forcing fluids into her as fast as he could to compensate for her blood loss. He looked over at Mrs. McCafferty again and she knew Beth was in real danger, but she still didn't know what to tell him to do. She shook her head to show her wavering.

Beth was lifted onto a gurney and Mike instructed them to follow behind the ambulance to Mercy General. Father Pat offered to drive Mary and Frank in his car. Mrs. McCafferty stayed at the house with Emmy. Emmy watched the van doors close from the living room window frozen in shock. Mrs. McCafferty brought her to the sofa and rocked her as she cried, telling her that her mommy would be okay.

Matt flew back and forth unnoticed in front of the screen room watching in horror as the paramedics wheeled Beth away. He followed them around front and watched the van speed off down the street with its lights and sirens blaring. "My God, Beth, what's happening? This can't be!" He looked up in the sky trying to find a sign from the Heaven he knew was up there. He shouted in a rage so deep that it could only come from someone connected to the pain of the tragedy. "This can't be happening! Tell me! Why is this happening?" Matt's mind panicked and he looped through the air trying to drive the anger and frustration from his small body. He was helpless. How would he know what happened to her? He began a vigil in the front of the house, waiting for Father Pat's car to return so he could find out what happened. He raced to his feeding ground one last time to prepare himself for the long night ahead. His body shook uncontrollably, as he thought about the consequences that loomed over him like a hatchet waiting to strike him down. His focus was not on the failed mission that would send him back to earth to live out another lifetime, but strictly on the fact that he may never see Beth again. Matt rested on a small dogwood tree out front and began to cry. His cry quickly turned into sobs that released the loneliness and helplessness that coursed through his soul. As the night sky turned dark and the stars appeared, the brightest star flickered continuously through the night. It was Anjella, but this time her presence did not bring Matt relief. It only made him feel more at a loss. He sobbed from a depth of his soul he had never known existed.

Frank and Mary felt helpless, too, in the chaos that surrounded them in the emergency room. They had run alongside the gurney, through the doors, as the paramedics shouted out Beth's vital signs to the doctor and nurse, who were waiting for them on the other side. "We have a twenty-two year old female, positive loss of consciousness, vaginal bleeding, uncertain history of pregnancy, report of one fall about two weeks ago, BP 70 palp. We have her on a 15 litre non-rebreather and a 16 gauge in her left AC with saline wide. We got her pressure up to 80. Sinus is 132..." The rest of the stats were muffled as Frank and Mary were left outside of the swinging doors to emergency room one. Justin and Mike came back out and wished them the best and left.

A nurse directed Frank and Mary to the waiting area. They were given forms to fill out for insurance purposes. The nurse told them she would update them on Beth's condition as soon as she could. Father Pat walked in just as they were paging Dr. Robinson from Obstetrics and Gynecology to the emergency room for a consult. He sat across from them in the waiting area as they began their own vigil. Mary was frightened. Everything was turning around for her family and in one moment's time her dream come true was shattered.

About ten minutes later, the doctor that received Beth came into the waiting area. He looked at Frank and Mary. "Are you Beth's parents?" he asked.

"Yes, we are." Frank answered, as they both stood to face the doctor.

"I'm Dr. Dole. Your daughter is hemorrhaging. It is too early to tell what may be causing it. We will have to perform exploratory surgery to find the cause and stop the bleeding. We need you to sign a consent form so we can get started. Dr. Robinson is our OB on staff tonight and a very qualified surgeon. I will be assisting him. We will be able to tell you more after we get a look. We don't have much time." The doctor looked compassionately at the grief stricken parents.

"Of course, go ahead." Frank told him and then signed the release form. Mary dropped down into her seat.

"How bad is it, doctor?" Her bottom lip quivered with her words, fearing the answer.

"I can't honestly tell you until we have a look. As long as we can get the bleeding under control, we should be out of the woods, but I can't promise anything."

Mary squeezed his hand. "Thank you."

The doctor rushed back into the emergency room. It would be two long hours before they saw him again.

Mary looked at Frank, "I know it was that fall she had. She just didn't want to worry us." He nodded his head to console her. He had his own reservations.

Frank and Mary were both grateful that Father Pat was with them. They were not religious people, but in such a helpless state there was no other source you could turn to except for God. No other person could help them now. Father Pat made the sign of the cross and began to pray. Frank and Mary clung to each other for support and waited what seemed to be an eternity for any news.

After one hour went by, Frank stopped looking at his watch. His mind kept drifting from the past two weeks to a long time ago when he held Beth in his arms as an infant. Both now and then, he felt completely helpless as her father. She was so tiny and frail as a baby and he thought about how tiny and frail she looked laying helplessly on the floor back at the house while they waited for help. In the last few weeks he saw Beth in a new light. Just when he began thinking he may have judged her so wrongly, this happened. Would she have the audacity to try and fool him into accepting another fatherless grandchild? The word bastard was on the tip of his tongue, until he thought about Emmy. He looked over at Mary, who was lost in deep thought, and hoped to God that he was wrong. He would rather feel like a heel for doubting her than deal with the reality of another lie. It would prove to him that you couldn't change bad blood. It was more than he could bear.

Mary leaned against Frank almost afraid to breathe. The minutes that dragged by brought horrible thoughts to her mind. Was she losing her little girl again? Why hadn't she acted on her instincts and told Beth the truth? Maybe all of this conflict in their lives could have been avoided. All these years she was so afraid of rocking the boat. Now, with her whole life capsized, she could do nothing but look back and regret. The sight of two doctors coming from the operating room interrupted her thoughts. One of them was Dr. Dole and the other was Dr. Robinson. They did not have encouraging looks on their faces. They sat down next to Father Pat and leaned forward toward Frank and Mary. Dr. Dole introduced them to Dr. Robinson.

Dr. Robinson spoke. "Mr. and Mrs. Harris. There are some complications that we discovered during surgery and I'm afraid I don't have good news."

Mary gasped and clung to Frank waiting to hear.

He continued. "Your daughter is alive and we were able to stop the bleeding for now, but we have discovered the cause of the bleeding, which is the bad news. Part of her bleeding was caused by a miscarriage. It was very early. She appeared to be about a month pregnant." Dr. Robinson watched Frank gasp and drop his head into his hands to cover his face. He dreaded giving them the next bit of news.

"But that was not the primary cause of her bleeding. In addition to the miscarriage, she has an advanced case of cervical cancer. We found a tumor the size of a half-dollar. This is what caused the hemorrhaging. The hemorrhaging may have caused the miscarriage, but it's not clear. We performed an exploratory laparotomy through her abdomen and found that the cancer had spread through her bowels and bladder. We are running tests to see if it has spread elsewhere. Normally we would perform a hysterectomy, but her cancer is so advanced that removing her organs would be futile at this point. We were able to temporarily stop the bleeding, but it could start up at any time because of the position of the tumor in the cervix. I'm afraid it does not look good. We are conferring with our staff Oncologist who will be out to talk to you shortly, but I'm sorry to have to tell you to brace yourself for the worst." There was an awkward moment of silence that Dr. Robinson always hated when he announced such devastating news, when the overwhelmed family stared in utter disbelief at him, and made him feel like a messenger from the underworld. Medical school did not prepare him for this everyday ordeal and it never got easier. He nervously felt obliged to offer a more detailed explanation. "Unfortunately, pain and systemic symptoms are late manifestations of this disease. Cervical cancer is a very serious type of cancer and one that is not easily controlled if not caught in the early stages. A PAP test usually detects early signs, but ten percent of all cases metastasize in less than three months time. Once again, I'm very sorry." The doctors awkwardly left the room.

Father Pat put his hands to his face and shook his head. "Oh, Beth." He thought. "You were so worried about covering up the rape, you ignored the warning signs of cancer." He rubbed his eyes to still the tears that began to flow.

Frank's stunned reaction turned to anger. Mary was startled by the sudden change. "So, she was pregnant!" Frank exclaimed. "She came home to dump another child on us. That was what she was up to. I told you Mary, I was right!" His voice turned bitter. "She'll never change. She came home acting all innocent, when in fact, she had gone out and played her games as usual, expecting us to clean up after her." Frank looked at Mary and then at Father Pat, "Maybe this is God's way of punishing her for being such a liar!"

"Frank, stop it!" Mary cried. "You don't know what you're saying. Didn't you hear the doctor? Beth is dying. We are going to lose our little girl and all you can do is condemn her?" Mary looked at Father Pat helplessly. She sank back into the chair and began to cry. Frank stood facing the wall in the corner of the waiting room.

Father Pat went over to Frank and put his hand on his shoulder. "Frank, I know the news is shocking. But try not to judge her until you find out the whole story. There *are* reasonable explanations for these things sometimes. Don't ruin what is probably your last chance to be close to your daughter."

Frank turned to him, pulling away from his hand. His eyes were filled with bitterness. "What daughter, Father? I don't have a daughter anymore." Frank walked out of the waiting area and went outside the emergency room doors. Mary yelled after him. "No, Frank! Don't do this!"

Father Pat moved over to Mary and tried to comfort her while they waited for further news about Beth. He was completely stunned by Frank's reaction now that he knew him. He wondered about what could possibly have happened between Beth and him to make Frank react this way.

Dr. Miller, the Oncologist, came out about thirty minutes later. He hated bringing such fatal news to loved ones. There was no easy way to tell the patient's family, so he was direct. He hesitated, looking around for Mr. Harris. Father Pat signaled him on, so he gingerly proceeded. "Mrs. Harris, I am so sorry about your daughter. I have checked over the findings from the

CAT scan and biopsies and the doctors are right. There is no sense in operating at this point. We couldn't possibly remove all of the cancer cells and it will only spread the cancer further. Your daughter has an acute case that is spreading rapidly. It's in Stage IV-B. In layman's terms, Beth's cancer has spread through the bloodstream. There is evidence of several lesions in her lungs. All we can do for her now is make her comfortable. We are moving her to a room in the Oncology Ward. We will do everything we can for her there. She will probably wake up in the next few hours and you can stay with her as long as you like. Mrs. Harris, does this type of cancer run in your family?"

Mary froze at the question. Her eyes darted over to the emergency room door where Frank was standing. She couldn't speak a word. Father Pat gently shook her. "Mary, are you okay? The doctor just wants to know if you have a history of this in your family." He looked at Dr. Miller for help. Mary seemed to be in shock.

"It's okay if you don't know, Mrs. Harris. Usually in these severe cases, there will be one or two close relatives that have had cervical cancer, especially on the mother's side. I was just going to suggest that you get checked out and keep an eye on this in the future."

Mary continued to stare at the door but murmured a thank you to the doctor.

Dr. Miller concluded. "Your daughter can remain with us in the hospital or you can arrange for another service, such as hospice care, if you think she would prefer to be at home."

Mary blinked for a moment when she finally registered what she heard. "Are you saying, Doctor, that she *is* dying?"

"Yes, Mrs. Harris, I am very sorry."

"How long does she have?" It took all Mary had to whisper the question. She clung to Father Pat for support. Her knees felt too weak to stand on her own.

"It is hard to tell. Each patient has a different tolerance in the final phase. She may live a few days, or maybe even two weeks, but I don't think you can count on much longer. At this stage Mrs. Harris, it is better to hope that she doesn't linger, for her sake."

Mary collapsed completely into Father Pat's arms. She began the mourning process that a mother goes through when hearing that she is about to lose her child. Only she didn't even have her husband there to cling to and face it together. Frank watched Mary's reaction from the glass entrance door to the emergency room. He knew by her body language what she had been told. He wanted to be with her now, but he just could not find strength to go to her. He had already started the mourning process himself, when he discovered his daughter had betrayed them.

Mary and Father Pat followed Beth up to her hospital room in the Oncology Unit. Father Pat called Mrs. McCafferty and told her the sad news and the strange course of events that took place. They cried on the phone together. He told her about Frank's reaction that added to Mary's misery and his own guilt became unbearable. "Good Lord, Gladys, how can I keep what we know from them?"

"We've never broken our promise before, Father."

"It has never been this critical before!"

"I know, Father. Maybe we need to pray on this. I know whatever happens, you'll do the right thing."

"Thanks, Gladys. I needed to hear you say that."

When she hung up the phone, it dawned on her that that was the first time he ever called her by her first name. Emmy stirred on the couch. Mrs. McCafferty thought it best to take Emmy up to bed in her own room. Emmy sat up and rubbed her eyes. The memory of what happened flooded back into her mind. "Was that my mommy?" she said despairingly.

"No, that was Father Pat. He said they will be at the hospital the rest of the night and for us not to worry."

"But you're crying? Why are you crying?" Emmy was a very observant little girl.

"Oh, I guess I'm just worried, like you. I love your mommy, too, dear. She is a very good person." Mrs. McCafferty gave Emmy a smile. "Now, I think it is best if you go upstairs and go to sleep. I will let you know as soon as I hear how your mommy is doing."

"Okay," Emmy said and started to walk upstairs.

Mrs. McCafferty swallowed a sob as she watched brave little Emmy march up to her bed. She was such a sweet child. It was so unfair that she was about to loose her mother.

Emmy changed into her favorite Barbie® pajamas that her mommy had bought for her and climbed into bed. Mrs. McCafferty asked, "Do you say bedtime prayers?"

"Yep, I do mostly with my Grandmom."

"Do you say a particular prayer?"

"No, we just talk to God about what's important to us." Emmy folded her hands and bowed her head and began her own little prayer. "Dear God, thank you for bringing to my family Father Pat and Mrs. McCafferty. I don't know what happened to my mommy, but I know you will take care of her. I love her and I know you love her, too. Love, your Emmy. Oh, and I almost forgot! A penny for your thoughts!" She looked up at Mrs. McCafferty to explain. "Mommy and me always say that when we pray together."

Mrs. McCafferty kissed her on the head and made no attempt to speak. The tears fell down her face as she tucked the little angel under the covers. She turned out the bedroom light and closed the door halfway. She wanted to make sure she could hear Emmy if she called out.

Mrs. McCafferty walked straight downstairs. She never noticed the light that illuminated Emmy's room after she left. She never heard Emmy's sweet voice greet her visitor.

Chapter 18

It was seven o'clock the next day when Father Pat and Frank wearily walked in the front door. Mary had insisted on staying with Beth. She slept on a cot that the nurses put next to Beth's bed, so she would be there the moment Beth opened her eyes. Beth drifted in and out of consciousness that night, but never stayed awake long enough to speak or hear clearly.

Mrs. McCafferty was asleep on the couch when they arrived. Emmy was still upstairs asleep in her bedroom. Frank went straight upstairs without a word. He arranged for time off at work, closed the blinds and collapsed on the bed. Mrs. McCafferty and Father talked about the situation. Father Pat had two meetings today. He could cancel his 2:00 dentist appointment, but he needed more than ever to keep his 11:00 appointment with Father Massey. In fact, he intended to go straight to Larry's office this morning. Mrs. McCafferty said she would stay at the house and take care of Emmy today. She was sure Mary would spend the entire day at the hospital.

Mrs. McCafferty was concerned about who would tell Emmy what was going on. Frank did not appear to be capable of such a task this morning. Father Pat told her to say nothing until he spoke to Mary. Emmy should hear the news from her family if it was possible. Mrs. McCafferty went into the kitchen to make him a pot of coffee, while he rested on the couch for an hour. It was enough of a nap to keep him going.

Matt dozed on and off throughout the night, awakening every time a car approached. When Father Pat finally pulled up, Matt was in a deep stupor. His tired body was not sure if it was asleep or awake anymore. The sound of the car doors closing jarred him into consciousness. He watched the two men enter the house by the front door. Matt moved down to the living room window but could not hear the conversation going on between Mrs. McCafferty and the priest. He could tell by Mrs. McCafferty's concerned look that the news was serious. He was desperate to find out what was going on, but didn't see how he could. He flew back up to the dogwood branch to think.

At nine o'clock Emmy bounced down the stairs. Father Pat was just waking up. "Good morning, Father!" Emmy exclaimed enthusiastically as she bounced by him.

"Good morning, Emmy." he replied, marveling at her cheerful demeanor.

Mrs. McCafferty came out of the kitchen quickly when she heard Emmy's voice.

"Good morning, Mrs. McC." Emmy smiled and climbed up on her chair swinging her legs back and forth under the kitchen table. "Can I have some cereal for breakfast?" Emmy smiled again, as if she were the cat who swallowed a canary.

"Well now," Mrs. McCafferty exclaimed, as she wiped her hands on the apron she had borrowed. "You are in a fine mood today."

"Yep. Where did you sleep last night?"

"On the couch. Would you like some juice with your cereal?" Mrs. McCafferty stared at Emmy out of the corner of her eye as she hunted through the cabinets for cereal. She looked at Father Pat quizzically and shrugged. Father Pat sat down at the table, too.

"Did you sleep here, too, Father Pat?" Emmy began carrying on a conversation fit for a twelve year old.

"No darling, I was at the hospital with your Grandmom and PopPop." Father Pat guarded his response carefully.

"Oh." Was all Emmy replied, as Mrs. McCafferty set the cereal and bowl in front of her and began to fill her bowl. Emmy ate two bowls of cereal and finished her orange juice. She climbed off her chair and went upstairs to dress.

Father Pat and Mrs. McCafferty looked at each other in amazement. Emmy seemed to be unperturbed by everything that happened last night. She made no inquiries about Beth. Her mood was so peaceful and content that they wondered if she might be in a state of shock or trying to cope with the situation through denial. Mrs. McCafferty assured him that Emmy didn't know anything about Beth's cancer.

Father Pat finished his coffee and one of Mrs. McC's cinnamon buns that she produced out of thin air. Father was too preoccupied to notice. He told her that he would stop by the rectory to change and meet Mary at the hospital after his meeting with Father Massey.

Matt watched Father Pat leaving by the front door. The suspense was now more than he could bear. He had to know what was going on. Without thinking Matt zoomed off the dogwood tree and swept by Father Pat circling in the air directly over his head and then hovered about six feet away directly in front of Father Pat's car. The priest was taken aback by the commotion until he realized it was a hummingbird causing the ruckus.

Father Pat stood staring at this amazing creature before him. He locked onto Matt's eyes and felt the same uncanny human to human connection that Beth described. He was in awe that such a miraculous creation now held the entire soul of a human being, even if it was a mistake. The intense depth of the bird's eyes made him feel certain that it was the same hummingbird that Beth had talked with.

Matt could speak no words to the priest. Only his eyes could convey his desperate need to know what was going on. Father Pat picked this up immediately.

"I'm afraid it is all bad news, my friend." Father Pat chose not to mince words with Matt. He knew they were all running out of time to help Beth. He looked sadly at the helpless soul who unintentionally handicapped himself in his grand mission. "Beth is dying, Matt." Father Pat shook his head at the very idea. "She has cancer that is terminal. They are giving her no more than two weeks, if that. She was pregnant from the rape and the cancer apparently caused a miscarriage. Her father believes she came home to burden them with another child and thinks she was trying to deceive them. He has disowned her. He doesn't know about the rape and I am sworn by the sanctity of the confessional not to disclose the truth. The only hope we have is that Beth will tell her parents the truth."

He looked at the bird's shocked expression and thought that he saw the tiniest tears drip off the bird's beak. "Matt, my heart is breaking, too." He said. "I think her father was about to renew their relationship and now this." Father Pat lowered his head feeling suddenly helpless and as small as the tiny hummingbird. He looked back up at Matt. "I know how hard you've tried to help patch things up between Beth and her father. I'm sorry for everything that has gone wrong." He began to get into his car and turned back to Matt. "Maybe you can ask God for me why things like this happen. It is a question I intend to address myself the first opportunity I get!" Father Pat felt a little anger rising in his throat with his last words.

Matt watched him drive off and went to the feeders for breakfast. He hardly felt like eating. The thought crossed his mind that dying might feel better right now. But his love for Beth urged him on and he forced himself to eat as much as possible before returning to the tree. He vowed he would not let Beth down like the rest of the men in her life had done. He would be with her to the end.

♥♥♥♥♥♥♥

When Father Pat burst into Father Massey's office an hour before their scheduled golf date, he knew Pat was there for more than a round of golf. In fact, when Pat threw his father's hat down on the corner of his desk, he pretty much wrote off the golf date completely. Pat never wore that hat unless he had serious business to attend to.

"What's wrong, Pat?" He also had a hunch that it would be about Beth.

Father Pat plopped down in the chair in front of him and covered his face with his hands. "It's Beth. She's in the hospital."

Father Massey frowned and buzzed his secretary. "Jennifer!"

241

"Yes, Father."

"Hold all of my calls, please."

"Yes, Father."

"What happened Pat?" He prayed it would be unrelated to Pat's previous actions, but he knew that was too good to be true.

"Mrs. McC and I went over to spend yesterday with her family. I told you Beth went home a few weeks ago." Father Massey held his breath waiting to hear his next words.

"Everything was going splendidly. Her parents are very nice people."

"What happened?"

"Beth was serving pie and she collapsed right out of the blue. No one saw it coming. It just came on so fast."

"What did?"

"A miscarriage." Father Pat watched Larry slump in back in his chair, breathing an exclamation. "It gets worse, Larry. It might have been caused by cancer. She has an advanced case of cervical cancer. The doctors give her two weeks max."

As terrible as it was to hear, Father Massey inwardly thanked God that there was a cause unrelated to her assault. At least the Church would be cleared of fault. He felt horrible for even thinking this, but he needed to protect the Church.

"Good Lord! I'm sorry Pat. I know how fond you have become of her."

Father Pat shook his head in agreement. "Yes I have Larry. That's why I'm in such a quandary."

Father Massey was surprised by his comment. "A quandary about what? Surely the cancer was there before she was assaulted. You can't blame yourself for this."

"No, not for the cancer or the rape, but I could have gotten her to a doctor sooner. I don't know, maybe that would of made a difference."

"Come on Pat, a month? If she's got less than two weeks, could it have really made a difference? I think you're being too hard on yourself."

"Well, whether I am or not, that's really not the problem I need your help with."

Father Massey braced himself. He knew Pat better than any other priest in the Diocese. They had been friends for a long time. Not one time in all of his escapades did he ever ask for his help. And there were many times when he wished he had asked. But this wasn't one of them. "What's the problem?"

"Beth won't tell her family that she was raped. Her father believes that she came home to dump another child on them to care for and he has disowned her. He wouldn't even come to her hospital room. I brought him home and in the car he didn't say a word! He was stiff as cardboard. I couldn't believe it. The doctors stood there and told him that his only daughter was gravely ill and all he could think of was that she had lied to him about the pregnancy. And you know, he's really a decent guy. I just don't get it! She's a good kid with a great big heart and love of life. It doesn't make any sense."

"Pat, we've come across this a dozen times before. Some people are stubborn, but he'll probably come around. They almost always do. It sounds like he's just in shock."

Father Pat rose from his chair and walked over to the window with his hands in his pockets.

"There's a lot more to this situation that I haven't told you. It's very complicated."

"When is anything you ever do simple, Pat!" Father Massey chuckled. "You might as well tell me everything."

And so Father Pat did. He told him about her attempt to run away and how she met Matt. He even told him that Matt had intended to enter his body, but entered a hummingbird accidentally and that he could only talk to Beth.

As the bizarre story unfolded, Father Massey was floored. He studied Pat, looking for signs of a breakdown and his disbelief was written all over his face.

Father Pat laughed when he caught the look. "What? You don't believe me? You think I'm nuts? Wish I were Larry." He rocked back and forth on his heels. "So now you see my quandary!"

Father Massey sat tapping his fingers together. "That's quite a story, Pat. And if you weren't such a close friend, I wouldn't believe you for a minute. Still, as crazy and unbelievable as this is, I still don't see what your problem is."

Father Pat looked out the window. "I want to tell her father about the rape. He needs to know."

"Well, that's not a problem, if you use discretion, unless it was a confession and then you know you can't do it."

"It was."

"I thought you said she confided with you in the living room."

"That was about Matt. She told me about the rape experience when she was still upstairs. The only way I could get her to say anything was to hear it as a confession."

"Then you can't, Pat. You know this. Once you offered to hear it as a confession, you swore yourself to secrecy. You shouldn't even be telling me this!"

Father Pat leaned on the back of the chair with both hands. "But she's a child and she doesn't know what she's doing! If she doesn't reconcile with her father, they all lose!"

"I know that upsets you, but it's her choice. You can't interfere. You took an oath! It didn't specify an age group. She's not a little girl."

Father Pat became upset. "Larry! Are you going to tell me that it is better to let her father live the rest of his life believing she deceived him, when all she did was make one mistake in trusting people too much? Larry, she's scared that if she tells him that he will not believe she's innocent, but I can back her up and *I know* he'll come around. For God's sake, she's dying!"

Father Massey rose from his chair and leaned over his desk. Their conversation became a heated debate. "As sad as it is that two people are unable to reconcile before one of them dies, you know the oath that you took by heart. *'You must love the truth and be faithful to the Magisterium of the Church! You are bound to absolute secrecy regarding the sins of the penitent. You can make no use of the knowledge that you receive and there are no exceptions to the Sacramental Seal!'*

"All I know, Larry, is that there is a lost soul out there who has a chance to be redeemed and I'm the only one who can help her. Not even the messenger from Heaven is able to do anything right now. I don't know if I can live with myself if I don't try."

"Pat, don't do anything crazy. Think about your career. What is it about this girl and her family that has driven you to the point of possibly giving up everything you've worked for? You have been so passionate about the oaths you made to serve God. What has happened to you?"

Father Pat was surprised by Larry's new tone. "Career? What are you talking about, career? I never saw my vocation as a career choice. If I wanted a career, I would have been on Wall Street! No, I became a priest to help people. Remember that word Larry, help? You might as well be wearing a three-piece suit and working in a tower across from City Hall! You speak of passion, where's the passion around here? The Chancery might as well be a law firm.

"It doesn't even feel like a church around here anymore. When's the last time there was a meeting to discuss developing a new social program? All I ever hear about is budget meetings, legal briefings, fund-raising and parish cuts. You're practically the only priest here who's ever worked in one of the diocese parishes. The people around here don't have any idea who they represent. Can't you see, Larry? That's why they created your job. So they didn't have to get their hands dirty with the little details, such as the welfare of their working priests."

Larry pounded his hand in response. "The Bishop had the best intentions for his priests when he created this job."

"He wouldn't have had to make *your* position if his staff were in touch with their own people!"

Father Pat went on. "And what's so special about this family I'm involved with? Everything! They are simply honest, hardworking people that are entrenched in this business we call life, twenty-four hours a day. You know, a priest's life isn't nine-to-five like the administrators want us to be. My parishioners don't stop living their lives after five o'clock each day. When they have a crisis, I stay with them all day and night if I have to. They *are my* life! And it isn't always easy for me to draw the line on where I need to stand. Sometimes, I have to let God draw it for me—not the Church!"

Father Massey waited a moment to let his friend cool down. "I'm sorry, Pat. I know you're hurting. Maybe I have been in this job too damn long. But, still, you can't break your vow! I've stood by and watched you bend the rules time and time again, but this time, it's too big! You know, I'll have to report you. I can't look the other way. You'll never be able to hear another confession again. How could you trust yourself? This is one of the most serious breaches a priest can make and I can't let it go. Not in good conscience."

Father Pat picked up his hat from the corner of Larry's desk and walked to the door. "I appreciate the warning, Larry, but you just made me realize that whatever I decide, it's already over for me. Thanks for your help. You've always been a good friend to me."

Before he opened the door, he turned to his friend with a wry smile on his face. "Funny, old man, I thought this office *was my confessional.* Maybe *now* you can understand the quandary that I'm in!" With a soft chuckle he opened the door and left. Father Pat always loved pulling the rug out from under his buddy.

Father Massey shook his head and swore to himself. "You sly, old son-of-a-bitch! How do you always manage to turn the tables on me?" He rubbed his temples and slapped his hands on his desk. "Jesus, what's this job come to?" He buzzed his secretary.

"Jennifer, get me an appointment with the Bishop as soon as possible." He got up and walked over to the window. His good friend was right; either way you go, you lose. It was time to get out of the confessional business, before he, too, had to make the same choice.

Father Pat arrived back at the hospital at noon. He found Mary sitting at Beth's side wiping her hair off her face. She was talking to Beth in a soft voice, so low that even Beth would not be able to hear her. "Mary, has she come around yet?" Mary turned, almost jumping at his voice.

"Oh, Father, you startled me a little. I'm so tired. Yes, she has been awake on and off for the last two hours, but we have not talked much. She knows she is in the hospital and has had surgery, but I haven't told her anything else. I was hoping that Frank would come along to help me with that." Her voice choked up. "I haven't had the strength to tell her myself. It's like my heart won't let me utter the words, hoping that will make it all go away." Mary turned to Father Pat and he embraced her weakened body. It felt soothing to have his support. Mary wondered if Frank would even come back to the hospital. She wiped her eyes again for the one-hundredth time and continued. "The nurse that was just in told me that someone would be stopping by to talk to me about the hospital's hospice program. They have an offsite hospice facility and a home program. She said that the home program is used the most, but I suppose we should let Beth decide where she would be more comfortable."

Father Pat sat down on the end of the cot across from Mary. "The at-home hospice service appears to be the best option given Beth's prognosis. It will give her the greatest dignity at the time of her death. It also helps the family through the transition. I know many of the staff and volunteers who are with the program. They are wonderful people. You should strongly encourage Beth to choose this as her best alternative." He looked at Beth lying so still in the hospital bed. Tubes and monitors were surrounding her, distorting her beauty. This was certainly no way to pass on to God's kingdom. The cold medicinal experience would leave scars on the hearts of everyone's memories of their precious loved one. Father was also hoping that being at home could possibly help Frank and Beth reconcile.

Just then, Beth stirred and opened her eyes. Mary was relieved to see that she appeared more cognizant than before. Barely able to move, Beth's eyes followed along the lines of the many tubes and wires connected to her body. She knew something bad had happened. Mary smiled at her and she managed a smile back. "Hi, Mom, you're still here. You should go get some rest." Beth tried to move but was too weak. She noticed Father Pat standing behind her mother and smiled again. "Oh no, you brought in the big cheese. I must really be in bad shape." She joked.

Father Pat moved around the bed and gently sat beside her, moving her hand aside so he would not jar her IV. "You didn't think you could get rid of me that easily, did ya?" He sounded more like a grandfather than a priest.

"So, is someone going to tell me how bad it is or do I have to guess?" Beth was hoping her bantering would ease the pressure for her mother. "By the way, how is Emmy? Is she really upset?" Mary looked over at Father Pat for help. She could not speak a word.

"Emmy is doing fine this morning." Father Pat jumped in. "She was in a great mood when she came downstairs. She hasn't been told anything yet."

Beth knew this meant that the news was serious. "So, what is it exactly that you're waiting to tell her?" Mary dropped her eyes and squeezed Beth's hand at the same time swallowing hard in an attempt to fight back the tears in her eyes.

"Beth, there is more news than what I told you earlier." Mary wiped her running nose with a tissue. "I told you that you were hemorrhaging and that is why they operated, but there was a reason for the hemorrhaging that I didn't tell you about."

Beth managed a dry swallow and braced herself. She had a foreboding sense that there was much more to her condition than when she first awoke. It was a feeling that she could not put into words. Her mother continued.

"The doctors said that you had a miscarriage. You were about one month pregnant." Beth shot a look over to Father Pat who was nodding affirmation to her mother's words.

"No, that can't be! Oh my God." Beth twisted her face away from her mother's sight in total horror at the thought that her rape resulted in a pregnancy. It was beyond belief. She closed her eyes and swallowed hard before her next question. "Does Daddy know?"

Her mother nodded and began to cry. Beth knew what that meant. She had come so far with her father and now he would have one more reason to continue his disappointment in her. It was over. She thought about Matt for a moment and what this meant to him. Her poor judgment had ruined it for everyone. Her heart sank at the news. Beth's thoughts were interrupted by her mother's voice once more.

"Beth, there's more news." Her mother was crying and Beth could not fathom what it could mean.

"Beth, the hemorrhaging was caused by cancer." She sniffed to clear her nose and wiped her eyes. "You have cervical cancer and it is in an advanced stage. There is no way for the doctors to remove it." Mary sobbed the last few words, "It's too late to fix. Oh, my sweet baby."

Father Pat held Beth's hand as she tried to grasp her mother's words. He watched the news register on her pale face. Tears began to form in her eyes as she contemplated the meaning of each word. "Are you saying I'm dying, Mom?" Her lips began to quiver.

Her mother could not answer, she just dropped her head and cried harder into her hands. She looked up and embraced Beth, holding on to her like a baby and wishing she never had to let her go.

All three of them cried together for a few minutes. Beth composed herself and began to think about Emmy. "No! Don't worry Mom. It's okay. You know how doctors get. They exaggerate! How many times have we heard of people who were told they would never walk again or had six months to live and they made complete recoveries. There are so many options available these days. We just have to do a little research. I don't want Emmy to know anything. After I recover from surgery, I'll be as good as new. We'll fight it, Mom. Don't worry." She squeezed Mary's hand and then she asked, "Does Daddy know about the cancer, too?"

Mary shook her head, "Yes, he does."

"Is he going to be here soon?"

Mary looked over at Father Pat for direction. He simply nodded for her to tell Beth the truth. "I don't know Beth. He was very upset to hear about the miscarriage. He thinks you were coming home so we could help you raise another child."

Beth shot a look of desperation at Father Pat. "No, Mom, I didn't even know I was pregnant! Please believe me!"

Mary patted her hand, "I do, Beth, I really do. I know you're a good girl. I've always known that. I should have stood up for you a long time ago. Please forgive me. But your father is different. He takes everything so seriously. I'll see what I can do."

"Mom, can you leave me alone with Father Pat for a moment? I need to talk with him about something." Mary looked surprised but honored Beth's wish.

"Okay. I'll go get a cup of coffee and call home. When I get back, I need to talk to you about a few things." Mary forced a smile and nervously left them.

Beth looked at Father Pat and said with a serious tone. "Father, you can't tell them I was raped. You simply *can't!*"

"Beth, are you serious? I don't think withholding the truth is wise for anyone. Don't you think it would help your father understand?" Father Pat wasn't surprised by her request. He knew she had a big stubborn streak like her father.

"No, you can't! I don't want them to ever know I was raped. You heard my mother. At least she has faith in me that I am a good person. She could understand me getting accidentally pregnant because I was involved with someone, but she would never be able to forgive herself for allowing me to leave home and end up being raped. Besides, my father would probably place the blame on me anyway. Can't you see? I can never win with him. No, I have a lot of work to do now and I don't need the extra confusion the rape would bring to them or to me." Beth was agitated, but now smiled at her reliable friend.

Father Pat shook his head as he thought about her words. "Okay, I'll do as you wish, but for the record, I don't believe it is a wise decision. Please take some time to reconsider. You don't know how your father will take the news." He looked at her and began to smile. "You know, little girl, you are a very stubborn person when you want to be!"

"I know, I guess I'm more like my father than I'm willing to admit." Beth's fatigue began to show. Her voice became a hoarse whisper.

Father Pat stroked Beth's arm lightly. "I think right now you need to get some sleep. Your mother and I will be close by. Get some rest, child. We'll work this out."

"Father Pat?" Beth pleaded with him. "I'm not really going to die, am I?"

Father brushed a tear off his cheek. His silent reaction told her everything she didn't want to know. But he was wrong, she thought. This wasn't happening. In a few days, everything would be back to normal. She'll show them all. And then she'll go off to California with Emmy and live happily ever after.

"No!" she whispered to him while her eyes closed. She wanted to say more but blackness took over and she slept.

Father Pat sat by her with his head hung low and wept holding his container of holy oil in his hand, but he didn't have the nerve to use it. "God, please don't make me use this!" he pleaded before slipping it back in his pocket and leaving the room to find Mary.

Almost a whole day had past the next time Beth woke up. A noise in the hospital corridor brought her back to her senses. The shades were drawn on the windows and the room was dark, except for the light over her bed. She canvassed the room looking for her mother, unable to guess the time. The cot next to her bed was empty. Slowly the conversation with her mother and Father Pat crept back into her mind. As she tried to digest everything she was told, she developed a lump in her throat that caused her to cough. It seemed that even her body was having a difficult time swallowing what she had heard. The coughing brought on a burning pain in her stomach, which reminded her that the surgery was real.

A quiet desperation enveloped her as she tried to move her body. Her legs felt like lead and her arms were restricted from the IV tubes. When she tried to roll over, she tugged on the catheter and drainage tubes that were tapped to her legs, causing another pain that froze her movement.

"Oh God! Why now?" Her mind returned to the Labor Day dinner. She was so happy, she thought. Everything was perfect. Her dad was laughing and he even smiled at her. She remembered right before the pain came that she was sure that he winked at her after he made the waitress comment. "No, no, not now!" She thought. She was so close. Then she remembered Matt and wished he were with her right now so she could ask him, "Why, why would God do this to me now?" Matt was the only one who could help her. "I have to get home to see him! He must know why this is happening. This must be why he's here. I need to talk to him and be with Emmy. Oh, my baby. God, I love her so much. This is all a big mistake! I'm going to live. All of this nonsense about cancer! It's just a scare. Maybe it's a test! When we get past this, everything will be alright."

The morphine that the nurse had put into her IV just before she woke up was beginning to take effect. The burning pain in her abdomen was fading. A sleepy feeling started to overcome her. Beth was having trouble staying focused. Just then, her mother walked into the room carrying a large styrofoam cup of coffee. Mary was glad to find her awake and rushed to her side. She looked exhausted herself.

"Good morning, sweetheart!" Mary placed her coffee on the table by Beth's bed and stroked Beth's hair gingerly, as if she were a china doll. "You slept a long time, it's morning. The nurses said that is to be expected after surgery. They said it takes the body a few days to adjust to the morphine that you're getting. But in a day or two, you won't feel so tired." Mary tried to act as normal as possible. She didn't know what else to do.

Beth forced her eyes to stay open. "How's Emmy, Mom? What have you told her?"

"I went home for a little while last night. I didn't tell her much. I told her that you were operated on and that you wouldn't be home for awhile. She wants to come and see you. She was working on a picture for you when I left to come back here."

"You slept here all night?"

"Yes, of course. I could never sleep at home. I wanted to be here when you woke up. Although, I didn't time my coffee break very well did I?" She snickered.

Beth smiled. "I had just opened my eyes, right before you came in." Suddenly Beth lost her train of thought.

They sat together in a moment of awkward silence. Mary didn't know how to bring up what she needed to discuss next.

"Beth, we need to talk about our options."

Beth noticed her mom's apprehension, even through the fuzzy lens of her drugged world.

"About what?"

"About what we do next. The doctors, they say," Mary began to wring her hands, "that there's nothing they can do to treat you here and by the end of the week, you would be in good enough shape to be moved."

Beth didn't understand what Mary was driving at. "Moved where? To a cancer center? Oh, I think we should ask the doctors which hospital in Philly has the best center. I know my insurance will cover any one of them and it won't be so far away from home." Beth coughed again as she was thinking about what Matt had told her about his mom's healing center. She was in a confused state that began to agitate her. She struggled to hold her eyes open. "There's a center, Mom, called the Healing Touch Center or something close to that. It helps people like me. They use other treatments with herbs and vitamins and stuff."

"Beth," Mary interrupted. "The doctor's were referring to a hospice program at home."

"Hospice! Isn't that for dying people?" Her own words began to sink in as she said them. "Mom, you believe the doctors?"

Mary scrambled for an answer. She wasn't sure what to say. "Honey, the doctor's say the cancer is very bad. Too bad to treat, in any way."

Beth started to cry. "So, they're just gonna send me home to die? In front of Emmy? They're not gonna try anything?"

"Beth, you don't have to go home. You can stay here, if you would feel more comfortable."

"But they're not gonna do anything!" Beth moaned from a pain in her stomach that she got from thrashing about in bed.

"Honey, don't get upset. Please lay still. I'll get a nurse."

Mary rushed from the room and ran into Father Pat in the hall. "Father, help me. I've upset Beth and I need a nurse. She's in pain!"

"Calm down Mary. I'll find one. Go back and wait with her."

A few seconds later, Father Pat and a nurse came rushing in. The nurse checked Beth's abdomen and her IV. "Everything looks okay. It was probably from twisting the drainage tube here." The nurse showed Mary the tube she was talking about. "Everything is very swollen right now. I'll get an ice bag for it. Just try not to move Beth. You'll feel better in a day or two. Before she left, she raised Beth up to an almost sitting position.

Beth avoided eye contact with her mother and Father Pat. Mary started to explain to him what happened when an attractive middle-age woman stepped into the room. She spoke to Mary.

"Good morning, my name is Michelle Green. I'm the hospital coordinator for Outpatient Services." Then she recognized Father Pat. "Good morning, Father. How are you?"

"Just fine, Michelle. This is Mary Harris." Michelle shook her hand.

"And this must be Beth." She moved to Beth's side. Beth remained silent.

"Yes." Mary replied.

"Hi, Beth." Beth looked at her but didn't respond. Michelle was used to this situation.

"Beth, I need to speak to your mom a minute and then we'll be back, okay?"

Beth said nothing and looked out the window.

Michelle signaled Mary and Father Pat to move into the hallway. They walked down the hall to a group of chairs and sat down. Mary was distraught.

Father Pat spoke. "Mary started to approach Beth about the idea of going home and she became very upset."

Mary added, "Beth assumed I was talking about going to a cancer treatment center, not going home to die. She thinks that the doctors are giving up on her, when there are other options. She mentioned something about a Healing Touch Center. I don't know, now I'm confused. Maybe she's right. Shouldn't we be looking at other options before we discuss hospice? I don't know any of these doctors. Maybe we need a second opinion."

"Mrs. Harris, I know this is terrible news for you and your family. Of course, you can get a second opinion. I've worked with Dr. Miller for many years and if he thought for one minute that there was something else that could be done, he wouldn't hesitate to act. When I spoke to him this morning, he was quite upset, too. He said that he never saw such an advanced case in someone so young."

"But what about this Healing Touch Center that Beth talked about?"

"I've never heard of such a place, but I'll be glad to check for you. In the meantime, please feel free to get a second opinion." Michelle reached for Mary's hand. "Please know that we all want to help Beth in any way we can. I'll go check out that name for you and call when I know something. Dr. Miller will be along shortly to see Beth. The two of you can ask him any questions you have. We'll hold off on any discussions until we get a second opinion."

Michelle left Father Pat and Mary alone. Father Pat comforted her the best he could.

"Any change in Frank?"

"No, not at all. Mrs. McCafferty says he sits on the back porch a lot. He hasn't said anything at all."

"I'm so sorry Mary. This must be hell for you. We must pray that he comes around."

Mary looked up at Father Pat. She began to cry. "What am I going to do, Father? I don't know how long I can handle all of this on my own!"

"Just take it one day at a time, Mary. That's all you can do. And pray! Pray for strength. Maybe Frank will come around soon."

"I can't lose her like this, Father. I don't know if I can watch her die."

"I know. I'll be here for you anytime you need me—night or day. Don't hesitate to call me for one second. I really mean that. I don't know how any of us will get through this."

They both rose from the chairs that they were in and went back into Beth's room. She was asleep. Father Pat pulled his rosary out of his pants pocket and began to pray. Mary sat quietly and watched her daughter sleep.

♥♥♥♥♥♥♥

The visit from Dr. Miller that morning was not promising. His explanation was awkward and clinical, but how else can you tell someone that there was no hope for their loved one. He agreed that a second opinion wouldn't hurt, especially if it helped Beth.

Michelle Green stopped by Beth's room at dinnertime and told Mary privately that she couldn't find anything on the Healing Touch Center. Beth slept on and off throughout the day and Mary didn't bring the matter of hospice care up again.

By Thursday morning, Beth was more alert and able to eat soft foods. She looked better, but new tests showed no improvement. A top oncologist from the University of Pennsylvania Hospital reviewed Beth's case and made the same conclusion. Any radical treatment for the cancer would probably be fatal. Beth's lungs were filling with fluid and the antibiotics were not working. They predicted that pneumonia would probably take over soon and there was nothing else that they could do for her.

On Friday, Mary knew it was time to talk to Beth about hospice care. Mary asked Frank to come to the hospital to encourage Beth to come home. He was adamantly opposed to the whole idea and said he wouldn't. The thought of someone dying in his house frightened him. He had distanced himself so much from Beth that he didn't even view her as family anymore. It was then that Mary found strength in herself from an unknown source and drew the line.

"Beth is coming home Frank! I don't care what you think and if you say anything to ruin this, I'll leave you! She is *my* daughter, too, and I will not have her die in a depressing hospital room, if I can help it. I want her here with Emmy and us, and I want to take care of her! I don't know why this is happening, but I'm not going to make another mistake with her. We may only have her with us for a little while longer and I want her home with me!" Mary began to sob.

Frank knew by her new tone that there was no sense in arguing with her, so he accepted it without a fight. Besides, he couldn't stand to see her so heartbroken. He wished it would all go away. "Fine, have it your way, but I'll not be a part of the decision. Don't expect me to do any more than this—I just can't."

"I'm sorry to hear you say that. I can't imagine why you would be so stubborn at a time like this. After all, Frank, she's your flesh and blood! If you don't come to peace with her, you're going to regret it someday!"

"Well that's my problem." Frank left the room and went outside to work on the lawn.

Mary watched him systematically gather his tools and wondered if he would ever come around. She also wondered how they would feel about each other later on. She gathered the items she was bringing to Beth this morning and went upstairs to kiss Emmy goodbye. Emmy was excited because Mary was coming back for her after lunch to take her into the hospital to see her mom. Mary's close friend from the quilting club, Brenda, was watching Emmy today and would be there any minute.

After saying goodbye to Emmy, Mary began to focus on the meeting with Beth this morning. Father Pat, Dr. Miller and Michelle Green would be there. As she pulled into the parking garage at the hospital, she felt a knot in her stomach. She expected to have the same battle with Beth that she had had with Frank. It didn't matter. She had a newfound courage and decided to follow her heart. Mary desperately wanted Beth home with her, no matter how hard it was going to be.

Father Pat, Michelle Green and another woman about fifty years old were waiting in the hall by the nurses station when Mary arrived. Michelle introduced Mary to the woman. "Mary, this is Emily Thompkins, the Hospice Program Intake Specialist. I thought it would be good to have her here to address any specific questions you or Beth may have about the program."

The women exchanged greetings.

Michelle added, "Dr. Miller will be here in ten minutes, then we can go in." She noticed Mary had come alone. "Is Mr. Harris parking the car?" Mary blushed with embarrassment. "No. He won't be coming, but he will sign any forms that you need." Michelle nodded and made a note in her file.

"Michelle, I think I should go in first to prepare Beth. I don't know how she is going to take this. Perhaps, Father, you can come with me?" Mary asked in a pleading tone.

Father Pat nodded. "Certainly." As they walked toward Beth's room, they heard a commotion going on inside. Beth was arguing with someone. Mary hurried in.

"Beth, what's wrong?"

Beth was sitting up in bed with a wet spot covering her hospital gown and the covers of her bed. A young nurse was wiping down Beth's bedrail.

"It's okay, Mrs. Harris. We just had a spill. I don't think Beth was ready for this."

The nurse gathered up her supplies. "I'll get you a new gown and cover." She left just as cheerfully as when she came in.

Beth had an indignant look on her face that was disrupted by a coughing fit. Mary helped her sip water through a straw. "Honey, what happened?"

"Nothing, Mom, really." She sank back down into her pillows. "I told her that I could do it myself! It wouldn't have happened, if she had listened to me."

"She was just doing her job. You should be more patient next time. She's a very nice girl."

"Believe me, there won't be a next time! Tomorrow I am getting a shower."

Father Pat laughed to himself at her stubbornness while looking at the row of drainage bags hanging off of her bed. "I think it may be a few days before that happens, Beth."

Beth snapped at him. "I wish people would stop acting like I'm an invalid! I just had surgery and in a few days I'll be walking out of this place!"

Mary looked at Father Pat for support. "I'm glad you brought the subject up, Beth. We do need to talk about going home. Dr. Miller and Michelle Green, the woman you met the other day, are coming to talk to us. They should be here soon."

Beth grew teary. "I told you I don't want to talk to her. I just want to go home."

"But she's going to help us with that, Beth. I don't want you in here one more day than you have to be either." Mary began to stroke Beth's forehead.

Beth flinched at her touch. "But they think I'm going home to die and I'm not. I asked you to get a second opinion and check out the Healing Touch Center and I'm not going to talk to them until you do!"

Mary began to tear up, too. She looked to Father for help. He sat down on the other side of the bed. "Beth, your mother did get a second opinion."

"Yes, from Dr. Julius Newman at the University of Pennsylvania Cancer Center. He's one of the best, but..." Mary tried to finish her sentence but couldn't.

255

Beth knew what she was going to say. Her heart sank. Her voice became a desperate squeak. "But there's the Healing Touch Center! They can help me."

"We checked, Beth, but there wasn't anything even close to that name. No one has ever heard of such a place. Are you sure you gave me the right name?"

Beth felt faint. Her mind reeled in confusion. "Yes, I gave you the exact name that Matt told me about!"

Mary was confused. "Who's Matt?"

Father Pat jumped in. "Beth, are you sure you are speaking of the right person?"

Beth closed her eyes to think. "Yes, Matt! Father you know Matt." Then her own words registered in her mind. "Oh God, maybe. I'm not sure. I can't think anymore." Beth became physically upset again.

"Never mind, dear. It's okay. We'll check on it again. But for now, we need to work on getting you home, right?" Mary patted her hand. Beth twisted nervously in the bed without answering. After a few minutes, she calmed down.

Beth stared off in space when Dr. Miller and the two women entered the room. She was resolved not to cooperate with them, unless they were going to help her.

Michelle walked over to the end of her bed. "Hi, Beth. This is Emily Thompkins and you know Dr. Miller. Emily is an intake specialist from the hospice program. She is here to explain to you some of your options for medical care."

Beth rolled her eyes in disgust. "Until I die, right!"

There was a silence again. Beth was beginning to deplore this now common reaction every time she said something. No one was jumping in to save her like she was hoping they would. Finally Emily spoke up.

"The hospice program is voluntary. We do not force our help on anyone, but before you say no, I would like to tell you what we do."

"Unless you say you're going to help me live, I don't want to hear anything!"

Emily smiled warmly, "But that's exactly what we do! We are here to help you live. No one in this room knows for sure how long that will be, but our job is to make whatever time you have left the most productive you want it to be. Our *first* priority is to provide you with the best pain management available and to help you stay as active as you possibly can be. We can also help your family with their daily routines so they can devote their time to being with you."

Beth was not consoled by Emily's lovely speech. "Until I die, right!" Her words dripped with sarcasm. Emily looked over at Mary and felt so sorry for both of them. She saw the pain that registered on Mary's face deepen with each of Beth's responses. "Yes, Beth. I'm afraid you're right—until you die. But whenever that is, it does not have to be a fearful experience. That is totally up to you."

Beth became furious. "Get out—everyone!" She looked at Dr. Miller who was standing sheepishly in the corner. "Why won't you treat me? All we hear about these days is how many miraculous treatments there are for people with cancer. So why not try one of them on me? I have a four-year-old daughter! Hasn't anyone considered that!"

Dr. Miller hid behind his clipboard as he gave her his answer. "I wish I could, Beth. But your cancer is so advanced that it would take large doses of radiation and drugs to attempt to treat you. Your body is in such a weak state that the treatments alone would kill you. Honestly, your chances of surviving the first round would be a million-to-one."

Beth and Mary were crying. Mary held her hand. Beth looked up at her mom before answering him. Her tone was quite meek now. "But, if I'm gonna die like you say I am anyway, why not try for a miracle!"

Dr. Miller dropped his clipboard down to his side. He tapped his pen against his leg while nervously rocking back and forth. "Because the side effects from the toxic drugs and radiation would make your days a living hell. I'm sorry. I'm very, very sorry."

A buzzing sound filled Beth's head as he answered her and she started to get sick. Emily helped Mary handle Beth until the nurse came in. Dr. Miller was paged and had to excuse himself from the meeting. The page came not a moment too soon for him.

When Beth was cleaned up and the nurse had left, Emily approached her again. She was sweet and sensitive, even after the way Beth had treated her. She took Beth by the hand. "Beth, dear, what is it that you *really want*?" Beth was shaking and sobbing. "I just want to go home and be with Emmy! And I just want everyone to stop treating me like I'm going to die!"

"Okay, sweetie, why don't you let me help you. I can help you get home and then you can decide what to do next. Okay?"

Beth nodded yes and turned her head into her pillow.

Emily whispered to her. "Okay, sweetie, I'll get you home."

Michelle and Emily left to get the paperwork started. Father Pat waited a few minutes and then kissed her on the forehead as he was leaving. "God Bless You, Beth." He whispered. Mary sat by stroking her head and then gently climbed up onto the bed and held her daughter. She sang to her softly while Beth cried herself to sleep.

♥ ♥ ♥ ♥ ♥ ♥ ♥ ♥

It took two days to get the paperwork processed. Emmy had visited Beth on both days and it seemed to help lift her spirits. Emmy was so excited about her mom coming home that Beth chose to put off telling her any part of the truth. Besides, she knew once she got to talk to Matt that everything would change.

On Sunday morning, the drainage tubes were removed and all that was left was the IV and the catheter. The catheter would be removed Monday morning before she went home at Beth's option. Beth was ready to rip it out. Beth and her mother had an admissions interview with Emily at ten o'clock and they would sign the required consent forms then.

Emily was there exactly at ten with a folder already an inch thick. It contained the forms, but also all of the hospital records and tests. She would bring it with her later that day when she had an interdisciplinary team meeting at her office. This meeting would include the Hospice Medical Director, who would be on standby if Dr. Miller could not be reached, the nurse assigned to Beth's case, a social worker and two patient care aides who would help Beth and her family with miscellaneous chores when needed.

"Good morning, Beth! Mary! I have all the forms that require your signatures and we can go through them one by one. Ask as many questions as you need to. I want you to fully understand the process. Mary, since you are going to be the primary caregiver, I will need you to witness Beth's signature on all the forms."

Emily started with a form that explained hospice care and gave a copy of it to Mary along with a list of office telephone numbers for her reference. Next, there were several insurance forms and a hospital release form. Mary signed a primary caregiver form. Emily explained what would happen as they went along.

"After our meeting, I will be meeting with our interdisciplinary team back at the office. This team includes everyone that will be involved with your care. All of their phone numbers are on your list Mary. I have assigned Mrs. Addie Snyder to be your nurse. You will love her. She has been in hospice care for twenty years, almost since it started at this hospital. She has a great sense of humor and loves children. Your daughter will have a good time with her. Addie will stop in after our meeting and give you a thorough physical assessment. Then she will make a list of supplies that you will need at home. We have a twenty-four hour medical supplier and she will fax them the list tonight. They will be able to make a delivery first thing tomorrow morning, so Beth can be home by the end of the day. Mary, it would be great if you could be at home to direct them to where the supplies will be going. Addie will be your coordinator with us from then on and she will help get you whatever you need. But, if you have a concern that you feel needs my attention, you have my number on the list I gave you also. Addie will keep me informed and I'll be in touch with you weekly for the first several weeks until everything settles down."

"What kind of supplies are you talking about?" Beth asked.

"Oh, the usual. Probably a hospital bed to make it easier for you to get comfortable; IV supplies, bedding supplies, a commode or bed pan, depending on how well you can move around..."

Beth interrupted. "A commode! I told you before that I am not going home to be treated like an invalid! I will be able to walk to my own bathroom as soon as all of this stuff goes away tomorrow!"

"Beth, you'll still have an IV line in for antibiotics and pain medication. That will make moving around difficult."

"Fine! I won't use them."

"But you have to or Dr. Miller will not let you go if you don't agree to an IV. He feels it's the best way to administer your pain medication. If you don't use the IV, then your mother will have to dispense the pain medication and it will add the burden of decision making on her. We use an IV drip system that Addie can program to release medication automatically and you can adjust it by yourself if you need more."

"And what if I over-medicate myself?"

"It can't happen. The unit is programmed for a maximum dosage in a certain timeframe, so if you use up your dosage, your mother can call Addie for help. Addie will explain it all to you." Emily saw Beth getting worked up. "Listen to me, Beth. This may be very temporary. As your condition improves, we can move you off the IV and you can take your medication orally. If you stay here or anywhere else, you'll have the same restrictions, but you won't be home with your daughter. Now, before you say anything, there is one more form you need to sign in order for us to take over your care.

Emily pulled a long, white, legal-sized form from her folder.

"This is a DNR form. It is a Do Not Resuscitate Order. You and Dr. Miller must agree in advance that no heroic measures will be attempted if your heart should stop beating."

Mary let out a quiet gasp. Beth's stomach dropped. Emily knew that this form would be difficult for Beth and her mother.

"I know this is a hard pill to swallow, but if you should take a turn for the worse, we will be there to help you both, but we will not take any action to save your life."

"Can we change our minds?" Mary asked her.

"Sure, you can. You can pick up the phone and call 911 if something should happen and we would simply release Beth from our care." Emily turned to Beth. "This is not a form that signs your life over to us, Beth. You can continue to seek out any form of treatment that you want. We do not take hope away. But, if you seek a treatment that we view as a medically-performed life-saving procedure, then you no longer qualify for our care."

"If you want to go home and have the most comfortable setting for healing, then you need to sign this form. You can *always* change your mind later. Otherwise, the hospital may require you to move to a nursing home facility or stay right here and wait and see what happens. My bet is that you'll do much better at home."

Beth read the document slowly to herself. It was filled with a lot of fancy words that really said *you are going to die soon!* When she finished reading it, she asked Mary for the pen she was holding and mechanically signed her name at the bottom of the page. She handed the form to her mother along with the pen and pointed to the witness signature line, while shaking her head yes. Mary scribbled her name in and handed it back to Emily. Beth remained silent as Emily packed up her things.

"It doesn't matter." Beth thought to herself. "When I see Matt, everything will be alright. I'll do anything to get home right now!" Emily said goodbye and Mary walked her out into the hall.

"I'm sorry Beth is being so difficult. She seems so agitated, but that's really not how she normally is."

"That's quite common, Mary. She is under a great deal of stress right now. It is very common for people to act that way. And they have every right to be like that, don't you think?"

"I appreciate the way you spoke about her recovery. Do you think she has a chance at getting better?"

"I've seen many miracles in my line of work. Some people have actually walked away from our program and lived many more years. I never rule out a miracle. But to be honest with you, it would take a very large miracle in her case."

Mary squeezed her arm. "I think I'm beginning to realize that, but I can't help but hope that she's right."

"Keep on hoping! Never give up hope! Beth needs that kind of reinforcement, but it needs to be honed in. She does need to realize that right now she has physical limitations to deal with or she's going to make things worse for herself. I can't imagine having to deal with her situation at such a young age! It's impossible to imagine what it's like to be told such devastating news, when you're at that fearless age. I'm praying for her! Call me if you need anything. Take care."

Emily left and Mary went back into the room. Beth was asleep. She looked at the forms and her eyes moved to the empty line for the second guardian. It had small words written in brackets below the line that said 'optional'. Frank's signature wasn't even required—just hers.

"Optional!" She thought. "As if any parent in their right mind would feel they had a choice!" She looked at her shaky signature and thought it very accurately represented how she viewed her life at this moment—shaky, falling apart and alone. Just like Beth's. She looked at Beth sleeping and wondered what tomorrow would bring when she came home. She wondered how she was ever going to survive this nightmare.

♥♥♥♥♥♥♥

When Emily got back to her office, everyone was assembled but Father Pat, who had agreed to be Beth's hospice chaplain. Since he was already intimately involved in her case and already knew everyone, his presence was not required. He had several church commitments that needed his attention and Emily agreed to call him later in the evening to give him an update.

Dr. Isaac Weinstein, the Hospice Medical Director, Olivette Brown, the social worker, Addie Snyder, the primary nurse, and Christine Thurston and Helen Edmundson, the patient care aides were assembled in the conference room. Emily distributed copies of a summary on Beth's case and gave Dr. Weinstein and Addie copies of her medical records for review.

Emily gave a verbal summary of the situation to everyone else. "Beth Harris is in her early twenties and has cervical cancer, stage IV and it's progressing rapidly. Dr. Miller gives her two weeks tops! Her latest test results are in the back of your packet, Dr. Weinstein."

He thumbed through the reports. "Yes, not good."

Addie added, "Her vitals are bad. I'm concerned about the lungs."

Dr. Weinstein frowned, "I don't even think she has that long. It doesn't say how long she's been treated?"

"Just since her admittance last week. According to her mother, she didn't show any serious signs until she collapsed on Labor Day."

"Can't imagine that's possible with the severity, unless she has an incredibly high pain tolerance."

"Her mother said Beth told her she was experiencing cramping a few times in the last month and had bruises from a fall in the bathroom, but that was it." Emily looked over at Addie.

"Addie, Beth is extremely agitated right now and is resisting anyone's help. She has agreed to our care, but she really is just using us to get home. She's determined to get out of bed the minute she gets there. That's going to

261

be your call after you see her. Maybe you can try it once. Perhaps sit her in a chair and see what happens. I feel so bad for her. She's so young. She objected to having the IV drip, but I think I sold her on it for now. As far as other assistance like a commode or bed pan, you're in for a fight."

Addie laughed. "I don't blame her, do you? A girl that young who's just been told that her life is over has to be devastated. We'll work it out."

Emily went on to another note she had made for herself. "The morphine drip is working really well—almost too well. She doesn't realize how bad off she really is."

Dr. Weinstein piped in. "If she becomes too difficult, maybe we should get Dr. Miller to reduce the dosage for a day, so she can get an idea of how bad off she is."

"Nonsense!" Addie protested. "I don't like playing games when it comes to pain relief. We should just be grateful it's working so well right now. The more comfortable we can keep her, the better. I can handle her!"

Dr. Weinstein defended himself. "I was just thinking that if she doesn't realize how bad off she is, she could end up hurting herself."

Emily interrupted them. "Okay, let's calm down. I know it's frustrating when we get cases with such a short timeframe. We don't have time to do anything very constructive. All we can do is the basics here. Let's make sure Beth is comfortable and Mary has all the help she needs. We may not be able to bring much closure on any personal issues the family may have, but, as always, we'll do the best we can."

"Are her parents going to be at the hospital when I visit?" Addie asked.

"Her mother probably will be. Mary's a sweet lady. But I haven't seen Beth's father yet. He didn't show up for any of our meetings and I get a feeling there's something wrong at home. That reminds me, Olivette, you need to arrange for a family support meeting as soon as possible, so we can see what kind of help Mary will have. She hasn't left Beth's side all week and she's really wiped-out. Beth has a four-year old daughter at home and we need to make sure Mary has help with her."

"Christine, why don't you come to the house tomorrow and help with the set up and Helen, you can wait until Christine sees what other help is needed. Then you two can work out a schedule." Both women nodded in agreement and Emily closed the meeting with a prayer.

At the end of the prayer she added as a source of hope, "Okay. I'll let Beth and Mary know the plan and we'll meet here next Monday for an update."

Everyone left wondering if there would even be another meeting.

Chapter 19

Addie Snyder burst into Beth's hospital room, as unexpectedly as a hurricane on a January morning. Her long blonde hair tossed all about her shoulders, as she marched straight over to Beth's bed and belted out a greeting. The flash of her smile and her vibrant aura could melt an ice cap. Still, Beth remained frozen in her bed, staring out the window.

Mary jumped up from her cot with a sigh of relief, as though saved by the cavalry. Beth had been in this somber mood since Emily left earlier and Mary was at her wit's end.

Addie turned to Mary undisturbed by Beth's indifference. "Hi, you must be Mary. I'm Addie Snyder."

Mary latched on to her hand and gave her a hardy shake. "Yes, I am. It's a pleasure to meet you." Mary felt Addie's strength right away and welcomed her presence. She had never known Beth to be so difficult.

Addie was fifty-one years old, but looked ten years younger. She was extremely attractive and fit. She credited her health and fitness to her two boys, who had kept her on her toes for the last seventeen years. She had stayed at home to raise her sons until they went to college and then went back to school to finish her nursing degree. She worked at Clark County Hospital as a scrub nurse for a few years, but felt unfulfilled until Mercy General launched their hospice care program. It was the first in the area and Addie knew it was where she wanted to be. Addie was a vegetarian and a yoga instructor and believed in the sanctity of all life. Hospice care fit in perfectly with her philosophy of community service, but more importantly, it gave her a wonderful opportunity to study people. She loved to interact with people. And in the last fifteen years of service, she acquired an incredible palette of colorful personalities that were rich and diverse enough to paint a spectacular picture of human life.

"Beth, I know Emily told you that I would be in to do a physical assessment so we can get you home tomorrow." Beth remained silent.

Addie put her clipboard down on the meal tray at the bottom of the bed and removed her stethoscope from around her neck. Beth was still facing away from her and Addie reached out and touched her shoulder. "Beth, I need to check your vitals, so if you can turn this way, it'll just take a few minutes." Addie put the stethoscope to her ears.

Beth turned her body around but fixed her stare straight-ahead at the blank wall. Addie ignored her response and felt for a pulse. She checked Beth over from head-to-toe. During the exam, she took time out to write detailed notes and talked to Beth the whole time, even though Beth never responded.

At the end of the physical, she made her final notes and put her clipboard down. She addressed Beth again. "Okay Beth. I've taken all the notes I can about your health, but now we need to talk!" She smiled at Mary. "Mary, could you please excuse us for a minute?" Mary was surprised by her request, but agreed.

"I'll go get a cup of coffee."

When Mary left, Addie walked to the foot of the bed and straight into Beth's line of sight. Addie saw Beth squirm a little and was pleased. "Now, the two of us are going to spend a lot of time together and I think we need to get a few things straight." Addie noticed Beth still wasn't making eye contact with her, but she continued.

"First, there are plenty of people in your position that wish they had a family who could agree to take care of them at home, *and they don't*. I hope you will consider what you are doing to your mom when you act this way. This is just food for thought." Beth began to give her an indignant look.

"Second, you have every right to be pissed off—really pissed off!" Beth's look changed from indignant to shocked. Addie just stood in front of her without saying another word.

Suddenly, Beth felt that she knew what Addie was up to. She folded her arms tight against her chest. "Oh, so you think if you come waltzing in here and act like you know how I feel, I'll want to be your friend."

"No. I was just making a statement. You have every right to be pissed off. I'm not trying to win you over. I don't have to."

"What do you mean, you don't have to?" Addie leaned forward as she answered Beth. "I've been working this program for fifteen years, Beth, and I've seen every kind of reaction to your situation."

"You mean my death sentence!"

"Okay, if you wish, your death sentence." Beth flinched at her harshness. "However you want to word it, you run this show. Everything I do will be your call. I am not coming in to run your life. If you want me to take care of the basics and split each visit, fine. I have nine other patients to keep me busy. But if you want more from me, great. I'll be glad to help you in anyway I can. Understand?"

Beth dropped her arms, "Yeah." All of a sudden, she felt a little foolish, but didn't want to admit it.

Addie picked up her clipboard and continued. "Okay. I need to go over where I think we stand on a few things. Emily told me you're not sold on the idea of the drip, but I must tell you, it's the best thing we have going. It's really a very simple set up. The morphine will be fed through a pump into your IV line and it will be programmed to feed a steady dose all of the time, in your case probably one or two mils every hour. But if you still feel pain, then you can press a button and the unit will add another dose into your line. You'll have an eight-minute lockout, which means you won't be able to get any extra morphine for eight minutes. This set up makes it easier to adjust your medication. I think you should give it a try and if it doesn't work for you, then we'll try something else. Also, you have a choice of leaving the catheter in or removing it."

"I'm not leaving it in. Take it out!" Beth interrupted.

"Let me finish. I would like to suggest leaving it in for two or three more days. There is some swelling of your pelvic floor muscles that will be aggravated if you move around too much and it will hurt like hell when you go, if you don't let it heal first. Again, it's your call."

Beth began to fidget. "But, I want to get up and move around and I don't want to use a bed pan or have to look all day at a toilet sitting in my room."

"We can remove it, but to be honest, you won't have the strength to walk to a bathroom for two or three days anyway. It would make things a lot easier for you and your family." Addie finished abruptly. "So what'll it be?"

Beth pulled her sheet up to her chest for some symbolic protection. Addie had a very clever way of putting the ball back into Beth's court. Now Beth didn't know what to do—say take it out and live with the pain just to make a point or agree to leave it in and claim defeat. She suddenly realized that she had no idea who she was messing with. She answered sheepishly. "Leave it in." Addie read off the rest of her list of supplies and Beth nodded in agreement to each item. She was beginning to feel very tired.

Mary came in shortly thereafter and Addie reviewed the list with her and explained everything that would happen. Mary would stay at home tomorrow morning and supervise the delivery. Christine would be there to help her. Addie would meet Mary at the hospital around three o'clock and they would have Beth discharged. Addie would go with Beth in an ambulance and Mary would follow them home. Beth fell asleep before their conversation was over. Mary noticed Beth seemed calmer and thanked Addie profusely for her help. Addie left and Mary lay down on the cot. A wave of nausea swept over her as she thought about the next day, but somehow she managed to get some much-needed sleep.

The prospect of going home did not seem to have a calming effect on Beth Monday morning. She obsessively scratched at her sheets making a sound like fingernails on a chalkboard. It was a common fixation among the very sick and the nurses were so used to it that they hardly noticed after a while. The morning dragged on forever for Beth.

As much as she looked forward to being in her own bedroom and being with Emmy, she dreaded seeing her father. And even though going home meant finally seeing Matt, Beth dreaded all the fuss that would be created by the hospice people and visitors. She knew that she wouldn't be able to tolerate it for very long, especially the reactions from her sympathetic friends. Beth was thinking about the looks that they would give her as they offered her their well-intentioned prayers or talked lightly about the weather. She hated to be pitied. She knew that look well now. Although no one would ever intend it, their eyes would not be able to cloak their own fears about dying and they would speak so clearly to her, 'thank God it's you and not me'.

Beth did not have time for that kind of support right now. It would take precious time away from seeing Matt and getting the help she desperately needed. She decided that she had to be concise and lay down the law when her mother came for her. But Beth grew increasingly lethargic and drifted in and out of sleep.

Mary and Addie arrived earlier than Beth expected and before she had time to gather her thoughts, she was being moved from the hospital bed to a gurney by two EMTs. Beth had fallen asleep before Addie had told Mary about her transportation home and this surprise was too much for her to handle. Beth began to kick when the young men tightened two restraining straps across her mid-section that were only meant to serve as a safety precaution.

"What are you doing to me?" she demanded.

Mary tried to calm her. "Beth, they are only doing their job. Please, it's okay!"

"Mom, where am I going? No one said anything about this to me."

"Yes, Addie did yesterday. You must have fallen asleep. You're going home in an ambulance, but it's okay, dear. It's the easiest way."

"No it isn't! I can drive home with you in the car. I'm perfectly capable of sitting in a car!" The two men were trying to hold Beth down to prevent her from pulling out one of her tubes when Addie came rushing in.

"What is going on?" She looked at one of the EMTs.

"Apparently, Miss Harris does not want to use our service."

Addie gave them an apologetic look. She turned to Beth. "What's wrong with this, Beth?"

Beth glared at her. "I don't want to be treated like an *invalid*!"

Addie smiled, "Oh, I'm sorry, Miss Harris. I thought we were treating you like someone *recovering* from surgery. But if this is not to your liking, fine." Addie looked at the men. "Take off the straps. Get a wheelchair and put it in the hall."

The two men looked at her as if she was crazy, but did as she asked. Mary stood by nervously watching Beth's reaction. Addie moved around the gurney and unhooked the IV bag and handed it to Beth. Then she went around to the other side and unhooked the half-filled urine bag and placed it in Beth's other hand. By this time the wheelchair was outside Beth's doorway.

"Very well, Beth. We can leave whenever you're ready. I'll be waiting for you at your wheelchair." Addie walked out of the room and stood behind the wheelchair.

Beth looked down at her hands, unable to figure out how to move. She threw her mom an incensed look. "Mom, help me up!" Mary didn't know what to do. She looked at Addie, but Addie remained silent. Mary tried to help Beth swing her legs over the bed, but Beth couldn't do it. "Take the bags, Mom and then I can do it." But when Beth threw her legs ungracefully over the bed, a sharp pain in her abdomen overwhelmed her and she fainted.

Addie walked over and checked on Beth and then took the bags from Mary. She signaled the young men to continue their work and remarked to Mary. "This is one stubborn child! She is really going to work you over, Mary, if you don't watch it."

Addie went with Beth in the ambulance and Mary drove home ahead of them. She cried her eyes out all the way home. Her tears flowed so heavily that she could hardly see the road. She didn't know if she could take any more complications. Between Beth's mood swings and Frank's complete rejection of the situation, she felt like she was losing her mind. Mary was uncertain of how she felt about the way Addie had treated Beth and unsure of how she was supposed to handle her sick daughter. She was beginning to believe she might have possibly taken on more than she could handle.

Meanwhile, Beth came to in the ambulance just as it was pulling up in front of her house. She was just as confused about her present world. Addie was writing something down on her chart when she noticed Beth staring at her. "Hey, we're at your house."

Beth ignored her. Addie felt bad about what she did, but she knew Beth was going to put up a big fight and it was better to get her home as quickly as possible. She laughed to herself about her hard-line tactics. Dr. Weinstein would have a field day if he ever found out about this one, in light of yesterday's heated debate about showing Beth how sick she really was.

The ambulance doors swung open and Beth closed her eyes. The butterflies in her stomach about being home made her temporarily forget about confronting Addie on what she did to her.

From the moment Beth entered her house, an unending swirl of confusion surrounded her and for the next three days Beth lost track of time. As she predicted, her home was filled with chaos as friends and neighbors swarmed around the rooms trying to be of some help. Everyone who knew Beth tried to visit her the first two days that she was home. Mr. Manley came by and assured her that her job was waiting for her when she got better. Beth felt comforted right up to the moment the tears began to fall down his cheeks and he made a flimsy excuse to leave. Her best friends, Katie, Rebecca and Amanda, tried desperately to cheer her up. Only they couldn't disguise the look of shock on their faces after seeing Beth for the first time since she was hospitalized. Beth had refused visitors while at Mercy General and no one expected to see her in such a debilitated condition.

Then there were Christine and Helen, the hospice volunteers, who seemed to be standing next to her bed every time she opened her eyes. Actually, they only visited her home once a day, but Beth had no idea how long she was sleeping.

Of course, her mother's friends came by, too, to offer support and their own opinions about Beth's care. One of Mary's quilting club friends became obsessed about Beth's lack of appetite and meals of all kinds began appearing at the house. Even Mrs. McC tried to tempt Beth with her cinnamon buns and some homemade oatmeal cookies, but Beth ate nothing and finally begged her mother to stop trying to force her to eat.

Something was happening to Beth's body that she couldn't stop and she was too tired and confused to do anything about. At first, she thought that it was just the ride home from the hospital that had exhausted her; or perhaps the medicine in the new drip machine that Addie hooked her up to was stronger and was causing her to sleep all the time. But it didn't explain the emptiness she felt inside. There were times when she felt as if she was becoming detached from her world. She felt spaced-out and it took a lot of energy to stay focused on anything.

Even visits from Emmy didn't give Beth the spark she needed to get moving and she knew that if she didn't do something soon, she would be swallowed up into a deep black hole that she might never climb out of.

On Thursday evening, Beth wearily glanced at her window and saw the shadow of something like a leaf dancing in the middle of the windowpane. It struck her as odd because there wasn't a tree outside her window. Just as she began to lose focus on what it could be, she heard a familiar voice call out her name.

"Beth, Beth can you hear me?"

By some small miracle the fog lifted from her mind and she remembered who it was. "Matt! Is that you?" Her thoughts were clear, but she still couldn't move to see him. She reached for a bell that Mary had put on the nightstand and rang it as hard as she could. Mary rushed in and Beth saw Matt's shadow disappear. Her voice was hoarse.

"Mom, open the window!" Beth was pointing to it. Mary didn't understand her. It was the first time that Beth had used the bell and Mary thought something serious was happening. Her heart was pounding in her chest. "The window is open, Beth. I don't understand. Mary handed Beth a glass of water with a straw in it and Beth sipped some water to help clear her throat.

"The screen, open the screen!"

Her request didn't make sense to Mary. "The window's open." But Beth became upset.

"Open the screen. I want the *screen* open!"

"But bugs will get in. Here, I'll open the window more." Mary went over and lifted the sash but Beth was still upset.

"No, no—the screen, please. I need the screen opened."

Mary thought Beth might be delirious. "Calm down, Beth. It's okay. The window *is* open. It's late and you need to rest. Close your eyes and rest. You'll feel better in the morning." Beth rolled her head back and forth in frustration, but finally gave up. Mary kissed her damp forehead and said good night.

When Mary felt Beth was calm enough, she left her room. As she eased the door shut, Frank appeared in the hall. "What was that all about?"

"Nothing. She wanted the screen opened for some reason. I think she was confused. I'll ask Addie tomorrow if the new medicine has anything to do with it. Maybe she's taking too much."

Frank shrugged his shoulders and shook his head in disapproval and went back into their bedroom. "Don't stay up late Mary. You need your rest." He called out over his shoulder. Mary went downstairs to straighten up before she went to bed. It was the only quiet time left in her day now.

Matt was the only one feeling any kind of happiness at that moment. The last week was more than an eternity to him. He couldn't have felt lonelier or more abandoned if he were shipwrecked on a deserted island. He wandered around aimlessly, without a clue of what to do next. Very little was being said at Beth's house, so it was impossible to learn what was going on. The slightly cooler nights were beginning to tax his body and he wondered about how much time he had left. He agonized over the thought that if Beth didn't come home soon, he might die from the cold or lack of food. Matt remembered Enon's warning that he now had a time constraint. He should have paid more attention to what he said. Maybe he would have pushed Beth sooner to talk to her dad. Maybe none of this would have happened if he had. But he could only guess what would have changed and he hated not being able to ask for help. Father Pat had not come back to the house since their encounter. Matt had no idea Beth was coming home until Monday morning when a rush of activity preceded her arrival. And then he had to wait and wait for an opportunity to see her. So many times he would come to her window and find her asleep. He watched her for hours and hours, hoping to make eye contact, until finally he could not hold back anymore. He had been hesitant to speak because he was afraid that she might not remember him, or was too sick to speak. But when it finally happened, hearing her voice put him in a tailspin. When she tried to get her mom to open the screen, he rejoiced. His Beth was back! Now they could be together!

Suddenly, all of his rejoicing halted when he considered. "To do what? How is this going to end?" Matt sank into the trunk of the apple tree and fretted. The only thing he could see both of them doing was going down together. The only comfort in that thought was that at least he would have her with him one more time. For the first time in over a week, he looked forward to tomorrow and a chance to be with Beth again.

♥♥♥♥♥♥♥

It was only seven o'clock in the morning when Matt flew to Beth's house the next day and already a big commotion was going on inside. Matt saw Frank reach for the phone in the kitchen and dial a number off of a piece of paper in his hand. He feared the worst and zoomed around the corner and up to Beth's window where the noise was getting louder. He could hear an argument going on. Beth's voice was louder and clearer than last night and she was yelling at her mother. Matt landed on the window ledge and listened.

"I just want the screen opened! I don't care about bugs in here!"

Mary sounded bewildered. "I don't understand. Why do you need it open? The air comes though just fine."

"I can't explain why, Mom. I just need it that way. I want it opened and I don't want anybody in my room this morning."

"Beth, this is bizarre. Addie will be here and I need to bring up breakfast. Emmy's going to want to see you and your friend Kate said that she'd be coming by this morning. And we need to look after you."

270

"I don't need looking after, Mom. And I don't want anything to eat! Of course, I want to see Emmy, but I don't want to see *anybody else*! Addie can check in on me tomorrow." Beth looked around her room with wild eyes. Flowers filled every corner with notes from well wishers. "And get these flowers out of here! My room looks like a funeral parlor."

Tears spilled out of Mary's eyes. She hardly recognized her daughter anymore, between the mood swings and her gaunt appearance. Beth realized how out-of-control she had become and softened her voice.

"I'm sorry, Mom. I know how hard you're trying, but I need you to listen to me. Please, keep everyone out of here this morning. It means more to me than I can say."

Mary's shoulders slumped in resignation. "We're only trying to help you, Beth. So many people want to help you. I don't understand why you fight everyone. You're even alienating Emmy."

Mary sniffled. "I'll leave you alone for now. Use the bell if you need me." She left Beth without opening the screen. Beth watched her mother leave, feeling horribly about how she had yelled at her and then realized Mary never opened the window and swore to herself. Maybe she could get Emmy to open the screen when she came in, she thought. Emmy was the only one who really listened to her anymore.

Mary crept into Emmy's room and found her little bundle of joy was still nestled snugly under her light cover. She kissed her on her cheek and crept back out of the room. Mary went downstairs to see if Frank had gotten through to someone on call at the hospice service. Frank was just being put through to Addie, so he handed her the phone.

"Hello Mr. Harris, this is Addie. What's wrong?"

"Addie, hi, it's Mary. Frank just gave me the phone. Beth is calmer now, but she woke up about a half an hour ago screaming about opening the screen window in her room. She wanted it open last night, but I can't understand why. I tried to explain to her that she wouldn't get any more air that way and bugs would get in and she went off on a tangent about so many things, and I don't know what to do."

"How was she when you left her?"

"She was calm. I think she may have gone back to sleep. Could this be from the medication?" Mary was hoping it was something that they could fix.

"No, the medicine in the drip is the same dose that she received at the hospital. I think that she is going through denial right now about her illness. She doesn't have much control over anything in her life, so something as simple as controlling how a window is opened may be very important to her right now. Did you open the window?"

Mary had to think, "No, as a matter of fact, we got off the subject and I never did open it."

"The next time she asks, do it. It may help her feel better. I know I hate bugs in my house, too, but this may pass over in a day if she gets her way. I'll be by after lunch. If Beth gets upset again, beep me. And expect a call from Olivette Brown this morning. I'm going to call her right after I hang up with you. She will want to set up a family meeting as soon as possible. Olivette will want to include everyone who is going to be involved with Beth's care, including friends. She's going to make sure you have enough help, Mary and she'll also try to help you with some of these issues Beth has. Does that sound okay to you?"

"Yes, thank you." The offer of help suddenly made Mary realize how tired she felt.

"You hang in there. How's Emmy doing?"

"She's fine. I just checked on her. Somehow she managed to sleep through the whole episode."

"Great. I'll see you in a little while." Addie hung up and Mary handed Frank the receiver. He didn't say anything at all. Mary was just glad that he was willing to make the call for her. She decided that that was all she could hope for.

♥♥♥♥♥♥♥

Matt couldn't believe the change in Beth's temperament since he saw her last. At least she was calm now. He expected her to notice him hovering in the window by now, but he was unaware that the angle of the screen from where Beth lay made it impossible for her to see the bottom of the windowsill. That was why she so desperately wanted the screen open, so she could see him.

"Pssst. Beth! Are you awake?"

Beth tried to lift her head. She reached around for the bed controls, but it had fallen off the bed during the night.

"Matt?"

"Who else would you be expecting outside your second floor window?"

Beth smiled for the first time. "Touché! I missed your rotten jokes. I could have used a few of them in the hospital." Beth coughed after she spoke and it lasted a long time.

Matt became concerned. "Are you okay?"

"Sure, peachy!" Beth waited a moment to allow her throat to relax.

"I was afraid something might have happened to you while I was gone. Run into any more cats?"

Matt laughed and shuffled his feet coyly. He had never acted like this around a girl in his life. "No, it's been pretty dull. I...It was hell not knowing what was happening to you. I really missed you!"

Beth began coughing again. "I missed you, too, angel. But we don't have much time to talk. The doctors say I have cancer."

"I know. Father Pat told me."

"He did? You spoke to him?" Beth was thrilled. Maybe this meant that Matt had more power than he originally told her.

"No. I didn't say anything. I just looked at him."

Beth's spirit deflated. "Oh, he didn't tell me."

"What did the doctors say about your recovery?"

"You don't know?"

"No, I just saw him that one time, early last week."

Beth laughed to herself. "Oh, just that it's hopeless and they put me on this hospice program and sent me home to die."

Matt's stomach dropped like a rock. "What did you say?"

"They say I'm dying. But I won't. You know that."

Matt was shocked and remained silent. His silence was like everyone else's reaction and it pierced her heart like a hot knife. She couldn't stand to think she was wrong about him. "You know that I'm not dying, right?"

Matt didn't know what to say. "I don't know anything, Beth. I told you before, they don't talk to me."

"But you said you came to save my relationship with my father and you very well can't do that if I'm dead!"

"They never mentioned anything about you getting ill, Beth. I'm sorry. I don't have an answer to that question."

Beth refused to hear his words. "But you do! Don't you remember? You told me about the Healing Touch place—you know your mother's center. You said that they took on people with all kinds of hopeless cases and they found treatments for them. I can go there! But my mom couldn't find anything on it. I probably remembered the name wrong. I told her it was the Healing Touch Center. That was right, wasn't it?"

Matt couldn't believe his ears. Beth was so confused. How could he tell her? "It doesn't exist, Beth."

"What did you say?" Beth stopped moving around so she could concentrate on his words.

"The Healing Touch Foundation, it doesn't exist."

"That's impossible! You told me yourself, back at the rectory on the back steps."

"You're confused, Beth. I was telling you about what I was shown in my review that *would have happened* if I stayed alive and possibly will happen sometime in the future, but it doesn't exist now."

Matt's words swirled around in Beth's thoughts and she went into the confusing, semi-detached state of mind that she had been experiencing on and off. Matt watched her clutching her sheets, as if she was trying to keep herself from falling off a spinning bed. Her stomach pitched and rolled, as she felt her whole world crashing down around her. "Not you, too, Matt!" She thought to herself. "You were my only hope. I thought you were different! I have no one left! I have no one left!"

Just when Beth felt like the black hole was about to swallow her up, the cloudy state left her as quickly as it came and the dizzying ride stopped. Beth lay still, breathing hard and covered in sweat. As her breath slowed down, she remained in a fixed stare at the foot of her bed.

"Beth, are you okay?" Matt whispered.

Beth remained silent.

"Beth, please, talk to me." Matt pressed the side of his head up against the screen.

Then Beth slowly looked toward the window in the direction of the hummingbird that she couldn't really see. Her eyes were like hollow wells of bitterness and despair. Her voice was dead cold. "Go away. Don't ever come back here."

"What are you saying? You don't mean it."

"I said *go away and don't ever come back here*. You're a liar. You said you came here to save me! You lied! You're just like all the rest, who've come to watch me die! Beth turned her back to Matt and refused to answer him again.

Matt pleaded with her. "Beth, please. Please don't do this. We'll think of something. Just, please talk to me." Addie's car pulled up in front of the house and Matt knew he had run out of time. He went back to the apple tree to think and to wait and finally, to pray. Matt felt sadder now than at the moment he had watched his mom receive word of his death and he never thought in a million years that could be possible.

Olivette Brown telephoned Mary after speaking with Addie and arranged to be at the house at one-thirty. She had already planned to talk to Mary today about scheduling a meeting. Usually she would give Addie three or four days to help her patient and the family get settled before she would attempt a family evaluation. She hated these critical cases because her work required time for the family to get comfortable with her and for her to single out the most urgent problems that needed closure. The absence of Beth's father and Beth's volatile frame of mind was an obvious clue that there was a lot of turmoil in this family.

Mary was able to gather together Father Pat, Mrs. McC, Christine and Helen, her neighbor, Ruth Anne, and her friend, Brenda for the meeting. She had other friends who had offered their help, but these were the people Mary most depended on for support. Frank, of course, refused to come and went to work instead. Emmy was sent down the street to play with one of her friends.

Addie had honored Beth's request for no visitors in the morning and came back for the meeting.

Olivette looked over Beth's file and Addie's new notes and felt very bad for the family. There was so little time left to do anything constructive for Beth. She might never come to terms with her illness. There wasn't much anyone could do, except pray for a miracle. What was most important now, was to help the family deal with this difficult situation and make sure that Beth, Mary, Frank and Emmy received all of the assistance they could get.

Everyone was gathered in the dining room. Olivette stood at the head of the table and passed out a packet to each person, except for the staff, to read later. She explained its content after greeting them.

"Thank you all for coming on such short notice. Normally, we would take our time and ease into this, but unfortunately things have gotten off to a rough start. I've included in your packets a list of reading sources on the subject of hospice care and some excerpts from many of them. Some of the books explain each of your roles in Beth's care and gives you insights into some things that may be going on in a patient's mind who is critically ill. It is very enlightening and is a reminder that none of us could possibly guess what it is like to be the patient in this situation. Most of us, although with good intention, treat the patient contrary to what they really need. It's really our nurturing nature and our own fears that get in the way and that's perfectly normal. Almost everybody does it.

"But it's great to have all of these resources available today to help us change and make this the best experience possible for Beth and ourselves."

Olivette sat down and took out a notebook and pen. Mary took the opportunity to introduce everyone in the room. Olivette had the kindest, warmest handshake. She was only forty years old, but her weathered dark brown hands showed signs of an already long and hard life. She raised two children, a boy and a girl, on her own, cleaning offices at night while they were little. Once they went to school, she worked a day job and attended a college at night. Her background gave her the compassion and patience needed to deal with the many different circumstances that came up in her emotionally demanding job. But because of her skin color, she was not always greeted by families with a warm reception; however, she always managed to win her clients over before she left them. She often said, "Given enough time, anyone involved with the dying process will whittle away their biases and come to a greater understanding of life. Even though sometimes it will be begrudgingly."

When Mary had finished her introductions, Olivette began asking her questions.

"Mary, the most important thing that we need to do is to bring some peace into this house. What has given you the most difficulties since Beth has been home?"

Mary didn't know where to begin. "I know it's only been a few days, but so many things have gone wrong." She began to wring her hands. "Beth has been so irritated at everything. Nothing anyone does pleases her. She hasn't eaten a bite in three days. We've tried everything. We've cooked all of her favorite foods and she pushes the plate away, every time." Mary stopped and took a breath. "And now she's refusing to see anyone. She wants me to take the flower arrangements out of her room, because she thinks it looks like a funeral parlor. She wakes up screaming about opening the screen in the window and I don't understand what for. She gets so mad and upset that you can't reason with her. I don't know what to do for her. I'm always wrong."

Olivette was scribbling notes and held her hand up for Mary to stop for a minute. She looked at Addie. "Addie, how's her pain medication working? Has there been any problems?"

"None. As far as I know, the morphine is working great. She hasn't added any doses herself or said anything to us about it."

"Maybe we should check and see if Dr. Miller could prescribe an antidepressant and see if that helps her. What do you think?"

Addie thought about it for a minute. "Yes. I think if she continues like this, it wouldn't be a bad idea. Mary would you have a problem with that?"

"Oh, I don't think Beth will agree. She's so paranoid right now."

"I know, but if she continues to be physically upset, as her primary caregiver, you have authorization to okay it, if you and Frank decide that Beth is no longer able to make her own decisions."

"Addie, I don't know if I could do it. Beth will fight it to the end."

"Mary, Beth signed her consent already. We could do it quietly, if we need to. It was one of the forms she signed in the hospital. You have a copy of it. It's form PC-2."

Mary was apprehensive. "Could we wait? I want to talk it over with Frank." She didn't know why she said that, knowing how Frank felt about all of this, but she wanted everyone to feel that he was somehow involved with Beth's care.

Olivette spoke. "Okay, we'll put that on hold. Let's go over these other concerns. First, about the eating." Olivette hated explaining this part to a grieving family. "In your packet, there is a list of symptoms that a patient may experience as time of death nears. It's the blue papers." She watched the expression in everyone's eyes as they searched for the sheets. Usually someone would begin to cry when they talked about this realization. Mary and Mrs. McC were the first to draw tissues from the box that appeared in the center of the table.

"Very often a loss of interest in food and drink will occur. This can go on for some time and may come and go for a while. You should offer, but don't force, food to Beth. Don't get insulted or take it personally in any way if she refuses, even if she is hostile about it. If someone brings you food for her, explain to them that she isn't eating much and don't, under any circumstances, try to give Beth the food in front of them."

Mrs. McC began to feel bad about bringing over the cinnamon buns and trying to tempt Beth into eating one. She was only hoping that they would work their magic and it was the first time that they didn't. She knew it was a bad sign.

Olivette continued. "Also, Beth may sleep a lot and continue to detach herself from visitors. Your efforts to comfort her may be rejected. The best thing you can do for her is to let her sleep. At this point in time, *being with her* is more important than doing things for her. She also may become increasingly restless and hear or see things that you can't. It doesn't matter if you believe what she says is happening. Just reassure her and keep saying your name if she's not responding. Playing soft music, especially something she favors, can help, too.

"Mary, if the flowers or anything else in the room bothers her, remove them."

"When this is happening to her, does she know she is dying?" Mary asked.

"Not always, especially if she is in denial. At times, this could be a very frightening experience for her. Just keep reassuring her and give yourself a break from it." Olivette looked around the room at Mary's friends. "This is where you will come in. It's going to be hard for Mary to pull herself away and you need to convince her to get out of the house and go shopping or do something else. If Beth gets worse, you may want to make a schedule so that someone is with her all the time. That way Mary will feel better about getting rest herself."

Everyone nodded in agreement.

Mary asked another question. "I'm really worried about Emmy. What is this going to do to her when she sees her mom like this? Did I do the wrong thing bringing Beth home?"

Father Pat put his arm around Mary, as she began to cry.

Olivette answered her. "Every child is different and most are more resilient than we give them credit for. Children Emmy's age can be more open-minded and they may even ask a lot of questions about what's happening. The healthier your attitude is about death, the healthier hers will be. I would like to start seeing her once a week and then I can make a better assessment. Let her tell you how much she can handle. If she gets too upset, you may want to limit her visits with Beth. And I would suggest continuing counseling for as long as she needs it."

Mary nodded and turned into Father Pat's shoulder. No one spoke for a moment.

Olivette closed the meeting. "I'd like to stop by and see Beth in the next day or two, if we can get her to agree. I think Addie's visit with her will be enough for today. If anyone has any questions, please call me. Thank you all for supporting Beth and her family. It is a wonderful thing that you are doing for them and for yourself."

Olivette left and was followed by everyone except for Addie, Father Pat and Mrs. McC. Addie went upstairs to see Beth. Father Pat hoped that she would stand a visit from him after Addie was done. He knew why she wanted the window open and he hoped that he could help calm her down by being someone that she could confide in.

About thirty minutes later, Addie came down shaking her head at Father and Mary. "She won't talk. Physically, there's no change and when I asked her if she was in pain, she shook her head no. I noticed the screen was still down and asked if she wanted it open. She shook her head no to that, too." Mary let out a sigh. She wondered if this was how it would be from now on. That whole fuss over the window was for nothing. Maybe she was hallucinating. "How am I going to deal with her like this," she asked herself. Addie told Mary that she would call first before coming over tomorrow morning. She gave Mary a hug before she left.

Father Pat looked at the two women. "Do you suppose it's worth a shot?" He was nodding toward Beth's room upstairs.

Mary couldn't speak. She nodded okay to him. Mrs. McC took her rosary out and sat down on the couch. "A few minutes couldn't hurt, Father. We need to keep trying."

Father Pat mounted the steps toward Beth's room. It felt like *déjà vu* and he remembered that moment at the rectory the first time and recanted the same simple prayer. "Lord, help me to say the right words and bless her with the courage to respond."

He opened the door to Beth's room and caught a glimpse of Matt sitting in the corner of her window. He smiled to himself and walked over to Beth.

Her back was to the door and she pretended to be asleep. Father stood quietly watching her until he saw her eyes open and close quickly.

"Did you think you could get rid of me that easily?" Beth ignored him and continued to pretend to be asleep. Father sat down on the bed. "I hear you've been having a hard time. Do you want to talk about it?" Beth remained silent.

"Your mother said that you were quite insistent about the screen being opened this morning. How come you don't care if it's opened now? Don't you want to see Matt anymore?" Just the mention of his name was enough to jolt a response from her. Beth rolled over and faced Father Pat.

"I never want to see him again!"

"Did you see him already?"

"Yes! And he's just like all the rest of you!"

"How's that?" Father Pat prayed she'd continue the dialogue.

"He's come to watch me die! All his talk about coming to help save my relationship with my father was probably just a cheap joke from God. A continued punishment for being who I am."

Father Pat threw his head up. "Oh really, Beth. You don't believe that. God would never do something that insidious!"

"How do you know, Father? Maybe my dad is right. Maybe I am just a bad person who deserves this."

"Never! God would never treat any of his children harmfully. Your Father in Heaven loves every one of us, regardless of our merits. He loves you, Beth."

"And this is how he shows it! By having me raped? By giving me cancer? By giving me a father who hates me? By sending me Matt?" Father winced and felt badly for Matt, knowing he could hear that last remark.

"Listen to me, young lady. How do *you* know what God's like? None of us knows why these things happen. I don't know whether we choose these things to happen to ourselves or whether it's just luck or what the mechanics are. What I *do* know is that bad things happen to good people and maybe we will never know why it has to be this way until we are with God again. Maybe we choose to see our experiences the way we want to see them and overlook God's real intent for us."

"So you think I'm *choosing* to experience my life filled with pain and disappointment. Maybe I chose to receive a messenger who has no power to save me! Maybe I chose that my father wouldn't love me!"

Father Pat shook his head. "No, not at all! I'm only saying that maybe we don't always see the kind of power or love God is sending us. I don't have a straight answer of why all of this is happening to you, but I do know it's not because God doesn't love you."

279

Beth was in tears. She couldn't grasp anything he was saying. "All I know, Father, is that God has abandoned me! And anyone who believes that I'm dying is abandoning me, too! It seems I can only count on Emmy anymore. I have no father. I have no God. And I have no messenger from Heaven. Even my mother has given up hope. Everyone I have ever loved has chosen to desert me." Beth looked away from him.

"Everyone has left you, huh? Your mother is downstairs beside herself in grief trying to figure out how to help you. Your friends have done the best they could to comfort you. God has sent you a whole house full of people to pray and care for you. Your father has grief so deep over what's happening to you that it's easier for him to find fault with you than to face losing you." Beth looked back at him when he said that and he nodded his head. "Yes, it's true. Your father is as deep in denial about his real feelings as you are about your illness. And I'll tell you another thing. There's a soul who cares so deeply for you that he's risked everything to help you and he's never left you for a moment. In fact, he's right outside your window waiting for another chance." Father moved over so Beth could see the window. She didn't want to look but she couldn't help it. She saw Matt's shadow in the corner.

Father Pat got up and walked over to the window and opened the screen. He smiled at Matt. "Before you give up on him, Beth, maybe you should reconsider the goal of Matt's mission. From what I recall you telling me, he is here to prove that he knows what love is, as well as to help you. Maybe you both have to work together to accomplish both goals."

Beth felt anger rising inside her again. It was coming from an origin so deep within her that she could not place the source. Believing what Father said would only mean accepting her death. She could not face dying. She could not accept it and no matter how much she cared for Father Pat, she could not agree with him. To her, it would mean giving up her life.

Father Pat came back over to her bed. He saw the anger in her eyes and was disappointed in himself. He had hoped that she would reconsider her feelings. He patted her hand and began to leave the room. "For the record, I love you, kiddo. I'm here if you need me and I'll never abandon hope in a miracle for you." He left without another word and cried while walking down the steps. When Mary saw him, she embraced him. "Her anger is so deep, Mary. God help us help her," he prayed out loud.

Beth watched the door close without remorse for her stance. "I have to be strong for myself. I will show them all. I am simply recovering from surgery. In a few days, I'll be as good as new and I can leave this place and take Emmy to California." Her defiance fed her self-confidence and adrenaline began to rush through her veins. For a moment, she forgot about Matt and the opened window.

"Beth, can I talk to you?" Matt carefully stepped inside the window and walked along the sill toward her.

Beth flung her head around and looked at him. She held her hand up in protest. "Don't say anything. I'm tired of listening to lectures."

"Beth, why are you acting like this?"

"How do you want me to act? Like the sweet naive fool I've been in the past! So I can fall on my face again! Or better yet, maybe I'll just fall into my grave!"

Matt couldn't believe what he was hearing. How could she change so much? He couldn't believe that this was even a part of her nature. He understood that she was afraid of dying, but why fight it this way.

"Why have you deserted us?" he replied. His words were such a surprise that Beth could only glare at him in response, at first. Matt continued. "Father Pat is right. No one has left you. Everyone is trying to help you! It's you who have given up on yourself. It's not death that you're worried about. It's losing control that's killing you."

Beth's throat was dry and her response was barely audible. "How dare you lecture me. I'll show you who's in control." She threw off her sheet and started feeling for her catheter line.

"Beth, what are you doing?" Matt realized what she was about to do and tried to stop her. "Don't do it, Beth. Please stop!"

Beth ignored him and reached under the sheets and yanked the catheter out from between her legs. The adrenaline that rushed through her and the morphine blocked most of the pain and she quickly grabbed her IV line and pulled it out of the back of her right hand. Blood began to pour down her fingers. She swung her legs over the bed and stopped when she remembered what happened at the hospital.

Matt was frozen in shock, but recovered. "Beth, what are you doing? You can't go anywhere. You're going to hurt yourself. Stop! God! Angels! Stop her!"

Beth ignored his shouts and drew in a breath to stand. It had been so long since she supported her own weight that she wobbled and caught her balance. The dresser was three short steps away and she lunged for it. Her legs shook and she leaned over the top of the dresser for support. Her head began to throb and pain coursed through her legs and abdomen. She could hear a rushing sound like a great tornado spinning inside her head that drowned out Matt's pleas. Matt flew over and hovered in front of her face.

"Stop, Beth, stop! This is insane!" He was crying. "You can't do this. It won't work. Listen to me! You're gonna hurt yourself!"

Beth was able to look into his eyes for a split second before her eyes rolled back and she crumpled onto the floor.

"Beth, Oh God, talk to me." Matt buzzed around her head. He shouted as loud as he could. "Help, someone, help her!" He zoomed frantically around the room. The door was closed and there was no way for him to get help. It dawned on him that no one could hear him call and he rushed back to Beth. He hovered close to her nose and mouth and felt her breath. "Thank God," he thought.

Then he had an idea. He used his beak to tap on the door hoping someone would hear it. Because he had to hover, it sounded like a faint Morse code that no one could hear downstairs. After he tired, he checked Beth's breathing again and it was faint, but still there.

As he continued to check her over, he swore in horror at what he saw. Beth had blood on her nightgown. She was bleeding between her legs. It wasn't much blood, but Matt feared the worse. He tried to calm himself down. "Maybe it was from pulling the catheter out." It didn't matter. He needed to get someone's attention. He looked around the room. He had to create a disturbance loud enough for someone downstairs to notice. He saw a vase of flowers on the edge of her bookshelf and raced over to knock it down, but the impact nearly flattened his beak and almost knocked him out. He shook it off and scanned the room again. The vase was too heavy. He knew he couldn't break the window. Then he noticed three perfume bottles on the dresser. He whisked over and landed next to the largest one. He used his beak to knock it over, but it hardly made a noise. "Damn, damn, damn!" He cursed his small size.

His own strength was fading and he backed up against the mirror on the wall behind the dresser. He was beginning to lose hope when he noticed a radio on the second shelf of the bookcase. A light bulb went off in his head. He flew over and looked at the controls. Lucky for him, it had an on switch that flipped down. He hovered over the switch, being careful not to brush his wings on the radio and landed as hard as he could on the switch. After two difficult jumps, the radio came on. The volume was too low for anyone to hear, so he found the knob, which he could reach by standing on the shelf. The knob had ridges for gripping and he used his beak to move it, one tiny notch at a time. It took all of his strength to pull down on the knob and his beak slipped off a lot. After a few minutes, his feathers were drenched in sweat and the music was loud enough to blow the roof off of the house. Matt shook the sweat off his feathers and flew to the windowsill and waited for someone to come.

In less than two minutes, Mary and Father Pat had clamored up the stairs and burst into the room. Mary let out a scream and Father Pat rushed to Beth's side. He checked her pulse while Mary turned down the screeching radio and left to call Addie. Father Pat lifted Beth into his arms and walked her over to the bed. Matt stood by experiencing his own *deja vu' from* the first day he came to Earth. Only there was no way to call on his angels for help and he was left to wait and see what would happen to Beth.

While Father Pat waited for Mary to return, he became thankful that the radio had alerted them to Beth's accident. It struck him finally that from where Beth was laying that she probably didn't turn it on. He turned toward the window and saw Matt panting in the corner. He walked over to the window and knelt down eye level with Matt. Matt was still panting. Father Pat looked him straight in the eyes and whispered to him as he reached up and touched his small head with the tip of his finger. "Thank you, my friend." Matt gulped and panted and replied, "you're welcome", but Father Pat only saw his beak move slightly. He was sure in his heart, however, of what Matt had said.

Father heard Mary running up the steps and he rose from his knees. "Stay close, Matt." Before he made it back to Beth's bedside, Mary burst through the doorway too upset to notice anything. "Addie's on her way. She'll be here in ten minutes. They both surveyed the bed. Beth's IV cord was hanging off the side and the medicine that was left in the tube was dripping onto the floor. Her catheter was under the sheets and they both felt ill as they imagined what she did.

Mary stroked her head. "Is she dying, Father?"

"I don't think so. Her breathing is shallow and her pulse is weak. I don't think her bleeding is serious, but I'm no expert. We shouldn't try to draw any conclusions until Addie gets here."

Mary tried to straighten Beth's sheets. "It was funny watching what women do to comfort themselves," Father Pat thought, as he observed. It reminded him of when Mary cleaned the pie off of Beth while the paramedics were working on her.

"What do you think drove her to this?" Mary asked.

"Probably her stubbornness!" he answered and they both laughed lightly.

"Yes, she is stubborn, isn't she." Mary replied. "Like her Father, huh?" Father said back. "She certainly didn't get that from you." He meant his comment to be a compliment.

Mary's eyes filled. "She didn't get much of anything from me."

Father Pat reached for her arm. "I didn't mean it that way, Mary."

Mary shook her head. "Oh, I know. I was just thinking out loud."

Their attention was drawn to the sound of the front door closing. It was Addie. Addie bound up the stairs, two at a time. She rushed in with her medicine bag clutched in one hand and they both moved back as she slipped

283

on her stethoscope and began her assessment. Addie shook her head when she saw Beth's hand and the stain on her nightgown. She examined her pelvic area. "Holy cow, you did it this time, Beth." She looked at Mary. "She'll be alright. She fainted from the pain of the fall. Let's give her a little time to come around. Her vitals are weak, but not dangerous at this point. I have to clean her up and redo her IV. I'll probably have to use the other hand. I think I should call Dr. Miller about prescribing a sedative for a day or two, if she remains in an agitated state when she wakes up. Unfortunately, it will make her sleep even more, but she has to be still or the bleeding may get worse. It isn't all from pulling out the catheter. She is bleeding slightly from the cervix. If it gets heavier, it may never stop. Are you okay with a sedative, Mary?"

Mary nodded yes. If it would mean a little more time with Beth, she'd do anything. She wasn't ready to give her up.

"Do you want to speak with Frank about this?"

"No. I'm fine making the decision."

Addie smiled. "Okay. If you don't mind, I'd like you both to leave us alone. Mary, I need a clean gown and some warm water, a washcloth and a towel. It shouldn't take too long."

Mary went ahead of Father Pat. He turned and looked at Matt, who was still crouched in the corner of the windowsill. He nodded once to Matt and watched him fly away. He left the window screen open and told Addie that he would wait with Mary downstairs until she finished. Addie returned to her work and watched Beth begin to move in her sleep. It was a good sign.

Chapter 20

When Beth collapsed to the floor, a sound like rushing wind with faint tinkling bells filled her surroundings. Her rattling breath was magnified and although she was aware of her surroundings, her eyes were closed. She could see a glowing light that began as a very small circle expand to fill her entire inner-vision and the rushing wind faded away, leaving only the sound of her breathing that moved in harmony with the rise and fall of her chest. She felt peaceful. Off in the distance she saw a blurred form of a person with long blonde hair walking towards her, until this womanly form stood over her blocking out most of the light. Her form was still blurry and Beth could only confirm that it was a woman by the sound of her voice as she began to speak to her.

"Do not be afraid."

"Addie?" Beth called out.

The woman did not acknowledge if she was Addie but continued speaking. "You are running out of time, Beth. You must go back and try again."

Beth didn't understand what she meant. "Try what? Are you Addie?"

The woman touched her forehead with her hand that was as soft as rose petals.

"You must talk to Matt. He can help you." The woman's form became blurrier as Beth replied. "Matt? He can't help me. He said so himself."

The woman smiled. "He is the only one who can help you. You are running out of time. Matt has the power within him. You must trust him and he will find the way." The woman pulled back out of Beth's view and Beth was flooded with the light. The woman started to turn away.

"Don't go!" Beth called out. "I don't understand. How will Matt help me?" The woman turned completely from her and continued to walk away. "You only have a few days left, Beth. Trust Matt." The woman disappeared into the light and then the rushing wind returned. Beth's breath grew louder and it echoed in her head. Beth kept calling out to the woman. "Don't go! Don't leave me! How will he help me?" The light began to fade and Beth was immersed in darkness again. She began to hear other noises around her and slowly came back to consciousness. Suddenly, her eyes were open and she was lying in her bed.

Beth first noticed that the IV line was now in her left hand and it was wrapped in so much tape that it looked like a cast. She was startled when Addie spoke to her from her right side. "You'll have to really work hard to pull that line out!" She teased Beth lightly. Addie was smiling, as usual, and

Beth remembered what she did and felt foolish. Her chest felt restricted when she breathed now and it took a lot of work to talk.

"You found me?"

"No, you mother and Father Pat did. They called me and I've been here ever since."

Beth started to ask for the time but began coughing and couldn't clear her throat. It felt like she was suffocating and she began to panic. Addie pulled her straight up and listened to her lungs. She frowned at what she heard, although Beth never saw it. Addie gently lowered Beth back down.

Beth felt better after that. She watched Addie carefully place the stethoscope in her bag and noticed for the first time how beautiful she was. She exuded such kindness and confidence when she worked. She really seemed like a very nice person. She was the kind of person that Beth had hoped to be like. Beth was sure, at this point, that Addie was the woman she had spoke to a little while ago and was curious about what she said.

"Addie, how do you know Matt?"

Addie looked up from writing on her chart with surprise. "I'm sorry, what did you ask?"

"How do you know Matt?"

"Matt who?"

"You know. You told me when I was waking that I had to speak to Matt, that he has the answer."

Addie sat quietly for a moment. "I'm sorry, Beth. I didn't say that. I don't know anyone named Matt."

Beth looked confused and disappointed.

"It was probably a dream. It happens all of the time. Don't worry about it." Then Addie remembered that so many times at this stage, her patients began seeing and talking to people no one else saw or heard. "Hey, but just because I didn't say it to you doesn't mean you didn't hear it. If it's good advice, take it!"

Addie gathered up her things. "It's getting late and I think your mom and Emmy want to see you if you're up to it." Beth nodded her head yes.

"I'll see you tomorrow. It's real important that you don't move around tonight. You were very lucky that your fall didn't cause you more harm than it did. You started bleeding from your cervix, where the tumor is. It's almost stopped completely, but if you try to get out of bed again, it may not stop the next time. Are you going to be alright tonight?"

Sheepishly, Beth nodded yes again. Addie turned to leave. "Addie." Beth called out. Addie turned back and faced her. "I'm sorry."

Addie smiled. "It's okay. You just hang in there and enjoy some quiet time with your mom and Emmy."

Beth nodded okay again and closed her eyes. After Addie left the house, Mary and Emmy came upstairs for a visit. Mary brought Beth a mug of tomato soup and Beth was able to drink almost half of it. Neither of them mentioned anything about what had happened. They spent a few hours playing Old Maid with Emmy. Mary noticed the screen was open and left it alone. She was grateful for the wonderful time that they were having. The only thing that disturbed her was Beth's stressful breathing and frequent coughing. She knew in her heart that it was a bad sign.

♥ ♥ ♥ ♥ ♥ ♥ ♥

Beth woke up the next morning to a stream of sunlight on her face. It reminded her of the light that she experienced yesterday, but that light was different and she couldn't place what the difference was, exactly. The conversation with the mystery woman played over in her mind. Of course, she thought, it must have been a dream, but the woman's final words were so chilling. Beth remembered her saying *you only have a few days left*, and it scared her.

She needed to see Matt again, but how? She looked to the window and saw that the screen was open. It had to be at least eight o'clock and there was no sign of him. She called out his name and waited, but he never came. Just then Mary came in with breakfast. It was a liquid instant breakfast drink. Beth was doing better getting liquids down and it made Mary feel better knowing she was eating something.

"Good morning." Mary looked happy this morning. "Emmy's downstairs finishing up breakfast. She'll be up in a few minutes and then she's going down the street to play with Tina. Addie will be coming by this afternoon, unless you need to see her sooner."

"No that's fine." Beth started having a coughing fit and Mary sat her up until it stopped. Beth looked down at the hand that was covering her mouth and noticed a tiny spot of blood-tinged mucus. She concealed it from her mother.

Mary stayed and helped Beth with her first few sips of breakfast drink. She was relieved that Beth was calm this morning, but something was different. Her skin seemed paler with a slightly bluish color tone. There were dried secretions on the corners of her mouth. The blue list that Olivette gave her mentioned both of these things, along with mental confusion that Beth had clearly demonstrated in the last few days. She swallowed hard to fight back her emotions and made up an excuse to go downstairs.

"I have a load of clothes to throw in the dryer. Your father's coming home early today. He has an appointment with Mr. Klein and he'll want to wear his blue shirt. I almost forgot to wash it!" Mary didn't realize what she was saying, until it was too late. Mr. Klein was their family lawyer and she hadn't brought Frank up to Beth since she came home.

"Why's Dad seeing a lawyer?"

"Oh, he just wants to go over some retirement options with him." The truth was that Mr. Klein held the deed to their cemetery plot and Olivette had suggested that they have all the documents on hand, in case something happened to Beth. Frank was also going to discuss drawing up a Will that would give them legal custody of Emmy and see if they needed to do anything else to protect themselves from losing her, if her biological father ever decided to try and get custody. Mary couldn't believe how stupid she was for bringing it up.

Beth wasn't sure if she believed her mother, but decided to let it go. She had something else more important to ask her.

"Is Daddy ever going to come and see me? I hear him walking by my door all the time. Is that why you keep my door closed? So he doesn't have to look at me!"

Mary felt torn. Beth was right. "No. I thought it would help you sleep better. There has been so many people visiting us at all hours of the day that I didn't want it to disturb you."

"But *is* Dad ever going to talk to me?" Beth stammered. "How sick do I have to get?"

Mary was at a loss for words. "I thought that it might be better to wait and talk to him when you're feeling better."

Beth shook her head in amazement. "He doesn't want to see me ever again! What if I don't get better, Mom? Then what?"

Mary was surprised at Beth's last comment. It was the first time she had ever spoke like this. *My poor baby*, she thought. She was beginning to resent Frank for what he was doing to them.

"We'll just cross that road if we ever come to it!" Mary fixed Beth's covers and patted her cheek. "I'll check back in a little while. Okay?"

Beth wanted to continue their discussion, but she was too tired. Instead, she nodded okay and closed her eyes. She planned on resting her eyes for a few minutes but slept the morning away. Matt came by two times and once flew over to her bed and tried to wake her up, but she didn't stir at all. He watched her sleep and listened to her raspy breathing for an hour until he heard someone coming up the steps and flew away to get something to eat.

Mary came into Beth's room and shook her gently. Beth opened her heavy eyelids. She blinked a few times to focus and saw her mom standing over her.

"Beth, honey. Can you wake up?"

Beth rubbed her eyes and nodded. "How long have I been sleeping?"

"All morning." Mary replied. "I know you said yesterday that you didn't want any visitors, but someone special has come to see you."

Beth pointed to the bed controls and Mary raised the bed so she was sitting up straight.

"Who is it?"

"It's Rachel." Mary exclaimed. "She's come all the way from Texas to see you!"

Beth was so taken aback that she lost the ability to swallow. A large lump caught in her throat. She tried to speak, but she wasn't sure what to say. Her heart began to race. At first, she was afraid of what Rachel might have said to her mother, but it was obvious by Mary's reaction that she hadn't told her anything.

Mary saw Beth hesitate and hoped that she wouldn't get upset. She whispered to Beth. "She's right outside your door, Beth. The least you could do is see her for a few minutes. It would do you good to talk to a friend. Besides, she's come all the way from Texas."

Beth squeezed her eyes shut. What did she want to do? She didn't have time to think. Why would Rachel come here?

"Beth," Mary whispered again. "We can't leave her standing out in the hall!"

"Okay." Beth answered. "I'll see her."

"Great." Mary opened her door and asked Rachel to come in. Mary had warned Rachel that Beth was very ill, but she didn't say from what. She was delighted to finally meet Rachel and hoped that her visit would cheer Beth up.

Rachel stepped past Mary in the doorway and Mary closed the door, leaving it open about an inch. Rachel was horrified when she saw Beth and gasped. She hardly recognized her.

"Oh my God! What did they do to you?" She half whispered in a high-pitched squeal and covered her mouth with her hand. Beth was almost as shocked at Rachel's appearance. She was dressed in jeans and a baggie sweater. Her hair was pulled back in a tight ponytail and she wore hardly any makeup. She had dark circles under her eyes. Beth would have never guessed that she was the same flamboyant, sexy girl she had lived with. Beth wondered what she must have gone through to change so much herself. It took a moment for Beth to respond.

"*They* didn't do this to me. I have cervical cancer." She thought Rachel would be relieved by her answer, but she didn't show it. Her hand was still over her mouth.

"How bad is it?" Rachel's voice was shaking.

"They say I'm terminal." Beth replied. She was surprised that she was able to say those words.

"I don't know what to say. It's only been a short time. When did this happen?"

Beth rolled her eyes. "I don't know exactly. I guess I had signs about six months ago, but I ignored them."

Rachel walked a little closer. She seemed so sad. She drew in a deep breath and asked, "What happened to you?"

Beth wasn't sure if she was talking about the cancer or the rape. "You mean with the cancer?"

Rachel nodded yes.

"I collapsed on Labor Day. I had been having sharp pains for a few weeks and my period was messed up before that."

"Why didn't you see a doctor? Was it because of..." Rachel started to cry. Beth began to feel bad for her. She came to realize that she wasn't the only victim that horrible night. She remembered Rachel's letter. It appeared to her that two young women's lives were ruined at that party. Rachel must have been telling the truth in her letter. "What did those guys do to her?" Beth wondered.

"Yes. I was afraid to go to the doctors. I didn't want anyone to find out about what happened. I didn't know if the doctor could tell. I know it seems stupid now, but at the time I was too scared to think straight."

"I'm so sorry. It's all my fault. If I hadn't introduced you to those guys, none of this would have happened."

"No, the cancer had nothing to do with that night. I don't know how much of a difference it would have made."

Rachel put her head down in shame. "I've done nothing but think about you since I left. I haven't been able to sleep or think. I did end up going home and staying with my mom. I kept waiting for the police to come and they didn't. I tried to forget what happened to you and what they did to me, but it wouldn't go away." Rachel wiped her nose with a tissue she pulled out of her pocket. "I might as well be in a cell."

"Tell me what you know about that night." Beth never thought she would ask such a question, but she felt she had to know.

She signaled Rachel to sit down on the bed.

"Do you really want to know?"

"Yes, I do."

Rachel wiped her nose again before she started. "Well, when Rick asked me to get ice with him, I had no idea what was going to happen. I don't think they really did either. Before we got the ice, Rick suggested that we stop by my place. He said that the party was gonna go on all night and he couldn't wait to, ya know." The thought of what she did with him now made her feel cheap. She went on.

"Anyway, like I said in my letter, we took a lot longer than expected and I kept asking him to leave because I knew I had left you alone there and I was worried about you. But Rick said that Mark was going to look after you. Hell, I thought, that was what you were hoping for, so I figured you probably weren't missing me at all."

"When I got back to the party, everyone was acting strange and you were gone. When I asked Mark, he said you left and he didn't know anything else. He was drunk and wouldn't answer my questions. I got mad because I knew you wouldn't do that and then a girl pulled me aside and told me what happened. She said that she was sitting next to you while you were talking to Mark. He started getting mad at something you said and she left the couch at that point. She said the next thing she saw was Mark bringing you a drink and everything looked fine, until a few minutes later when you passed out. Jack and Brian caught you as you were falling and Mark helped them carry you outside. About twenty minutes later, Mark rushed in and got a beer from the kitchen and ran back outside, but came right back in. Jack and Brian came back a half an hour before I arrived."

Rachel looked into Beth's eyes. "I was really worried about you. Like I said in my letter, I started to call the police, but Rick stopped me. And that's when he dropped a bomb on me. After he told me what they were up to, I wasn't sure what kind of people I was dealing with anymore. I was so afraid of what was going to happen to me, if I called the police. I went crazy and I wanted to know what they did to you. I started yelling and screaming and Rick finally told me everything, just to shut me up." Rachel shook her head. "And then I was more afraid for my own life."

So far, Rachel did not say anything that Beth hadn't already suspected. She wanted the details. "Rachel, what did they do to me. I only remember bits and pieces. I want to know everything."

"Okay, I'll tell you exactly what Rick told me." Rachel began to nervously tear pieces of her tissue as she spoke. "He said that Brian is a real strange character and has a nasty temper, although no one would guess it to look at him. If he got really mad, he had been known to up and split town and not come back for a long time. He also had trouble, obviously, getting dates. Mark and Rick needed him to stay around, so they would help get him dates from time to time, as a favor. Evidently, they had been striking out lately and Mark was afraid if you said no that night that it would send Brian over the edge and he would take off. So Mark devised this plan and got this drug called liquid Ecstasy. It's one of those date rape drugs on the street. Supposedly, it's odorless and tasteless and can easily be slipped into a drink. It produces sedation and amnesia and makes it impossible for someone to identify whoever used it."

"Mark got really mad at you because it forced him to give the drug to you. He had never used it before and was so nervous that he forgot how much he was supposed to put in your drink. When they got you into the van, Mark came outside to see what was happening and he couldn't believe that you were awake while they were having you." She couldn't bring herself to say the word rape. "Anyway, he panicked and got another drink to give you. But after they fed you the drink, you went limp and they were afraid that you were OD'ing. All Rick knew was that they drove you someplace and left you on the side of the road, but I don't think he would have told me where you were even if he knew. They didn't want me to go look for you."

So now Beth basically confirmed what she thought had happened, but something didn't make sense to her.

"Why did Rick tell you about the drug? Wasn't he afraid that you would eventually go to the police with his confession? What if I had gone to the police? What you knew was more damaging than any information I had."

Rachel laughed to herself. "Because he knew that I couldn't even if I wanted to."

While Rachel was talking to Beth, Frank had come home from work. Mary told him about Rachel coming from Texas to see Beth. He mumbled under his breath and went into the kitchen to make himself lunch, before he went upstairs to change for his meeting with Mr. Klein.

Meanwhile, Beth was studying Rachel as she spoke. Her sincerity made Beth feel better; knowing now that Rachel had not betrayed her like she thought. She had to know what Rick and the others were holding against her.

"What could they possibly have on you Rachel?"

Rachel laughed sarcastically. "Well, girl, if a fool's born every minute, I've probably taken up a whole hour for sure!" She got up and walked around the room with her arms folded tightly across her chest. "Now that I look back on everything, I realize I was such a moron. I can't believe how gullible I was. I guess, when I first moved here, I was scared. I'm sure you've noticed that I don't make girlfriends very easily. I didn't know anyone in town and when Rick showed an immediate interest, it felt good to latch on to someone.

"Well, anyway, remember how Rick used to come to the office on the nights I would work late?"

"Yes."

Rachel laughed again, "I thought that it was sooo sweet of him to hang around and wait all those boring hours while I worked. Remember, I was working on those cash account reports that were missing money, trying to find out where it all was going. Stan had discovered the discrepancies right before he hired me and he asked me to dig into the salesmen's expense reports to see if I could find any abuse. He already suspected one of the sales guys, but I couldn't find anything wrong with his reports. So he asked me to keep looking. The records were so sloppy that it was going to take me a long time to work through them.

"Rick would hang over my shoulder while I thumbed through the reports and, being the genius that I am, I would explain to him what every account was for. He even started making xerox copies for me when I needed them. I thought that he was an angel! Oh, I couldn't have been further from the truth!"

"While he was making copies of the accounts for me, he conveniently made copies for himself and slipped them into his pocket. Within a few weeks, he was able to get all of the bank account numbers and even some pin numbers out of me as well. He'd give them to Brian and Jack and they somehow found ways to set up fictitious accounts for themselves at the same bank that General Life uses. Then they made telephone transfers from the company accounts to the fake accounts and then disguised themselves or paid others to make small cash withdrawals at ATMs every day. They've taken thousands of dollars!"

Rachel covered her face with her hands and rubbed her eyes. "It's the perfect crime! I could've probably sat at that desk for another two months and no one would have suspected that I was involved at all. Shoot, I wouldn't have suspected myself! The money was already disappearing before I came. The guys kept the withdrawals low so they wouldn't raise any red flags!"

Beth was astonished. "Oh my God! But why can't you go to the police?"

"Rick said that if I ratted on them that all three of them would swear it was my idea. They would say that I made up the whole scheme to rip off General Life and that I was part of everything else they had going on. And to convince me, he showed me records that one of the accounts was in my name. I could go to jail! They had me completely fooled into believing that they were the nicest guys in the world and I have no doubt that they are cunning enough to pull off framing me with the police. It would be my word against theirs. I wasn't sure I would win."

Beth kept shaking her head. She never would have guessed that these guys were such creeps. Who knows what level they would stoop to if they became desperate? "Why did you come back?"

"Because I can't live like this. It haunts me everyday! I told my mom what happened and she supports me. She came with me and I have a lawyer. I can't let them get away with this. Especially what they did to you! I'm going to the police and telling them everything I know. Hopefully, they will believe me."

By this time in the conversation, Frank had mounted the stairs and was passing Beth's door. Neither Beth nor Rachel heard him. Beth's response caught Frank's attention.

"You can't tell the police everything! No one can ever know what happened!"

"But it's the right thing to do!"

"I don't want my parents to ever find out about it. Think about what it will do to them! I don't want Emmy to know this about me. Besides, I don't think I could take the interrogation. Please, Rachel, don't say anything to the police!" Beth started to cry.

Rachel grabbed Beth's hand and whispered to her, "You're the only one who can vouch for me!"

Beth whispered back, "I know and God, I'm sorry, but I can't let my family know. I don't want this to be the last thing they remember about me, especially Emmy!" Beth squeezed Rachel's hand and pulled her closer to her face until she could feel Rachel's breath on the back of her hand and continued to plead with her eyes.

Tears were dripping off Rachel's nose onto Beth's cheek, as she asked faintly. "Are you sure that's what you want?"

Beth smiled through her tears. "Yes, it is!"

"Okay. I won't say anything."

"Thank you."

Frank couldn't make out what they were saying but he had heard enough. He was growing hot under the collar just thinking about it. "So she's in trouble with the police, too." Frank marched into his room to change.

Rachel stayed for a few more minutes and then said goodbye. "Well, I guess I should be leaving. You look tired." She wiped her eyes and tried to look presentable.

"Are you really going to the police?" Beth couldn't believe her courage. She wondered if they would believe her story. She hoped so.

"Yes, tomorrow. What's the worst that could happen—ten years in jail?" They both laughed nervously. "You take care, now, ya here! Maybe I'll be by in a few days to see how you're doing." Rachel realized while looking at Beth how unlikely that would be. She wasn't sure what would happen to her without Beth to back up her story, but she certainly understood Beth's position. She hoped that leaving her out of the story would show Beth how sorry she was for the trouble she had caused her.

Before Rachel left she embraced Beth. "Bye, darling. Give your little girl an extra hug for me! I'm sorry I never did get to meet her."

"I will. You take care of yourself, too. Thank you! This means so much to me."

Rachel hurried out of the room and ran straight out of the house crying. Mary saw her from the kitchen and ran up to Beth's room to see if everything was okay. She found Beth weeping softly.

"Rachel left in a hurry. I didn't get a chance to say goodbye. Is everything okay?"

"Yeah, just fine."

"She seems like a nice friend!"

Beth smiled and took a tissue from the box Mary held out to her. "She's a very nice friend. I hope everything works out well for her!" Beth lay back and began to cough. Mary frowned to herself. The more relaxed Beth was becoming, the sicker she seemed to be. Mary didn't know what to hope for anymore.

When Mary left the room, Beth thought about everything that had happened to her in just a few short weeks. She thought about her miscarriage and finding out she had cancer. She thought about Rachel and wished she could help her, but knew that she couldn't. She thought about dying for the first time and she felt a fear rumbling up from the pit of her stomach that was so deep it was almost unbearable. She couldn't believe it was happening to her. She didn't feel like she was dying. But what was dying supposed to feel like? The words that the lady had spoke to her echoed in her head. Was she really running out of time? Every time she drew a deep breath, her restricted lungs warned her it was so, but she could never accept that it was death calling. Her heart yearned for a second chance to do everything right. She looked at the empty windowsill and wondered if Matt would come back. Maybe she had ruined her only chance for a miracle. Sleep was calling to her and that faint tinkling sound was playing sweetly inside her head. It lulled her softly into the inner-world where she felt so content.

♥ ♥ ♥ ♥ ♥ ♥ ♥

After dinner that evening, Mary held Emmy's hand as they walked into the bedroom. She was not sure how Emmy would react to the changes in her mother, who was looking frightfully pale. In one short day, it became obvious that the cancer was winning. Emmy smiled at the first glimpse of her mother and ran to her bedside. She was careful not to lean on the IV or catheter tubes as she climbed on her bed. You would have thought by her reaction that her mother was just staying in bed with the flu. Emmy was not disturbed by anything she saw.

"Mommy, I love you!" She laid her head gently on Beth's chest, almost intuitively knowing what areas of her body to avoid.

Beth wrapped her arms carefully around her little girl's head and treasured the feeling of her warmth next to her own skin. She wondered if she would be able to remember this feeling if she died. "Hi there, precious, how's my little girl?"

"Oh, I'm fine Mommy. You know what?" Emmy smiled up at her with her angelic eyes.

"What, sweetie?"

"You're the most beautiful Mommy in the whole wide world and I love you more than anything in the world!" Emmy closed her eyes and snuggled as close to her mother as possible. Beth wondered how much of her situation Emmy understood. She looked at her mother through tears. Mary was crying into a tissue, but shook her head and shrugged her shoulders, wondering where this was coming from, too.

"Thank you, Emmy. I think you are the most beautiful little girl any mom could possibly dream of having and I love you very much." Beth pushed Emmy away so she could look directly into her precious eyes. She emphasized her last words, "I will love you forever and ever, no matter how far apart we are, will you remember that?"

Emmy shook her head in agreement and through her own tears replied. "Yes, I will." Beth pulled her back into her body and kissed her head, as she exchanged questioning looks with her mother again. Mary quietly left the room and closed the door so they could be alone.

After a while, Beth asked Emmy to sit up because they needed to talk. She took a long deep breath and fought for the courage to let her little girl know the unbearable news she must tell her. There was precious little time left. She felt her body's energy draining as the hours went by.

"Emmy, sweetheart, I have something to tell you." Emmy sat straight up and listened carefully. "Emmy, Mommy is very sick. Very, *very* sick." Emmy nodded her understanding and Beth went on. "Mommy has a thing called cervical cancer. Do you know what cancer is?" Emmy nodded yes which surprised Beth a little. "Well, many times, if a person discovers they have cancer early enough, the doctors are able to make them better." Beth squeezed her eyes together tight to fight back the impending tears. "In Mommy's case, we didn't find out early enough, so the doctors can't help me get better." Beth watched Emmy's reaction to see if the meaning was sinking in. Emmy glowed with a soft smile that sent an eerie chill up Beth's spine and she continued. "This means I'm not going to be with you much longer. I will be going away. Kind of like that trip we talked about earlier, except I can't take you with me."

Emmy smiled at her mother, "I know, Mommy, you're going to Heaven." Beth was surprised at her response.

"Yes, I guess I am. How did you know that?"

"The pretty lady told me. Don't worry Mommy, you will be happy there. Heaven is beautiful and God will take care of you until I get there."

Beth's heart began to race. They hadn't talked much about God and Heaven before. "What lady told you this?" Beth asked, trying not to seem too surprised.

"The pretty lady who visited me the night you went to the hospital. Don't worry Mommy, she said you would be a little afraid of going but that everything would be alright. Heaven is really a beautiful place filled with sparkly castles and angels and God, of course." Emmy said it so matter-of-factly that Beth forgot about her grief for a moment.

"How do you know that Heaven is beautiful, did she tell you this?"

"No, well, yes she told me, but then she took me there and explained why everything was happening and why I could not come with you."

Beth was shocked. "She did? Why did she say this had to happen and where did she visit you?"

"She came to my room after Mrs. McCafferty tucked me into bed that night you got sick. At first, all I saw was this pretty white light and then she kind of walked out of it into my room. She smiled at me and I said hello and we started to talk—she's nice."

For a moment, Beth was totally confused until she remembered that she, too, had a messenger from Heaven. Could Emmy be telling the truth or could this be her way of dealing with the trauma of her mother's illness, she wondered.

"So what did she say, exactly?" Beth tried not to appear too anxious for answers. She didn't want to frighten Emmy and make her afraid to tell her story.

"Well, she told me not to be afraid, that she was sent by God. Then she told me that you were real sick and that you would have to go to Heaven soon, so you can be better. I began to cry because I was scared. So she asked me if I would like to see Heaven, so I could know where you were going and be happy about it. I said yes and she took me by the hand and we flew into the light. Then I was in Heaven and it was beautiful. There were angels everywhere and people were always smiling. And the flowers danced to music and there were colors I never saw before. You will be sooo happy there, Mommy. I asked if I could go, too, but she just shook her head and said it wasn't time."

By now, Beth was crying. Emmy held her and patted her shoulder trying to comfort her like she was the mommy and Beth was the little girl. She continued her story. "So the pretty lady told me that you would come to Heaven first, but I have to stay here with Grandmom and PopPop and live my life. She told me that I was very special and I had to do something important while I was on Earth for God. She said you would be really happy that I stayed here when you found out what it was. When I was done, I could come to Heaven and we would be together forever and ever."

Beth's tears flowed freely now. She was almost afraid to ask the next question. "Did the lady tell you why Mommy must go to Heaven now?"

"Yes she did Mommy, but she made me promise not to tell you yet. She said you have to find out something first for yourself. It's a surprise!" Emmy thought about what she had just said and didn't like not telling her Mommy the whole story and added, "I really want to tell you Mommy, but she said it was really important that I keep it a secret."

Beth smiled at her daughter. It didn't matter whether Emmy's story was real or not. It was wonderful if it helped her daughter accept her death. She decided not to continue questioning anymore and just remained contented holding her close. The two of them fell asleep for a while.

When Matt came to the window, he saw the two girls sleeping together. To his surprise, the screen was still open. Beth was pale and sickly, but all Matt could see was her beauty. Peacefulness enveloped her as she cradled her little girl. He could not imagine what was going on inside her mind right now. Beth opened her eyes and looked at the window and smiled when she saw him. She let out a sigh of relief that he was finally here and nodded for him to come inside. He looked around the room before he flew over to the bed and landed on the bed rail. Beth remained still so that Emmy would not wake up.

"You've come back! I'm so glad. I'm sorry for everything I said to you. I thought I lost you forever."

"Not a chance! I've been here. You've been sleeping a lot."

Beth snickered at his comment. "It doesn't look very good for either of us right now, angel."

"I don't care what happens to me, Beth. I just care what happens to you." Matt's voice quivered as he spoke.

Beth started to reminisce. She was shaking her head. "On Labor Day, I was on cloud nine. My dad got along with Father Pat so well and he even started speaking directly to me. I was so happy at dinner that I thought I was going to cry in front of everyone. And now, look at me! I'm dying, my father will never speak to me again and I ruined your chances of staying in

Heaven. My poor, sweet Emmy will grow up without a mother." Beth looked down at her daughter and stroked her hair.

"Matt, Emmy just told me that a pretty lady who came out of a bright light, visited her the night I was taken to the hospital and explained everything to her. She said the lady even took her to Heaven and showed her around. Did you have anything to do with that?"

"No, I don't know anything about it. Like I've said before, I can't communicate with them. Are you sure she isn't making it up?"

Beth looked up at Matt, "I don't know. She's taking the news so calmly. It was like she already knew every detail before I told her. Anyway, how can I not believe her? When I'm laying here talking to a hummingbird who was sent by God!"

"Touché! You've got a point there." Matt looked at Emmy. "So what happened?"

Beth explained Emmy's adventure to Matt.

"Did she tell you why this is happening?"

"She knows but the lady told her not to tell me yet. I need to find out some things for myself. This Heaven business is full of mystery isn't it?"

"Yeah, more of a mystery than I ever imagined." Matt replied.

Beth felt sleepy again and fought to stay focused. "There's something else I have to tell you."

"What is it."

"When I took my fall and passed out, a lady with blonde hair spoke to me. She was blurry and I couldn't see her face and I thought it was my nurse, Addie. It's funny, now that I think of it; she sort of came out of a bright light, too. Anyway, she said that I was running out of time and that I needed to come back and talk to you. Do you think I was dying when it happened?"

Matt was puzzled by what she said. "I don't know, but it doesn't matter. You're here and we have some work to do." He was glad to see Beth so calm about what happened.

"So, when are you planning to tell your father about the rape?"

"I'm not going to." Beth avoided Matt's eyes by watching her hand caressing Emmy's curls.

"What do you mean you're not going to tell him? He needs to know, Beth! You still have time to resolve your relationship."

"To him there *is no relationship*! He knows how bad my illness is and he hasn't come to visit me once. He would rather stew in his contempt for me than hear my side of the story. *He* made the choice to stay away from me and I can't change that. If he really loves me, then he will come to me. After all, I am the one that is dying here!"

"Well, I guess *he's* just as stubborn as *you are*, so you can die leaving it a draw!" Matt swooped down in front of Beth's face to get her attention and softened his voice. "You know, I've been thinking about it and there had to be something more than just a forged report card that would make him hold such a grudge against you. Did you ever think about that?"

Beth started to look annoyed. "Sure, I thought about that, but what in the world could I have done as a little girl that would warrant this kind of rejection? And why wouldn't I remember it?"

"Well, maybe you were too little to remember." Matt was grasping at straws. He didn't want to see Beth die without fixing her relationship with her father. He knew how awful it was at the review to look back on your life through your father's eyes and see the pain that you inflicted on him unknowingly.

Beth was growing tired. "What can I do to prove to my father that I'm not so deceptive and cunning as he thinks? Are you sure that he will believe my rape story? Even if Father Pat backed me up, he could twist it around to be my fault. He does that all the time, I know him. It would take a miracle to change his heart. *A real miracle!*"

Matt knew he was pushing her and he didn't want to in her fragile state, but time was running out. "Beth, if you believe that Emmy really saw an angel and was taken to Heaven and that you spoke to an angel yourself, then you have to have faith that there is something greater at work here." He saw Beth's eyes gaze out the window as she pondered the notion. "Maybe a miracle is exactly what's required! Maybe that is what your father must experience for himself!"

Beth began to smile again. "You know, you may be right, but what miracle could happen that would convince my dad that everything I'm telling him is the truth?"

Matt began to get caught up in his own idea. He hovered in front of Beth's face and made direct eye contact with her. "I don't know, but we'll think of something."

Beth looked into her friend's eyes and felt a deep stirring of love that she had never felt before. As he moved backward, she felt her soul connect with his for a single moment. She looked intensely into his eyes and saw a transparent vision of a young man's face, framed with brown hair and chiseled features. She put both hands up and cupped the young man's face. Matt hovered at the same time between her two hands in the center of the vision. He felt her hands on his face, too, although she physically did not touch the bird's body. When Matt landed in the palms of her cupped hands, the vision disappeared like a popped bubble. Beth looked at him for a moment and asked, "What color is your hair?"

"Brown." He was puzzled by the question.

Beth smiled again and her face almost glowed. "Okay, angel. Let's find a miracle." They decided to talk again the following day. They both needed time to think about the conversation they just had.

Matt flew back to the apple tree in the back yard to sit and think. It was quiet in the backyard and it gave Matt a sense of serenity. He began to think about everything that Beth told him. First about Emmy and then about the visit from an angel. He wondered if the pretty lady was Anjella. He pondered why Emmy was told not to tell her mother the reason she was dying. Was dying the only way that Beth and her father could forgive each other? It didn't seem like things were heading naturally in that direction. Why did she have a cancer that could spread so quickly in a short time? Fast enough to make it impossible for the doctors to save her life. And what happened when they made eye contact? How could he feel her hands on his face? Matt realized most of his questions could not be answered with simple explanations. The events seemed too synchronistic to call them coincidences. He started from the beginning and recalled the original objectives of this mission and realized that it had two distinct parts. First, he was supposed to help Beth patch up her relationship with her father. Second, he was supposed to prove to the Elders that he understood and experienced unconditional love.

Matt thought about Beth and her father's relationship and how it related to his own experience with his father. There were striking similarities. His father and Beth were what he called for argument's sake the good guys. He and Frank were the bad guys. Matt's father tried hard to do what he thought was best for his family. He tried to please Matt and make up for the times Matt thought he failed him. He fought hard to keep a relationship going until he got tired of fighting and gave up. Beth did the same thing. She tried all her life to please her father, but finally decided she did not have the strength to try anymore and similarly gave up. Matt never realized how many times his father tried to make up for his supposed disappointments and even began to hurt his father on purpose to "get even". Frank never saw anything Beth did as worthy and even began looking for trouble along the way, until he could not see anything but failure in Beth.

Matt's father, however, had a change of heart and began to try again. After watching his friend almost die from a heart attack, he realized what he wanted more than anything was to heal the conflict that he had with his family, especially with Matt. So he was about to offer to buy Matt the motorcycle to get him started with his dream of racing. Suddenly, Matt was aware that that thought alone made it sound like a shallow attempt to buy Matt. There was something more to what he saw in his view of what the future could have been. Stephen was not just giving Matt a motorcycle; it was an olive branch, an attempt to make peace with his only son.

Matt sat on the branch awestruck at the revelation he was making. His father wasn't just buying him a toy to appease him; he was allowing Matt to be who he wanted to be and not his father's version of what he thought a son should be. He was allowing him to follow his dreams. There was no guarantee that night when he told his family of his plans that that would renew a close relationship between the two of them. Stephen was setting Matt free, unconditionally. Maybe that is when a miracle is made possible. "That is it!" Matt realized, "That is the meaning of true love. To allow the one you love to be who they are and love them with no guarantees that their love will be returned. It's unconditional. It is the only way to set both souls free."

"Oh my God!" Matt thought, "That is how Beth's relationship with her father can be saved. She needs to tell her father the truth and allow him to react as he may, loving him even if he chooses not to believe her! Then she will create the opportunity for a miracle to happen. The power is in learning the meaning of true love." It was so clear to him. The revelation felt like a light going off in his head, except the light was coming from the wisdom of his soul. It was pure truth he was experiencing. Matt could not wait to talk to Beth tomorrow. When he showed her how she could allow both of them to win, without changing who they were, it would make sense to her, too. And it was possible that the mere action of telling the truth could create the circumstances that would facilitate her father's change of heart. It was the miracle of the power of love. Matt was higher than a kite and could not sit still. He flew over to his feeder for a nightcap before calling it a night.

Anjella and Enon looked down on Matt with elated smiles. Even Enon could not hide his delight at Matt's success. He finally discovered the meaning of true, unconditional love. There was a celebration in the control room. The Council would be pleased at the news. Matt had no idea what this revelation meant for him that night, but he slept more contentedly that evening than he had since the mission began.

Chapter 21

Thursday morning, Matt awoke feeling anxious. He couldn't stand the waiting. He wanted to see Beth desperately. First he fed and then waited for a sign to go to Beth's room. He buzzed by several times when the nurse or a volunteer was attending her. She looked worse today. Her continued decline was more of a shock to him than seeing her drastically changed appearance for the first time yesterday. Beth spent the morning trying to sleep through the nausea and sweats that she was now having.

Her night was long and restless, but she used the time to think about her conversation with Matt. She was haunted by the voice of the blonde-haired woman and what she said. She also went over in her mind what Emmy told her. She came to the deluded summation that the reason Emmy couldn't tell her why she was dying was because she wasn't going to die. The woman told her that Matt had the power inside of him and that she had to help him find it. *He* could heal her cancer if he believed he had the ability. Beth tried to convince herself that this was the truth, in spite of the fact that this morning she felt more detached from her body than ever. She felt a sensation like fire coursing through her veins. She was running out of time and knew of only one way to convince her father that she was not a liar. She was so sure she could convince Matt of her plan that she went ahead and asked her mother to sit and listen to her wild story.

She started, first, by telling her mother about meeting Matt the hummingbird, who was sent by God to help save her relationship with her father. She told her mother that she stayed with Father Pat for a few days when she was sick, because it did not work out with Rachel. She conveniently left out the rape. She also told her mother most of what Emmy had said. Mary's reaction to her story was cautious. Beth anticipated that she would assume the medications were affecting her mind, but she assured her mother she could prove it all and asked her to tell her father and bring him into her room at five o'clock. *She was going to show him a miracle!* When he saw her proof, she was sure that he would realize she was not a liar and they could finally find peace and live happily ever after.

Mary left Beth's room exasperated. She didn't know how to tell Frank such a far-fetched story and ask him to believe it, when she wasn't sure she could believe it herself. Mary quietly took Emmy aside and asked her if she had an angel visit. Emmy delightfully said yes with a twinkle in her eyes. At this point, Mary wasn't sure who was going mad from the stress. She realized she had no choice but to honor Beth's request. Addie had reported this morning that Beth's vital signs were very poor and that the pneumonia had taken a drastic turn for the worse. Beth could go at any time. All Mary wanted was for her daughter to die in peace.

Mary marched into the kitchen where Frank was sitting drinking a cup of coffee. "Frank, we need to talk." Her look was so upsetting that he reached for her hand, expecting to hear the worst. What he heard instead was beyond belief. After Mary finished telling Beth's wild tale of a soul coming from Heaven to save her and accidentally entering a hummingbird's body, and Emmy's trip to Heaven, and how she planned to provide proof of everything to them through a miracle, Frank shook his head.

"Mary," He said, as he rubbed his hands through his hair, "It's obviously the drugs. She is hallucinating. She probably told Emmy the angel story and Emmy is just too upset to understand what's going on."

"Frank, it doesn't matter. Don't you see? Your daughter, delusional or not, is so desperate to make amends with you that she is willing to try anything." Mary hesitated before she said her next words, "Besides, Frank, what if she is telling the truth? What if God did send some messenger to help the two of you get back together? That would explain how she mysteriously became friends with Father Pat. You know, I have never believed that Beth is the liar you think she is. I have always thought that you usually exaggerated, when you accused her of lying. Beth is a strong girl and I don't think she would become a victim to a breakdown or succumb to some kind of mental stress. I know it is a far-fetched story, but our little girl is dying. Don't you owe her one more chance?" Mary's eyes were pleading with him.

"Mary, she is playing *you* for a fool! She is not as innocent as you think. I wasn't going to tell you this, but yesterday I overheard a part of her conversation with that girl, Rachel. She was pleading with her to not go to the police about something involving her. Who knows what other trouble she was bringing home to us! I told you that the apple doesn't fall far from the tree."

Mary became enraged at Frank's comment. "I don't care what she has done! Did you ever think that maybe she's a product of *our* own deceit? Why don't you ever see what we have done to her as wrong? Maybe the tree she is standing next to is you!"

Frank could not find words to counter Mary's attack. He did not want to think about the past anymore. He pushed back a horrible surfacing thought that maybe he was hoping that Beth's dying would finally bury his painful past. He slumped back into his chair in resignation. "I don't know if I can handle another fabrication, Mary."

"Frank, we can handle anything together. I will not have any peace if I felt that we let Beth down before she died. I couldn't live with myself if I found out somehow that it was all the truth! I have to live with enough guilt for never trying to get the two of you to work out your differences before something like this happened."

Frank placed his head in his hands and leaned on the table. "Alright, I'll go to Beth's room this afternoon. For your sake, Mary, because I love you and Emmy."

"And Beth!" Mary chided him. "*You will do this for Beth*!"

Frank wiped tears from his eyes and stood up. "And for Beth," he said, and went outside to work on the lawn, to take his mind off of the memories the pain had resurrected.

It was about three o'clock when Matt finally was able to see Beth alone. Both of them were so excited that they didn't want to wait to tell their news. Matt finally let Beth go first.

"Matt, I've done it! I figured it all out! I have a plan and it's simply brilliant! I can't wait to see their faces when I show them." Beth was sitting up in bed, fiddling with the pain medication dispenser and increasing the morphine. She had a nagging suspicion that her time was shorter than they thought. Her bleeding was heavier and she constantly found blood in the mucus she coughed up so often. Her lungs were so restricted that every breath hurt. The morphine wasn't relieving the pain anymore.

"That's great Beth, but I have made an incredible revelation that you need to hear first."

"No, Matt, listen to me. We don't have much time. I'm scared. I feel it in my body." Matt was hovering but landed on the bed rail when he heard what Beth was saying.

"You mean, you think you're going to die?" He asked for clarification, even though he did not want to hear her answer.

"Yes, I think I am." Beth took a deep breath before continuing. "But I'm not going to die and *you* are the reason. Anyway, my plan is fantastic and you have to hear me through, okay?" She did not wait for an answer. "First, my father is pretty stubborn and he is the type of guy that needs physical proof. Well, in all of my trouble with him in the past, I could never physically prove anything. But now, I have proof. I can prove that God wants us to heal our relationship before I die, and then he will see that I am not the horrible person that he thinks I am." Beth was glowing with pride at the thought.

"So, how are you going to prove all this to your father?"

"Well, I'm not, really, you will." Beth was about to go on with her plan but Matt interrupted.

"What do you mean, me? I can't talk to him. I told you before; I can only talk to you. Anyway, last night I realized the secret of true love and you will know it, too, when I tell you."

305

"No, Matt, my plan will work. The angel, who visited me, told me that the power was in you and if I trusted you, that you would find the way. You are the miracle! When you confront my father, you will be able to talk. And if you have the power to talk to him, then you also have the power to heal me. Besides, at first you won't really be talking to him, you will be talking to me, *in front of my father*. You can do that now. And think of everyone's reactions, when they hear you talking about what you were sent to do." Beth was visualizing the whole scene as she spoke.

"It won't work, Beth. It won't!" Matt yelled at her. "Listen to me! It's a big mistake. It's not possible for me to speak in front of you, since your intention is to have the others hear us speaking to one another. You have to change his heart on your own. Now, please, let me tell you what I have discovered."

Matt began to tell her the wonderful revelation that came to him last night, and how he came to the conclusion that it is the unselfish act of accepting others as who they are that creates the circumstances for miracles to happen. He stressed that it was imperative that she tell the whole truth about her experiences with Rachel and her friends and especially about the rape. This would enable her father to make a clear judgment. Matt explained that even if her father did not accept her truth that they both would still win in the eyes of God, especially Beth, for loving her father unconditionally.

Beth disagreed completely. She did not see how she could come from a place of unconditional love. That meant she had to accept his rejection and love him, in spite of it. She could not see how that was going to create a miracle. Her idea seemed easier and this way, she could avoid telling her parents about the rape altogether.

"Matt you don't understand. I know the real miracle will happen when they see *you* speak. I just know it! You have the power! That's what the lady meant, I'm sure. Look, I only have one chance here. I feel the life draining from me. Only you can save my life! Please, please, please do it my way!" Beth gave Matt a look of desperation so heart-wrenching that he felt totally helpless in her gaze. The look was so pitiful that he lost all will to disagree. He loved her too much to say no.

"God help us, Beth! I'll do it but I don't think you're right." Matt resigned himself to failure. His mission would be over soon and he would go on to living another life on Earth. He felt truly powerless and not powerful. His heart had taken over and he realized how deeply in love he had fallen for this beautiful girl, who lay withering before him. He decided that he would rather fail in his mission than to let her down before she died. He did not want to follow the same path that every other man who supposedly cared for her had taken. The thought occurred to him that neither one of them would succeed at experiencing unconditional love in this lifetime. Perhaps Beth would be required to return to Earth to live the lesson all over again. Maybe they would find each other during their next life on Earth, if Beth was coming back, too. Something brought him back to a question that was bothering him for a long time.

"Can I ask you something before I leave?"

"Sure, angel." Beth had rolled over onto her side and her face was half pressed into the pillow. She sounded so tired.

"Remember when we were talking that night on the porch? When I told you that I would go out with you?"

"How could I forget. You were my secret admirer, right?"

Matt blushed. "Right. Well, you said something about no matter who says they love you, even if they really do, they always leave you. I know you've had a lot of bad experiences with men, but I kind of got the impression that there was someone who really loved you that you were talking about."

Beth lifted her head to say something and then laid it back down on the pillow. She was having trouble gathering her thoughts.

"In all my life there's only been one man who has ever showed me that he loved me, and it's hard for me to talk about it."

Matt's heart skipped a beat. He was right, he thought, she was in love with him.

Her pain was getting worse, so she reached up to increase the morphine dosage, but it was already at the maximum level. She sank down into her pillow and mumbled. "His name was Brandon."

Matt's heart plummeted into his stomach. "What did you say?"

"His name was Brandon. I met him after I had Emmy, when I first went to work at General Life. He was a dream come true. Brandon was so wonderful with Emmy. She was so tiny in his hands, but I could..." She flinched from the pain. "I could tell."

Matt could hardly speak himself. Of course, this made more sense. What was he thinking? "Tell what, Beth."

"Tell that he loved us. We were so happy together."

"What happened?"

"I don't want to talk about it." Beth looked like she was falling asleep.

Matt had to know. "Please tell me."

"He died. Car crash. His brother's bachelor party. There I said it. He left me, too."

"I'm so sorry."

"It's okay. It wasn't your fault." Beth was drifting to sleep. "At least I got you now, right angel?"

"Yes, you do. You'll always have me. I will never leave you." Matt realized that she needed her sleep.

"What time do you want me back here? I don't have a watch you know, so I could be a few minutes early or late."

"I told them to be in the room at five o'clock." Beth bit her lower lip for a second. "Thank you Matt! You don't know how much this means to me! I'll never forget everything you have done."

"I'll never forget you either, Beth." Matt heard a noise outside Beth's door and took off for the window. He turned to her, "I have to go to the feeders before I come back, it's just a few blocks away. I'll be back in plenty of time." He left her bedroom and rested in the apple tree, first. He was still reeling from what Beth had told him about Brandon. Matt imagined different scenarios in his mind of how this meeting could result. He was never able to envision Beth's dream coming true. In one vision, he even saw himself getting squashed by Beth's father. He shuddered at the thought. It was four o'clock when he left for the feeders.

Chapter 22

Summer was fading. The temperature outside had dropped ten degrees in just a day and the humidity that long wilted the flowers was lifting and was replaced by a freshness in the air. Summers ended as quickly as they started in this part of the country.

Matt flew along the suburban streets heading toward his nectar haven. The summer flower season had ended and nectar was scarce in their centers. Nature had begun its rejuvenation cycle and every tree and blade of grass began the preparation for a long winter's sleep. Matt was grateful for the artificial supply of food that was provided by the hummingbirds' gracious fan, Mrs. Wendell. Her garden stood as a tribute to the smallest, most delicate creatures of God. It was a haven to birds, butterflies, and bees alike.

Matt moved through the air gracefully now that he had mastered the intricate art of flying. He swooped and circled in a special dance of freedom today, as he thought about his closing time here on Earth in the form of a hummingbird. He knew he would have to return, however, and braced himself for the confrontation with the Council. All he could tell them was that he did his best and realized, far too late, how this business of love is meant to operate here on Earth. Matt decided to ask the Council if he could somehow be involved in a ministry on Earth the next time around that was devoted to relationships. Regardless of what he came back to do, he hoped they would allow him an attraction to hummingbirds, so he could learn more about them and appreciate their beauty. He would definitely keep a feeder overflowing in his backyard.

Matt changed his thoughts from daydreaming to the task at hand, as he neared his feeding grounds. He had not seen the other two birds at all this morning and wondered where they were. He had never entered the property without one of them whizzing over his head to make their presence known. He was glad this would probably be the last time he fed, because it was during this time that the little bird's body fought most fiercely to migrate, while his concentration level was low. The little bird's urgings to find food supplies further south were difficult to overcome.

Approaching Mrs. Wendell's driveway, Matt detected a change in the surroundings. It was quiet in the yard. Normally, birds were singing and busying themselves at their own feeders around the garden. When he rounded the corner of the house to the backyard, Matt watched with horror as he discovered the reason for the unusual silence.

Mrs. Wendell merrily hummed as she took down the last of the three feeders and carried them into the house. Matt moved over to the screen door and watched her empty the feeders, one by one, into the sink in the laundry room. She washed the feeders, dried them and put them into a box. "Until next year, little angels!" she sang, "Have a safe winter in the south!" Mrs. Wendell placed the box up on a storage shelf, wiped her hands dry and headed into the house.

Matt looked around the garden, hoping that there would be one more feeder, miraculously missed, but there were none. His heart sank further as he moved from flower to flower that remained standing in the garden and found them all dry. A few of them had small amounts of nectar, but not nearly enough to recharge his body. Matt roamed through the connecting backyards, only to find the same thing in every tired flower patch.

"This really doesn't matter, I suppose." He contemplated. "I will be done with my job in just a few hours and will probably be back in Heaven by the end of the day anyway, if Beth's father doesn't send me there sooner. I'm sure I can hold on until then." He thought about Beth sadly and wondered if she really would move on today. He would go to Beth very soon and hope by some miracle that she was right, and he would magically speak in front of everyone. Whether this would really do anything to help her father, he could not begin to guess. Anyway, he did not feel like this miracle would happen. It relied too much on the chance of a blessing from Heaven and not from personal power from within. Didn't the angels tell him specifically that Beth needed to create the change herself? Beth was not coming from the truth this way. She was still lying to herself. It was hard for him to concentrate on Beth when his energy was sapped. Especially since he would need energy, just to fly the few blocks home.

Matt decided to survey a few more yards and sup whatever nectar he could just to be safe. About a block from Mrs. Wendell's yard, a public park had a single patch of bright orange daylilies. The daylilies reminded him of the rectory and he smiled, reminiscing about his grand adventure with the scruffy cat. He swooped in and began to feast on the remaining supply of nectar. Matt became so involved in his present task that he dropped his guard, while reveling in his stroke of luck. He never heard the buzzing directly behind him.

Matt busily drained the last of the nectar from the base of the lily. It was only then that he felt and heard the eerie presence of the worker bee. The presence felt like it was above his head. He carefully moved straight down toward the lilies long green leaves that arched to the ground. Matt looked straight up and saw the angry expression on the bee, as it began its descent toward him.

Alarms went off in Matt's head as his body registered the impending attack, and he dipped down, almost touching the grass. Just as quickly, he reversed direction and began ascending over the top of the bee. The angry bee made chase, nearly catching him and he flew across the park, almost running into a sapling by a pond. Matt glanced backwards losing sight of the bee and rested in a pine tree for shelter, while he scoped out the area for signs of his adversary.

Matt's heart was racing at nearly twenty-five hundred beats a minute, which was twice the bird's usual accelerated rate. It was a wild feeling that coursed through his body and his mind. He took a few minutes to compose himself before carefully setting out for home. "Whoa!" Matt exclaimed, as he remembered how aggressive bees became at this time of year. "That was close! I cannot believe how big that bee was. The stinger was big enough to go right through me." Matt breathed a sigh of relief. He had had enough of cats and birds and bees for one lifetime. He checked his surroundings and carefully headed out of the park.

Matt flew cautiously, looping every so often to cover his back. He relaxed as he exited the park, seeing the top of Beth's house in sight. As he made his way across the empty street, a shadow loomed above him briefly blocking out the sun. When he looked up, he saw, again, the yellowjacket dive toward him, this time too quickly for Matt to evade. The angry bee lurched at Matt, placing its front legs on Matt's shoulders while its deadly stinger pierced through the middle of Matt's back injecting its poison into the little bird's body. Matt began a spiraling descent, as he fought to throw the bee off of his back, before the bee finished his lethal injection.

A fire blazed through his body and he tried to right himself. The bee disengaged, flying off in the direction of the park. Matt fought frantically to keep his wings beating against the pain that began to drown his consciousness. He panted as he rounded the corner, seeing Beth's house straight ahead of him. To his relief, he saw that the second floor window was still open.

The pain seared through him and he struggled with every ounce of strength and courage to keep control as he neared the house. "I just have to get up to that window!" He thought to himself, but it was about ten feet higher than he was flying. Matt arched his back in a final attempt to fly upwards toward the window. He struggled against the numbness from the bee sting that seemed to paralyze his efforts. He fought to fly higher and higher. He was just two feet away from the window ledge as his wings seized and the last of his will drained from his body. He blinked tears away, while his body spiraled towards the ground. As he raced toward the brown earth, he thought about the consequences of his failed mission and what it would mean for Beth. Mercifully, he entered the blackness of a semi-conscious state before his body hit the ground. He landed between two rose bushes next to the house. His wings were instantly broken and he began to bleed internally.

♥ ♥ ♥ ♥ ♥ ♥ ♥ ♥

The sound of Matt's wings breaking echoed in the control room like a crack of thunder. Every angel stopped in their tracks and bowed their heads in silence. Just a short time ago, they were rejoicing at Matt's revelation about the meaning of true love. The angels were busy making return preparations for both Matt and Beth. Matt's discovery had invoked such a positive chain of events that they were sure nothing could go wrong. Anjella and Enon watched with sorrow, as their most incredible success story diminished before their eyes. Everyone knew that Matt had succeeded in understanding the meaning of true love, but a shadow would loom over the return celebration, because his mission was cut short by the death of the bird.

Anjella put her hands to her face as she looked down on her sweet friend. "Oh, Matt! You were so close!" She turned to Enon who was still staring at the screen. "Why did that happen, Enon? He had so much power of unconditional love within him."

Enon was studying the screen, looking for something. He tilted his head toward Anjella without moving his eyes off the screen. "Matt's message of true love would have manifested during the meeting with Beth's father and mother. He would have been able to create his own miracle, using the intentions of the three souls, Beth's, his own and her father's, as they gathered to honor her final request. There would have been a moment when the father's surprise at the sight of a hummingbird in the room would have opened a small spot in his heart. It would have been just large enough for his soul to administer an infusion of forgiveness and acceptance. The actual miracle would not have been as either Beth or Matt envisioned, but the result would be the same. Matt's power could not change the realm of the physical world, however. He still had to live by those rules. It was an unfortunate situation that he stumbled upon and one that could not be anticipated or prevented."

Anjella sighed as she looked at Matt lying on the ground. "Is he dead?"

"No, not yet." Enon shook his head. "It will be soon, though. Once the bird dies, we will go to receive him."

"Well, I guess I better inform Human Affairs." Anjella walked away to instruct an angel to begin preparing for Matt's return.

Enon remained staring at the screen. His heart went out to the courageous soul that lay still on the ground. The bird's breast moved up and down slightly. There was a trickle of blood seeping from his beak. The once skeptical angel stood frozen in front of the screen reviewing all the rules of the operation in his mind. There was no possible way to intercede on Matt's behalf this time. Enon was about to admit that the case was hopeless when a shadow appeared in the corner of the screen and it caught his attention. The human figure never entered the screen, but Enon could tell immediately who it was. "It's not over yet!" He smiled to himself. He quickly scanned the rulebook and looked back at the screen with delight.

♥ ♥ ♥ ♥ ♥ ♥ ♥ ♥

At four-thirty, Beth felt a strange premonition of danger for Matt. An image of Matt being chased by something flashed in her mind. At the same moment, she felt a stabbing pain in her heart. It was different from the burning pain that coursed through her body from the cancer. The fiery pain was becoming more frequent and almost unbearable now, and it was hard to tell what was real anymore. She fought hard to remain conscious. Her lungs felt heavy and breathing was raspy. Her mother had checked in on her several times, asking her if she was sure she wanted to go through with her request. Beth was in no condition to experience anything upsetting. Mary hoped that she would change her mind, but Beth was adamant every time.

Addie had stopped by and reported that Beth's lungs were almost full of fluid. Beth had used all of the morphine allowed this morning so she increased the pump to allow five mils whenever Beth hit it. There was nothing left that she could do for her. Addie said that she had to visit another patient, but would be back after dinner and would stay the night with the family, if they wanted. She told Mary that it was up to Beth's will now.

Mary let Frank know, then called Father Pat and asked him to come over. She told him briefly about Beth's mysterious request for Frank's presence at five o'clock and her claim that God sent a messenger to patch things between them. Father Pat did not tell Mary anything he knew, but told her he would be right over and asked if Mrs. McCafferty could come, too. Mary was glad to have her company. When Mary hung up the phone from talking with Father Pat, she called her two sisters and Frank's brother who were all in different states to tell them about the graveness of Beth's illness. Her oldest sister lived in upstate New York and the other in New Jersey. They said that they would drive down together early the following morning. Frank's brother lived in the Midwest and would catch the first flight he could in the morning but would probably not arrive until late afternoon. Mary numbly used preparation for her guests as a distraction from her worst fears. She was losing Beth.

Emmy visited her mother at four-thirty and lay on Beth's shoulder. Beth cried softly as she tried to imprint the feel and smell of Emmy's hair and skin into her memory. She told Emmy that she did not think it would be long before she began her new journey. Emmy told her she understood and would try to be brave. She told her mother one more thing about her visit from the angel. The pretty lady said that she would visit her when Beth was gone and give her special graces to be strong when her mother left. Emmy thought Beth would feel better knowing this. It gave Beth solace to know that special graces would help Emmy deal with her death, but it did not erase the pain of the impending separation. After a while, Beth asked Emmy to go downstairs. She needed to be alone. She was so tired. It was exactly five o'clock and Beth hoped Matt would come before her father, so they could talk by themselves. Beth was beginning to feel groggy from the increased dose of morphine and it was very difficult to keep her senses clear. When Emmy left, she stared at the window and felt that sense of danger again. She tried not to think about how afraid she was.

Father Pat arrived exactly at five o'clock, too, and Emmy skipped merrily past him out the door. She greeted Mrs. McCafferty outside and hugged her before heading toward the backyard. Father Pat exchanged a heart-felt look with Mrs. McCafferty and Mary. Mary explained to him what Beth told her about staying with them while she was sick because things did not work out with Rachel. She said that Beth claimed to meet a hummingbird sent by God to patch up the relationship with her father. Mary was desperately confused. She told Father Pat that Frank agreed to go to the room, but she feared Frank's reaction, if this turned out to be Beth's wild imagination.

Father Pat was in a quandary. He struggled to listen to his heart and hear what God would have him do. He knew about Matt, and had encountered him twice, but the bird did not speak to him. Beth did not tell the whole truth to her mother and never mentioned how they actually came to know each other. Mary was too upset to sort through the plausibility of the situation. He feared that telling them the truth would cause more complications. He asked to speak to Beth alone. Mary agreed that it would be a good idea.

Frank was in the screen room, nursing a beer for courage. He toiled over the mix of emotions that he was experiencing. Addie said Beth was dying. Beth was talking to hummingbirds; Emmy was talking to angels. None of it made sense. He felt like he was living a bad dream, but could not wake up. His heart began to break knowing his little girl was dying and, at the same time, anger bubbled in his throat for the way she seemed to be using her final moments to manipulate Mary. He had been used before and Beth had succeeded in forcing those painful memories to the surface again.

Beth was staring blankly at the window when Father Pat walked in. She glanced over at him, too numb to speak. Father Pat smiled at her and sat down on the bed. It felt like *deja vu*. He took her hand, just like before and squeezed it gently. "So what are you up to Beth? Your mother tells me you are about to reveal your secret companion to her and your father."

Beth looked over at the window. Her optimism was waning inside but she put on a good act. She was losing her strength and her words came out very slowly. "Matt will be here shortly. I told him five o'clock, but he doesn't have a watch, you know." She continued to stare at the window.

"It sounds like you haven't told your mother the entire truth. Are you planning to tell them everything?" He gave her a stern look.

"After Matt tells them why he is here, my father will be ready for the truth!" She said it more to convince herself than Father Pat.

Father Pat rubbed his chin with his hand. "Back at the rectory, I thought you said he could only talk to you? Has that changed?"

"Well, Matt suggested that with everything going on, something big was working here. An angel told Emmy why I was leaving, but that I must discover the reason for myself. So, we figured that maybe there is some kind of miracle about to happen and I think the miracle will be my father's ability to hear Matt and finally believe me. And if he believes that God wants us to forgive each other, then he will change his mind about me." Her voice trailed off as she looked back at the window, "and hopefully I'll be cured."

Father Pat rubbed her arm gently. "What does Matt think about all of this?"

Beth rolled her eyes. "He doesn't think it will work either. He believes that if I tell my father the entire truth and love him regardless of his reaction, that a different kind of miracle can happen, because I have loved unconditionally and that act will create a miracle."

"Matt sounds like a wise little hummingbird." Father Pat watched Beth, as she closed her eyes for a moment.

"I can't do that Father. I don't think I can love my father unconditionally if he rejects what I tell him one more time. I just can't." Beth looked out the window, becoming anxious for Matt's appearance.

"So you plan to go ahead with your way?"

"Yes, I plan on it. Matt will be here shortly. Can you please get my parents for me, Father?" Beth bit her lip and stuttered, "I don't think I can hang on much longer." Her eyes were pleading for approval. Father Pat melted just like Matt. What could he do?

"Okay, Beth, I'll get them." He left her room and she heard his footsteps trail off down the stairs.

315

Father Pat returned a few minutes later with her mother and father. They looked nervous and apprehensive. Beth smiled at them and tried to sit up. The medicine was making her groggy, but Beth was more afraid that it was a sign that her body was failing. She was determined to see this through. Mary came to the right side of her bed, farthest from the window and sat down in a folding chair that was set up next to the bed. She was crying and could only kiss her daughter's hand, until she composed herself to speak. Mary looked over at Frank and Father Pat and smiled, "We are all here, Beth, just like you asked."

Frank looked at his daughter closely for the first time in weeks. He barely recognized the shell of a body that days ago chased his granddaughter around the house. A sob caught in his throat. He did not know what to make of this entire sequence of events. Beth smiled at him through her own tears and thanked him for coming with a faint, hoarse voice.

Father Pat stood directly behind Frank, hoping he would feel his support. Frank walked over to the bottom of Beth's bed. "Hi," was all he could think to say.

Beth looked at the window praying Matt would come. The clock said it was five-fifteen. Beth began to panic inside. She could not imagine that Matt would let her down now. He was not like the other men in her life. She watched her father begin to pace back and forth staring at the floor.

"I'm sure he'll be here soon!" Beth gave a look over to Father Pat as if to say "please help me out here".

Father chimed in. "Beth, perhaps you would like me to explain everything that has happened, so your parents can understand."

"No!" Beth screamed out, but it only came out as a whisper and made her cough. "He will be here soon, and then I will tell them." Beth looked over at her mother, who was patting her hand. Mary grew more nervous watching Frank pace back and forth.

"Beth, why don't you tell your father what you told me while we are waiting. I'm not sure I explained it very well." Mary was hoping she could start some kind of dialogue between the two of them.

Beth looked over at her father, "Dad, first, I know that I have told some lies before. But I never intended to hurt you. I was just a kid doing kid things. But you have to believe me now. God has sent us a messenger to help us heal our relationship." Beth had to stop for a moment and take a deep breath. Her lungs were feeling tight and it was difficult to talk. Her voice came out as a strained squeak. "Anyway, you will see soon that this messenger is a hummingbird and he can talk. He will tell you what God wants us to know. And Emmy, she really was visited by an angel. I know we're not religious, but it's true. She knows why I'm dying but that's not what's important here. What's important is that you believe me."

Frank stopped pacing and looked at his daughter. He wanted to believe her but he felt like he was hallucinating. It felt like she had created a fantasy world and was trying to draw everyone into it. She lied about why she had come home and now she has this wild story about a hummingbird. So many lies, he thought to himself. He was torn between wanting so much to believe her and feeling that her mind may have deteriorated as a byproduct of the sudden illness. Since she was born, he had felt unsure of whom to trust. There was no guarantee you could trust a loved one. Hadn't he already learned that lesson? Maybe they were the least trustworthy of all. His fear welled up in his belly and he began to feel skeptical again. He would not let go of the doubts he had had for all these years. "Beth, where is this messenger from God?"

Beth looked at the window. She felt her stomach turning in panic. This was not going well at all. "He will be here, I promise!" She looked at Father Pat as her mind raced to recover. "Dad, you've got to believe me, he is from God!"

"When was he supposed to be here?" Frank's voice was dry.

"At five, but he is a hummingbird, he doesn't have a watch." She smiled, hoping he would see the humor.

"I doubt God's messengers need one, Beth. Maybe you are confused. Sometimes things seem more real than they are." He turned to walk out of the room. He could not watch her deterioration. It was too painful.

"No, Daddy, don't go, he is coming!" Beth had a coughing fit. Mary stood and tried to calm her down. Frank kept on walking out of the room. Beth began to weep tossing her head back and forth. "No, don't Daddy, please. I'm not asking you to believe in angels! I'm asking you to believe in me!" Her words faded along with the sound of Frank's footsteps going down the stairs. Beth sobbed into her mother's arms.

Father Pat moved to the bottom of the bed and whispered to Beth. "Please tell him, child! Don't do this to yourself!" Beth did not respond, so he followed Frank downstairs. Mary continued to rock Beth, trying to calm her down, and wondering what on earth Father meant. Beth looked up at her mother. "What's wrong with him Mom? Why is he acting this way? What in the world could have ever hardened his heart that he cannot make peace with me? Something must have happened to Matt! He would never let me down like this, never!" She buried her head into Mary's chest and looked back up. "I don't think I can hold on much longer! What am I going to do?" Mary held Beth as tight as she could. Tears ran down her face and dripped onto Beth's hair.

"I don't know, sweetheart. Maybe you should just let it go. I love you! Emmy loves you! And whether your father shows it, *he* loves you, too. Maybe I should get Emmy to come up here. She will make you feel better, don't you think?" Beth nodded in agreement and closed her eyes. Mary went to the top of the stairs and called down to Mrs. McCafferty to ask Emmy to come to her mother's room. Mrs. McCafferty knew what was happening by the look of urgency on Mary's face. She cupped her hands over her mouth and fought back the tears before going to the front door to call Emmy. "Emmy, dear," she called, "Where are you?"

"I'm in the backyard!" she chimed.

"Your mother would like to see you." she tried to sound as normal as possible.

"Okay, I'm coming!" Emmy skipped through the yard and tried to open the screen room door, but it was jammed. She shrugged her shoulders and walked toward the front of the house. As she hummed to herself, she ran her hands over the leaves of the bushes that lined the side of the house. A flash of light caught her eyes, as she wandered past the rose bushes. She knew, instantly, what it was and bent down to investigate. "Oh!" she exclaimed. "Wait 'til Mommy sees this!"

Chapter 23

Frank went straight to the kitchen and grabbed a beer. He popped the top with his shaking hands and sat down at the kitchen table. Father Pat walked down the stairs and went over to Mrs. McC, who was sitting on the couch. He spoke to her softly, so Frank could not hear him. "Gladys, is there anything left in your bag of tricks?"

Mrs. McC took his hands in hers and shook her head no. "Nothing comes to me Father. Dear God, I wish it would."

Father smiled at her. "Thanks, anyway." He started to get up and head for the kitchen.

"Pat." Mrs. McC whispered. He turned to face her. "You *will* do the right thing. I'm sure of it."

He walked into the kitchen and reached for a beer, too. He sat down across from Frank and sipped his beer. He contemplated his next action. What choice did he have? Betray the honor of his sacred vow, or watch a family crumble in despair. In all of his years as a priest, he never doubted the sanctity of his vows, but now, sweet Jesus, how could they make sense? Beth was just a child. A beautiful, uncut jewel, lacking the wisdom and insight that comes with time and forms an exquisite, precious diamond. How could he stand by and let her make the biggest mistake of her life? He felt that he knew Frank well enough to know that he would certainly come around, if he heard the circumstances surrounding her pregnancy. If Frank did not reconsider, then so be it. He would be damned by his own foolishness. But if he did have a change of heart, there was still a little time left to bring some kind of peace to these good people.

He made up his mind and decided to take the risk. It was time Frank knew the whole truth. Beth was now in a life or death situation. "Frank, it's time we talked." Frank looked up at him and nodded. He was grateful to have him as a friend. It was one of the only positive things he could credit Beth with lately. He needed a friend right now, before he lost his mind.

Father Pat was about to tell Frank how he really came to know Beth and what had happened to her; but he was interrupted when Emmy burst into the kitchen holding something cupped in her hands. "Look, PopPop! Look at what I found in the garden!"

Emmy opened both her hands all the way to show the two men. In her left palm was a shiny copper penny that gleamed brilliantly without a scratch on it. In the other hand, a battered hummingbird lay breathing shallowly. The tiny bird had blood trickling onto Emmy's hand from its beak. The bird opened its eyes and tried to focus at the blurry shadows that

319

loomed over him. As his sight cleared, he recognized the two men, but his vision dimmed to black again.

"Where did you find them?" Frank asked Emmy with a shaky voice.

"Between the two rose bushes, PopPop. Right under Mommy's bedroom window." Emmy's face grew sad as she inspected the bird's broken body. "He's really hurt."

Frank looked at Father Pat with a stunned expression. "This couldn't be, Father! It's just a coincidence." Father Pat shook his head no. He knew it was Matt.

"No, Frank, this does look like the hummingbird Beth described." He hesitated but decided to take the plunge. "I have seen him before."

Frank looked down at the bird and his thoughts swirled in confusion. "Does he speak, Father?"

Father Pat smiled, "He can only speak to Beth. That is what he told her. He was sent to help her mend her relationship with you. It is a long story, but he was not supposed to be a hummingbird. He's a human soul on a rescue mission from Heaven and was supposed to enter my body and work through me. However, he made a mistake and accidentally entered this bird's body instead. He has spent the last month or so trying to work a miracle despite impossible circumstances. It looks like it was too great a challenge for such a small creature." Father Pat rolled the bird's body gently over and saw a piece of stinger protruding from Matt's back. "It looks like he fell prey to a bee of some kind. Poor fellow." Father Pat looked at Emmy and smiled, "Emmy, I think your mother needs to see Matt now. She should know what happened to him." Emmy nodded with a sparkle in her eyes. She seemed to have wisdom far beyond her years. He knew this little girl would be alright.

Father Pat took a deep breath and began to explain what really happened to Beth. He knew he was violating his sacred oath, but he could not allow Beth to pass on under these pretenses. Frank sobbed until his body was exhausted, after he heard what really happened to his little girl. Father Pat consoled his friend as much as he could. Frank reached in his back pocket for a hanky and cleaned his face.

He looked at Father and prepared his own admission. "Father, I have my own confession to make. I have been keeping my own secrets for far too long." Frank began his soulful confession, as Father Pat sat quietly and listened. It all became clear to him what had caused Frank's animosity towards his own daughter. When Frank finished, he patted him on the back.

"Frank, I can understand how hard these years have been for you. We all are blinded by fear sometimes, when the ones we love the most hurt us the worst. However, I think it is time Beth knows the truth, don't you? You will both feel at peace when the truth is revealed."

"You know, Father, she has spent all her life trying to get me to forgive her for things that she didn't even do. Do you think she will be able to forgive *me,* when she knows the secrets her mother and I have been keeping?"

Father Pat smiled, "I think Beth will be grateful to know the truth, Frank. All she ever wanted was your love. The truth won't take that away."

♥ ♥ ♥ ♥ ♥ ♥ ♥ ♥

Beth was lying quietly in her mother's arms when Emmy entered the room. Emmy's smile beamed like a ray of sunshine. She knew now that everything the angel told her was true. When she reached her mother's side, she gently opened her hands.

"Mommy, I found your friend outside, he is hurt." She raised her hands and rested them on Beth's lap carefully.

Beth moved away from her mother and looked down at Matt. She gently lifted his body into her hands and brought him closer to her face. "Oh, Matt what happened?" She scanned his body and saw the blood and the stinger. She looked at Mary. "He was stung by something, Mom. I knew he would never desert me. He kept his promise, after all." Beth sniffed her tears back as she stroked his head. Matt opened his eyes and focused in again. He saw sweet Beth's face smiling down at him. She looked weaker than the last time he saw her.

"I'm sorry Beth," he managed to whisper, "I got attacked by a bee trying to get back here." He tried to make light of his doomed predicament. "And I thought the *cat* was a challenge!" Closing his eyes, he tried to speak again. "I just want you to know…" he swallowed and tasted blood. He felt the bird's body fading. "I just want you to know, that, that I love you."

Beth raised her hand even closer to her mouth to make sure Matt could hear. "I love you, too, angel. You gave your life for me today. I think, now, I know the meaning of true love. Thank you, Matt." She kissed his head tenderly and Matt opened his eyes to speak but breathed his last.

Beth continued to stroke his head for a moment and folded her hand closed over his body. She knew he was gone. Mary could not hear Matt speak, but knew he did in her heart. She saw Beth's face light up with a loving expression and felt relieved that, at least, she would have this wonderful memory in her last moments.

When Matt closed his eyes, he heard the familiar rushing sound and felt his soul free itself from the little bird's body. In a blink of an eye, he was standing in the corner of Beth's bedroom with Enon and Anjella on each side. She smiled at him and hugged him. All three looked at the three girls on the bed. Matt felt tears rolling down his cheeks. He turned toward Enon. "I really screwed everything up, didn't I?"

"I wouldn't consider your mission a complete failure, Matt. After all, you did discover the meaning of true love. You should be proud of yourself." He patted Matt's shoulder.

"But I thought you said, if I kept her from going to California, I would save her life?"

"No, Matt, we didn't say your mission was to save her life. We said it was to save her soul!" Anjella and Enon both smiled at each other and then looked back towards Beth. "Anyway, Matt, your mission hasn't failed yet. Why don't we wait and see how it turns out." The three of them watched intently.

Emmy laid her head on Beth's leg, alongside the hand where Beth gently held onto her hummingbird friend. Beth began to stroke Emmy's hair. "I love you Emmy. Don't you ever forget that."

"I will always love you, too, Mommy." She opened Beth's hand and lightly stroked the body of the little bird. She leaned over to her mother's ear and whispered so only Beth could hear. "Now you know why you need to go to Heaven!" as she pointed her chubby little finger at Matt.

Beth looked at her hand and then at Emmy and whispered back. "Are you telling me rugrat that I am leaving you for another love? I could never love anyone more than you!"

"I know Mommy. But there are lots of people who are waiting for you in Heaven." Emmy looked straight into her mother's eyes with a look of glowing anticipation. "You know when I said that I had a surprise for you?"

"Yes, I do."

"Well, I can tell you now." She moved so she could whisper in Beth's ear. "I saw Brandon! He's waiting for you!"

Beth could not believe her ears. "Brandon! How do you know it was him?"

"He told me. He's up there waiting with a lady called Aunt Katherine and Great Grandmom Georgina and Uncle Alex. You need to be with them now. It's where you belong." Emmy smiled and added, "Grandmom and PopPop and I will be just fine. Someday soon, we will all be together again."

Beth leaned back against her mother's arm filled with relief. She looked at Mary, "Yes, Emmy, I can't wait for the day we are all together again." Mary smiled and kissed her head.

The door to her room opened wide, as Frank and Father Pat entered. Frank's eyes were swollen and red. He appeared nervous. Father Pat

322

remained at the back of the room, as Frank walked over and sat on the bed next to Emmy.

"Emmy, would you mind if Grandmom and I talk to your mommy a minute? You can wait over there with Father Pat." Emmy quietly left Beth's side and stood by Father Pat.

Frank took Mary's free hand and squeezed it tight. His eyes told her what would come next. "Beth, I have something I would like to explain to you. Father Pat told me everything that happened to you, including the rape." Beth shot a look of panic at Father Pat. He smiled and nodded that it was okay. Mary gasped and Beth turned to look up at her. "It's okay Mom."

Frank continued. "I saw the hummingbird when Emmy brought it in. Father Pat told me it was the one you were talking about." Frank swallowed hard and squeezed Mary's hand before he continued. "Anyway, I have my own confession to make. I need to explain to you why I foolishly treated you the way I did. And I only hope you can forgive me." Frank looked at Mary and she squeezed his hand back in approval. It was time that the truth be told.

Frank cleared his throat. Beth sat still, completely clueless about what her father was about to tell her. Frank started his long story.

"Beth, first, I want you to know that your mother and I have never meant to hurt you. At first, we thought keeping this a secret was the right thing to do. Later, it just got harder and harder to tell you. I was afraid of what it would do to all of us. When I was in my early twenties, I lived in New York City. I used to go to the local jazz clubs on the weekends. At one of the clubs, there was a singer named Bridgette Marquise. She was beautiful, her voice was like something out of a dream, and I fell head over heels in love with her. Bridgette was from France and her visa was expiring. When we started dating, she only had a month left before she would have to go back to France. I was so naïve and in love with her, that after four dates, I proposed to her. She accepted and we were married by a justice of the peace a few weeks later. She got pregnant immediately and that seemed to change her. We had planned on concentrating on her singing career for a few years before we had children. I thought we had been careful, but we were both young and took too many risks. Bridgette hated being confined to the apartment during her late months of pregnancy. Back then, women could not sing in clubs after their pregnancy began to show. I thought her depression was just part of being pregnant. After the baby was born, Bridgett ran away. She just left me with a four-week-old baby to care for. In her goodbye letter, she told me she never really loved me and had used me to stay in the country. She was planning to leave me right after we married, but then she got pregnant. That baby was you." He paused for Beth's reaction. She looked at Mary in confusion. Mary nodded affirmation anxiously to Beth.

323

Frank continued, "Well, I was beside myself. I tried hard to take care of you and hold down a job at the same time. The daycare expenses became too much and I was overwhelmed. Your mother, Mary I mean, was a close friend who lived with her parents in the same apartment building. I knew Mary was attracted to me before I married Bridgette, but I never really took the time to see how wonderful she really was." He smiled at Mary and kissed her hand. "Anyway, she began coming over to help me in the evenings and we became close. It was obvious that we could not continue like this, because it did not look proper to have her coming and going every night. Your birth mother, Bridgette, filed for a quick divorce, thankfully, and as soon as that came through, we were married. I heard a rumor that she went to Las Vegas, but I never saw her again. She never tried to make contact with me or inquired about you. Mary and I decided that it would be better if we moved someplace else and started a new life. So I found a job here and we moved."

Beth looked at Mary, "So, you're not my birth mother? Why didn't you tell me what happened? I would have understood." She was too spent to be angry.

Mary looked into Beth's eyes. "I know we should have, and we were going to tell you. But I discovered a few years into our marriage that I couldn't have any children. Your father was afraid that if we told you, you might reject me and he didn't want to see me get hurt."

Beth nodded. It made sense to her. "But what does this have to do with your not trusting me, Dad?"

"The part about marrying Mary has nothing to do with it. It was the best thing that ever happened to me. Everything was fine when you were a little girl. As you became a teenager, your looks changed and you became the spitting image of your mother. And your voice, whenever you would sing, it would haunt me because you sounded so much like her. You even had the same interest in jazz music! Sometimes, I would look at you and almost talk to you as if you were Bridgette. Then there were a few times when you lied to me and I thought that you were becoming deceptive and untrustworthy just like Bridgette. I was afraid to trust you anymore. She hurt me so bad that each time you lied, I could feel the knife she had left in my back twist. I guess I never did get over what she did to me and I began to punish you for her mistakes. I'm sorry." Frank looked away from Beth and began to cry.

Mary added, "Beth, I'm sorry, too. I was so afraid of losing you! I was afraid to involve myself when your father would overreact. I didn't want to rock the boat. If the truth came out then, you may have decided to run off in pursuit of Bridgette. So I stayed quiet until it became impossible to muster the courage to tell you." Mary's voice tightened, "I just didn't want to lose my little girl, forgive me!" She sobbed into Beth's shoulder.

Beth closed her eyes and tried to reason. Mary was not her real mother. Her father held this deep secret from her and even blamed her for her real mother's mistakes. "Oh Matt," she thought, "I wish you were here." Then Beth remembered what Matt told her earlier that morning about loving unconditionally. Her heart filled with the most loving feeling as she looked at her parents. Thank you, Matt, she thought.

After a few moments of excruciating silence, Beth spoke softly. "Mom" Mary looked down at her. "I love you. You are the only mother I will ever have." Mary kissed Beth's head and cheek and held her tight.

"Thank you, Beth, thank you. You will always be my precious girl!"

Beth looked over at her father and touched his hand. "Dad, I love you. I'm sorry that you were hurt so badly. I wish I knew earlier, but I can understand your reasons. I forgive you." Her father kissed her hand, as his tears rolled onto the sheets.

"Thank you, Beth. I'm so sorry for everything. I feel responsible for what happened to you, please forgive me for that."

"No, Dad, that was not your fault. I did that to myself. I should have used better judgment. We all have to make choices in our lives, and we are responsible for the decisions we make. I'm glad that you chose to keep me, and I'm glad that Mom came along for both of our sakes." Beth was tired. Time was running out. She could feel her breath getting shallower. It was becoming hard to think. Her parents' voices were beginning to fade in and out.

Beth looked at Emmy who stood patiently with Father Pat. "Father Pat, could you bring Emmy here?" The two of them approached the other side of the bed. He lifted Emmy onto the end of the bed. Beth struggled with her IV and grew frustrated trying to work around it to hold Emmy. Father Pat asked if she wanted her IV line removed. She nodded yes and he went and got Addie. She disconnected the tube from the machine and laid it along side of Beth, out of the way. Beth squeezed Addie's hand and Addie kissed her forehead and said goodbye. She went back downstairs with Mrs. McC. Emmy was able to snuggle in close. Mary continued to hold on to Beth as she hummed her favorite song, Amazing Grace, while rocking her gently. Frank held both of their hands.

Beth slept on and off for the next two hours. Suddenly, she opened her eyes wide looking past everyone on her bed. By this time, she had no strength left and could hardly make an audible sound. She tried to talk. Mary moved close to her to listen.

"Confession." Beth whispered. She was looking at Father Pat.

"Confession?" Mary repeated louder.

Father Pat walked over to the bed. "Beth, do you want me to hear your confession?" Beth was looking past him in the corner. She seemed frightened.

"Yes." She whispered again. "Mom, I love you. Take Emmy down." Was all she could get out.

"Okay." Mary whispered back. She knew what was happening. She looked at Frank and nodded for him to get Emmy. Frank leaned over, unable to speak, and kissed Beth on the forehead and then on the cheek. He began to sob leaning against her face. She reached up and caressed his face. He picked up Emmy in his strong arms and held her so that Beth could kiss her once more before they left and went downstairs. Mary leaned over and mouthed I love you, then kissed Beth on the lips and left the room crying.

Father Pat walked over and sat down next to her. "Please forgive me for breaking my promise, kiddo. I couldn't bear to see all of you suffer. I'm sorry I betrayed your trust."

Beth tried to smile and nodded okay. "You knew better." She whispered.

"Do you really want a confession, Beth?"

She was so weak. It took her a minute to form her words. "No, angel."

"Angel?"

Beth raised her hand barely an inch and pointed to the corner of the room. She could not talk.

Father Pat knew what she meant then. The angels seemed to work over his shoulders a lot lately. "Do you see an angel?"

Beth nodded. "She...says...it's time."

"Time to go?"

Beth nodded again.

Father Pat smiled. "Well, it sounds like you're in good hands now, Beth."

Beth looked frightened. "I'm scared." She whispered.

"Scared of what, kiddo?"

"I don't," she swallowed and tried to finish, "know how to die."

Father Pat took her hand. He squeezed it hard. "I think I can help. Just close your eyes, feel God's presence in your heart, and have no fear. Don't think of it as dying. Think of it as a new journey, where no one will *ever* hurt you again." He reached into his pocket and took out a small metal container with the letters OI inscribed on it. He had fought using this on her since she was in the hospital. He never wanted to admit to himself that she could be dying. He was secretly hoping that she would be right about a miracle. After all, anything was possible. Regretfully, he unscrewed the cap

326

and took out a cotton ball that was soaking in the holy oil. He proceeded to perform the Sacrament of the Anointing of the Sick.

He began by anointing her forehead. "Through this holy anointing, may the Lord in his love and mercy help you with the grace of the Holy Spirit. Amen." Then he anointed both of her palms while saying, "May the Lord who frees you from sin, save you and raise you up. Amen."

Mrs. McCafferty came into the room, knelt down at the bottom of the bed, and began to say a silent rosary. Beth opened her eyes one more time and looked over at the angel standing in the corner of the room. She nodded once to her and looked up at Father Pat. She used all the strength left in her to say one more thing to him. "Tell Emmy my story. All of it."

Father Pat whispered yes and kissed the back of her hand. Beth smiled at him one last time, closed her eyes peacefully and took her last breath.

Matt, Enon and Anjella clung to each other as they watched Beth's spirit rise from her body and leave the bed. The angel in the corner disappeared and two angels in brown robes and a young man appeared by her side. Beth embraced the young man, looked at herself lying in bed, and realized she had died. After a quiet moment, she turned to go with them. For a second, she saw Matt with his angels and blew him a kiss before fading away. Matt looked at Anjella and asked who the young man was, although he already knew it was Brandon. His heart sank and he signaled that he was ready to go. He wondered if he would meet up with Beth in Heaven, as the three of them began to fade into the air.

One by one, Beth's family came in and kissed her softly on the cheek. Father Pat said a brief prayer for those grieving. Mary, Frank, Addie and Mrs. McC left the room together clinging to one another for support. Father Pat asked Addie to call the coroner's office. Beth looked as though she was quietly sleeping and he straightened out the sheets, but left them off her face. She had had a peaceful passing and it showed in her radiant expression. As Father Pat fixed her arms so that they would lay neatly over the sheet, the little bird's body rolled out of her right hand and landed next to her right leg. He looked closer at the bird, taking in its delicate features. Such a beautiful creature with feathers that glimmered iridescent green and red. He wondered if the little bird knew what a grand sacrifice that it had made to save two special souls. He gently picked the little thing up and placed it back in Beth's hand. He would make sure that the bird went along with Beth and received a fitting burial. He knelt beside the bed and thanked God for allowing him to witness such a marvelous miracle. He rose, made the sign of the cross, and left the room to join the family.

Chapter 24

Beth walked silently through the plain hallway holding Brandon's hand, with an angel at each side. She remembered what Matt had told her about this hallway and where it led. Dying did not seem to be as scary as most people expected. The angels who greeted her when she left her body enveloped her with so much love that Beth never felt anything but joy from that moment on. She instinctively knew that her family would be alright. She would miss Emmy so much, but she no longer feared the separation. She was so happy that she retained the memory of the smell and feel of Emmy's skin and hair. It was even more vivid than Beth could ever experience on Earth.

Beth felt so happy walking hand-in-hand with Brandon. They had hardly spoken a word to each other and, yet, Beth felt a lifetime of conversations had gone between them, the moment their hands touched. The two angels signaled Beth to stop and turn toward the plain wall. An archway appeared before them and they entered the beautiful courtyard that Matt had described to her. It was even more spectacular than he had described and Beth gasped at the sight.

The angels asked her to follow them, as they walked around the courtyard and entered the hallway labeled Human Affairs. Beth walked down the hallway and recognized the room off to the right that said Inspiration Room. She asked her two angels, Daphne and Israel, if she could browse a minute. The angels were delighted to give her a tour. As Beth and Brandon walked around the room, she spotted many of the inventions Matt told her were there. She giggled when she saw the set of plaques with the inventor's name and that of the sponsoring spirit. What a marvelous place this is, she thought to herself. This room and everything about Heaven reminded her of Matt.

"Do you know if Matt is here?" She whispered to Israel.

"Yes, I believe he went straight to the control room where he was dispatched. It is not in this building, but the one next door."

"Will I be able to see him again?" Beth asked reluctantly. She could not imagine experiencing disappointment in such a grand place.

"You may see anyone you wish here. You can request a meeting with any friend or relative that is here. It will all be explained to you by the Council." Daphne replied.

Beth was relieved. They entered the main room in Human Affairs, walked past the large screen, went to the right and stood in front of the second booth. This was as far as Brandon could take her. "Beth, it's so good to see you."

"It's good to see you, too." Beth replied.

"I can't go in with you, but we'll catch up later. We have so much to talk about." Brandon kissed her cheek and walked into a small cloud that appeared behind him and faded away. Daphne directed Beth into the booth. "Everything is exactly as Matt described," she replied to her angels, "I feel like I have been here before."

Israel and Daphne both laughed lightly and looked at each other. "Well, Beth, you've been here more times than you think!"

"I have? Why don't I remember?" Beth was puzzled and a little scared by the thought.

"You will remember everything after the meeting with the Council. They will determine if you are ready to move on here or return to Earth. Do not be frightened, it is far from a negative experience. The Council members are wise and understanding. I think you will enjoy your session." Daphne looked over at the angel, Stefan, who was in the booth when they entered. "We are ready for processing." Stefan took Beth through the entire procedure and left to arrange a Council review. When he returned, Beth's angels escorted her to the conference room. Two large doors swung open and Beth entered with them. They directed her to sit in the chair facing the twelve smiling faces of the Council. Beth prayed to herself that they would not send her back before seeing Matt. Her review was quite a surprise.

The man directly in front of her began to speak, "Welcome, Beth, we are so glad to see you."

"Thank you. I'm glad to be here." She thought that sounded corny and showed her nerves. Beth flipped her hair behind her left ear and bit her lip slightly.

"From the reports we received, you had quite a time during your last days on Earth." The Elder smiled and folded his hands. There were no papers to review in front of him; he seemed to know all the facts already. "I have to tell you, we never thought that young Matt would have pulled off such a miraculous feat. He is quite a character." All of the members of the Council smiled and laughed softly.

"He is a very special person, sir." Beth relaxed at the positive beginning.

"Well, now, you are a very special soul, too. It appears that you have learned a valuable lesson this time on Earth about the meaning of true love."

"Yes, I have. I owe it all to Matt. It was not until I saw what he went through for me that I realized what he said about unconditional love was true. He knew my plan would not work and yet he went along with it. He could have refused and possibly avoided his terrible encounter with the bee. He went along anyway, because he loved me, unconditionally. Even though

I was wrong. And because of that, I was able to forgive my father even though he was wrong."

The Elder smiled and nodded his head with approval. "Yes, Beth, you are right. And did you feel the power of God's presence that came over you when you forgave your parents?"

"Yes, I did feel this overwhelming feeling of perfection in that moment!"

"Well, it is that miracle you created out of love that will remain with your family and allow them to heal and get on with their lives. Love is the energy on Earth that can conquer the deepest sorrow."

"I see that. It is wonderful." Beth felt freed from the weight of her life in that revelation.

The Council took Beth through her review and opened the screen on the table before her eyes. She saw her past lives, so she could remember herself completely. After that, she saw the course that Emmy would take on her special mission in life. She was breathless as she watched her little girl grow into a strong, loving woman. The first scene was of Emmy kneeling at her grave with her grandparents. Emmy was running her fingers over the cold marble headstone. It had beautiful hummingbirds carved in each corner. Emmy smiled with delight as she traced her little index finger over the word 'Mommy' that was formed by shiny copper pennies. It was PopPop's idea. Beth could feel the love each one had inside them and knew that they had found peace. She saw Emmy graduate from high school and college with honors and then the incredible mission that God assigned to her. She saw several disappointments that Emmy would have to bear and cried out in anguish when she saw the horrible experience that Emmy would have to endure in her mid-twenties. She sighed with relief, when she saw her perform an incredibly brave act that would help correct a terrible error that men were making at this point in time. She could hardly believe that her Emmy would be responsible for such a great accomplishment. She was grateful to know that it was partly because of the lessons that Beth had helped her learn through her own death. Beth realized how critical it was for Emmy to have this foundation in order to achieve her mission that would help mankind move forward after the turn of the millennium. Beth saw that her own death was necessary to lead Emmy to the place where she would become most effective in her life, and it made perfect sense. She was so proud of her little girl and humbled by the honorable part she contributed to Emmy's incredible achievements. Tears of joy and thanksgiving formed in her eyes. The Elders also showed Beth how happy her parents' final years would be.

When the review was finished, Beth stood silently waiting for her orders. The Elder clasped his hands together and began to speak. "Beth, you have come a long way in this lifetime. Unless you would prefer to return to Earth to live out another experience, we see no reason why you cannot stay in Heaven and move on to the next level of the soul's evolution."

Beth almost jumped out of the chair with joy, "I would love to stay here and move on. What exactly does moving on involve?" She could not imagine what could come next in this place.

"It is customary for those moving forward to receive a special reward for their accomplishments. In your heart, you already know your deepest desire. At the eternity window, you will be shown what that is and it will manifest for you here in Heaven, for as long as you like. When you are ready, you can move on to various projects or even return to Earth, again. It will be totally up to you."

"So what do I do at the eternity window?"

"Nothing, just look into it and it will read your soul. If you are pleased, your angels will escort you to that destination. It is as simple as that!" The Council rose to their feet. The meeting was obviously over.

"Excuse me sirs!" Beth interrupted, "Is it possible for me to meet the real Matt?"

The Elder who led the meeting turned back to her and responded, "If it is your soul's deepest desire, I'm sure you will." He winked at her and walked through a private exit following the other members.

Beth stood up. "What did he mean by that?" She thought. Israel and Daphne came forward and led Beth out the side door of the conference room. When they entered the hallway, they turned left and headed back toward the main processing room and walked through the ropes that led to the eternity window. There was another human soul with his angels at the window. Beth and her angels waited in line, as if they were queued up for a movie.

"What did he mean when he said that I would see Matt again, if it was my soul's deepest desire? I thought meetings could be arranged here." Beth directed the question to Daphne.

"Perhaps that will be possible, if Matt is to remain here in Heaven." The window was free and Daphne directed Beth to stand at the viewing station.

Beth moved slowly up to the screen. She had forgotten the possibility that Matt would have to return to Earth. She assumed that if she were able to move on, that Matt would, too. He did accomplish his mission! Maybe the answer lay in what their deepest desires truly were. "Would he be led in a different direction? Was his love for her too new to be part of his deepest desire? What would Heaven be like without him?" She wondered. As she looked down into the screen, she discovered the answers to her questions.

331

♥♥♥♥♥♥♥♥

Matt appeared in the control room with Enon and Anjella. Angels scurried by chattering excitedly. What a terrific mission, everyone thought. There had never been a time so exciting in the control room. Even Enon was caught up in the moment, until he discovered Matt and Anjella were watching him. He stiffened up and called the troops to order.

"Everyone, pay attention!" All the angels stopped in their tracks. Enon had a reputation for being such a fussbudget at times. "I think we should all calm down," he began to say and looked at everyone in the room. A smile crept over his face as he thought, what the hell! He continued, "Calm down, everyone, long enough for me to say…well done!" Applause went up in the air from the angels. Enon turned to Matt. "Let's not forget who made this wild mission possible!" and he pointed to Matt. "Well done, Matt!" Enon patted him on the back. All of the angels came up to Matt and shook his hand or gave him their own pat and congratulated him.

After the angels cleared the room, Matt, Anjella and Enon sat down at the table. Matt could not believe the change in the old stuffed shirt. Enon was almost giddy.

"So, Enon, you seem like a new angel yourself, what gives?" Matt queried his friend. Anjella sat by quietly shaking her head. Even she could not believe the change in her mentor.

"Matt, I've got to tell you, before you came along, my job was beginning to become a pile of monotonous tasks. I was beginning to think of retirement. However, after seeing your determination against the wildest of odds, I realized how *presumptuous* I have become. You taught me a great lesson my friend. I forgot how inspiring the human soul could be, when it succeeds victoriously against all odds. After years of processing the usual cases with the basic everyday human soul, I lost sight of the rare courageous soul whose undaunting persistence could change the history of man. You have reminded me that I must stay alert to nurture those great souls that are entrusted to my care. I am grateful." Enon shook Matt's hand and then stood and gave him a hug.

Anjella hugged Matt and then looked at Enon. "Oh, what the heck!" she blurted and gave Enon a great big hug. The three of them laughed together.

Enon gestured to leave, "Matt, I guess it's time to see the Council. After you!" Matt walked to the control room door and walked out of the building. As he walked to the Human Affairs center, he saw the Kingdom. It was more fabulous than he remembered. He turned left through the wall of roses back into Human Affairs. Stefan was waiting for them in central processing. He beamed as they approached.

"You sure have everyone buzzing around here, Matt. Welcome back." He gestured to enter the second booth. After some basic questions, Stefan left to arrange the meeting with the Council. Matt felt breathless anticipation as he waited to hear of his final destination.

"Do you think the Council will let me stay?" He asked his caseworkers.

"We cannot speak for the Council, Matt, but I hope they do." Anjella said.

"Do you know where Beth is now?"

"She has been processed and has moved on to her eternal rewards." Enon replied, trying to console his friend.

"Oh, I guess that's that." Matt suddenly did not care what the Council would say. He thought about how much love he felt for Beth his last days on Earth and would not trade it for the world. Not even for Heaven!

Stefan returned and the three headed toward the conference room. The same angels were standing guard as before and the great doors opened when they approached. The Council had already taken their seats. The Elder seated center left spoke first when Matt sat down in front of him.

"Welcome back, Matt, welcome back. I must say on behalf of the entire Council, it was a job well done!" The other men nodded in agreement. "So, you thought when you left us that you understood the meaning of true love and relationships. We are glad that you discovered the truth during your mission. That was our intention. But I must say, you managed to do everything the hard way!" The Elders all laughed.

"Thank you, Sirs," Matt said, "I do have a way of steering off course at times."

"Well, all is well that ends well, someone once said." The Elder straightened in his chair and put on a more serious look. "Since you were able to accomplish both the task of saving Beth's soul and realizing the true meaning of love, we are pleased to allow you to move on here in Heaven. If you still feel that is what you want." The Elder gave a cunning grin along with his last remark.

"Yes, I do want to stay here, of course." Matt looked down at the table sheepishly, "I was just hoping that I could stay here with Beth, but I heard that she has chosen to move on."

"Yes, that is correct. You should feel very proud that you were able to save such a fine soul from a damaging experience that would have set her back quite a bit in her search for the truth. Beth moved on because of you. She has gone to the eternity window and discovered her reward."

The Elder leaned forward as if he was talking privately to Matt. "When you were here last time, you did not get a full explanation of the window, so let me proceed. When you successfully complete a level of growth, you receive the opportunity to look into the eternity window. The window will look deep into your soul and show you your truest desire. It is something your soul has yearned for all of your lives on Earth and finally, as a reward, you can experience this dream for as long as you choose. Now, for many people, they are surprised when they see what it is that they have been yearning for, but always, they are delighted to experience it." He pulled back into his chair.

"Whatever Beth has discovered to be her reward, it is what she has searched for all her life. She lived a long time before she had the fortunate opportunity of meeting you, Matt. So, bless her reward and be happy for her." He slowed his words down to make his point. "It is part of unconditional love!"

Matt shook his head and laughed to himself. He was well aware that the Council could hear his thoughts, too. "If I was willing to die for you, Beth, then I guess I can let you have your dream, even if it is without me. But I will always love you…always!"

"And so you should, Matt!" The Elder exclaimed. "Love has no endings. It is eternal. The memory of a loved one from every life you have lived will come back to you when you move on. Now, go and find out what it is that you have desired to experience. We haven't had a disappointed customer yet!" The Elder rose along with the other members and left through their exit in the wall behind them, leaving Matt and his angels alone in the room.

Anjella sensed Matt's disconsolation regarding Beth. "Matt, I can't wait to see what your deepest desire is! Let's go see." She pulled on his arm.

Matt looked at Enon and shuffled his feet, "I don't think any desire could make me forget how I feel about Beth."

Enon smiled and put his arm around Matt's shoulder. "It is not supposed to Matt. Your eternity will be a rewarding experience here. What you are about to see is a reward, not a punishment!" He laughed at the turn of events. "You will be able to visit with Beth any time the two of you want. There will be many opportunities to experience this kind of love. Your problem is that you still are very connected to the physical realm. In time, your physical experience will wear off, and you will experience your existence through a higher level of cognizance. As this happens, the love that you feel for Beth and others from your past will meld together and you will experience that same dimension of love in everything you do here. If you miss physical love, then you can return to Earth for the physical experience. There are no limits here. Time is nonexistent. You can go backward or forward. You can experience the full spectrum of love alone or as it is experienced with others. There are so many projects to work on here that I hardly believe you will become the least bit bored. Now, are you ready to experience the Heaven you so desperately wanted to stay in or have you changed your mind?"

Matt smiled, "No, let's go and see what my reward is."

Matt, Enon and Anjella exited through the door that led to the eternity window or to the outside. Although they were turning left, Matt's eyes were drawn in the other direction.

To his surprise and delight, he saw his Great-grandmother Anna, a white-robed angel and a young girl about fifteen years old, standing at the doorway to the outside. The young girl was beautiful and it did not take Matt a second to figure out who she was.

"Sarah?" Matt took a few steps closer and turned to Enon for permission to go further. He smiled and nodded to go. Suddenly, Matt was flying across the floor to her and she opened her arms to embrace him.

"Matthew, it's so good to see you." Matt remained in her arms speechless and they rocked gently together. His heart was singing with joy. He pulled away and held her face to study her. She looked angelic herself. "Sarah, it's really you!" He knew Sarah only as a frail five-year-old, when she died; but, now, she was standing here as a beautiful, young lady and the spitting image of her mother. An aura of sweetness surrounded her and her wisdom and grace shown like a bright star gleaming off of her image.

"Why do you look like this?" Matt asked.

"It's how I like to be seen here." Matt remembered Anna saying the same thing and it turned his attention to her. "Gram, I did it!"

"I know. I'm so proud of you! We all are!"

Matt was so excited that he did not know what to say next. Sarah spoke. "Matt, I have to be going. It's almost time."

"You're going back, now?"

"Soon, but I need to prepare." Sarah took both of his hands in hers. Her smile was so lovely.

Matt wished that they had more time. "Sarah, will you do me a favor?"

"If I can."

"Will you give Mom and Dad a hug for me. I know you will be forgetting everything and it may not be possible, but if it is, could you somehow let them know that I'm okay and I love them."

Sarah smiled. "I will. I intend to bring your spirit with me! If you watch us closely and pray for us, we will feel it. Now, will you do me a favor, big brother."

"Anything! Even if it's not possible, I'd find a way."

Sarah laughed. "Oh, I'm sure you would!" Then she became more serious. "When I come back, will you greet me!"

335

Matt kissed both of her hands. "It would be an honor!" They embraced one more time and Matt embraced Anna.

"We have to be going, Matt." Anna said. "But I'll be in touch later."

Matt watched the three of them walk back down the path and go to the right. Sarah and Anna turned and waved. Matt waved back and walked back to his angels. They strolled casually down to the eternity window. There were no other souls waiting in line so they went directly to the viewing station. Matt stopped a few feet away to gather his courage. He looked at Anjella and Enon, took a deep breath and stepped up to the screen.

The screen was blank when he approached and, as soon as he saw his reflection in the glass-like material, the screen began to change. First clouds appeared swirling around, creating a center dot. The dot grew wider and wider and an aerial view of an Earth scene appeared before Matt. The screen zoomed in on the most incredible racing complex Matt could ever imagine. The scene was a magnificent valley full of winding paved roads that wandered up and down the mountainside. Motorcyclists were racing through the gently curving paths that passed spectacular displays of wooded areas next to streams and ponds. Tiny cottages dotted the hillside and parks filled with children laughing, as they played on swings and monkeybars. To the right side in the valley was a giant complex of buildings and four motorcycle and racecar stadiums, ten times larger than any racing stadium on Earth.

Some of the buildings looked like factories, but were immaculate with gleaming iridescent white walls. The sky was cerulean blue with puffy white clouds bouncing by. It was more beautiful than any place on Earth that Matt had ever seen.

"What is this place?" He asked Enon and Anjella.

Enon was more than happy to explain. "This is called Racing Valley. It is one of the many kingdoms here in Heaven. This is where all of the development takes place for the next generation of motorcycles and racecars for use on Earth. You certainly have a strong desire for speed and this is where every dream you ever had about racing will come true. You will be assigned as one of the chief test drivers for the current motorcycles being developed by the Universe's top racing mechanics."

Matt was so excited. "Did you guys know about this all along?"

"No," said Anjella, "In Heaven, we always stay in the present moment."

"So, how does it work? Do I report for work like a job on Earth?"

"Yes, just like that, only there are no alarm clocks here. You will just know when you are to report. You will be summoned through thought. You will be free to explore the valley or other kingdoms that interest you in your spare time. You will reappear where you are needed. If you want to go back to what you were doing, you will pick up right where you left off. You will be surprised how wonderful it is not to have the constraints of physical time."

Matt could not believe his eyes. The beauty of the valley and the excitement of the racing complex helped him forget his disappointment, until he looked at the quaint cottages on the hillside. He wondered if something as wonderful as this could fill the void of separation from Beth.

"So where do I go to begin? Where will I live? Is it the same as on Earth, where everyone has their own home?"

Enon moved closer to Matt. "If that is part of your dream, then it is. Without a physical body, there is no need to lodge in any particular place. You can rest just by thinking about it. Your soul will automatically wake when the rest cycle is completed. You will find after a very short while that rest is not required much in this realm. There are too many things to explore. When you looked at the valley, was there a particular place that called to you?"

"Why yes, that house down by the stream, right outside the complex. It has a wonderful garden that reminded me of my hummingbird friend. I think Beth would have loved it." He stammered his last words. He could not believe how natural it sounded to him.

Enon smiled at Anjella, "Well, no sense in dragging this out. Why don't we go down there together and show you around? After we see the cottage, we will let you stay there a while, and then take you over to the racing complex for a tour. Everyone is excited about meeting you after what they have heard. You're already a legend around here."

Enon and Anjella placed one hand on Matt's shoulder and in an instant, they were standing in the driveway of the little cottage Matt had pointed out. It was a charming little home with a one-car garage attached to it and a beautifully maintained grass lawn that was lined with a flower garden bordering the perimeter of the yard. Matt could see the sparkling walls of the complex from the backyard.

"It's all very nice, you guys. I am really excited about this. All my life I have dreamed of working with the elite of the motorcycle world. Who would have guessed that I would be working with the best in the Universe someday." Matt looked at both angels full of love and gratitude. "I could never have completed this mission without you. I don't know how to thank you."

"Just enjoy your rewards Matt." Anjella answered. "I think you will be surprised at just how many you have coming to you!"

Matt looked at the two of them suspiciously, "Wait, I know you both a little too well. You haven't shown me everything yet, have you?"

Anjella shrugged her shoulders and rolled her eyes. Enon looked toward the house, as the garage door began to open automatically. Parked in the middle of the floor stood the most incredible motorcycle Matt had ever seen. Its sleek silver body was molded to fit the contours of a cyclist's chest and legs. The handlebars extended from the sides, which allowed the driver to lay across the top of the bike. This allowed the cycle and driver to become one. Enon explained that the symmetrical design, along with the lightweight alloy body, allowed for increased velocity. The bike could easily be handled at speeds of two hundred and sixty miles an hour and had an engine design that could go from zero to one hundred miles an hour in three seconds.

Matt was hoping they were going to tell him that he could see Beth, but the incredible piece of machinery in front of him still left him speechless. He walked over to the bike and ran his hands over the body and the handlebars. He mounted the bike and leaned onto the soft supple leather seat. The padding immediately molded to his chest and the position of the handlebars felt comfortable to his back and shoulders. There was a special padded chin rest extending from the seat that the bike helmet conformed to perfectly, with a special gel shock-absorbing system to relieve the stress on a racer's head while racing at high speeds. Matt got off the bike and stepped back. "Amazing!" He walked around the bike two times, checking out the tires and gauges. He looked at his friends.

"There has never been anything like this on Earth! Who would believe that technology could go this far. This is *incredible*! They found a way to build the driver right into the bike!"

Enon chuckled softly. "Why do you think they call this Heaven?"

Matt laughed, throwing his head back. "Touché! Angel, touché!"

The two angels walked outside with Matt. "Well, I'll tell you," Matt exclaimed, as he rubbed his right hand through his hair, scratching his head. "This is terrific, but I still feel that there is one more thing that would make this a dream come true."

A sultry voice came from the garage behind him, "I hope you're talking about me!"

Matt froze staring at Enon who winked at him and gestured for him to turn around.

Beth walked forward from the shadows of the garage smiling and holding something cupped in her hands. Matt turned and stared at the long legged beauty that sauntered toward him. She was wearing a light green floral dress that molded to her waist and flared softly at the hips, emphasizing her provocative figure. Matt remembered the girl in the gift shop that he saw during his review.

"You are the girl I saw in the gift shop! I do not believe it! How could this be?"

Beth laughed at Matt's bewilderment. "Yes, I am. I was supposed to pick up my girlfriend, Amanda, when she got off from work there. We were going to meet Katie at the movies on the same day that you were supposed to go to dinner with your family. Amanda was the girl behind the jewelry counter in the gift shop. Instead, I went to the party with Rachel and you went to the tracks. It seems we both share a stubborn streak that gets us into more trouble than it's worth. If we had listened to our hearts, perhaps we could have met under different circumstances."

Matt was more amazed than ever. He could not believe the level of synchronicity that was behind every moment of their lives on Earth. He could only assume that this must be the reason that Beth had to die. She was his soulmate. The Council knew this all along, when they sent him off on the mission. They *knew* what the outcome would be. *It was a setup!* They did not allow him to see Beth's face in his review, so he could fall in love with her naturally. The Council was more ingenious than Matt had given them credit.

When they were arms distance away, Beth held out her hands and opened them to reveal the ruby-throated hummingbird sitting peacefully inside. It lifted off her hands and hovered in front of Matt's face, twittered a few times, as if to say hello, and flew off to the flower garden on the side of the house.

Matt watched the hummingbird fly away and looked back at Beth, uncertain if he should ask his next question, but he had to know. "What about Brandon? Aren't you supposed to be with him?"

Beth smiled. "I will always love Brandon. He gave me a taste of real love when I was at one of the lowest points in my life. But we both knew when we reunited that our love was more about friendship. He is very happy where he is now and he wishes us the best."

Matt breathed a sigh of relief and drew her close to him. She studied his face, running her hands over his chiseled features that she had seen clearly in her vision. "I forgot to ask you what color eyes you had!"

"They're grayish-blue."

"That's what I thought!" Beth kissed him softly on the lips and then put her arms over his shoulders and embraced him lovingly. As their lips met once more, they formed a deep bond that would last for all eternity. When their tender embrace was over, they turned to the two angels who were beginning to fade.

"Thank you!" Beth called to them.

Matt gazed into their eyes. He wasn't sure words could ever express how deeply and eternally grateful he was for such a wonderful gift. "Now this feels more like a dream come true!"

Enon and Anjella both smiled, "We'll be back later, you two!" Anjella said. "We have so much to show you!" The two angels faded away arm in arm.

Matt and Beth embraced each other around the waist and walked through the backyard to the stream. They had a lot to talk about.

♥ ♥ ♥ ♥ ♥ ♥ ♥

Enon and Anjella returned to the Control Room to prepare a summary for the Council. "Enon, there's just one thing I don't understand." Anjella inquired.

Enon answered her distractedly, "What is that, Anjella?"

"Well, when we were watching the viewing screen and Matt fell between the rose bushes, there was no shiny copper penny laying right next to him."

"There wasn't? How unobservant of you!" Enon tried to pretend that Anjella was mistaken.

"Oh, no you don't, I specifically remember, and need I remind you that I could replay it for you on the screen. That copper penny was not there. So what gives?" Anjella began to tap her fingers impatiently on the table.

Enon looked up at her in resignation. "Alright, if you must know, the rule book specifically states that we could not interfere with Matt's mission by creating anything that could be considered miraculous, thereby aiding the soul in accomplishing its mission in an unnatural way." He looked back down at his clipboard.

"So, how did the penny get there?" Anjella was relentless.

Enon pushed the clip board aside. "If I tell you this, you must promise never to tell another angel or soul ever!"

Anjella nodded in agreement.

"When you left the screen after seeing Matt's fall, I noticed a shadow in the corner of the screen and recognized that it must be Emmy. Knowing that she had a particular fondness for copper pennies, I simply arranged a good deed gift through her guardian angel. Her angel found no harm in expending a minute portion of grace to create such a reward."

"So, you cheated!" Anjella was shocked at her once uptight, by-the-rules teacher.

"I did not! I merely observed an opportunity to reward a little girl for her courage in the face of losing her mother. Now, not another word!" Enon was beginning to regret telling her. Trainees were a constant source of aggravation.

"Okay, but technically you still cheated."

Enon began to protest again but Anjella held up her hand to stop him. "Don't worry, Enon, this will be our little secret, I promise."

The two of them returned to the task of officially closing the case that would stand as the most extraordinary accomplishment of their now famous careers. Behind them in the Control Room, Sage was preparing for the next assignment and only the quiet rustling of angels could be heard.

The End

About the Author

Helen Heinmiller lives in Chester County, Pennsylvania with her husband and two daughters. For the past nine years, she has been studying comparative religion in a spiritual quest to understand the reason why we are all here and the real meaning of unconditional love. Her experiences have led her to write her debut novel, *The Rustling of Angels*, which explores the meaning of unconditional love in our closest relationships. She is working on a sequel that will expand this concept to include our global relationships.

Printed in the United States
5650